STUDIES ON
THE SELF
AND SOCIAL COGNITION

STUDIES ON THE SELF AND SOCIAL COGNITION

Aix-en-Provence, France   18–20 March 1991

Editors

M-F Pichevin
M-C Hurtig
M Piolat

CREPCO / Univ. of Provence

World Scientific
Singapore • New Jersey • London • Hong Kong

Published by

World Scientific Publishing Co. Pte. Ltd.

P O Box 128, Farrer Road, Singapore 9128

USA office: Suite 1B, 1060 Main Street, River Edge, NJ 07661

UK office: 73 Lynton Mead, Totteridge, London N20 8DH

STUDIES ON THE SELF AND SOCIAL COGNITION

ISBN 981-02-1237-2

Printed in Singapore by Utopia Press.

v

" [...] *Now there is no problem that is more central, to Anglo-American philosophy particularly, than the problem of other minds: how do we know other minds. How do we get a fix on what they are thinking, what they are intending, etc., and as you all know, there has been an enormous amount of study over the last decade dealing with this problem of other minds, and it starts, as these things always do, at some distance in the past, particularly in the work of George Herbert Mead. G. H. Mead made the point that you do not develop a sense of yourself until you begin to develop, at the same time, a sense of the other: you begin to get a fully developed sense of self when you begin to relate to something which he spoke of as the generalized other – which was a matter that interested J.-P.Codol a great deal. Mead was basically a social philosopher and didn't do much in the way of empirical work, much of his work was very suggestive. You get a real changes however, when you get the Meadian notion, the notion that self develops by virtue of a person relating himself to other and relating himself to a generalized other [...]. So now, in 1991, as we look at the issue of self and other and self and other evaluation, we recognize that this is not a phenomenon that is laid on top of the way in which ordinarily human beings respond one to the other, but rather is it the very heart of the problem, the very heart of the question of the way the individual enters into his social world, that representation of the self and other and their evaluative relation, so that today we recognize that the problems that J.-P. Codol was dealing with were not just problems in social psychology or in one branch of social psychology, but live right in the center of the major area that is psychology and the human sciences as a whole. It is at the heart of the process involved in meaning-making. [...]"*

Jerome Bruner

Aix-en-Provence, Mars 1991
Opening address to the conference
in honour of Jean-Paul Codol

PREFACE

In March 1991, the CREPCO (Center for Research in Cognitive Psychology, CNRS, University of Provence, France) organized an international conference in honor of its ex-director, Jean-Paul Codol (1944–1989). Jean-Paul Codol was an internationally renowned social psychologist, whose ongoing endeavor was to integrate the cognitive and social perspectives in psychology; our goal in organizing this conference was to further that purpose. On the first day of the conference, following a videotaped opening address by Jerome Bruner, four lectures were given respectively by Miles Hewstone (*Social Cognition and Stereotyping: Concepts, Measures, and Models*), Anthony Greenwald (*Implicit Self-Reference: Indirect Measurement of Self-Cognition and Self-Esteem*), Serge Moscovici (*Que faire des représentations sociales?*), and Robert Zajonc (*Cognition and Communication: A Paradigm Missed*). Two round tables were held on the last day of the conference. The participants in the first round table on *The Cognitive Approach to the Study of the Self* were Willem Doise (University of Geneva, Switzerland), Anthony Greenwald (University of Washington, U.S.A.), Maria Jarymowicz (University of Warsaw, Poland), Jacques-Philippe Leyens (Catholic University of Louvain, Belgium), and Hazel Markus (University of Michigan, U.S.A.). The participants in the second round table on *Cognition and Social Cognition* were Claude Bastien (CREPCO/University of Provence, France), Jean-Paul Caverni (CREPCO/University of Provence, France), Jonathan St. B. T. Evans (Polytechnic South West, England), Claude Flament (University of Provence, France), Miles Hewstone (University of Bristol, England), Jean-Marc Monteil (University of Clermont-Ferrand, France), Guy Tiberghien (University of Grenoble, France), and Robert Zajonc (University of Michigan, U.S.A.). In the interim, forty-five papers and posters were presented. This book offers a selection of the above papers, as well as a few additional contributions, notably the introduction to each section.

There are two ways of understanding the book's title, *Studies on the Self and Social Cognition*. Each corresponds to one of the goals set by the editors: (1) to emphasize the contribution of social cognition to the new trend of research on the self, and (2) to add to the debate concerning the status of social cognition in cognitive psychology.

In the history of psychology, the withdrawal from the psychological realm, of self-awareness and of phenomena revealing the idiosyncratic functioning of human beings has constituted one of the epistemological conditions for the establishment of the general laws of behavior. This separation, a basic foundation of behaviorism, has survived throughout the progression of cognitivism (the computer metaphor probably has something to do with this), and may still appear for some to be one of the prerequisites of the development and validation of models of mental processes. However, as long as no theoretical or methodological consideration can be found to oppose it, the nomothetic approach to self-awareness, as a fundamental property of the human mind, can only grant greater validity to our models of thought and behavior.

The new approaches to the study of the self in psychology and more particularly in social psychology are a relatively recent advancement which resulted from a very specific change: the application of the information processing paradigm to the study of person-related information in research on social cognition. Accordingly, research on self-related information and its encoding, organization in memory, and subsequent activation in the self-regulation of behavior, has been flourishing since the end of the seventies.

Given that the human agent of cognition is a subject who (a) himself/herself is the object of knowledge, (b) exercises control over his/her own individuality, and (c) bases his/her judgments on a system of values, then what are the consequences of these properties of the human information processing system on human cognitive functioning?

This question is not raised with the same acuteness in all areas of cognition. Granted, cognitive psychologists are no longer ignorant of the important roles played by certainty, the feeling of knowing, and other metacognitive variables in the self-regulation of information processing. Nor do child psychologists doubt that the construction of the self is a necessary condition for the development of cognitive functioning. But since the breakthrough initiated by Allport in 1943, social psychologists have been responsible for the most striking theoretical advances. They have also done the most empirical work on the question of the self. It was the social cognition trend which, by focusing on cognitive and motivational biases, pointed out the structural and functional properties of the self as an *object of knowledge* and a *knower*. A major research theme in this trend has been social comparison and self-reference, also a central issue in Codol's work. The first objective of this book is to give the reader an idea of both the coherence and diversity of these cognition-oriented studies on the self.

Organizing a debate on the status of social cognition — the second objective of this book — inevitably leads us to raise the recurring question of whether social cognition should be granted a specific status, or whether it should be considered as just one of the forms of cognition, subjected to the same human information processing factors as those affecting all forms of cognition.

We can point out three opposing standpoints which clearly outline the terms of this debate:

(1) Researchers in the field of social cognition, while using the principles and methods of the cognitivist approach to study social information processing, claim that social objects are not processed like other objects, because (a) they are more ambiguous and have more unstable properties than non-social objects, (b) the subject-object relationship is usually reciprocal and interactive, (c) there is generally conscious or unconscious ego-involvement in social information processing, and (d) cognition and affect can rarely be completely dissociated.

(2) Advocates of a "purely" cognitive approach dispute this alleged specificity of social objects, contending either that their properties (a) are nothing but simple modulators of cognitive functioning which do not affect its laws and general principles, or (b) should be investigated using an approach which cannot be viewed as strictly cognitive.

(3) Finally, some social psychologists who do not necessarily reject the principles of the cognitive approach in social psychology have criticized researchers in social cognition along three main lines: while still claiming to be social psychologists, they (a) utilize models which account exclusively for intraindividual functioning and thereby completely ignore interindividual and collective phenomena, (b) limit their explanations to effects which can be ascribed to the internal properties of the cognitive processing system (more specifically, to cognitive biases), and (c) neglect the effects attributable to factors such as the subject's social insertion in socially valued and meaningful contexts.

The book is divided into three parts. The first, entitled *The Anchoring Function of the Self in Social Judgments*, is introduced by A. Greenwald and M. Jarymowicz. The papers in this part are representative of the approach which considers the self as a cognitive reference point in the perception of persons and interpersonal relations. The second part, entitled *Cognitive Effects of the Intergroup Structure and Representations of Self-Other Relations*, is introduced by W. Doise. It focuses to a greater extent on the social conditions of the processes under study, adding the dimensions of group membership and intergroup relations to the preceding perspective. The third part is entitled *Questioning the Social Cognition Approach*. It is introduced by J.-M. Monteil and includes theoretical and empirical work on the issue of the validity and limitations of a strictly cognitive approach to social behavior. This part also includes papers dealing with the issue of the value in the cognitive sciences of a specifically sociocognitive approach.

The studies on the self found in the first two parts of the book — which deal with the intraindividual or interindividual effects of self/others relations — form a particularly coherent body of research. In these studies, the reader will find a common set of references, now the "Classics" of the Anglo-American literature on the self. This common reference base is a testimony to the proximity of this work to the American research responsible for the theoretical renewal of the study of the self. But their unity is not limited to this common foundation. It is also based on a name, one which continues to appear throughout a great majority of the chapters in the book, either as a starting point for defining an issue, or as a theoretical landmark. This name is Jean-Paul Codol. The reader must not be mistaken here, for this is not a rhetorial exercise which duly complies with the rules of any social tribute. If tribute there is, it is a scientific tribute, in recognition of the position this researcher held as an initiator of a specifically-European research trend.

We shall not retrace the scientific career of Jean-Paul Codol, originally a sociologist, who was to affirm his position in social psychology as a rigorous and creative experimentalist. Instead, we would like to emphasize the ever-increasing originality of his topics of research, which ingeniously combined remarkable continuity of focus and great diversity of content: social influence, social representations, social norms and conformism, self-images and the quest for singularity, social comparison and perception, personal space, similarity judgment, estimation of interpersonal physical distance, cognitive schemas and biases. Yet amidst this diversity, there is one ever-present element: the self. And one recurring issue: identity. Codol's work on this issue culminated in his doctoral thesis entitled *"Semblables et différents. Recherches sur la quête de la similitude et de la différenciation sociale"* (Being both similar and different. Research on the quest for social resemblance and differentiation). Personal identity, a notion which found theoretical and empirical sustenance in this thesis, emerged in the center of a set of images in mirror: the self vs. others, the individual vs. the social, comparability vs. incompatibility, differentiation vs. undifferentiation, etc. According to Codol, these oppositions (pairs of antonyms) form the basis for the cognitive construction of identity, with no gap between cognition and motivation.

It was the discovery and interpretation of the PIP effect (*Primus Inter Pares*) which led Codol into the field of personal and social identity. Aiming to show as he said in his thesis that "the quest for differentiation is rooted in the strength of the social link, and is both complementary with and opposite to the search for similarity between oneself and others" (*our translation*), Codol turned his attention towards situations involving the affirmation of one's similarity to — or difference from — others. It was during his work on the perception of self/others similarity and difference that he discovered asymmetry effects in interpersonal comparison, depending on the point of reference. The study of such asymmetry phenomena became the focal point of his final work, which led him to hypothesize the existence of a self-centered assimilation process, and even to go so far as to consider the self as a categorial prototype. This field of study, newly opened up by Codol, was rapidly explored and extended by many European researchers, as this book clearly reveals.

Codol's work itself, as well as the research it inspired, is illustrative of one of the particularities of European research in social psychology. This particularity, which distinguishes it from American social psychology, is its more specifically *psychosocial* orientation, its more affirmative focus on *sociocognitive* processes. In this psychosocial context, the question of identity is ever-present, be it in the foreground or in the background. And the study of the processing of self-related information generally includes personal and social valuing phenomena, the social insertion of subjects into the social space, and the social significance of the objects processed. But this common approach is far from implying uniformity of viewpoint. One example is the ongoing debate on the issue of individual identity vs. social identity, initiated by the research on intergroup relations conducted within the Bristol school.

As we shall see, this sociocognitive approach to mental processes has made it possible to define the issue of cognition versus social cognition in different terms.

Mario Franco Piohovin
Marie-Claude Hurtig
Michel Piolat

ACKNOWLEDGEMENTS

The editors are grateful to Vivian Waltz who translated or checked the English for some of the papers. This book benefited also from the help of Thierry Bollon (Université de Provence) and Anne Debray-Decory (CREPCO). We would like to thank all three of them.

CONTENTS

PART ONE

THE ANCHORING FUNCTION OF THE SELF
IN SOCIAL JUDGMENTS

INTRODUCTION

Maria Jarymowicz

University of Warsaw, Poland

Anthony G. Greenwald

University of Washington, U.S.A.

1. Searching for the Self-Concept

In one of his "Tales of Sameness" ("A Syrian Tale of a Sparrow and a Weasel"), Leszek Kolakowski portrays a perplexing dilemma. A small sparrow is witnessed overcoming a large weasel in a race. The defeated weasel can not believe her eyes, feels undone and submits the matter to the owl for adjudication. The owls agrees that the sparrow deceived the weasel, and when the sparrow protests, the owl argues:

> "[...] you deceived the weasel", screamed the owl.
> "I said nothing", the sparrow protested.
> "You deceived her with your appearance", repeated the owl.
> "That's the way I was born", the sparrow reported, "and I cannot be responsible for the way I look."
> "Whether you are responsible or not is beyond the point ", blared out the owl [...].
> "Suffice it to say that you look as you do and your looks deceived the weasel!"
> "Perhaps my looks deceived the weasel but I did not deceive the weasel", bawled back the sparrow, red in the face with anger. "I am not my appearance!"

For the sparrow, being identified with his appearance was more disturbing than the prospect of losing his prize. The sparrow was red with anger because he felt that others were mistaking his looks for his self.

What's worse, in the sharp exchange of opinions, the sparrow eventually lost self-certainty:

> *"Well, who is your appearance?"* asked the owl caustically, confident now, because she knew the sparrow was becoming more and more muddled-up.
> *"Nobody is,"* answered the sparrow, uncertainly.

This tale reflects some important phenomena and dilemmas. The sparrow loses self-confidence, but even the owl's wisdom is insufficient to decide whether the appearance of the sparrow is part of his "self", or what the essence of the "self" is.

Could the owl find the necessary answers in contemporary psychological literature? Would she discover them if she began to study the research literature on the role of the self in social information processing? Can we help her with any useful hints?

Many famous names in past and contemporary psychology are associated with the idea that the self is not a unitary entity, but consists of several functionally distinct subsystems that are transformed in the course of development (James, 1890; Freud, 1923; Erikson, 1956; Gergen, 1971; Epstein, 1980; Tap, 1985; Markus & Nurius, 1986; Wyer & Srull, 1989). Labels such as the self as agent or knower, object or concept, public, private, and collective facets of the self, and actual vs. ideal vs. possible self, etc., identify what are presumed to be developmentally and functionally differentiated domains of the self. However, these labels cannot capture the full richness of empirical investigations of the self. Despite the long psychological traditions represented by these various labels, they still require further articulation. Therefore, we start by briefly reviewing the historical background of theorization concerning facets of the self.

In reviewing philosophical and psychological treatments of the self, James (1890) distinguished the *self as knower* ("pure ego") from the self as *object of knowledge* (the "empirical self" or me). James described the empirical self as consisting of material, social, and spiritual aspects. While believing that the self as knower belonged in empirical psychology (and deploring the mystery attached to various conceptions of "pure ego" in philosophy and theology), James could do little to provide the self as knower with an empirical existence. Apparently, James believed that the famous metaphor of the stream of consciousness was a route to bringing the self as knower into empirical psychology. In retrospect, that route can be judged to have been unproductive.

In a more eclectic theoretical overview of the self, some 50 years later, Gordon Allport (1943) described eight senses of self or ego, listing the self as knower first among these. Although Allport (1961) later abandoned the attempt to bring the self as knower within empirical psychology, nevertheless the extended treatment of ego-involvement in Allport's 1943 article previewed the manner in which self as knower has subsequently been given an empirical existence.

In reviewing the explosion of research on the self that started in the 1970s, Greenwald and Pratkanis (1984) concluded that the self as knower had at last become firmly established as a topic of empirical investigation. The major areas of such investigations included research on the role of the self in memory and on ego-related biases in jugdment, as well as Codol's (1985) discovery of asymmetries in judging physical distance between self and others. Greenwald and Pratkanis further proposed that the psychological concept of *schema* was capable of accommodating the dual (knower/object of knowledge) nature of the self; they defined the self as "a complex, person-specific, central, attitudinal schema" (p. 166).

Recent advances in the conception of the self as object of knowledge have taken the form of hypothesizing multiple sub-entities within the self-concept. Markus and Nurius (1986) proposed that the person typically possesses multiple "possible selves" and Higgins (1987) similarly elaborated the possibility of multiple "self-guides". These views have theoretical antecedents in previous concepts of social roles and in the distinction between actual and ideal self that developed as an outgrowth of the Freudian distinction between ego and superego.

Markus and Higgins have used their respective theories to explain motivational functions of the self. In each theory, discrepancies between perceived characteristics of the current actual self and an alternate self-representation (e.g., a possible self for Markus or an "ought" self for Higgins) provide the basis for approach or avoidance motivations; the approach or avoidance is understood as psychological movement toward or away from these alternate representations. In contrast, several other theories attribute motivational functions to the self-as-knower aspect of the self-schema by focusing on the self's function in maintaining self-esteem, (e.g., Aronson, 1992; Brown, in press; Greenwald, 1982; Steele, 1000, Swann, 1990; Tesser, 1988).

In the context of these modern theoretical and empirical developments in self theory, the chapters of Part 1 take their place in continuing the modern psychological evolution of the concept of self as knower.

2. Self-Related Principles of Social Information Processing

One cannot overrate the usefulness, for the understanding of human behavior, of knowledge concerning different subsystems of the self. In the course of laboratory research it had been possible to establish several subtle and significant effects. One important factor is type of code of self-knowledge (imaginal/experiential vs. conceptual/verbal) activated by research procedures. Winczo (1991) found that subjects are less susceptible to the pressure of public opinion when imaginal rather than conceptual representations of the self are activated. Trzebińska (1991) found that affiliative tendencies toward assimilated members of a minority are more negative following activation of a conceptual (compared to experiential) self-representation. These research findings seem both practically important and theoretically interpretable.

The ego is a source of defensive motivation that causes biased data processing (Grzegołowska-Klarkowska, 1986). To perceive others in order to confirm one's self-knowledge, to maintain one's self-esteem, to make a better impression – these are basic goals of the totalitarian ego (Greenwald, 1980) and manifestations of self-serving biases (Dymkowski, 1989). The self, in turn, as a system of self-knowledge, may provide the foundation for knowledge of other people (e.g., due to generalization), despite the lack of motivational premises. Whether social perception will be guided by one or the other subsystem depends on the contingencies. However, these two subsystems frequently cooperate. This led Greenwald and Pratkanis (1984) to the formulation of their global definition: the self is "a complex, person-specific, central, attitudinal schema". Do all our research endeavors fit, however, into this definition (e.g., the concepts of "independent and interdependent self" – cf. Markus & Kitayama, 1991)?

What can be gleaned from the research described in this volume for the understanding of the self in social judgments?

Obviously, the works included in Part 1 are not representative of the whole problem area. There are some topics of particular focus, especially studies on asymmetry in judging physical distance or psychological similarity between self and others. The authors present research related to the studies of Jean-Paul Codol. However (or, perhaps, thanks to this) many important issues have been taken up.

Several studies deal with two assumptions concerning the role of the self-schema. According to the first assumption, the self-schema functions as a prototype in social information processing. According the second (less specific) one, the self-schema is a habitual reference point and as such is a source of cognitive and motivational determinants of social judgments.

2.1 The Self as a Prototype in Social Perception

Data presented by **Durand-Delvigne** support the claim that other people are perceived in terms of categories that are basic dimensions of self-schema. Adult women used self-dimensions in describing others but still distinguished self from others (these findings for adult women are consistent with results reported by Markus, Crane, and Siladi, 1978). These data were gathered in conditions for which the "other" was a familiar (known) person, selected by the subject, suggesting a role of the self-schema in the formation of relatively *stable* representations of other people, based on automatic information processing.

Hardoin and Codol (1984) found a relatively high convergence between the description of another *unknown* person and a previous self-description, whereas when the two descriptions were done in the opposite sequence (first description of the other, then the self-description) the convergence was significantly smaller. It is worth noting that such relationship between the self-schema and other-perception is most apparent when the perceived object is an unfamiliar other. In this case the self-schema is often the principal basis for inference. However, other, more complex relationships, including derivatives of the *assimilation/contrast* mechanism, have been observed.

Jarymowicz and Codol (1979) presented students with a fragment of an unfamiliar person's diary. The subjects were then asked to complete an adjective checklist that was previously used for self-description, to describe this new stimulus person. The obtained descriptions were remarkably diverse: the target person was described by some subjects as passive and shy, and by others as active and provocative, etc. When the relationships between self- and other-descriptions were analyzed, it was possible to detect a specific assimilation/contrast mechanism: the intensities of the traits attributed to the other were either very similar or very dissimilar to the self.

Kodilja and Arcuri present findings that indicate far-reaching implications of the process of referring social information to the self-schema. Subjects described themselves by means of an adjective checklist. After their self-schemas were thus activated, they were asked to rate the evaluative coherence of the social desirability of adjective pairs. As hypothesized, subjects made their evaluations significantly faster when both adjectives in a pair described self-attributes, than when one adjective was, and the other adjective was not, a self-attribute.

2.2 Ego-Involvement and Social Perception

Poeschl and Doise report findings that reflect the meaning of ego-involvement and the related *Primus Inter Pares* phenomenon, described by Codol in the 1970s (Codol, 1975). Subjects indicated that various attributes of broadly conceived intelligence describe self more accurately than they describe "people in general". Poeschl and Doise conclude that people perceive themselves as adhering to socially accepted standards to a greater extent than do most other people. Thus, the familiar tendency to perceive self in positive terms was observed. However, the data of Poeschl and Doise indicate yet another significant feature of processing, a context dependency. The intelligence ratings were more favorable, both for the subjects themselves and for other people in general, when ratings were made following previous estimation of animal's intelligence. But, this context effect was significantly smaller for self-ratings than for ratings of people in general. It was also found that the variance of self-ratings was much smaller than the variance of people in general, irrespective of the conditions. This consistency of self-ratings and their relatively greater independence of context, suggest that the principles of self-evaluation are more stable and universal, and hence the underlying ego-involvement mechanisms are really powerful factors. This conclusion is consistent with the general position that cognition is in the service of emotions (Plutchick, 1980), i.e. in the service of the ego.

The relationship between ego-involvement and subjects' judgments of physical interpersonal distance is intriguing (Codol, 1978). **Yinon and Amit**'s findings (obtained on very young subjects) show that the acceptable distance of others to the self is greater than the distance at which something induces the subject to stop when approaching other people. This difference is most clearly apparent when somebody aproaches from behind. The authors suggest that these effects depend on important personal needs such as security or control. They also claim that results are consistent with the tendency – found in studies that require judgments of physical distance between self and others (Codol et al., 1989) – to rate the distance from others to self as smaller than that from self to others. If we understand correctly, this consistency can be interpreted as follows: as a consequence of overrating the distance from the self to others, a greater acceptability of one's own closeness (without violation of somebody's personal space) may occur. The illusion manifest in evaluation asymmetry should therefore have its behavioral consequences.

Among the papers presented in his part of the volume, we find another intriguing result concerning physical space. **Kamińska-Feldman**'s subjects, who had to rate self-to-others or others-to-self distance, showed a different degree, or even a different direction, of asymmetry when the rated objects (presented on diagrams) were more or less dense. When density was low, subjects displayed so-called allocentric asymmetry: they estimated the distance of others to self as greater than the (objectively identical) distance of self to others. When density was high, the degree of so-called egocentric asymmetry increased: subjects had an impression that the distance of others to self is smaller than the distance of self to others. In the same task, where subjects (estimating self-others distance) worked with a small drawing of space, the shift of attention from low density to high density led to different biases in distance rating.

We cannot comment further on Kamińska-Feldman's findings at this point. We will merely note that rating of physical distance and space provide a very promising domain for studying the relationship between nonsocial and social cognition. Relevant findings (Holyoak & Mah, 1982) seem to imply that both purely cognitive skills and motivational processes related to the subject's needs and rules of social evaluation can be involved.

The experiential ego (self as knower) and the conceptual self (self as object), functionally combined in the self-schema, provide a solid basis of "knowledge" and evaluation of other people. Social stereotypes and prejudices, thus rooted in the self-schema, must be very resistant to attempted modifications. But are the ego and the self as powerful as implied by the findings of many social studies?

3. Limits of the Totalitarian Functioning of the Self

We cannot deny Allport's statement (quoted earlier) that "ego-involvement, or its absence, makes a critical difference in human functioning". However, the important question concerns the types of consequences of ego-involvement. Under what circumstances does ego-involvement lead, not to egocentric outcomes but, on the contrary, to nonself-serving or even nonself-related focus on others? Also: under what circumstances does ego-involvement invoke "totalitarian power" of the ego/self and in what situations does the ego/self submit itself to the domination of other structures and regulating forces?

Do La Haye and Lauvergeon studied the functioning of the self-schema as a prototype in interpersonal perception. The subjects were youths (17-to-20-year-olds), who were asked to rate similarities between eight indicated familiar people and themselves. According to the criteria adopted in their analysis, prototypical self-functioning was observed in only about one quarter of the subjects.

This outcome led to a simple assumption concerning the limitations of the totalitarian functions of the ego/self: if the self-schema is to function as a prototype it must be developed (this takes years but even in adults it may be inhibited – cf. Markus & Kitayama, 1991). When ego functions without the mediation of the self-schema, its principles of egocentric operation are not the same: ego may be guided by hedonistic principles or external pressures (cf. Greenwald, 1982), and the effect on social information processing is different.

The ego/self does not always play a dominant role. Emotional-motivational and cognitive processes may be triggered by external factors, internalized norms, or other, nonself-related schematic representations, as is indicated by some of the studies of asymmetry in self-others similarity/distance rating that are presented in this volume.

The asymmetry effect has been studied both with respect to physical distance and similarity judgments (Rosch, 1975; Tversky, 1977), and for various categories of objects: colors, letters, numbers, geometric figures, social objects, and interpersonal relations. Convergence of outcomes, despite such considerable diversity of object classes, suggests that some pervasive cognitive mechanism determines the observed asymmetries. Series of experiments have yielded the following general principle: nonprototypical objects and/or less salient ones seem closer (physically close, more similar) to prototypical or more salient objects than the reverse. Codol's finding, that in self-other comparisons it is the others who seem more similar to the self (and also closer in terms of physical distance – cf. Codol, 1984a, 1984b, 1987; see also Holyoak & Gordon, 1983; Srull & Gaelick, 1983), has led to the formulation of the hypothesis whereby the self-schema functions as a prototype in person perception.

Several studies on the asymmetry called egocentric (whereby similarity or physical proximity of others to the self is rated as greater than that of self to others) have corroborated the hypothesized prototypicality of the self-schema. Greater asymmetry of this type is found in people in whom we may suspect a well-developed self-schema: people with a high level of private self-consciousness (Srull & Gaelick, 1983) or people with considerable self-we-others distinctiveness (Jarymowicz, in press; Kamińska-Feldman, 1992; Szuster-Zbrojewicz, 1989).

However, the same studies have also shown that some persons do not reveal any egocentric (or groupcentric) asymmetry. This would suggest that in some people the self(we)-schema does not function as a prototype.

A reversed asymmetry effect has been observed in many studies on rating self-others similarity/distance. Kamińska-Feldman (1988) found a reversed asymmetry effect when she focused her subjects' attention on other people: she called this the allocentric asymmetry effect. It is worth noting, on the basis of Kamińska-Feldman's studies (and several dozen other studies completed at the University of Warsaw – cf. Jarymowicz, 1989) that, irrespective of the experimental contingencies (facilitation of attentional focus on the self or facilitation of attention to others), some subjects reveal the allocentric asymmetry pattern.

The self may be powerful or it may be limited depending on the specific characteristics of the self-schema or other cognitive schemata, as well as situational factors, facilitating the actualization of one or the other (Jarymowicz & Kamińska-Feldman, 1988).

Holyoak and Gordon (1983) have shown that when attention is focused on relatively nonstereotyped objects this was accompanied by egocentric asymmetry, whereas focus on objects with very well-developed stereotypes led to what we call allocentric asymmetry. In **Karyłowski**'s studies, the egocentric asymmetry effect emerged in the self-primed but not in other-primed condition.

Vermunt and Extra obtained a reversed asymmetry effect by manipulating objects' prototypicality. Their data showed the susceptibility of the asymmetry effect to situational factors, including social ones.

The presented studies on asymmetry in self-others comparisons appear to confirm Tversky's claim, based on research on comparison of other classes of objects: [...] the direction of asymmetry is determined by the relevant salience of the stimuli so that the less salient stimulus is more similar to the salient than vice versa. In particular, the variant is more similar to the prototype than the prototype is to the variant, because the prototype is generally more salient than the variant." (Tversky, 1977, p. 333). The implication of this statement is the conjoncture that asymmetry in rating of psychological or physical distance is determined not only by cognitive mechanisms, but also by social factors. These affect the direction of attention and hence lead to an increase in the object's salience.

The susceptibility of self-others asymmetry effects to various factors, manifest in the ease with which the direction of asymmetry can be reversed, may thus indicate limitations on the totalitarian power of the ego/self in relation to other sociocognitive schemata.

References

Allport, G. W. (1943). The ego in contemporary psychology. *Psychological Review, 50,* 451-478.

Allport, G. W. (1961). *Pattern and growth in personality.* New York: Holt, Rinehart & Winston.

Aronson, E. (in press). The return of the repressed: Dissonance theory makes a comeback. *Psychological Inquiry.*

Brown, J. D. (in press). Self-esteem and self-evaluation: Feeling is believing. In J. Suls (Ed.), *Psychological perspectives on the self* (Vol. 4). Hillsdale, NJ: Erlbaum.

12

Codol, J.-P. (1975). On the so-called "superior conformity of the self" behavior: Twenty experimental investigations. *European Journal of Social Psychology, 5,* 457-500.

Codol, J.-P. (1978). Espace personnel, distance interindividuelle et densité sociale. *Revue de Psychologie Appliquée, 28,* 43-68 and 129-147.

Codol, J.-P. (1984a). La perception de la similitude interpersonnelle: influence de l'appartenance catégorielle et du point de référence de la comparaison. *L'Année Psychologique, 84,* 43-56.

Codol, J.-P. (1984b). Quand Dupont ressemble à Dupond plus que Dupond à Dupont : l'asymétrie de la similitude perçue entre personnes semblables. *Psychologie Française, 29,* 284-290.

Codol, J.-P. (1985). L'estimation des distances physiques entre personnes : suis-je aussi loin de vous que vous l'êtes de moi? *L'Année Psychologique, 85,* 517-534.

Codol, J.-P. (1987). Comparability and incomparability between oneself and others: Means of differentiation and comparison reference points. *Cahiers de Psychologie Cognitive / European Bulletin of Cognitive Psychology, 7,* 87-105.

Codol, J.-P., Jarymowicz, M., Kamińska-Feldman, M., & Szuster-Zbrojewicz, A. (1989). Asymmetry in the estimation of interpersonal distance and identity affirmation. *European Journal of Social Psychology, 19,* 11-22.

Dymkowski, M. (1989). *Samowiedza a psychologiczne konsekwencje ocen.* Wroclaw: Wydawnictwa Politechniki Wrocławskiej.

Epstein, S. (1980). The self-concept: A review and the proposal of an integrated theory of personality. In E. Staub (Ed.), *Personality: Basic issues and current research.* Englewood Cliffs, NJ: Prentice-Hall.

Erikson, E. H. (1956). The problem of ego identity. In M. R. Stein, A. J. Vidich, & D. M. White (Eds.), *Identity and anxiety.* Glencoe, IL: Free Press.

Freud, S. (1923). Das Ich und das Es. In S. Freud, *Gesammelte Werke.* London: Imago.

Gergen, K. J. (1971). *The concept of self.* New York: Holt, Rinehart and Winston.

Greenwald, A. G. (1980). The totalitarian ego: Fabrication and revision of personal history. *American Psychologist, 35,* 603-618.

Greenwald, A. G. (1982). Ego-task analysis: An integration of research on ego-involvement and self-awareness. In A. H. Hastorf & A. M. Isen (Eds.), *Cognitive social psychology* (pp. 10-147). New York: Elsevier/North-Holland.

Greenwald, A. G., & Pratkanis, A. R. (1984). The self. In R. S. Wyer & T. K. Srull (Eds.), *Handbook of social cognition* (Vol. 3, pp. 129-178). Hillsdale, NJ: Erlbaum.

Grzegołowska-Klarkowska, H. (1986). *Mechanizmy obronne osobowości*. Warszawa: PWN.

Hardoin, M. & Codol, J.-P. (1984). Descriptions de soi et d'autrui : influence de l'ordre des descriptions sur les catégories de réponses utilisées. *Cahiers de Psychologie Cognitive, 4,* 295-302.

Higgins, E. T. (1987). Self-discrepancy: A theory relating self and affect. *Psychological Review, 94,* 319-340.

Holyoak, K. J., & Gordon, P. C. (1983). Social reference points. *Journal of Personality and Social Psychology, 44,* 881-887.

Holyoak, K. J., & Mah, W. A. (1982). Cognitive reference points in judgments of symbolic magnitude. *Cognitive Psychology, 14,* 328-352.

James, W. (1890). *The principles of psychology.* New York: Holt.

Jarymowicz, M. (Ed.) (1989). Spostrzeganie samego siebie. *Studia Psychologiczne* (special issue). Wrocław: Ossolineum.

Jarymowicz, M. (in press). An attempt to operationalize "social versus personal identity" constructs. In M. Jarymowicz (Ed.), *To know self – To understand others.* Delft, The Netherlands: Eburon.

Jarymowicz, M., & Codol, J.-P. (1979). Spostrzegane podobieństwo ja – inni ludzie a formowanie obrazu nieznanej osoby. *Przegląd Psychologiczny, 16,* 73-88.

Jarymowicz, M., & Kamińska-Feldman, M. (1988). "Totalitarian ego" and cognitive biases: Is the asymmetry effect related to the self prototypicality in social perception? In *Proceedings of the CREPCO European Conference on Cognitive Biases* (pp. B1-B10). Aix-en-Provence: Université de Provence.

Kamińska-Feldman, M. (1988). Conditions of social deindividuation and asymmetry in rating self-other distance. *Polish Psychological Bulletin, 19,* 241-248.

Kamińska-Feldman, M. (1992). The self status and the asymmetry effect in interpersonal distance rating. In L. Arcuri & C. Serino (Eds.), *Asymmetry phenomena in interpersonal comparison : Cognitive and social issues* (pp. 61-69). Napoli: Liguori Editore.

Markus, H. R., Crane, M., & Siladi, M. (1978, May). *Cognitive consequences of androgyny.* Paper presented at the meeting of the Midwestern Psychological Association, Chicago.

Markus, H. R., & Kitayama, S. (1991). Culture and the self: Implications for cognition, emotion, and motivation. *Psychological Review, 98,* 224-253.

Markus, H. R., & Nurius, P. (1986). Possible selves. *American Psychologist, 41,* 954-969.

Plutchik, R. (1980). *Emotion: A psychoevolutionary synthesis.* New York: Harper and Row.

Rosch, E. (1975). Cognitive reference points. *Cognitive Psychology, 7,* 532-547.

Srull, T. K., & Gaelick, L. (1983). General principles and individual differences in the self as a habitual reference point: An examination of self-other judgments of similarity. *Social Cognition, 2,* 108-121.

Steele, C. M. (1988). The psychology of self-affirmation: Sustaining the integrity of the self. In L. Berkowitz (Ed.), *Advances in experimental social psychology* (Vol. 21, pp. 261-302). New York: Academic Press.

Swann, W. B. (1990). To be adored or to be known? The interplay of self-enhancement and self-verification. In E. T. Higgins & R. M. Sorrentino (Eds.), *Handbook of motivation and cognition* (Vol. 2, pp. 408-448). New York: Guilford.

Szuster-Zbrojewicz, A. (1989). Poznawcze wyodrębnienie własnej osoby a przejawy asymetrii w ocenianiu dystansów ja-my-inni. *Studia Psychologiczne, 27,* 55-71.

Tap, P. (1985). *La société Pygmalion ? Intégration sociale et réalisation de la personne.* Paris : Dunod.

Tesser, A. (1988). Toward a self-evaluation maintenance model of social behavior. In L. Berkowitz (Ed.), *Advances in experimental social psychology* (Vol.21, pp. 181-227). New York: Academic Press.

Trzebińska, E. (1991, September). *Attitudes towards minority group members as a result of problems with own national identity.* Paper presented at Changing stereotypes Symposium, Paris.

Tversky, A. (1977). Features of similarity. *Psychological Review, 84,* 327-352.

Winczo, M. (1991). *Kody reprezentacji a odporność na nacisk społeczny: pomiędzy hipotezą zgodności kodów a hypotezą genezy kodów.* Unpublished PhD Thesis, University of Warsaw.

Wyer, R. S. , & Srull, T. K. (1989). *Memory and cognition in its social context.* Hillsdale, NJ: Erlbaum.

SELF, OTHERS, AND GENDER MODELS OF THE PERSON

Annick Durand-Delvigne

Charles de Gaulle University , Lille , France

This research concerns the homology of cognitive organization specific to the representation of the self and the representation of others. To be more precise, our aim is to assess the links and gaps between the representation of others, self-representation, and the stereotyped gender representations, and to analyze the possible causal factors which connect these three representational products.

1. Theoretical Questions

This study raises the question of the status of the self in social cognition. Is the self an autonomous, generative entity of the representation of the social word, or is it, on the contrary, a dependent structure whose organization and content are determined by supra-social factors, and which is related to functions of social control?

1.1 The Self as a Particular Cognitive Structure
The growth of cognitive psychology has made it possible to look at this question from a different angle, an empirical one. From a cognitive viewpoint, the self is seen as a prototype or a set of higher order schematas whose elements (general components as well as specific components based on traits[1] and behaviors) are organized hierarchically. This approach has generally brought about a conceptualisation of the self as a powerful integrative cognitive structure (Markus & Sentis, 1982) which acts as a prototype for processing personal information (Rogers, 1981; Rogers, Kuiper, & Kirker, 1977; Rogers, Rogers, & Kuiper, 1979;) and upon which the perceptions and representations of the social world

---

[1] Consequently, the data collection method generally involves using a list of personality traits (technique validated in an experiment by Gara and Rosenberg, 1981).

16

depend. Indeed, even if some of the authors believe that the representation of the self and the representation of others bring the same mechanisms into play and depend on similar structures (Wegner & Wallacher, 1977), it is at present a relatively accepted opinion that the self is a unique structure, of a different nature (Kuiper & Derry, 1981; Kuiper & Rogers, 1979), which has a very definite influence on interpersonal perception and social interaction (Markus, 1977; Markus & Smith, 1981). For Markus and Sentis (1982), the self is not only a different structure, but certainly the central and primary structure through which information is processed.

So when it comes to relating self-perception to the perception of others, most authors agree to acknowledge the prominence of the self.[2] The self is assumed to determine the parameters in which others are perceived, which results in an isomorphism of the representational products.

However, while numerous theorists contend that there is complete interdependence between self-perception and the perception of others, and see the self as a pivot in the whole process of the perception of people, the claimed direction of the relation (self → others) is not the same in all cases.[3] Indeed, in the analysis of the relationship between self-perception and the perception of others, one must consider two aspects: (1) the aversion individuals feel to similarity; (2) whether the others are familiar or not.

1.1.1 Hardoin and Codol (1984) showed how individuals have a prototypical conception of themselves: they see themselves as the model for any interpersonal comparison. But, so as to defend their own identity, they seem to strive to be different from others. The experimental paradigm used by these authors involved two steps: the subjects described themselves, and then described a person in a photograph, or vice versa. The results showed that subjects in the first situation acted as models; the descriptions were similar. Conversely, subjects in the second situation (describe someone, then describe oneself) described themselves differently from the way they described others.

---

[2] As noted by Hamilton (1981) who gave Bruner and Tagiuri (1954) as an example, the idea that the perceiver's cognitive structure could influence the way she or he perceives others is not new, by the way.

[3] It must be noted on this subject that in a 1985 text, published in collaboration with other authors, Markus slightly alters her first theorization on this theme. On the other hand, recent works such as de La Haye and Lauvergeon's (see their chapter in this book) show that as far as the representation of the self and others goes, the correlations are not as strong as suggested in the literature, and to be more precise, the isomorphism may apply to girls only and not to boys.

Codol's former works, especially those on the *Primus Inter Pares* (PIP) effect (1975, 1979) brought to light the way individuals make use of differentiation strategies when they find themselves in a situation of great comparability (these strategies consist of asserting that oneself conforms more closely to the norms of the group, a behavior referred to by Codol as the superior conformity of the self). For Codol, behaviors which differ from the norm are connected to the feeling of personal uniqueness. This search for uniqueness "depends itself on a more general and more powerful factor which determines behavior: affirming a certain picture of oneself" (1979, p. 254, *our translation*).

A dual mechanism therefore intervenes in interpersonal perception with an assimilation process centred on the self (others are like me) and a differentiation process stating uniqueness (I am different from others). The self is the core of interpersonal comparison and thus descriptions of others are similar to descriptions of the self. However, in situations where one's sense of identity is threatened (similarity imposed by a third person, others given as a point of reference), the distance between the self and others will be greater. In this case incomparability prevails (Codol, 1987). For Jarymowicz, the results obtained by Codol, as well as those she obtained in collaboration with him, claim the existence in self/others perception of an interplay of general (self-related) and subjective (self-serving) biases which she refers to as egocentric asymmetry (see Leyens, 1990; see also Jarymowicz, 1988). This egocentric asymmetry will determine differentiation or similarity in self/others perception, depending on whether or not the conditions are favorable to the person's identity.

1.1.2 Research on the perception of others shows that previous knowledge of the target person may have an influence on the subject's assessments. Although some authors have shown that the same trait structures were used for a familiar person and for a stranger (Passini & Norman, 1966; Wiggins & Blackburn, 1976), others emphasise that, depending on the degree of familiarity, structural differences are brought to the fore, and that it would be advisable to make the distinction between familiar persons (non-strangers) and intimate persons (father, mother, self, lover and to a lesser extent best friend). Indeed, as demonstrated by studies on the perception of others, the former do not elicit cognitive productions which are organized differently from those produced for a stranger, while the latter bring forward particular responses (Gara & Rosenberg, 1981).

We also need to stress that, according to Ostrom, Pryor, and Simpson (1981), only target persons who are known and familiar can be construed through a local implicit personality theory (IPT). For these authors, only familiarity produces organisation of information about the target person. In the case of unfamiliar persons, information would be organized in another cognitive mode (by semantic closeness of traits, by reference to categories, by reference to the perceiver's spatiotemporal experiences, by the self).

The question of whether or not the target person is familiar is also relevant to the study of the relationship between self-perception and perception of others. As pointed out by Markus, Smith, and Moreland (1985) most of the research on perception of self/others uses an experimental condition where the target person is not well-known to the subject (in which case, as mentioned previously, we observe a structuring effect of the self on the way the others are perceived). However in the case of a known target person, the situation is different, since the other person, as an unambiguous and rich stimulus, may be expected to bring into play specific cognitive structures. Indeed, when the other person is poorly known or ambiguous, the self controls the abstraction process, thus allowing the information available about the other person to be summarized. The self then has an "embellishment function": it uses the content of its prototype to "dress up" the way the other is represented. When the target person is known, things work differently. If this person is familiar, two elements come into play: on the one hand, there is more information available, on the other, the element of familiarity makes the construction of a specific cognitive structure possible (Kuiper & Jones, 1978, quoted by Rogers, 1981 ; Kuiper & Derry, 1981).

1.2 Cognitive Representations and Social Cognitive Representations of People

Is the representation of people purely a question of cognitive elaboration, or is it a social cognitive product of a mainly social origin? Are representations of the self and others specific and autonomous developments? Could there be some more general representations of the person and what would their roles be in social perception?

Since Asch (1946), an extensive amount of research about interpersonal perception has provided some answers to these questions.

One body of research grew out of the notion of implicit personality theory (Bruner & Tagiuri, 1954), an expression which suggests that social perception takes shape from preestablished postulates made possible by rules which organize the information perceived. In everyday life, the individual is assumed to implicitly use those theories in the course of her/his social interactions. The perception of others is thus organized from preexisting structures (Passini & Norman, 1966). According to some authors such as Cantor and Mischel (1977), it is with the aid of abstract prototypes, unified categories of specific personality traits, that the individual effectively processes information about others and ends up "knowing" them (cf. Paicheler, 1984).

Another body of research was established to study the effects of these structures. It addressed the question of how social schemas[4] govern the encoding, organization, and retention of information (cf. Taylor & Crocker, 1981). Going along with this view, Hamilton (1981) maintained that the processing of information about the self and about others takes place within an organized and general conceptual framework. Hamilton and Leiner (1979, cited in Hamilton, 1981) proved through experiments that perceivers use the same schemas in order to process information on the self and others.[5] According to Hamilton, there exists a unique set of schemas related to the nature and content of personality, a worthwhile set of schemas which can be used for the self and others. He does not state what might be the origin of this superstructure.

A different approach to social cognition validates the hypothesis that the origin of this superstructure is as much, if not more, of a social nature than a cognitive one. Indeed, an essentially European trend of research which criticizes the social cognitivism of psychology for concentrating too much on the study of individual mechanisms, incorporates social and ideological factors into its analysis of the question of interpersonal and social representations (Deschamps, 1973; Moscovici, 1982; Paicheler, 1984). Seen from this angle, the problem becomes understanding the social causes and functions of the identified mechanisms, and their interdependence with the individual causes and functions. The function of the reciprocal relationship between "the ideological" and "the cognitive" is thus a definite prospect. To be more precise, social models which draw their ideological origin from the social organization are thought to affect interpersonal perception structures whose cognitive implementation would act as a guardian of the social order. The study of the "psychologization" of social utilities (Beauvois & Joule, 1981; Aldrovandi & Gryselier, 1986) provides a good analysis of the way social utilities (a set of values and behaviors necessary for social order and the proper functioning of organizations) change into "natural" personality traits which are classified in implicit personality theories, and which, through daily use, render legitimate each person's place in the social fabric.

---

[4] That is to say the cognitive constructions related to the way the world functions. These can be summed up in three general classes: person schemas, role schemas, and event schemas.

[5] In their experiments, "other" is an unspecified other, "a person" (see previous discussion).

This postulate, which links interpersonal representations to a social and ideological process, may be equally relevant to self-representation (cf. Wicklund, 1982).

Generally speaking, one could make the assumption that the person's normative social models, as they are formed in a given culture, generate and structure the perceptions and representations of others and of the self. These models may not be general, that is, they may not have the same relevance for everyone. They may not stand for the ideal model of the human being, in which case such an assumption would be trivial. They are not the product of the ontological identity mentioned by Deconchy (1987).[6] Instead, they are thought to be linked to social positions and to specify desirable personality characteristics according to social positions. Moreover, more than simple reference norms, they form the functional elements of the mental system creating knowledge on the self and others.

The self can be seen as a mediator between these social models and others: social models are assumed to generate a representation of the self which in its turn influences the way others are represented.

It seems to us that gender, seen as a unit of representational and attributive meaning which underlies a major social categorization, makes it possible to operationalize the ways in which ideological factors influence the processes of social perception and self-perception.

2. The Experiment

2.1 Objective and Procedure

A former study with a "raw" sample enabled us to conduct an independent and comparative analysis of the specific content of self-representations, representations of others, and gender stereotypes (Durand-Delvigne, 1989). The aim of the present study was to examine the potential relationship between these three types of representations for a better defined sample, and to test a model which includes the social representations of the person – attained through gender stereotypes in this case – as a causal factor.

The data collection procedure consisted of three phases aimed at obtaining expressions of: a) implicit theories or representations of the personality of a familiar other; b) implicit theories or representations of the self; and c) gender-related stereotypes.

---

6 The ontological identity refers to a general idea of the person "without any reference to a particular system." (Deconchy, 1987, p. 153, *our translation*).

To this end, we used the long version of the Bem Sex-Role Inventory [7] (Bem, 1974) translated into French, which includes sixty personality traits. The same list was used in each of the phases.[8] Each item was followed by a six-point scale. The subject expressed his or her degree of support for each item from "never true" (point 1 on the scale) to "quite true" (point 6) for the tasks involving other- and self-representation, from "not at all desirable" (point 1) to "quite desirable" (point 6) for the expression of gender stereotypes.

The instructions for these phases were the following:

"You are going to think of someone you know: we would like to know the impression you have of the chosen person's personality" (for the other-representation phase).

"We would like you to think of yourself and describe yourself with the following list of characteristics" (for the self-representation phase).

"We would like to know if, in your opinion, it is desirable for women in our society to possess the following characteristics" (for the gender stereotype phase).

In each phase the instructions were followed by explanations of how to use the scales.

The sample consisted of thirty adult women. Each subject performed the three phases in the following order: representation of the other person, self-representation, characteristics desirable for women.

The data were processed using three techniques. Factorial correspondence analysis was done in order to study the specificities and similarities of factor structures in each phase. A multiple factorial analysis was used to assess the relative importance of each of the three groups of data, as well as the discrepancy between them. Lastly, a dependency analysis was used to study the possible causal relationships between the three representational products.

---

[7] In this study, the Bem Sex-Role Inventory (BSRI) was used as an inventory of personality, and not as a measure of the subjects' gender orientation. We used the French version as the survey population was French.

[8] With an independent sample, we tested for the possible order effect with the chi-squared test. Results showed that the answers to each item and the set of all answers to all items had nothing to do with the phase order.

3. Results

3.1 Factorial correspondence Analysis
The rates of inertia processed by the first factors are given in Table 1.

Table 1
Rates of Inertia (%) for the First Three Factors in Factorial Correspondence Analysis, by Phase

Factors	Other	Self	Stereotype
F1	25.71	15.44	25.11
F2	10.90	12.24	12.16
F3	7.90	9.73	9.03
Total	44.51	37.41	46.30

The first factor of the other-representation phase and the first factor of the gender stereotype phase are more consequential than that of the self-representation phase (they account respectively for 25.71%, 25.11%, and 15.44% of the total inertia).[9]

This difference between the rates points out in particular that the subjects' representations of others were less diversified than their self-representations (although the targets were just as diverse; cf. the instructions "think of someone you know"). Likewise, the representation of characteristics desirable for women involved a limited number of dimensions.

It will become apparent that the multiple factorial analysis goes along with this analysis by showing that self-representation relies on a greater number of dimensions.

A comparison of the data organization in each phase uncovers some similarities and some differences. The similarity is based on the fact that the first factors in each phase have an assessment value and that, for their negative pole, they are determined by sets of relatively similar items carrying a negative connotation. There were some differences however. For example, the item "masculine" appears in the self and stereotype phases, but not in the other phase (see Table 2).

---

[9] We found the same difference between the rates of inertia for the first factors of the three phases on other adult sample. This is not true for samples of 16 to 18 year-old female students.

23

Table 2

Items Contributing the Most to the Negative Pole of Factor 1 in the Correspondence Analysis, by Phase

Other		Self		Stereotype	
Items	CTR	Items	CTR	Items	CTR
conceited	10.0	jealous	11.2	childlike	10.8
aggressive	6.8	childlike	10.0	inefficient	9.1
moody	5.8	gullible	6.5	moody	7.4
gullible	5.8	moody	5.3	unsystematic	6.9
unpredictable	5.0	inefficient	4.4	flatterer	6.5
childlike	4.5	unsystematic	4.3	solemn	6.0
flatterer	4.3	secretive	4.1	unpredictable	5.5
inefficient	2.3	shy	3.8	masculine	4.6
		masculine	2.6	conceited	4.3
				jealous	3.6

CTR = contributions

On the other hand, at the opposite pole of the factors, the data from the three phases generated different organizations which bring into play positively connotated items with different meanings. More precisely, a difference was observed between other-representation on the one hand and self-representation and gender stereotype on the other.

Indeed, at this pole, the first factor of the other-representation phase consists of an item expressing a positive social attitude whereas the first factors of the self-representation and gender stereotype phases are determined by items connected with agency. There appears to be a greater similarity, for the first factor, between these last two phases, even if there are some features specific to each (use of items traditionally associated with femininity in the stereotype phase, and use of items connected with assertiveness in the self phase; see Table 3).

Table 3

Items Contributing the Most to the Positive Pole of Factor 1 in the Correspondence Analysis, by Phase

Other		Self		Stereotype	
Items	CTR	Items	CTR	Items	CTR
tactful	3.9	makes decisions easily	8.3	willing to take risks	3.2
		acts as leader	6.8	has leadership abilities	2.4
		self-reliant	5.5	understanding	2.1
		has leadership abilities	3.4	does not use harsh language	2.1
		willing to take risks	2.2		

The difference between other-representation phase and self-representation and gender stereotype phases appears again in all of the other analyzed factors (first three factors).

The factors of the other-representation phase are indicative of social evaluation whereas those of the self-representation and gender stereotype phases bring into play traditional gender orientations (communion and agency).

3. 2 Multiple Factorial Analysis

The multiple factorial analysis[10] was used to compare the data groups found for the different phases of the study. In the following text, group 1 refers to other-representation, group 2 to self-representation, and group 3 to gender stereotype.

The comparative study of the histograms of the specific values obtained through partial analysis showed that group 2 was the "richest" group, with the greatest number of factors brought into play (pluridimensionality of the self). Comparing these histograms with those obtained through general analysis showed that they were similar. This is an initial indication of the strength of self-related data and their role in the general structure.

The first eigen value of general analysis could be 3 since we have three data groups. This would mean in this case that the first factor of general analysis would be common to the first factors of the three groups and therefore these three factors would be perfectly identical.

In our study, the eigen value of general analysis was 2.03. One can therefore conclude that the first factor accounts for a large amount of the total variation of the three groups, although each has its own specific margins.

By studying the correlations between the canonical variables (factors of the partial analysis) and the general variables (factors of the general analysis) we can see that the first factor of the general analysis is closely related to the first factor of groups 2 and 3, and consequently this factor is common to them (see Table 4). Note also that the second factor can be declared common to the three groups (equally high correlation indices). Lastly, we find that group 2 strongly influences the third and fourth factors.

---

[10] The data from all the weighted groups were processed as a whole by a analysis into principal components (general analysis), and the first factors from the data of each group (partial analysis) were treated as additional variables (canonical variables).

Table 4

Correlations between the Canonical Variables and the General Variables for the First Four Factors of the Multiple Factorial Analysis

Groups	F1	F2	F3	F4
Group 1	.76	.84	.74	.90
Group 2	.92	.82	.84	.92
Group 3	.94	.90	.79	.76

Note that :
(1) Whereas groups 2 and 3 are jointly strongly present on the first axis and therefore close to each other for this factor, group 1 is not as strongly concerned;
(2) factor 2 is common to all groups;
(3) group 2 influences all factors;
(4) group 3 appears very strong for the first two factors.

The partial analysis and the general analysis thus yelded similar results indicating a connection between the groups. However this connection is not complete. In particular, group 1 is set apart from the rest. Besides, the self appears as a fundamental structure (group 2 was active for all factors). Finally the self and gender stereotype are close (at least for the first two factors).

One part of this analysis was confirmed by studying the coordinates of the three groups. The coordinates of one group can be interpreted in a multiple factor analysis as the absolute contribution of the variables of this group to the relevant factor of general analysis (Escofier & Pagès, 1988). We can thus discover the groups which have most influenced the factors in the general analysis, which provides further evidence of a connection. Generally the groups' contribution to the first factor is fairly balanced. This finding was not borne out in our case, which stresses the specificity of our results. Indeed, for the first factor, a large discrepancy between the coordinates of groups 2 and 3 (respectively 788, % of var. – 90.78, and 826, % of var. = 40.65) and those of group 1 (418, % of var. = 20.57) was observed (see Table 5). So groups 2 and 3 largely contributed to the first factor whereas group 1 was barely concerned. On the other hand, group 1 contributed to a larger extent to factor 2 than groups 2 and 3 did (611, % of var. = 45.13 vs. 485, % of var. = 35.82 and 258, % of var. = 19.05 respectively). Let us mention that group 2 also contributed to factor 4, which indicates its strength again.

Table 5

Coordinates of the Groups on the First Four Factors of the Multiple Factorial Analysis

Groups	F1	% var.	F2	% var.	F3	% var.	F4	% var.
Group 1	418	20.57	611	45.13	387	34.83	264	26.40
Group 2	788	38.78	485	35.82	347	31.23	487	48.70
Group 3	826	40.65	258	19.05	377	33.93	249	24.90
Eigen-value	2033		1356		1111		1001	

These indications confirm and complete the previous interpretation: groups 2 and 3 contributed jointly to factor 1, group 1 was essentially concerned by the common factor, factor 2.

The study of the coordinates of the partial axes (correlation between the axes of the general analysis and the partial axes of each group) also indicates that the first axis of analysis in the principal components of group 2, and the first axis of analysis in the principal components of group 3 are strongly correlated to the first axis of the general analysis (cos^2 75.4 and cos^2 68.3) but this was not true of group 1 (cos^2 25.2).

Processing the data by multiple factor analysis allowed us to conclude that there is a gap between the structure of the representation of a familiar other and the structure of the representation of the self and the gender characteristics. Moreover the representation of the self appears as a fundamental structure.

3.3 Dependency Analysis

The aim here was to work out and test a causal structure which account for dependency relationships between the three types of representation. We used the dependency analysis method which enabled us to assess the validity of recursive causal graphs (no feedback).[11]

Dependency analysis was conducted on the factorial coordinates of the individuals in the correspondence analysis (which was carried out on the replies to the three phases). That is to say, we calculated the correlation matrix between the factorial coordinates on the first three factors of the three analyses in a given theoretical order. In connection with the theoretical analysis of the link between the social models of the person and social perceptions, the reference model is:

---

[11] The program was developed by Chirol (1976) at C.R.E.S. of Vaucresson. The dependency analysis was carried out in this case on the first three factors of the correspondence analysis of the three phases.

Gender Stereotypes (St) → Self (S) → Others (O). We can therefore expect the graph showing the most powerful causal links start from the Stereotype condition factors (St1, St2, St3), go through Self condition factors (S1, S2, S3), and end on the Other condition factors (O1, O2, O3). We nevertheless studied all the possible models in order to retain the one that carries the most dependencies. This involved checking all the possible orders and combinations between factors.

The results did not validate the theoretical model of reference. In fact, the orientated graph St → S → O brings out certain dependencies which go in the same direction as the hypothesis (St1 → St3, St3 → O1, St3 → S2 → O2 and O3, St1→ S3 → O2, for coefficients of dependency > .50). But above all it shows an effect starting from S. This effect is also found on graphs oriented in a different way.

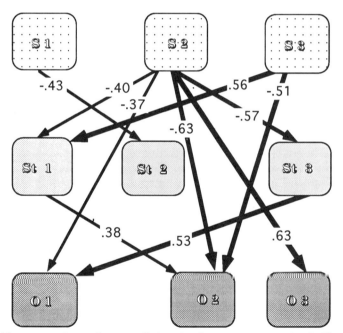

The connections whose coefficient is above .30 are retained. The connections whose coefficient is above .50 are highlighted. (S = Self, St = Stereotype, O = Other).

Figure 1. Dependency analysis for the first three factors of the correspondence analysis of the three phases (graph orientation: Self → Stereotypes →Others).

Therefore, causality is mainly organized with the self as a starting point. In particular, factors 2 and 3 of this phase were on all graphs, the most powerful causal sources. Notably a powerful causal effect of Self on Others has been identified. It is expressed in particular by the dependency of factor 2 of the Self phase (S2) on the three factors of the Other person phase (O1, O2, O3). The coefficients of dependency are for the most part negative (see figure 1). There is therefore a connection between the factors which organize the self-representation and those which organize the representation of others, but the axes are inverted. For the items affected by these factors, the subjects' answers placed others and the self at different poles.

These graphs prove the "centrality" of the self and stress a strategy of differentiation in relation to others to a larger extent than they prove the major influence of stereotypes on representations of the self and others.

4. Conclusion

Data relating to the representation of a familiar other, self-representation, and gender stereotype were collected from a sample of adult women using an inventory of personality and processed by means of three different methods. They testify to the strength, central role and influential position of the self in social cognition.

The analysis of the data (factorial analysis of correspondence and multiple factorial analysis) showed that the representation of the self and gender stereotypes are close in meanings. The factors which organized the data in both correspondence analyses were similar in content. The multiple factorial analysis confirmed this similarity and showed that, in a general analysis, these two conditions are linked. Furthermore it indicated that the representation of the self is the decisive structure.

The dependency analysis, a quantitative method, confirmed this central role of the self, uncovered by the multiple factor analysis. For the subjects in this study, other representations, especially that of other persons, are based on dimensions which are active in self-representations. In the representation of others, dependency is mainly organized by a principle of differentiation from others.

The direction of the dependency relation found in this sample is consistent with Codol's theoretical and empirical work. It stresses the effect of "self-centering", and through the differentiation process which was uncovered, it evokes the asymmetry of the representational products relating to the self and others.

In our case, this effect of egocentric asymmetry (to restate Jarymowicz' formula, 1988) appeared in connection with a familiar other, whose representation depended on the structures of the self. Even if specific factors organize the representation of a familiar other, as revealed by the factorial analysis of correspondence, they are linked to those which structure the representation of the self. To sum up, for this sample, the hypothesis that representations of the self and others are dependent on gender models of people was not confirmed. Models of the self and of gender were found to have similar organizations but, as far as "functionality" is concerned, the representation of the self is the active structure in social cognition.

References

Aldrovandi, M. & Gryselier, M. (1986). Théories implicites de la personnalité professionnelle. *Psychologie Française, 31,* 123-127.

Asch, S. E. (1946). Forming impressions of personality. *Journal of Abnormal and Social Psychology, 41,* 258-290.

Beauvois, J.-L. & Joule, R. V., (1981). *Soumission et idéologies.* Paris : Presses Universitaires de France.

Bem, S. L. (1974). The measurement of psychological androgyny. *Journal of Consulting and Clinical Psychology, 42,* 155-162.

Bruner, J. S., & Tagiuri, R. (1954). Person perception. In G. Lindsey (Ed.), *Handbook of social psychology* (Vol. 2, pp. 634-654). Reading, MA: Addison-Wesley.

Cantor, N., & Mischel, W. (1977). Traits as prototypes: Effects on recognition memory. *Journal of Personality and Social Psychology, 35,* 38-48.

Chirol, Y. (1976). *L'analyse de dépendance : modèle théorique, pratique des calculs.* Vaucresson : Centre de Recherche de l'Education Surveillée. Unpublished manuscript.

Codol, J.-P. (1975). On the so-called "Superior Conformity of the Self" behavior: Twenty experimental investigations. *European Journal of Social Psychology, 5,* 457-501.

Codol, J.-P, (1979). *Semblables et différents. Recherches sur la quête de la similitude et de la différenciation sociale* Unpublished doctoral thesis, University of Provence, Aix-en-Provence, France.

Codol, J.-P. (1987). Comparability and incomparability between oneself and others: Means of differentiation and comparison reference points. *Cahiers de Psychologie Cognitive/European Bulletin of Cognitive Psychology, 7,* 87-105.

Deconchy, J.-P. (1987). Conduites sociales, comparaison sociale et représentation du patrimoine comportemental commun à l'homme et à l'animal. In J.-L. Beauvois, R. V. Joule & J.-M.

Monteil (Eds.), *Perspectives cognitives et conduites sociales* (Vol. 1, p. 151-186). Cousset : Delval.

Deschamps, J.-C. (1973). L'attribution, la catégorisation sociale et les représentations intergroupes. *Bulletin de Psychologie, 27*, 710-721.

Durand-Delvigne, A. (1989). Schéma de genre et cognition sociale. *Revue Internationale de Psychologie Sociale, 2*, 467-481.

Escofier, B. & Pagès, J. (1988). *Analyses factorielles simples et multiples.* Paris: Dunod.

Gara, M. A., & Rosenberg, S. (1981). Linguistic factors in implicit personality theory. *Journal of Personality and Social Psychology, 41*, 450-457.

Hamilton, D. L. (1981). Cognitive representations of persons. In E. T. Higgins, C. P. Herman, & M. P. Zanna (Eds.). *Social Cognition: TheOntario Symposium* (pp. 135-159). Hillsdale, NJ: Erlbaum.

Hardoin, M. & Codol, J.-P. (1984). Descriptions de soi et d'autrui : influence de l'ordre des descriptions sur les catégories de réponses utilisées. *Cahiers de Psychologie Cognitive, 4*, 295-302.

Jarymowicz, M. (1988). Distance perçue entre soi et autrui, et altruisme. *Revue Internationale de Psychologie Sociale, 1*, 275-285.

Kuiper, N. A., & Derry, P. A. (1981). The self as a cognitive prototype: An application to person perception and depression. In N. Cantor & J. F. Kihlstrom (Eds.), *Personality, cognition, and social interaction* (pp. 215-232). Hillsdale, NJ: Erlbaum

Kuiper, N. A., & Rogers, T. B. (1979). Encoding of personal information: self-other differences. *Journal of Personality and Social Psychology, 37*, 499-514.

Leyens, J.-P. (1990). Jean-Paul Codol's approach to social psychology. *Revue Internationale de Psychologie Sociale, 3*, 253-272.

Markus, H. (1977). Self-schemata and processing information about the self. *Journal of Personality and Social Psychology, 35*, 63-78.

Markus, H., & Sentis, K. (1982). The self in social information processing. In J. Suls (Ed.), *Psychological perspectives on the self* (Vol. 1, pp. 41-70). Hillsdale, NJ: Erlbaum.

Markus, H., & Smith, J. (1981). The influence of self-schemata on the perception of others. In N. Cantor & J. F. Kihlstrom (Eds.), *Personality, cognition, and social interaction* (pp. 233-262). Hillsdale, NJ: Erlbaum.

Markus, H., Smith, J., & Moreland, R. L. (1985). Role of the self-concept in the perception of others. *Journal of Personality and Social Psychology, 49*, 1494-1512.

Moscovici, S. (1982). The coming era of representation. In J.-P. Codol & J.-P. Leyens (Eds.), *Cognitive analysis of social behavior* (pp. 115-150). The Hague: Nijhoff.

Ostrom, T. M., Pryor, J. B., & Simpson D. D. (1981). The organization of social information. In E. T. Higgins, C. P. Herman, & M. P. Zanna (Eds.), *Social Cognition: The Ontario Symposium* (pp. 3-38). Hillsdale, NJ: Erlbaum.

Paicheler, H. (1984). L'épistémologie du sens commun. In S. Moscovici (Ed.), *Psychologie sociale* (p. 277-307). Paris: Presses Universitaires de France.

Passini, F. T., & Norman, W. T. (1966). A universal conception of personality structure. *Journal of Personality and Social Psychology, 4*, 44-49.

Rogers, T. B. (1981). A model of the self as an aspect of the human information processing system. In N. Cantor & J. F. Kihlstrom (Eds.), *Personality, cognition, and social interaction* (pp. 193-214). Hillsdale, NJ: Erlbaum.

Rogers, T. B., Kuiper, N. A., & Kirker, W. S. (1977). Self-reference and the encoding of personal information. *Journal of Personality and Social Psychology, 35*, 677-688.

Rogers, T. B., Rogers, P. J., & Kuiper, N. A. (1979). Evidence for the self as a cognitive prototype: The "false alarm" effect. *Personality and Social Psychology Bulletin, 5*, 53-56.

Taylor, S. E., & Crocker, J. (1981). Schematic bases of social information processing. In E. T. Higgins, C. P. Herman, & M. P. Zanna (Eds.), *Social Cognition: The Ontario Symposium* (pp. 89-134). Hillsdale, NJ: Erlbaum.

Wegner, D. M., & Vallacher, R. R. (1977). *Implicit psychology: An introduction to social cognition.* New York: Oxford University Press.

Wicklund, R. A. (1982). How society uses self-awareness. In J. M. Suls (Ed.), *Psychological perspectives on the Self* (Vol. 1, pp. 209-230). Hillsdale, NJ: Erlbaum.

Wiggins, N. H., & Blackburn, M. C. (1976). Implicit theories of personality : An individual differences approach. *Multivariate Behavioral Research, 11, 267-285*

THE ROLE OF SELF-SCHEMATA
IN THE DESCRIPTION OF OTHERS

Renata Kodilja

University of Trieste, Italy

Luciano Arcuri

University of Padova, Italy

1. Introduction

The everyday "social" thinking activity mainly involves judgments about the self, others and self-other comparisons. No doubt this phenomenon is relevant, considering that the persons with whom we interact and the relationships we hold play an important role in our social experience. The scientific approach to the study of social phenomena is well aware of the importance of this primary naive experience: in fact the self-other relationship has been a privileged topic in the social psychology research tradition. A review of the current literature reveals that a great deal of effort has been devoted to the comprehension of the multiple aspects of the self-other relationship, but that many questions are still left unexplained.

One of the most intriguing aspects of the theoretical analysis of this issue concerns the cognitive counterpart of the self-other interaction. Sometimes, the underlying cognitive processes are different in that they deal with either self-representation or the representation of others. Other times, there is a large overlap between self-related and others-related cognitive processes. We wish to present some empirical evidence on representational content and cognitive processes in self-other comparison.

1.1 Self- and Other-Knowledge

In a study on the differences between self- and other-representation, Prentice (1990) holds that self-other differences are due to a "familiarity effect". The author shows that a continuum of representations exists, with the self, familiar others and unfamiliar others located on this continuum, according to the richness and availability of information. Self-schemata and other-schemata, i.e. the cognitive structures deemed to represent social knowledge, are different in the kind of information they hold. Self-knowledge is expressed by means of internal dimensions: personality traits, thoughts, feelings; other-knowledge is expressed mostly by means of external dimensions: physical characteristics, social behavior (Codol, 1988; Hardoin & Codol, 1984; McGuire & McGuire, 1986).

During social inference processes, actors grant more relevance to affective information originating from their own experience than to information obtained from observers. Johnson (1987) found that people believe they can conceal their own emotions better that others do. Moreover, people think that familiar others feel emotions more deeply but that they show them less than unfamiliar others do.

Some studies indicate that people usually describe others using self-relevant dimensions. Markus and colleagues (Markus & Smith, 1981; Markus, Smith & Moreland, 1985) maintain that the self-concept has an interpretative function that helps observers give meaning to others' behavior. Lewicki (1983, 1984) demonstrates that the more a certain dimension is desirable in self-judgment the more that dimension will be relevant in others' perception. This phenomenon was defined as the self-image bias in person perception.

From this pattern of data we can infer that there is a strong link between self-knowledge and other-knowledge. Self-knowledge is used in order to identify the conceptual and affective dimensions on which judgments of, and comparisons with, others are carried out. Depending on the specific self-other comparison situation, self-knowledge will favor either the differentiation or similarity process.

1.2 Judgment Asymmetry

When two objects are compared, usually one of them is taken as the model and the other plays the role of compared object. Given that each of two equivalent objects belonging to the physical world can be held as model, the symmetry role takes effect. In the psychological realm, when two people are compared, this role is not the same: the subject can play the role of comparison model or of compared object (Codol, 1987; Hardoin & Codol, 1984).

Holyoak and Gordon (1983) demonstrated that subjects judge a friend more similar to themselves than vice versa, whether physical or social dimensions are considered. Therefore, the self-concept acts as a reference point in the processing of social knowledge. The activation of self-knowledge occurs by a "default" procedure when a judgment is required about unfamiliar social objects (categories, stereotypes, people). On the other hand, when familiar objects are judged or compared, the cognitive structures that represent these objects assume the role of reference points (Holyoak & Gordon, 1983; Markus, Smith, & Moreland, 1985). Codol (1987) maintains that if an explicit reference point is lacking, a spontaneous self-centering schema effect occurs. To conclude, when other strong cognitive structures are not available, the self is used as anchor or reference point during the perceptual or cognitive processes applied to social information.

1.3 The Importance of Self-Schemata

The self is deeply involved in the whole process of perceiving and judging others. If we consider the conception of the self as a reference point (Holyoak & Gordon, 1983; Markus, Smith, & Moreland, 1985), Codol's theory of self-centered assimilation processes, the self-image bias in person perception (Lewicki, 1983, 1984; Epstein & Feist, 1988), the false consensus effect (e.g. Sherman, Judd, & Park, 1989), the role of the self in attributing importance to emotional experience (Johnson, 1987; Johnson, Struthers, & Bradlee, 1988), we can see a pattern of empirical data that consistently establish the role of the self in these processes. It stands out that the self-concept is also a powerful and active structure in the retrieval of social information. Refering to the studies on the self-reference effect (Rogers, Kuiper, & Kirker, 1977; Kuiper & Rogers, 1979), a consistent result which emerges from the experiments is that relating information to oneself enhances its memorability. Many studies demonstrate that the self-reference effect is extended to others (Bower & Gilligan, 1979; Keenan & Baillet, 1980; Kuiper & Rogers, 1979): information about familiar others is easier to remember in comparison to information about unfamiliar others. A frequently suggested explanation for this effect refers to the self-schema as a high-level structure that overrides other structures because of its degree of centrality and complexity. Therefore, a self-reference task mobilizes a cognitive structure, the self-schema, which is capable of efficently ruling over the coding and retrieval of relevant information. In the same way, other-schemata, when others are well known or familiar, may act as well as self-schemata in social information processing (Klotz & Alicke, 1989; Wells, Hoffman, & Enzle, 1984).

1.4 Automaticity

Higgins, King and Mavin (1982) maintain that people hold a limited set of "cronically accessible" categories, selected on the basis of everyday experience. These categories may be used in processing social information which refers to both the self and other social objects. Bargh and Pietromonaco (1982) consider the relevance of the self-information as a criterion for the assessment of its accessibility. As the information relevant to a social category is present in the environment, according to these authors, this category will be automatically activated. For example, the social desirability of a stimulus is a feature which is relevant to the self; it will produce the processing of the stimulus in an automatic way.

Other results confirming the hypothesis of the automaticity of cognitive processes related to the self are present in the literature. In this regard we stress the distinction proposed by Hastie and Park (1986) between memory-based and on-line processes: the former refer to the retrieval from memory of already acquired information (memory-based); the latter are involved in the immediate processing and *ex novo* transformation of incoming information (on-line).

According to this theoretical distinction, it can be hypothesized that a given category of stimuli, which is durably accessible, will imply an on-line process, and that this process will, by definition, be automatic. On the basis of previous research findings, we could maintain that the conceptual content of a self-schema represents a preferential category of stimuli: we would perhaps conclude that this occurs because it implies an on-line process. This conclusion could explain, for example, why judgments about the self are less time-consuming than judgments about other social objects. Or, on the contrary, this model could suggest the hypothesis that judgments about unfamiliar others imply a conscious information retrieval process (memory-based) and therefore that these judgments have longer response latencies.

1.5 Social Desirability

In many situations of everyday life people spontaneously produce judgments about the social desirability of traits describing personality, behaviors, habits, and so on. Some research findings show that positive social information, i.e. highly desirable for the self, is processed automatically (Bargh & Pietromonaco, 1982; Bargh, 1984). It does seem to be true that besides the descriptive dimension ("this trait does or does not describe me") every adjective which refers to the self includes a very important desirability dimension ("this trait means either a positive or a negative evaluation of myself"). This latter dimension could either interfere with the first one or facilitate its activation.

In the field of social judgment and, in particular, in self-other comparison situations, there is another important effect due to the social desirability dimension. A clear and significant difference in social desirability emerges from the comparison made between self-descriptions and other-descriptions, producing a systematic judgment tendency (self-other bias). This bias refers to the fact that positive traits are judged, in general, as more descriptive of the self than of others, whereas negative traits are considered, in general, less descriptive of the self than of others (Alicke, 1985; Brown, 1986). Bearing in mind the extent to which people actively and firmly act in order to keep a positive self-conception, the self-bias seems to be easily explained.

2. The Experiment

The aims of the experiment presented in this paper are the following:

(1) To evaluate the differences between self-descriptions and other-descriptions, through the comparison of the number of traits used and decision response times. On the basis of previous research findings, we may predict that the number of adjectives people use to describe themselves will be greater than that used to describe another unfamiliar person. Furthermore if the hypothesis that a relation exists between the rapidity of the judgment and the organization and richness of the schema involved is correct, we may predict that the decision times on the self-description task will be shorter than those on the other-description task. If the other person is unfamiliar (not a close friend) the corresponding schema will probably not be as detailed; therefore the subjects will need not only longer decision times than those needed for the self, but they will utilize a search strategy based on the activation of a memory process. In contrast, for decisions concerning the self, the process will be on-line.

(2) To investigate the effect of social desirability on self- and other-descriptions. According to previous research findings, a self-other bias may appear: a greater number of positive than negative traits should be attributed to the self.

(3) To test the hypothesis that the self acts as a reference point. On the basis of empirical evidence (cf. Codol, 1984) an asymmetry in self-other judgment is expected to appear. In particular we may predict that if the subjects are requested (a) to perform a description task concerning another (unfamiliar) person in the first phase and then to describe themselves, or (b) to produce the same descriptions in the reverse order, there will be a difference in the decision times of the second phase tasks. According to Codol's model, a description of the other person implicitly elicites the self-schema, taken as a reference point, and this facilitates the decisions the subjects will make to describe themselves in the second task. The reverse should not be true.

2.1 Method

The experimental procedure is divided in four phases:

(1) *Description task*. Half the subjects were requested on the first task to produce a self-description; the other half described a not-close friend. The subjects were given a list of 120 traits (60 positive and 60 negative) selected from Anderson's list translated and scored for the Italian population (Colpo, 1976). Traits appeared in random order on the screen of a VDU and the subject was requested to respond as soon as possible to the question *"Does this adjective describe yourself?"* (or *"Does this adjective describe your friend?"*). Decision time was recorded. At the end of this task the adjectives were divided into four different categories according to the answers given by each subject. The following categories were considered: positive descriptive adjectives (PD); positive non-descriptive adjectives (PnD); negative descriptive adjectives (ND); negative non-descriptive adjectives (NnD).

(2) *Judgment task*. The traits belonging to the four categories were combined in order to obtain 10 different pairs of stimuli, according to the following list:

Pair 1: PD - PD	Pair 6: ND - PnD
Pair 2: PnD - PnD	Pair 7: PnD - NnD
Pair 3: PD - PnD	Pair 8: ND - ND
Pair 4: PD - ND	Pair 9: ND - NnD
Pair 5: PD - NnD	Pair 10: NnD - NnD

In this phase the subjects were instructed to compare the social desirability of the two traits in the pair and to judge whether their desirability was the same. If the subject judged both adjectives to be either socially desirable or not, the YES button was to be pressed; if the pair was judged as made up of a positive and a negative trait, the NO button was to be pressed. Decision times were recorded.

(3) *Description task*. The group of the subjects that had first performed the self-description task, had to describe a not-so-close friend in the present phase. The reverse occurred for the group that in the first phase had described a not-so-close friend. In sum, the two groups of subjects performed the description tasks in two different orders:

order 1= self-description,then other-description
order 2= other-description, then self-description.

(4) *Judgment task:* On the basis of the answers obtained in the second experimental phase, the traits belonging to the four different categories were combined in order to obtain 10 pairs of traits to use in the judgment task. The subjects were requested to judge the homogeneity of the traits presented. Reaction times for this task were recorded.

2.2 Subjects

Forty-two students of the University of Padova (Italy) participated in the experiment.

3. Results

For the purposes of the present paper, the data concerning the judgment of the social desirability of the trait pairs will be omitted. We will describe and interpret the data obtained for the description phase only. As Table 1 shows, the subjects used a greater number of traits to describe themselves than to describe the friend ($t = 5.18$; $df = 41$; $p < .001$). An analysis of variance carried out on trait attribution frequencies, with a two between-subject factor design (two levels of descriptiveness and the target person) showed a statistically significant interaction between the two factors ($F(1,41) = 26.85$; $p < .001$).

This result confirms that the self-representation of the subjects is richer and more complex than the representation of the friend.

Table 1

Frequency of Traits Considered as Descriptive and Non-Descriptive in Self- and Other-Descriptions

	Description	
Traits	Self	Other
Descriptive	62.45	57.00
Non-descriptive	57.54	63.00

An inspection of the desirability of the traits attributed to the self and to the other person (see Fig. 1) revealed an ego-defensive bias more than a self-other bias. In fact the subjects tended to use the positive traits more than the negative ones as descriptive. According to the self-other bias, this strategy is used only for self-description; on the contrary it was also adopted here in the description of the friend.

A $2 \times 2 \times 2$ analysis of variance (self vs. other description task; descriptive vs. non-descriptive traits; desirable vs. non-desirable traits) showed two significant two-way interactions: one between type of task and descriptiveness ($F(1,41) = 26.85$; $p < .001$) and the other between descriptiveness and trait desirability, ($F(1,41) = 202.43$; $p < .001$).

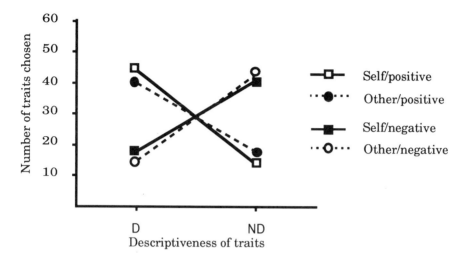

Figure1. Number of traits (positive and negative) used for the self- and other-description.

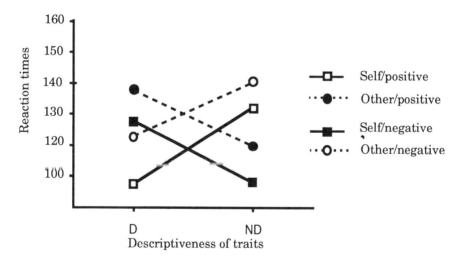

Figure 2: Reaction times for the self- and other-description tasks. The data are presented independently of the order of the task and are expressed in 1/60 ths of a second.

As predicted, the decision times for the self-description were significanly shorter than those for the other-description (see Fig. 2).

Considering the order in which the two tasks were performed, the decision times were nearly the same in each type of description for order 1, where the experiment started with the self-description (see Fig. 3). In contrast, the decision times were significantly different ($t = 5.03$; $df = 41$; $p < .001$) in the case of the order 2, where the subjects first described the friend.

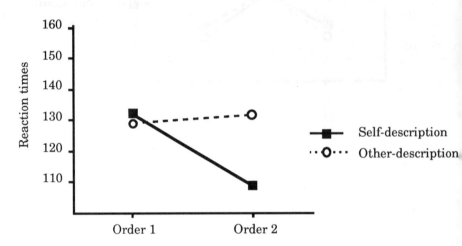

Figure 3. Mean RTs for self- and other-description according to the order of the tasks (order 1: self-description first; order 2: other-description first).

4. Conclusions

Different aspects of the self-other relation were analyzed in order to highlight the similarities and differences in the underlying processes and content. In many situations the judgments people make about others seem to be mediated by self-knowledge and self-reference processes. In other cases a strong tendency towards the differentiation of the self, the observer, and the observed other occurs. No doubt it is an important achievement to determine the conditions under which a similarity or a differentiation effect takes place. In this respect, it seems to us that some interesting conclusions may be drawn from the present experimental study. The result concerning the number of adjectives used for the self- and other-descriptions supports a well-known finding in the literature.

Subjects tend to describe themselves in a more detailed way than they describe others. In this experiment we did not take into account the important effect due to familiarity between the subject and the other person, but the effect of this factor was controlled by choosing a low familiarity level for the evaluated other. Both the quantitative (number of traits used) and the qualitative (faster response times which point to a qualitatively different process) superiority of self-description compared to other-description is a coherent index of an actual "superiority" of self-knowledge structures. This superiority is made clear by the richer content and greater availability in self-description. A tentative explanation may be that since self-description is very detailed, continually updated and progressively enriched by everyday experiences, it also creates a notable and continuous load on information processing. On the other hand, as other-description is more stereotyped and stable across time and situations, it should be more easily and more quickly processed. So, in self-description, information processing times should be significantly longer than in other-description. Why is the data pattern exactly the opposite of this prediction?

A very plausible explanation could be the already mentioned distinction between on-line and memory-based processes. During on-line processes, judgments are based on the analysis of the information available at that particular time; the subject does not need to activate any retrieval processes and the judgment is therefore immediate. In our opinion this kind of process underlies self-description. When subjects have to describe an unfamiliar friend, the judgment will result from a memory-based process. There is in fact no reason for subjects to keep an active schema on an unfamiliar person and they must therefore retrieve from memory the information needed to make the judgment, when required. This retrieval process necessarily takes more time.

The analysis of the social desirability of self- and other-description provides interesting conclusions. People are motivated to present themselves to others and presumably also to themselves in a positive and desirable way. This positivity bias, however, does not seem to exist to the detriment of others: in a relatively "neutral" situation people want to give a good image of themselves, but do not need to differentiate themselves from others in a "good" way.

A further finding concerns the "order" effect, which leads us to consider the topic of cognitive reference. Two explanations are possible. According to Codol's theory, Fig. 3 data could be explained: in the case of order 1, the subjects initially take the self as the reference point and therefore "assimilate" the other person, making him or her similar to themselves. In the case of order 2, the subjects are indirectly induced to use the other as the reference point, and in the subsequent self-description, feel they must differentiate themselves from that reference point. Nevertheless, the plausibility of this interpretation can be challenged, as the methodology we used in the present experiment was different from Codol's. There is a more plausible explanation: the self-concept may be the mediator in the whole process of social judgment. The self can be seen as a continually available and active structure which affects judgments and inferences about others. From this point of view, we can suppose that in order 1 the previous activation of the self-concept mediated and affected the other-description. In order 2, we can suppose that the activation of the other-schema implied an automatic and unconscious comparison with the content of the self-schema; in this case, a subsequent unexpected request to describe oneself would be an extremely easy and therefore quicker task. In conclusion, all the obtained data confirm the role of knowledge structures as a powerful agent of social judgment.

References

Alicke, M. D. (1985). Global self-evaluation as determined by the desirability and controllability of trait adjectives. *Journal of Personality and Social Psychology, 49,* 1621-1630.

Bargh, J. A. (1984). Automatic and conscious processing of social information. In R. S. Wyer & T. K. Srull (Eds.), *Handbook of social cognition* (Vol.3, pp. 1-43). Hillsdale, NJ: Erlbaum.

Bargh, J. A., & Pietromonaco, P. (1982). Automatic information processing and social perception: The influence of trait information presented outside conscious awareness on impression formation. *Journal of Personality and Social Psychology, 43,* 437-449.

Bower, G. H., & Gilligan, S. G. (1979). Remembering information related to one's self. *Journal of Research in Personality, 13,* 420-432.

Brown, J. D. (1986). Evaluation of self and others: Self-enhancement biases in social judgments. *Social Cognition, 4,* 353-376.

Codol, J.-P. (1987). Comparability and incomparability between oneself and others: Means of differentiation and comparison reference points. *Cahiers de Psychologie Cognitive/European Bulletin of Cognitive Psychology, 7,* 87-105.

Codol, J.-P. (1988). On self-centered assimilation processes. In J.-P. Caverni, J.-M. Fabre, & M. Gonzalez (Eds.), *Cognitive biases* (pp. 387-400). Amsterdam: Norh Holland.

Colpo, P. (1976). *Tarattura italiana dei giudizi di piacevolezza di 555 tratti della lista di Anderson*. Unpublished doctoral dissertation, University of Padova, Italy.

Epstein, S., & Feist, G. J. (1988). Relation between self- and other-acceptance and its moderation by identification. *Journal of Personality and Social Psychology, 54,* 309-315.

Hardoin, M. & Codol, J.-P. (1984). Descriptions de soi et d'autrui: influence de l'ordre des descriptions sur les catégories de réponses utilisées. *Cahiers de Psychologie Cognitive, 4,* 295-302.

Hastie, R., & Park, B. (1986). The relationship between memory and judgment depends on whether the judgment task is memory-based or on-line. *Psychological Review, 93,* 258-268.

Higgins, E. T., King, G. A., & Mavin, G. H. (1982). Individual construct accessibility and subjective impressions and recall. *Journal of Personality and Social Psychology, 43,* 35-47.

Holyoak, K. J., & Gordon, P. C. (1983). Social reference points. *Journal of Personality and Social Psychology, 44,* 881-887.

Keenan, J. M., & Baillet, S. D. (1980). Memory for personally and socially significant events. In R. S. Nickerson (Ed.), *Attention and performance* (Vol. 8, pp. 651-669). Hillsdale, NJ: Erlbaum.

Kuiper, N. A., & Rogers, T. B. (1979). Encoding of personal information: Self-other differences. *Journal of Personality and Social Psychology, 37,* 499-514.

Lewicki, P. (1983). Self-image bias in person perception. *Journal of Personality and Social Psychology, 45,* 384-393.

Lewicki, P. (1984). Self-schema and social information processing. *Journal of Personality and Social Psychology, 47,* 1177-1190.

Markus, H., & Smith, J. (1981). The influence of self-schemata on the perception of others. In N. Cantor & J. F. Kihlstrom (Eds.), *Personality, cognition, and social interaction* (pp. 233-262). Hillsdale, NJ: Erlbaum.

Markus, H., Smith, J., & Moreland, R. L. (1985). Role of the self-concept in the social perception of others. *Journal of Personality and Social Psychology, 49,* 1494-1512.

McGuire, W. J., & McGuire, C. V. (1986). Content and process in the experience of self. In L. Berkowitz (Ed.), *Advances in experimental social psychology* (Vol. 21, pp. 97-144). New York: Academic Press.

Prentice, D. A. (1990). Familiarity and differences in self- and other-representations. *Journal of Personality and Social Psychology, 59,* 369-383.

Rogers, T. B., Kuiper, N. A., & Kirker, W.S. (1977). Self-reference and the encoding of personal information. *Journal of Personality and Social Psychology*, *35*, 677-688.

Sherman, S. J., Judd, C. M., & Park, B. (1989). Social cognition. *Annual Review of Psychology*, *40*, 281-326.

Wells, G.L., Hoffman, C., & Enzle, M. E. (1984). Self versus other referent processing at encoding and retrieval. *Personality and Social Psychology Bulletin*, *10*, 574-584.

ONE'S OWN INTELLIGENCE
AND HUMAN INTELLIGENCE IN GENERAL

A "SUPERIOR CONFORMITY OF THE SELF" EFFECT

Gabrielle Poeschl and Willem Doise

University of Geneva, Switzerland

1. Introduction

The name Jean-Paul Codol will remain associated with major currents in social-psychology research, such as the experimental study of social representations (SRs) and studies of the "superior conformity of the self " and of asymmetry in the ratings of similarity and difference in comparison with the self. For each of these currents, Codol conducted a series of original studies enabling him to better describe the processes involved and the conditions under which they emerge. With great intellectual rigor, he repeated his studies to make sure the results were valid and did not attempt to generalize beyond the conditions incorporated into his research paradigms.

To study the *"primus inter pares"* effect (PIP effect) or the "superior conformity of the self " phenomenon, he compared the behaviors and characteristics which individuals attribute to themselves or other ingroup members. He strived particularly to verify the following central proposition: " *For a given set of individuals, there generally is a strong tendency for each one to assert that he conforms more closely to the norms prevailing in this set (as these norms are perceived or experienced) on the whole than do the other participants. The greater the degree of normativeness of these norms, the stronger will be this tendency. "*(Codol, 1975, p. 463).

We wish to make it clear that studying the *"primus inter pares"* effect was not the primary aim of our research. It focused instead on the effects of anchoring in the SRs of intelligence. Borrowing a paradigm used by Deconchy (1987) in his work on ideological filters, we wanted to show that opposing human intelligence to animal intelligence remains a major anchoring process for the representation of intelligence (in this connection, see Doise, 1990). More specific results concerning the problem of anchoring and problems concerning the representation of animal intelligence will be discussed by Poeschl (1992) elsewhere.

However, the results of the present study led us to conclude that there was good reason for examining them in the light of Codol's ideas, although we were not in a position to apply his model rigorously. In fact, our research included neither interindividual comparisons nor attribution of characteristics to the self, since we asked our subjects to attribute characteristics to their own intelligence or human intelligence in general before or after describing animal intelligence. As for the normative aspect, we do know that all of the characteristics associated with intelligence are part of a normative universe in our society. However, our research also included conditions in which this normativeness could be accentuated by comparing humans with animals. Is intelligence not specific to man? And should this specificity not be made more salient when describing animal intelligence?

Our first hypothesis therefore was that the characteristics associated with one's own intelligence would be more consistent with this normative view than those attributed to human intelligence in general.

This study is also part of another problem: social stereotypes. We know that a stereotype exists when there is a broad consensus among group members about the attribution of characteristics similar to most, if not all, of the members of a given social group. Empirical studies, however, usually focus on the perceived homogeneity of the stereotype's object, while the degree of consensus or agreement between group members in their manner of asserting a stereotype receives far less attention.

Our attention, however, was attracted by an unexpected regularity in the agreement between group members (Doise & Lorenzi-Cioldi, 1991). An inspection of the indices of between-subject variation showed that the variations were generally no greater when subjects attributed certain traits to themselves than when they attributed these traits to their ingroup or an outgroup. In concrete terms, there was no more variation in the way Genevan pupils described themselves on scales than in the way they described the Swiss in general or foreigners in general. Pupils of foreign extraction attending the same Genevan schools gave more consensual definitions of themselves than of the foreigners or the Swiss in general.

At first glance, such results seem to contradict a number of ideas prevalent in social psychology, notably those which, in line with the work by Tajfel and Turner, postulate the existence of a continuum opposing individual variety to group homogeneity. Those results are also incompatible with general conceptions according to which idiosyncrasy and striving for originality are more characteristic of attitudes toward the self, while attitudes toward groups are more uniform, since criteria used for defining a group are necessarily fewer and simpler than those employed for defining a specific individual.

Intrigued by this issue, Doise reviewed the results of several other studies to reach an initial conclusion that is quite trivial: the authors reporting the self-descriptions and descriptions of groups rarely give indices of intersubject variation for responses to the specific scales used. This shows that, in social psychology, the study of interindividual variations has been neglected in favor of that of variations between groups or experimental conditions. It turns out, however, that, when such information is available, the variations between individuals in their self-descriptions are seldom greater than the variations in their descriptions of ingroups. In our view, this result is less trivial.

But does this agreement in self-descriptions contradict the results of Codol's research on the "superior conformity of the self " effect? We do not think so because, while it is true that one strives for originality and difference while maintaining a certain degree of similarity, this effort, if made on the same normative dimensions in a group, may well lead individuals who believe themselves to be different to actually describe themselves in a similar manner. In this sense, the *"primus inter pares"* effect would have to be considered a response-homogenizing effect, at least when subjects are unaware of the responses of others.

From this viewpoint, our second general hypothesis predicts that subjects will describe their own intelligence more consensually than human intelligence in general.

2. Method

The 30 items of the questionnaire used in all experimental conditions were selected from three sources: (1) the propositions presented in Poeschl's previous research (1992) on the SRs of intelligence, (2) the literature on animal intelligence, and (3) a survey conducted among our students to determine what traits they judged characteristic of animal intelligence. The items were the following:

1. Knowing how to stay calm; 2. Learning from experience; 3. Choosing an environment favorable to the development of one's children; 4. Acting with a purpose; 5. Being able to acquire new knowledge; 6. Leading a healthy life; 7. Having a good memory; 8. Grasping what is at stake in a situation; 9. Communicating easily with others; 10. Exercizing one's physical capacities; 11. Being shrewd; 12. Being able to assert oneself; 13. Being curious; 14. Acquiring automatisms; 15. Knowing how to protect oneself from bad weather; 16. Possessing a concrete intelligence; 17. Evaluating the consequences of one's acts; 18. Knowing how to behave in society; 19. Acting promptly; 20. Leting oneself be guided by one's intuition; 21. Being able to fight as well as to yield; 22. Choosing competent leaders when organizing important tasks; 23. Knowing how to seduce; 24. Being responsive to others; 25. Being able to adapt to changing conditions; 26. Not wasting one's energies; 27. Knowing how to rear one's children; 28. Protecting one's rest area; 29. Creating novel responses; 30. Being able to store memories.

The questionnaire was divided into two parts. Each part contained the same list of 30 items accompanied by a seven-point scale ranging from −3 (totally irrelevant) to +3 (quite relevant) and subsequently recoded to range from +1 to +7. Half the subjects were instructed to describe human intelligence and animal intelligence. Each stimulus appeared in first or second position. The other half were asked to define their own intelligence and animal intelligence. The order of presentation of the scales varied in the same proportion.

Our study involved 66 men and 66 women, aged 13-70 (34 on average) and living in the Geneva area. The breakdown of the sample population was as follows: 45 students, 75 employees in a variety of sectors and 12 housewives. Ninety-seven of them were Swiss. Half the survey population had a domestic animal, while the other half had none.

This population was recruited by students attending a research seminar. Depending on the circumstances, subjects were questioned collectively during evening or private school courses or in their workplaces. Each student was instructed to alternate the four experimental conditions, and we obtained the following breakdown:

Human intelligence/animal intelligence:	30 subjects
Animal intelligence/human intelligence:	34 subjects
One's own intelligence/animal intelligence:	35 subjects
Animal intelligence/one's own intelligence:	33 subjects

3. Results

3.1 Mean Relevance of Characteristics

Table 1 shows the mean relevance attributed to the 30 characteristics for describing one's own intelligence and human intelligence in general in the different experimental conditions. Analysis of variance of the effects of order (before/after description of animal intelligence) and targets (self/mankind) showed a simple effect for order of entry. When traits were presented after evaluation of animal intelligence the means were higher ($F(1,131) = 4.756$; $p = .031$). A nearly significant trend resulted in more relevant traits ($F(1,131) = 3.804$; $p = .053$) for the description of the one's own intelligence than for the definition of human intelligence in general.

The "superior conformity of the self" compared with human intelligence in general was clearly confirmed through the results of a principal-component factor analysis of the 30 items. After varimax rotation, the first factor grouped the items pertaining to instinct and sociability, while the second grouped the variables measuring mental aptitudes and mobilization. These two factors had an eigenvalue in excess of 3 and accounted jointly for 41% of the total variance. Table 2 shows, for each of these two dimensions, the items whose saturation levels were greater than or equal to 0.50, as well as the means and standard deviations obtained for these items.

Table 1

Means Attributed to the 30 Items for Describing One's Own Intelligence or Human Intelligence in General before (1) or after (2) Description of Animal Intelligence

Abbreviated items	Mankind (1) $N = 30$	Self (1) $N = 35$	Mankind (2) $N = 34$	Self (2) $N = 33$
17. Eval. consequences	5.93	6.23	6.44	6.06
29. Novel responses	5.50	5.29	5.53	5.03
8. Grasping sit. stake	5.47	6.09	6.21	6.00
25. Adaptable	5.37	5.91	6.18	5.91
5. Knew knowledge	5.13	6.34	6.03	6.06
13. Curious	5.10	5.69	5.97	5.03
24. Responsive	5.10	5.46	5.26	5.64
26. Saving one's energies	5.03	4.97	5.09	5.09
16. Concrete intelligence	5.00	5.69	5.56	5.67
4. Acting with purpose	4.93	5.74	5.88	5.52
6. Healthy life	4.77	4.89	4.68	5.15
9. Easy communication	4.73	5.03	5.35	5.82
22. Choosing leaders	4.70	5.00	5.38	5.00
11. Shrewd	4.60	4.46	4.85	5.39
2. Learning from exper.	4.57	6.03	5.97	5.94
7. Good memory	4.53	5.14	4.62	5.24
20. Intuition	4.47	4.97	4.35	4.97
28. Protecting one's rest	4.47	4.34	4.03	4.70
12. Asserting oneself	4.47	4.80	4.71	5.46
1. Staying Calm	4.37	4.57	5.18	5.85
3. Envir. favor. to childr.	4.37	5.29	4.82	5.61
21. Fighting/yielding	4.23	4.91	4.85	5.21
23. Know. how to seduce	4.23	4.29	4.41	5.00
27. Rearing children	4.20	4.83	5.35	5.48
19. Acting promptly	4.13	4.43	4.71	5.03
18. Competent in soc. life	4.10	4.80	4.97	5.36
30. Storing memories	4.07	4.66	4.59	5.00
10. Exerciz. phys. capac.	3.73	3.97	3.68	4.33
15. Bad weather protect.	3.47	3.66	3.74	3.88
14. Acquir. automatisms	3.07	3.00	3.62	3.45
M	4.59	5.02	5.07	5.26

Table 2

Items which Saturated the Two Principal Dimensions Describing One's Own Intelligence and Human Intelligence in General at the Threshold of .50. Means and Standard Deviations Calculated in the Four Experimental Conditions

Items	Scores	*M*	*SD*
Factor 1 (29.6%): Instinct and Sociability			
10. Exercising one's physical capacities	0.73	3.93	1.89
28. Protecting one's rest area	0.70	4.38	2.07
12. Being able to assert oneself	0.70	4.87	1.78
18. Knowing how to behave in society	0.69	4.83	1.81
9. Communicating easily with others	0.66	5.24	1.74
15. Knowing how to protect oneself from bad weather	0.66	3.69	2.13
27. Knowing how to rear one's children	0.65	4.98	1.86
6. Leading a healthy life	0.63	4.87	1.79
19. Acting promptly	0.58	4.58	1.83
14. Acquiring automatisms	0.58	3.29	1.83
26. Not wasting one's energies	0.55	5.05	1.57
24. Being responsive to others	0.53	5.37	1.59
3. Choosing an environment favorable to the development of one's children	0.51	5.04	1.87
23. Knowing how to seduce	0.51	4.48	1.85
1. Knowing how to stay calm	0.50	5.00	1.83
M		4.64	1.83
Factor 2 (11.3%): Mental Aptitude and Mobilization			
5. Being able to acquire new knowledge	0.83	5.92	1.55
8. Grasping what is at stake in a situation	0.83	5.95	1.30
17. Evaluating the consequences of one's acts	0.78	6.17	1.07
25. Being able to adapt to changing conditions	0.78	5.86	1.30
2. Learning from experience	0.66	5.66	1.63
4. Acting with a purpose	0.61	5.54	1.69
13. Being curious	0.50	5.46	1.58
M		5.79	1.45

Whereas the analysis of variance performed on the factor scores of subjects showed no differences between the various experimental conditions on the first factor, it indicated that the means attributed to the items of the second factor (see Table 3) exhibited significant differences across the four experimental conditions ($F(3,131) = 3.58; p = .016$).

Table 3
Mean Factor Scores Calculated for the Second Factor in the Four Experimental Conditions

	Order	
Target	Before	After
Mankind	− .48	+ .26
Self	+ .17	− .02

It was found that the subjects describing human intelligence in general without being in a comparison situation attached significantly less importance to the cognitive variables than the subjects in the other three experimental conditions did ($p < .05$ according to Duncan's multiple range test). The significant interaction between order of entry and targets, ($F(1,131) = 7.47; p = .007$) suggests that individuals are likely to have a clear-cut view of their own intelligence in accordance with the norms (cognitive mechanisms being generally recognized as specific to human intelligence), while a comparison of general human intelligence with animal intelligence is necessary for the former to approach this normative view.

3.2 Convergence and Stability of Judgments

To compare the extent of agreement in the subjects' responses according to the "target" to be described, we studied the standard deviations of these responses for each of the 30 scales and compared their means in the different experimental conditions. In other words, we considered the variations on the different scales to be independent of each other, and the 30 standard deviations to form the basic per-condition data for the analysis of variance.

Table 4 shows the mean standard deviations calculated on the 30 characteristics for the description of one's own intelligence and human intelligence in general before and after description of animal intelligence.

Table 4

Mean Standard Deviations for the 30 Items Describing the Intelligence of Different Targets According to Order of Description

	Order	
Target	Before	After
Mankind	1.86	1.65
Self	1.64	1.59
Animal	2.01	after mankind: 1.99 after self: 1.84

The results of the analysis of variance clearly showed that the standard deviations were smaller ($F(1,116) = 5.62$; $p = .019$), i.e. that the mean agreement per scale was greater, when one's own intelligence was involved than when human intelligence in general was involved. Moreover, the order of description played a significant part ($F(1,116) = 4.73$; $p = .032$), while there was less agreement in the descriptions provided before evaluation of animal intelligence than in the descriptions made after evaluation of animal intelligence. Since this order effect of entry was insignificant in the description of animal intelligence, it cannot be reduced to simple familiarization with the content of the scales.

Moreover, and although the interaction between description order (before/after) and targets (mankind/self) was insignificant ($p = .142$), the order effect was nonetheless less pronounced for the description of one's own intelligence. The standard deviations remained remarkably stable when the responses before and after description of animal intelligence were compared. To highlight the effects of order of description on the two targets (mankind/self), we calculated and compared the differences in absolute value between the standard deviations before and after evaluation of animal intelligence. It turned out that these differences were significantly greater ($t = 2.28$; $df = 29$; $p = .030$) when subjects described human intelligence in general (mean difference: .371) than when they described their own intelligence (mean difference: .224). The agreement in the descriptions of one's own intelligence thus turned out to be significantly more stable than the agreement in the descriptions of human intelligence in general.

Analyses of the standard deviations thus clearly showed greater agreement among subjects in their descriptions of one's own intelligence, and this agreement was not subject to variations by description context.

One question that might be raised is whether or not the effects observed are some sort of artifact associated with a ceiling effect. Agreement may be greater in the description of one's own intelligence because subjects used a greater number of high scores in these responses. Analyses of the correlations between the means and standard deviations and an analysis of covariance between the two variables suggested that this was in fact the case. It should be noted, however, that the existence of such a covariation by no means invalidates our interpretations in normative terms. The existence of a norm led in this case to more extreme responses and involved smaller variations on the proposed scales.

By way of comparison, let us also note that the mean standard deviations for animal intelligence were greater than the standard deviations for one's own intelligence or of mankind in general (2.01 when the evaluation was made outside a comparison situation and 1.99 and 1.84, respectively, when this evaluation followed the description of human intelligence and one's own intelligence). Everything seems to indicate that we have a new case here in which the stereotype of the self seems more consensual than the stereotypes of groups, even if the latter, in this case, concerned very large populations.

4. Conclusion

The entry conditions of our questionnaire on one's own intelligence and human intelligence in general were, of course, different from those used by Codol. A major difference was that our research included no interindividual comparison because the descriptions concerned either one's own intelligence or human intelligence in general. Moreover, these two descriptions were not made by the same subjects. Despite these differences, the results of our research appear compatible with the "superior conformity of the self" model, and illustrate the implication of Codol's model concerning the stereotyped aspect of self-representation. This implication has not been studied much. If there is "superior conformity of the self" in a large number of members of a group, they necessarily agree in their responses.

Apparently, no intergroup comparison is needed for observing a relatively high degree of agreement in responses concerning one's own intelligence. These responses were undoubtedly already worked out in many previous normative comparisons. The responses concerning the whole group, while reflecting these norms, nonetheless leave some room for the "superior conformity of the self" effect to appear. This effect cannot appear with the same intensity when an intergroup comparison has been made. This brings us to another current of research – the one initiated by

Deschamps (1984) on covariation between intergroup differentiation and intragroup differentiation. The "superior conformity of the self" effect has received little attention in this theoretical framework.

References

Codol, J.-P. (1975). On the so-called "superior conformity of the self" behavior: Twenty experimental investigations. *European Journal of Social Psychology, 5,* 457-501.

Deconchy, J.-P. (1987). Conduites sociales, comparaison sociale et représentation du patrimoine comportemental commun à l'homme et à l'animal. In J.-L. Beauvois, R. V. Joule & J.-M. Monteil (Eds.), *Perspectives cognitives et conduites sociale : Vol. 1, Théories implicites et conflits cognitifs* (p. 151-185). Cousset : Delval.

Doise, W. (1990). Les représentations sociales. In R. Ghiglione, C. Bonnet & J.-F. Richard (Eds.), *Traité de psychologie cognitive* (Vol. 3, p. 111-174). Paris : Dunod.

Doise, W. & Lorenzi-Cioldi, F. (1991). L'identité comme représentation sociale. In V. Aebischer, J.-P. Deconchy & E. M. Lipiansky (Eds.), *Idéologies et représentations sociales* (p. 273-286). Cousset : Delval.

Poeschl, G. (1992). *L'intelligence : un concept à la recherche d'un sens.* Unpublished Doctoral Thesis, University of Geneva, Switzerland.

THE RELATIONSHIP BETWEEN
THE NEED FOR CONTROL, EXTROVERSION,
AND ACTIVE VERSUS PASSIVE PERSONAL SPACE

Yoel Yinon and Gil Amit

Bar-Ilan University, Israel

Personal space is usually defined as an imagined, portable boundary around us into which invasion by others arouses a sense of uneasiness (Hayduk, 1983).

Perusal of the personal space literature reveals a considerable amount of inconsistency among the findings obtained by various studies. Hayduk (1983) suggested that the primary reason for the absence of a clear picture in this area is a methodological one. There are several techniques for measuring the size of one's personal space. These techniques can be classified into two paradigms. The first one measures the passive personal space (PPS) and includes situations in which subjects are in a static position and are being approached by someone (an experimenter, a confederate, a stimulus person using indirect techniques). The frequent and typical case features a confederate who slowly approaches a subject, up to a distance which would be presumably perceived as an irregular penetration to the subject's personal space (Altman & Visel, 1977). Subjects reactions to the assumed penetration are observed and measured. These could be fleeing from the situation, bending down, turning around, avoiding eye contact, verbal comments, and reports about felt uneasiness.

The second paradigm measures the active personal space (APS) and includes situations in which subjects are allowed, or are instructed to approach and/or penetrate the personal space of another person (e.g. Knowles, 1973). In these studies also the minimal distance kept by subjects while approaching the other person is measured, and is considered as an indication of the size of their personal space. Additional responses, such as avoiding eye contact and speed of fleeing from the situation, are also observed.

These two paradigms are treated in the literature as equivalent and substitutional. The present study turns the equivalence assumption into a hypothesis, stating that the size of the personal space of people might be different when they are being approached than when they initiate a penetration into another person's personal space.

Hartnett, Bailey, and Gibson (1970) found that there is a difference in the size of the personal space of the same subjects measured when approaching the experimenter and vice versa. The conclusion reached by Hartnett, Bailey, and Gibson (1970) was that subjects let the experimenter approach them more than they approached the experimenter. However, this finding cannot be generalized to natural situations of human interaction, for two reasons: a) in the Hartnett study, when subjects approached the experimenter, they were following his instructions rather than being the initiators of this behavior, and consequently had the feeling of reduced control over the situation; b) when the experimenter approached the subjects, they had a relatively high degree of control (in contrast to natural situations); they could stop the experimenter at any moment, and they had an explanation for this behavior.

In one of their recent publications, Codol, Jarymowicz, Kaminska-Feldman, and Szuster-Zbrojevicz (1989) report an asymmetry in interpersonal physical-distance evaluations as a function of the evaluator's perspective. When requested to estimate how far they were from another person, subjects' judged distance was larger, as compared to their judged distance when requested to estimate how far the other person was from them. Of course, the real physical distance was identical in the two cases. In other words, people have the feeling that others are located closer to themselves, than they are located to those others. The behavioral implication of these feelings might be that people would get closer to others than they would let others get to them.

The studies conducted by Hartnett et al. (1970) and Codol et al. (1989), show that when personal space is measured, we cannot assume that it makes no difference whether the subject approaches another person or is being approached by another person. However, the conclusions one might draw based on these studies are inconsistent. According to Hartnett et al.(1970), people let others approach them to a closer distance than they approach others. The results reported by Codol et al. (1989) suggest exactly the opposite.

At any rate, at the individual level, we can ask whether there is a correlation between the sizes of the active and passive personal spaces. The assumption of the present study is that the active and passive personal spaces reflect psychological states which differ in both their cognitive and emotional aspects. Therefore, the size of the active personal space is not necessarily correlated with the size of the passive personal space. The essential difference between active and passive personal spaces lies in the identity of the initiator of the interaction. An individual approaching another person on his/her own initiative has an advantage. He/she knows the purpose of this approaching, what his/her intentions are, and where he/she will stop. In contrast, when a person is being approached, all the information available in the former situation is lacking, and consequently the level of certainty or confidence enjoyed is relatively low.

The literature does not refer at all to the question of the correlation between active and passive personal spaces. However, all definitions of the personal space concept are formulated from the point of view of the person being approached, and never refer to the individual who approaches the other person.

It is therefore suggested here that a distinction should be made between active and passive personal spaces of a given individual. Assuming that these two are not necessarily correlated, one can expect any random sample of people to fall into four categories when their active and passive personal spaces are measured:

1) People whose active and passive personal spaces are both relatively small. These people approach other people, and let other people approach them, up to a relatively small distance.

2) People whose active personal space is relatively small, while their passive personal space is relatively large. That is, they let other people invade their own personal space to a relatively lesser degree than they invade the personal space of others.

3) People whose active personal space is relatively large, while their passive personal space is relatively small. These people let others invade their own personal space to a relatively greater degree than they are ready to invade others' personal space.

4) People whose active and passive personal spaces are both relatively large. These people keep a relatively large distance when approaching as well as when being approached by other people.

Thus the first goal of the present study was to determine empirically whether people fall into the above four patterns, or whether there is a perfect correlation between the size of the APS and the PPS.

Assuming that such patterns do exist, our second goal was to identify personality variables which might be related to the various relationships between APS and PPS.

In order to arrive at these personality variables, we consulted Wiggins' circumplex structure of interpersonal behavior (Wiggins, 1988). The vertical dimension in Wiggins' circumplex, called "dominant-submissive" is a personality variable which presumably should be correlated with patterns of correspondence between APS and PPS.

Burger and Cooper (1979) developed a scale aimed at measuring individual differences in the need for control over others and the environment. They found that individuals whose need for control is high are also dominant, assertive, determined, active, try to influence others, and seek the leader role when participating in group activities. Those who have a low need for control are unassertive, passive, undetermined, less desirous of influencing others, and prefer following the decisions made by others. Burger, Oakman, and Bullard (1983) indicate that behavioral differences between people who are high and low in their need for control are a function of the interaction between the level of the need for control and the situational conditions. They report that when subjects were assembled into a crowded room from which they could not get out, and therefore didn't have control over the situation, the personal space of subjects whose need for control was high was larger than the personal space of those whose need for control was low. This finding can be interpreted as reflecting the fact that when people are approached by another person, they have minimal control over the situation. Therefore, people whose need for control is high will keep those who approach them at a larger distance than those whose need for control is low.

When people approach others, they are in control of the situation, the speed of approaching, and the stopping distance. A deeper invasion to the other's personal space reflects active and assertive behavior, capturing the other's space, and reducing his/her space of free movement. It is therefore predicted that people whose need for control is high will tend, when the opportunity arises, to invade the personal space of others to a greater extent than people whose need for control is low.

In contrast, it is also reasonable to expect that people whose need for control is low will let others invade their own personal space, allowing them to control the situation, to a greater extent than people whose need for control is high.

In sum, our prediction is that people of high need for control will keep a relatively smaller personal space when they initiate the invasion, as compared to a situation in which they are approached by others. People of low need for control will behave in exactly the opposite manner.

This prediction is an attempt to relate a personality variable, i.e. the need for control, to those individuals who are characterized by the lack of correspondence between their APS and PPS.

An additional personality variable is required in order to explain the behavior of individuals who are characterized by a high degree of correspondence between their APS and PPS. We chose the extroverted/introverted dimension from Wiggins' circumplex of interpersonal variables, which seems to be a reasonable one for this purpose.

There is some evidence (Williams, 1971) showing that an extrovert is a person who approaches the objects in his environment, while the introvert tends to avoid them. Thus it can be expected that extroverts will keep a smaller active and passive personal space than introverts, whose APS as well as PPS will be relatively large.

1. Method

1.1 Subjects

One hundred and seventy-six high-school students participated in the study. They were 16-17 years old, and composed of 112 girls and 64 boys.

1.2 Instruments

1.2.1 Active and Passive Personal Space. For measuring the size of an individual's active and passive personal spaces, the Comfortable Interpersonal Distance (C.I.D.) questionnaire, developed by Duke and Nowicki (1972) was used twice. The instructions employed for the PPS requested subjects to imagine that they were standing at some central spot and that someone of their own sex was approaching them, and then indicate at which point they would stop him/her. The instructions for the APS requested subjects to imagine themselves approaching someone of their own sex who was located at the central spot, and indicate at which point they would stop.

1.2.2 The Need for Control was measured by Burger and Cooper's (1979) questionnaire called "The Desirability of Control". It is composed of 20 items, specifically related to the need of people to control their environment as well as other people.

1.2.3 Extroversion - Introversion was measured by Eysenck's (1970) scale, based on the Maudsley Personality Inventory. The scale is composed of 24 items pertaining to the extroversion dimension. The higher the score a person obtains on this scale the more extroverted he/she is considered to be.

2. Procedure

The study was conducted in two stages:
1) Subjects responded to the Extroversion and the Need for Control questionnaires, and then completed the C. I. D. questionnaire under the original instructions designed to measure PPS.
2) Two weeks later, subjects were administered the C.I.D.Q. under instructions aimed at measuring APS.

3. Results [1]

3.1 Personal Space
Each subject indicated 8 active and 8 passive stopping distances. Accordingly, subjects had 16 scores each, which were then collapsed and averaged. For the active and passive personal spaces separately, each subject was given 4 scores:

- Front personal space (the mean distance from the subject in the 0°, 45° and 315° directions).
- Back personal space (the mean distance in the 135°, 180° and 225° directions).
- Side personal space (the mean distance in the 90° and 270° directions).
- Overall personal space (the mean distance from the subject in all 8 directions).

The intercorrelations of the distances for each of the 8 directions within the active and passive personal spaces were computed separately.
It was found that the further the point of invasion to the personal space was located from the front (0°), the smaller the correlation with the front entrance, all the way to the back entrance (180°), where the correlation with the front entrance was the lowest. Then the correlations began to increase again. This was true for both the APS (lowest $r = .42$) and the PPS (lowest $r = .23$).
In addition, as for the other entrances, it was found that the stopping distance at a given entrance was more highly correlated with the stopping distance at the symmetrical entrance located on the other side of the front-back axis (45° with 315°; 90° with 270°; 135° with 225°), than with any other distance.

---

[1] Two thirds of the participants in the present study were females. Therefore all the data analyses examined sex differences. Since none were found, the findings are presented for the entire sample, regardless of the subject's sex.

62

It can therefore be concluded for both APS and PPS that: (1) People keep a similar distance at the right and left sides of their personal space, and (2) people do not keep the same distance regarding the front and back entrances to their personal space.

Figure 1 presents a diagram based on the mean active and passive personal spaces.

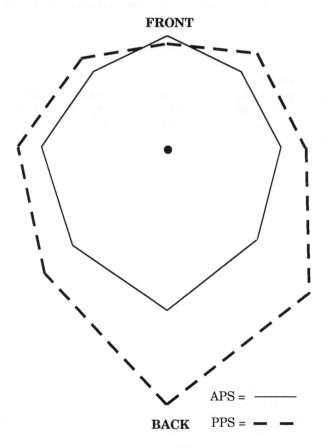

FRONT

APS = ———

BACK   PPS = — —

Figure 1. Mean stopping distances (enlarged twice) at 8 entrances for active (APS) and passive (PPS) personal spaces.

As can be seen in Fig. 1, the personal space has an elliptic form, which is almost symmetric along the front-back axis.

It was found on the average that the passive personal space (PPS) (M = 28.3 mm) is significantly larger than the active personal space (APS) (M = 22.1 mm) (t = 5.40; df = 175; $p < .001$). However, upon comparing the size of the APS and the PPS for each of the 8 entrances, we found significant differences for the back and side entrances but not for the front entrances (See Table 1).

Table 1

Mean Distances from Subjects (in mm) to the Entrances of the Passive and Active Personal Spaces

	Front			Back			Sides	
	0°	45°	315°	135°	180°	225°	90°	270°
Passive PS	17.60	21.10	20.60	35.70	43.90	35.70	25.70	26.30
Active PS	18.50	20.10	18.70	23.80	27.70	24.80	21.80	21.40
Difference PPS–APS	–.90	1.00	1.90	11.90	16.20	10.90	3.90	4.90
t	.71	.78	1.65	7.61	8.03	6.92	2.85	3.44
p	ns	ns	.10	.001	.001	.001	.01	.001

When the 176 subjects were classified on the basis of whether they were above or below the median size of both the APS and the PPS, 64% were found to be either above or below both medians. The remaining 36% were found to be above the median on the APS and below it on the PPS, or vice versa.

3.2 Extroversion-Introversion and Personal Space

The correlations between the extroversion score and the sizes of the APS and PPS were all negative and significant as expected. They are presented in Table 2.

Table 2

Correlations between Extroversion, Need for Control, and Sizes of Active and Passive Personal Spaces

	Active Personal Space				Passive Personal Space			
	Front	Back	Sides	Gen.	Front	Back	Sides	Gen.
Extroversion	−.26*	−.18*	−.28*	−.26*	−.21*	−.15*	−.19*	−.21*
Need for Control	−.22*	−.16*	−.25*	−.22*	−.10	−.06	−.09	−.09

$N = 176$ for all correlations; * $p < .05$.

These correlations suggest that the stronger an individual's tendency towards extroversion, the smaller the APS and PPS he/she tends to maintain.

3.3 Need for Control and Personal Space

The correlations between the need for control score and the size of the APS are presented in Table 2. As can be seen in this table, it turns out that the subject's need for control gets higher as his/her active personal space gets smaller. However, the correlations between the need for control scores and the size of the passive personal space turned out to be very low and non-significant, which was against expectations.

4. Discussion

In general, the results obtained in the present study suggest that when investigating personal space one should distinguish between active and passive PS. Although we think that APS and PPS are cognitively and affectively distinct, they have some common elements.

The most salient common element is the general elliptic form of both the APS and the PPS, with the person located in the center facing the shortest radius. As can be seen in Fig. 1, the front area of the PS is smaller than the back area. The findings in the literature regarding the difference between the front and back areas are inconsistent. Some studies (e.g. Strub & Werner, 1982; Aono, 1981; Aston & Shaw, 1980) reported a somewhat larger front area than back area. Others did not find any difference between the two (e.g. Leventhal, Schanerman, & Maturro, 1978; Roger & Schaekmp, 1976). Still others reported that the back area was larger than the front area (e.g. Curran, Blatchley, & Hanlon, 1978; Beck & Ollendick, 1976), as found in the present study. Research on this issue should focus on identifying the variables which might explain these inconsistent findings.

The question of the absolute size of the APS vs. the PPS might be solved based on the findings of the present study. We found that in general, the PPS was larger than the APS. This finding is in line with the ideas which emerge from the Codol et al. (1989) data, and corroborates the conclusion stating that people generally keep a smaller PS when they invade the PS of others than when their PS is being invaded by others. This is true for all entrance directions except the front ones, for which there was no difference between the APS and the PPS.

Apparently, the difference in size between the APS and the PPS is a function of the direction of invasion. The largest difference in size was found in the back area, which can be interpreted as stemming from the difference in the perceived degree of control characterizing the APS vs. the PPS. When people approach another person behind the other person's back, they have a high degree of control over the situation. In contrast, a person who is being approached from behind should be on the alert. He/she does not see the approaching person, and cannot estimate the exact location of that person so he/she keeps a larger safety area than in the front area.

The hypotheses about the personality variables associated with the relationship between APS and PPS were mostly supported. The negative correlations between extroversion scores and the size of both the APS and the PPS supported the prediction that as people become more extroverted, both their APS and their PPS become smaller. This kind of relationship holds true for all the measured directions of invasion of the personal space.

The prediction regarding the relationship between the need for control and the size of the APS and the PPS was only partially supported. It was expected that when invading another person's personal space, people with a strong need for control would keep a smaller personal space than people with a weak need for control. The opposite would happen when others were the invaders. In this case, people with a strong need for control would keep a larger personal space than people with a weak need for control. The results only partially supported this prediction. People with greater need for control did indeed keep a smaller APS. However, no link was found between the size of the PPS and the need for control.

The latter finding may reflect the influence of an uncontrolled variable, namely, the level of self-confidence of the subjects. People lacking self-confidence may be quite defensive (Bauer, 1970), and are often motivated to avoid making mistakes (Barach, 1974). Assuming that there is not necessarily a correlation between the need for control and self-confidence, one may speculate about the behavior of subjects in the present study who scored relatively high on the need for control when given PPS instructions. When a strong need for control is accompanied by a lack of self-confidence, the person keeps a relatively large PPS in order to defend himself and to maintain control over the situation. In contrast, when a strong need of control is accompanied by high self-confidence, the person is not worried about losing control when people approach him, and thus keeps comparatively small PPS. Subjects with a weak need for control should be less affected by their level of self-confidence when dealing with their personal space.

It is possible that the level of self-confidence contaminated the relationship between the need for control and the size of the PPS. This would explain why we found almost no correlation between these two variables.

This lack of correlation might also be the result of a methodological problem concerning the measurement of the PPS. It might be argued that the C.I.D.Q. is not an adequate psychological simulation of the real situation in which a person encounters a stranger approaching him. Unlike in reality, subjects using the paper and pencil technique developed by Duke and Nowicki to indicate the stopping distance of a stranger in their simulated PS have some degree of control. Although subjects do not know the motives of the approaching person, they are the ones who decide where to stop him, which is not the case in real situations. It is possible that this problem added its share to the low correlations between the need for control and PPS size.

In sum, it seems that the personal space is a multi-faceted concept. The present study has made new conceptual and methodological refinements, by showing that the size of the personal space is dependent on who is the initiator of the invasion, as well as on some personality dimensions. The results of our study suggest that when investigating the size of the personal space, one should distinguish between active and passive personal spaces, because a person who invades the personal space of an other person is in a different psychological state than a person whose personal space is being invaded by others.

References

Altman, I., & Vinsel, A. M. (1977). Personal space: An analysis of E. T. Hall's Proxemics framework. In I. Altman & J. F. Wohlwill (Eds.), *Human behavior and the environment: Advances in theory and research* (Vol. 2). New York: Plenum.

Aono, A. (1981). The effect of sex and dominance upon personal space. *The Japanese Journal of Psychology, 52,* 124-127.

Ashton, N. L., & Shaw, M. E. (1980). Empirical investigations of a reconceptualized personal space. *Bulletin of the Psychonomic Society, 15,* 309-312.

Barach, J. A. (1974). *A resolution for conflicting theories and data concerning generalized self-confidence and persuasibility.* Paper presented at the APA meeting, New Orleans.

Bauer, R. A. (1970). Self-confidence and persuasibility: One more time. *Journal of Marketing Research, 7,* 256-258.

Beck, S., & Ollendick, T. H. (1976). Personal space, sex of experimenter and locus of control in normal and delinquent adolescents. *Psychological Reports, 38,* 383-387.

Burger, J. M., & Cooper, H. M. (1979). The desirability of control. *Motivation and Emotion, 3,* 381-393.

Burger, J. M., Oakman, J. A., & Bullard, N. G. (1983). Desire for control and the perception of crowding. *Personality and Social Psychology Bulletin, 9,* 475-479.

Codol, J.-P., Jarymowicz, M., Kaminska-Feldman, M., & Szuster-Zbrojewicz, A. (1989). Asymmetry in the estimation of interpersonal distance and identity affirmation. *European Journal of Social Psychology, 19,* 11-22.

Curran, S. S., Blatchley, R. J., & Hanlon, T. E. (1978). Relationship between body-buffer zone and violence as assessed by subjective and objective techniques. *Criminal Justice and Behavior, 5,* 53-62.

Duke, M. P., & Nowicki, S. (1972). A new measure and social learning model for interpersonal distance. *Journal of Experimental Research in Personality, 6,* 119-132.

Eysenck, H. J. (1970). The questionnaire measurement of neuroticism and extroversion. In H. J. Eysenck (Ed.), *Readings in extroversion-introversion* (pp. 100-127). London: Stamples Press.

Hartnett, J. J., Bailey, K. G., & Gibson, F. W. (1970). Personal space as influenced by sex and type of movement. *Journal of Psychology, 70,* 139-144.

Hayduk, L. A. (1983). Personal space: Where we now stand. *Psychological Bulletin, 94,* 293-335.

Knowles, E. S. (1973). Boundaries around group interaction. The effect of group size and member status on boundary permeability. *Journal of Personality and Social Psychology, 26,* 327-331.

Leventhal, G., Schanerman, J., & Matturo, M. (1978). Effect of room size, initial approach distance and sex on personal space. *Perceptual and Motor Skills, 47,* 792-794.

Roger, D. B., & Schalekamp, E. E. (1976). Body-buffer zone and violence: A cross-cultural study. *The Journal of Social Psychology, 98,* 153-158.

Strub, M. J., & Werner, L. (1982). Interpersonal distance and personal space: A conceptual and methodological note. *Journal of Nonverbal Behavior, 6,* 163-170.

Wiggins, J. S. (1988). Psychometric and Geometric Characteristics of the Revised Interpersonal Adjective Scale (IAS-R). *Multivariate Behavioral Research, 23,* 517-530.

Williams, J. L. (1971). Personal space and its relation to extroversion-introversion. *Canadian Journal of Behavioral Science, 3,* 156-160.

SELF-SALIENCE VERSUS OTHER-SALIENCE AND AUTOCENTRIC VERSUS ALLOCENTRIC ASYMMETRY EFFECTS

Marta Kamińska-Feldman

University of Warsaw, Poland

1. Theoretical Framework

Tversky (1977) showed that objects perceived as prototypical (e.g. the Soviet Union among communist countries) are seen as more distinct from nonprototypical objects than nonprototypical objects are from prototypical ones. This finding is consistent with earlier results offered by Rosch (1975) on the asymmetry of perceived distance between more and less prototypical objects. Tversky's explanation is the following: "The variant is more similar to the prototype than the prototype is to the variant, because the prototype is generally more salient than the variant" (p. 333).

Such an asymmetry effect in self-other distance ratings was described by Codol (1984, 1986). He found that this distance is perceived as greater when the self is compared with another person than when the other person is compared with the self. We have called the asymmetry effect described by Codol autocentric asymmetry. The autocentric asymmetry effect suggests that the self plays the role of a prototype; this effect is a manifestation of self-prototypicality.

Codol also found that this autocentric tendency increased as the number of persons in the defined space increased (i.e. in high social density conditions), even though the objects are the same and therefore their prototypicality is also the same!

The question thus arises: What is the mechanism underlying the phenomena revealed by Codol?

Analyzing his own findings, Codol interpreted them in motivational terms of affirmation and defense of personal identity. When the social density is high, subjects feel that their identity is threatened, and this induces stronger egocentric tendencies.

However, the asymmetry phenomena may be assumed to have another nature: that the mechanism of the autocentric asymmetry effect is the same as that mentioned by Tversky (1977) and is related to the object's salience. The self often functions as a habitual reference point and therefore it may be more salient than the others. When the social density is high, the relative salience of the subject may be reinforced.

However, there are some theoretical premises (e.g. Regulative Personality Theory by Reykowski; Reykowski & Kochanska, 1980) and empirical results (Holyoak & Gordon, 1983; Kamińska-Feldman, 1988, 1992; Karyłowski, 1990) which show that, although the self may be the largest and perhaps the most social of all prototypes, it is not the only one, and the cognitive representations of others can function in a similar way.

For example, Holyoak and Gordon (1983) showed that these social concepts can serve as habitual reference points whose stereotypes are especially familiar and about which a great deal is known, while the self may serve as a reference point with respect to relatively unfamiliar stereotypes. Also, the results obtained by Karyłowski (1990) showed that other people can serve as habitual (or transient) reference points in self-perception during comparisons of oneself to others in judgements involving the prototypical traits of the others.

If we assume as a general rule that the asymmetry effect is related to compared-object prototypicality, the autocentric asymmetry effect (as described by Codol) in interpersonal distance rating would disappear or be reversed (giving the allocentric asymmetry effect) if the self cannot play the role of a prototype in social perception. Namely, we predicted the following:

(1) The asymmetry effect depends on the situational salience of different cognitive representations; (a) the effect is weaker in low self-salience conditions, and (b) the effect is reversed in high other-salience conditions.

(2) The asymmetry effect depends on the object's schema status; (a) the effect is weaker if the self-schema is not well formed, and (b) the effect is reversed if the other's schema is well formed, especially when the other is familiar.

Our study concerns a social context as a modifying factor of the asymmetry effect. It was expected that the direction and magnitude of the asymmetry effect would depend on the level of the situational salience of the self versus that of the other object, i.e. the actualization of the self-schema versus the other's schema.

The following hypothesis was formulated: In low self-salience and high other-salience conditions, the autocentric asymmetry effect is weaker or reversed into allocentric asymmetry in comparison with high self-salience conditions.

2. Procedure

Two independent studies were run among university students, aged 20-23: Study 1 (by Kamińska-Feldman) with 113 subjects, study 2 (by Sereda) with 102 subjects.

2.1 Asymmetry Effect Measurement

Taking into account that the asymmetry effect is related to the reference point, we sought a technique to control this variable. A graphic technique for distance rating was constructed by Jarymowicz and Kamińska-Feldman (Kamińska-Feldman, 1988). This method allowed us to measure the difference between estimations of the self-to-other and other-to-self distances (actually the same) within the same person, using a technique other than Codol's.

2.1.1 Technique

Subjects estimated the physical distance between themselves and others. They received two diagrams (see Fig. 1), each on a separate sheet of paper in randomly rotated order. One diagram was a mirror image of the other.

Each diagram was a 17 × 11 cm rectangle containing 18 points identified by a letter of the alphabet representing persons, 12 on one side (high density) and 6 on the other side (low density) with a central point marked self (ME) placed slighty closer to the denser side.

The subject was asked to imagine that he/she and other people were waiting for their trains in a railroad station in two different cities. The task was presented as an ability test. The subject was asked to estimate the distance, in real space, taking into account that 3 centimeters in the picture was equal to 1 meter in reality.

The subject estimated a series of distances between him/herself and the others. Each distance was estimated twice, but each time the question was formulated in the different direction, depending on which of the two compared objects, the self or the other person, served as the point of reference. The direction of comparison between "ME" and "other" was reversed on every question for both diagrams. For instance (Fig. 1), if on the first diagram the subject was asked about the distance from R to him/herself (ME), on the second diagram he/she was asked about the distance from he/herself (ME) to P. The distances R/ME and ME/P were the same. Thus, for each distance, the subject (ME) was the point of reference every other time.

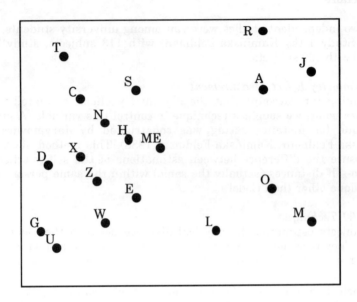

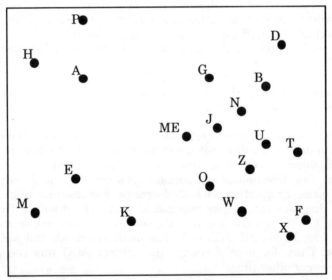

Figure 1. Diagrams used for asymmetry effect measurement (reduced diagrams).

2.1.2 Indices

Differences between every two estimations of the same objective distance for a given pair of persons in which the self was or was not the point of reference were calculated as follows:

AS = (self-to-other distance) − (other-to-self distance)

Thus, positive values indicate autocentric asymmetry, and negative values indicate allocentric asymmetry.

Two asymmetry indices were applied for each subject: (a) ASLD for the low density condition and (b) ASHD for the high density condition.

2.2 Manipulation of Self-Salience and Other-Salience

In both studies the level of self-salience and the other person's salience were manipulated by varying the conditions of centration on the self or the other person.

In study 1, the low and high self-centering conditions were manipulated by written instructions before the distance rating task. Two experimental conditions were set up: (1) in the high self-centering condition (individuation condition (I) n = 60), high self-uniqueness was emphasized; subjects were treated as individuals with personally addressed instructions, questionnaires signed with the individual's initials, information that subjects were personally selected to assess unique capacities, etc; (2) in the low self-centering condition (deindividuation condition (DI), n = 53), decentration was triggered. Subjects were treated anonymously with impersonally formulated instructions, questionnaires marked with numbers, information that subjects were randomly selected to assess general capacities of people, etc. Subjects were randomly assigned to groups I and DI.

In study 2, the manipulation of self-centering and other-centering was applied to the same subjects, in two stages. These stages were as follows: (1) other-centering condition (social task condition, SC) in which social centration was triggered by giving subjects a "social task" where they were asked to invent the arguments for egalitarianism and elitism. Then they were requested to perform the distance rating task (stage I); (2) self-centering condition (egocentric condition, E), in which high self-others similarity was emphasized by informing subjects that a) the profiles of the attributes they gave in the first stage of study were similar in 90 to 95% of the cases to the typical profile, and b) this typical profile was defined on the basis of the analysis of data compiled from 10.000 subjects. In the next step, subjects again performed the distance rating task (stage II). There was a one-week break between stages I and II.

3. Results

The data from the two studies were input separately into a 2 × 2 analysis of variance: high self-centering vs. low self-centering (or other-centering) × low vs. high density.

3.1 Data from Study 1

The data of 113 subjects were analyzed (DI: $n = 53$, I: $n = 60$). The results are shown in Figure 2.

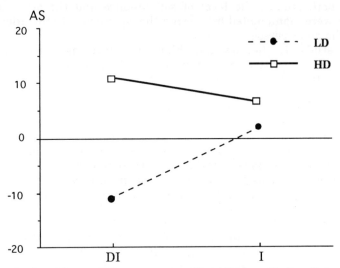

Figure 2. Study 1 Means of the asymmetry effect (AS) in self-other distance rating in self-centering (I) vs. other-centering (DI) conditions, for low (LD) vs. high (HD) social density.

Analysis of variance revealed a main effect of the level of self-centering: subjects in the low self-centering condition (DI) exhibited allocentic asymmetry whereas in the high self-centering condition (I) the autocentric effect was obtained ($F(1,111) = 3.13$; $p < .08$). This result confirms our hypothesis.

The second main effect was obtained for the social density. When the level of social density was low the asymmetry measures were allocentric, whereas when the level of social density was high the asymmetry measures were autocentric ($F(1,111) = 17.12$; $p < .000$).

Analysis of variance revealed a significant interaction between self-centering and social density : $F(1,111) = 7.44$; $p < .007$. But simple effects analysis showed that (1) in high density conditions, subjects in both groups obtained AS scores, signifying autocentric asymmetry (regardless of the self-centering conditions: n.s. differences), and (2) in low density conditions, the high self-centering group exhibited autocentric asymmetry, whereas the low self-centering group obtained scores suggesting allocentric asymmetry.

3.2 Data from Study II

The data of 102 subjects were analyzed (social task condition or SC in stage I of the study and egocentric condition or E in stage II; within-subject design).

The results are shown in Figure 3.

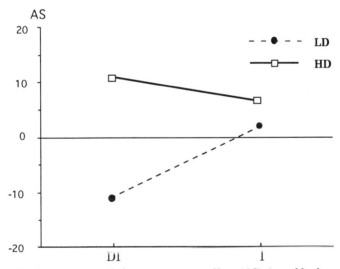

Figure 3. Study 2 Means of the asymmetry effect (AS) in self-other distance rating in the self-centering (E) vs. other-centering (SC) conditions, for low (LD) vs. high (HD) social density.

Analysis of variance revealed a main effect of self-centering versus other-centering: the same subjects in the other-centering conditions obtained significantly higher allocentric asymmetry indices than in the self-centering condition ($F(1,101) = 5.07$; $p < .027$). Taking into account the different starting point of this Study 1n comparison with study 1, this result seems to be consistent with our assumptions.

The second main effect was obtained for the social density level of the compared objects. When the level of social density was low the asymmetry was allocentric whereas when the level of social density was high, asymmetry was nearly attained ($F(1,101) = 5.15$; $p < .025$).

The interaction effect between self- and other-centering and the social density of the compared objects was nonsignificant. The simple effect analysis revealed, however, that: (1) in high density conditions, subjects obtained a weak allocentric asymmetry effect in other-centering and a weak autocentric effect in self-centering (nonsignificant differences), and (2) in low density conditions the asymmetry was significantly less allocentric in the egocentric situation than in the previous social task.

4. Discussion

As a whole, the results of our studies seem to confirm the assumption that the direction and magnitude of the asymmetry effect depend on the transient point of reference, which is related to various situational conditions of self- vs. other-salience.

The results of Study 1 seem to confirm our hypothesis quite clearly: in the low self-salience condition an allocentric asymmetry effect occurred, while in the high self-salience condition an autocentric asymmetry effect was obtained.

However, if we consider the different starting point of study 2 in comparison with Study 1, it seems justified to treat the results of study 2 as also confirming our assumption. The same persons participated in both stages of this study. In stage I, other-salience (social task condition) was triggered and in stage II, self-salience (egocentric condition) was triggered. The results show that the allocentric asymmetry effect in stage II (where egocentricity was provoked) was significantly weaker in comparison with the previous social task conditions.

In both studies, our hypothesis was only confirmed, however, in the low social density conditions. This result suggests, as mentioned previously in our theoretical assumptions, that high density of compared objects leads to an increase in self-salience. However, we believe that the explanation of the source of this self-salience as a defense of personal identity is not necessary. It is obvious that the object's prototypicality may be revealed only in the presence of the other objects. Our assumption is that the greater the number of other objects, the more distinct and salient the object's prototypicality. Thus, if the self is the prototype, its salience is greater in the presence of larger numbers of other objects, and for that reason high social density increases self-salience (Jarymowicz & Kamińska-Feldman, 1988).

Finally, note that our results also show that although the level of social density may have played an important role in determining subjective self-salience, its meaning is not the same in all conditions. The results obtained suggest that in conditions of actualization of the self-representation, the social density level has no effect (in both studies, the observed differences between the low and high density indices were nonsignificant): self-salience is quite enough. In contrast, the social density level is clearly a modifying factor in low self-centering and other-centering conditions (significant differences between the high and low density indices): the presence of a large number of other people accentuates the self and increases self-salience.

References

Codol, J.-P. (1984). L'asymétrie de la similitude perçue entre des personnes diversement stéréotypées. *Cahiers de Psychologie Cognitive, 4*, 605-610.

Codol, J.-P. (1986). L'estimation des distances physiques entre personnes : suis-je aussi loin de vous que vous l'êtes de moi? *L'Année Psychologique, 85*, 517-534.

Holyoak, K. J., & Gordon, P. C. (1983). Social reference points. *Journal of Personality and Social Psychology, 5*, 881-887.

Jarymowicz, M., & Kamińska-Feldman, M. (1988). "Totalitarian ego" and cognitive biases: Is the asymmetry effect related to self-prototypicality? In *Proceedings of the CREPCO Conference on Cognitive Biases* (pp. B1-B10). Aix-en-Provence: Université de Provence.

Kamińska-Feldman, M. (1988). Conditions of social deindividuation and asymmetry in rating self-other distance. *Polish Psychological Bulletin, 19*, 241-248.

Kamińska-Feldman, M. (1992). The self-status and the asymmetry effect in interpersonal distance rating. In L. Arcuri & C. Serino (Eds.), *Asymmetry phenomena in interpersonal comparison: Cognitive and social issues* (pp. 61-69). Napoli: Liguori.

Karyłowski, J. (1990). Social reference points and accessibility of trait-related information in self-other similarity judgments. *Journal of Personality and Social Psychology, 58*, 975-983.

Reykowski, J., & Kochanska, G. (1980). *Szkice z teorii osobowosci.* Warszawa: Wiedza Powszechna.

Rosch, E. (1975). Cognitive representations of semantic categories. *Journal of Experimental Psychology: General, 104,* 192-233.

Tversky, A. (1977). Features of similarity. *Psychological Review, 84,* 327-352.

SELF-IMAGE IN JUDGMENTS OF SIMILARITY BETWEEN PERSONS

Anne-Marie La Haye and Guy Lauvergeon

René Descartes University, Paris, France

1. Introduction

In studies bearing on self-image, it is commonly held that self-perception is tightly linked to the perception of others. This idea has been developed along two lines of research which could be qualified as an "analytic" approach and a "global" or "configural" approach.

1.1 The Analytic Approach

1.1.1 In the analytic approach, one particular feature of the self-image – usually a personality trait – is given special attention, and its impact on person perception is studied. The hypothesis is that features which are important in self-definition are also given priority in judging other persons. This kind of analysis can be found in studies by Lewicki (1983, 1984) and Markus (Fong & Markus, 1982; Markus & Smith, 1981; Markus, Smith, & Moreland, 1985). For Lewicki (1983, 1984), the relationship between the self-image and person perception is an evaluative one. The more positively someone evaluates him/herself on a given dimension, the more important that dimension is in judgments of others (Lewicki, 1983); the traits on which we rate ourselves positively are readily attributed to persons we like, and readily denied to persons we dislike (Lewicki, 1984).

Hazel Markus' analyses do not deal directly with the content of the judgments but with the judgment process. Following her reasoning, when a person has developed a given self-schema, this cognitive structure will also operate for processing information about others. Developing a schema on a given dimension means giving oneself an extreme stand on this dimension and feeling this dimension as important for self-definition. Those persons who have a schema for a given dimension are conceived of as experts in processing information along that dimension. They should be able to more quickly detect any schema-relevant information, and process it more easily and in a more complex way if necessary (Markus, Smith, & Moreland, 1985).

1.1.2 Though it has been demonstrated that we use the same traits when judging ourselves and judging other persons, the significance of the phenomenon must not be overstated. Prentice (1990) showed that this is mainly true for descriptions of unfamiliar persons. Moreover, studies on causal attribution have shown that we resort less frequently to traits for explaining our own behaviour than for explaining the behaviour of someone else. We are aware that our behaviour is variable across situations, and less aware of the same fact when someone else's behaviour is at stake (Baxter & Goldberg, 1987). Consequently, self-descriptions usually include contradictory traits, while this is much rarer for descriptions of others (Sande, Goethals, & Radloff, 1988). Thus, the function of traits as person descriptors is not the same when the self is described as when others are described.

1.1.3 Furthermore, we think that the person perception field would be regrettably limited if we were to consider only personality traits. Our cognitive representations of ourselves and other persons as well are not composed solely of traits. A few recent studies have shown that the primary dimensions of person categorization most probably are age and sex (Brewer & Lui, 1989) or social categories (Bond & Brockett, 1987). It seems that personality judgments are used to differentiate within large categories, but that traits do not themselves function as categories. It is thus justified to ask whether the reciprocal dependency of self-perception and perception of other people, which has been found in studies on personality trait judgments, still holds true at the level of more primary categorizations such as age, sex, and group membership. The following study is an initial approach to this question.

1.2 The Configural Approach

In another line of research, which can be called the "configural" orientation, the self-image as a whole is supposed to play some role in person perception.

1.2.1 Kuiper and his co-workers (Rogers, Kuiper, & Kirker, 1977; Kuiper & Rogers, 1979) were the first ones to study the self-reference effect in cognitive functioning (for a review see Kihlstrom et al., 1988). It has been more recently demonstrated that the phenomenon is open to reinterpretation (Klein & Kihlstrom, 1986). However, Kuiper was one of the first authors to have conceived of the self as a particular reference object, and to have formulated the hypothesis that the self has a prototype function. This hypothesis has found further support in studies on similarity judgments.

1.2.2 Studies on similarity judgments between persons has brought to light a now well-known phenomenon, i.e. the asymmetry of perceived similarity to the self. This phenomenon was simultaneously studied by Codol (1984, 1986, 1987) and other authors (Srull & Gaelik, 1983; Holyoak & Gordon, 1983). It consists of the following: when a subject is asked to estimate the similarity between him/herself and someone else, the estimated similarity is greater when the judgment is made in reference to the self ("How similar is this person to you?") than when the reference point is the other person ("How similar are you to this person?"). The analogy between these results and those observed in similarity judgments between objects is unescapably striking. Asymmetries are observed in perceived similarity between objects from the same category when the objects are not all equally typical of the category. In this case, perceived similarity is greater when the judgment is made in reference to the more typical object (Tversky, 1977). So, asymmetries in perceived similarity to the self directly suggest the interpretation that the self is a usual reference point in judgments on persons, and presents functional properties which are analogous to those of a prototype. But is it possible to go one step further, and assert that *the self is a prototype*? Up to now, available evidence is only indirect. The asymmetry of perceived similarity to the self does not by itself prove that the self is a prototype. We know that unequal prototypicality between objects induces asymmetries in perceived similarity. It does not logically follow that the inverse is true, that is to say, that any asymmetry in perceived similarity results from unequal prototypicality. In the present study, we intended to bring new pieces of evidence to the case.

2. Goals of the Study

This study tackles two problems, one which is in keeping with the analytical line of research, and the other, with the configural line.

2.1 Self-Categorization and Categorization of Other Persons

We intended to broaden the scope of our understanding of the relationship between the self-image and person perception by considering the problem from the point of view of social categorization. We examined the relationship between the weights of the same dimension, for the same subject, in two different kinds of judgments: categorizing other persons and categorizing oneself.

2.1.1 On this question, it seems necessary to distinguish between Turner's formulations and our own (see Turner, Hogg, Oakes, Reicher, & Wetherell, 1987). Turner makes a sharp distinction between two levels of self-categorization: the personal level, where the self as an individual is contrasted with the other ingroup members, and the ingroup/outgroup level, where all members of the same group are assimilated to each other, and the differences between groups are accentuated. In the following study, both kinds of categorization we distinguish are of the ingroup/outgroup type. What we call self-categorization is not aimed at distinguishing the subject from the members of the same group or category, but to contrast two categories: the one to which the subject belongs, and the one to which he/she does not belong. This operation can be called self-categorization, insofar as self-reference is central in defining the categories. What we call categorization of other persons is also a contrast between two categories but this time the definition of the categories makes no reference to the subject. Thus, our question is the following: Does a given subject grant the same weight to a given dimension of categorization (1) when he/she uses it to define him/herself as a member of a category in contrast with another category and (2) when he/she uses it for distinguishing between these two categories without considering his/her own membership.

2.1.2 As far as we know, this question has not yet been studied. A plausible hypothesis on this point would be that the most pertinent dimensions for self-categorization are those which allow subjects to distinguish themselves from their current surroundings, that is to say, dimensions which introduce sub-categorizations into the groups to which they belong. This would be in line, for example, with the fact that groups are generally perceived as more internally diverse by their own members than by outgroup members (Brewer & Lui, 1984; Judd & Park, 1988; Linville, Fisher, & Salovey, 1989; Park & Rothbart, 1982). On the other hand, the categorizations which do not refer to the self make use of more general dimensions. Thus, our hypothesis was that self-categorization and categorization of other persons are not as tightly linked as are self-image and person perception, when personality judgments are at stake. But this hypothesis was not specified in detail. We were expecting either no correlation at all, or weakly positive correlations between the weights of the same dimensions in the two realms. The weights of the categorization dimensions were estimated from a set of similarity judgments between pairs of persons. This procedure is based on the postulate that if a subject does categorize along a given dimension, the objects which fall into the same category along that dimension are perceived as more similar than the objects which fall into different categories along that dimension.

2.2 Is the Self a Prototype?

Our second aim was to provide new pieces of evidence concerning the question: "Is the self a prototype?"

Rosch's works on the structure of natural categories (see for example, Rosch, 1978) have shown that an object's membership in a category is not an all or none matter, but may vary by degrees. All the objects which fall into the same category are not equally typical of it. The prototype of a category is the most typical of all: it may be a real object or an inner representation which combines the features most typically found among the category members, though these typical features do not coexist in any real object. The fact that typicality is a variable characteristic among objects of the same category can be assessed in a number of ways. A direct measure of it is the answer to the question: "Is the object a good example of the category?" But several other parameters show correlations with this first one: these are accessibility of the object as an example of the category (operationally, the rank of its appearance in a list of examples), the number of descriptive features common to the object and other category members, the mean perceived similarity between the object and other category members, and finally, the similarity to the prototype.

The point that makes Rosch's demonstration so impressive is that all these independent indices systematically converge to firmly establish the graded nature of category structure. By the same token, the hypothesis that the self is a prototype should be examined through two different indices of the underlying structure of a set of similarity judgments. We considered (1) self-other similarity judgments, and (2) judgments of similarity between others. If the self is a prototype, then the more a person is perceived as similar to the self, the more he/she should be perceived as central among the others. Thus, there should be a correlation between the perceived similarity of each person to the self, and the mean perceived similarity of the same person to all the others.

3. Method

A questionnaire was given to high school students (45 girls and 27 boys, ages 17 to 20). The questionnaire consisted of two parts. In the first part, subjects were asked to make a list of persons who met some precise requirements. These had to be real persons, and the subjects had to have met them in person, though a deep personal relationship was not required. The persons should not be members of the subject's family. Each person had to fit a given definition involving three characteristics: the target's sex, the target's age (similar to the subject's age, i.e. difference no more than 5 years vs. older than the subject, i.e. minimal difference 15 years), and the quality of the subject's relationship with the target (good vs. not so good). These three dichotomous criteria generate 8 definitions.

When the subject had completed the list, he(she) added a ninth person: him/herself.

In the second part of the questionnaire, subjects were asked questions about the similarity they perceived between the targets. The wording of the question was: "How similar is X to Y?" The responses were given on a 9-point scale, ranging from "extremely similar" (+8) to "not at all similar (0). The question was repeated 72 times, which means that every possible pair of targets, including the subject him/herself, was considered twice: once in a given order, and again in the reverse order. This list of 72 questions was presented in pseudo-random order; each pair appeared once in the first half of the list, and a second time in the other half of the list; the questions were arranged so that a given target never appeared in two consecutive pairs.

4. Results

4.1 Self-Categorization and Categorization of Other Persons

4.1.1 Let us start from the following definition: a given criterion is used as a dimension in categorizing *other* persons whenever the subject perceives greater similarity in pairs of targets that are identical on that criterion than in pairs of targets that differ on that criterion. So, for each criterion and each subject, we calculated the following index, which measures the weight of a given dimension in the categorization of other persons:

(mean perceived within-class similarity) – (mean perceived between-class similarity)

A given criterion is used as a dimension in *self*-categorization whenever the subject perceives him/herself as more similar to the members of one category on this dimension than to members of any other category on the same dimension. So, we calculated the following index, which measures the weight of a given dimension in self-categorization:

(mean perceived self-other similarity within one category) – (mean perceived self-other similarity within the other category)

The differences were calculated so that positive values corresponded to:
- greater perceived similarity of self to persons with whom the subject has a good relationship;
- greater perceived similarity of self to persons of similar age;
- greater perceived similarity of self to persons of the same sex.

4.1.2 Table 1 gives the mean weights for each dimension in the two categorization domains. All these values differ significantly from zero. This means that each dimension is in fact used by our subjects, both when categorizing themselves and when categorizing other persons. In other words, for each dimension, subjects perceive more similarity between persons who are similar in that respect, than between persons who differ in that respect. They also perceive themselves as more similar to people of the same age, to people of the same sex, and to people with whom they have a good relationship, than to people of the other category. However, the three dimensions have very different weights. In both domains, the "good/not so good relationship" dimension is largely the heaviest determinant of similarity judgments. Though significantly different from zero, the weight for the "age" dimension is weak in both realms, and the weight for the "sex" dimension is extremely weak.

Table 1

Mean Weights of Categorization Dimensions (with Student's t Values for Comparisons with Zero)

Dimension	Categorization of others		Self-categorization	
	M	*t*	*M*	*t*
Quality of relationship	2.39	19.36	3.60	20.91
Age	0.52	6.82	0.81	5.61
Sex	0.22	4.38	0.44	4.13

The mean weights were also found to be greater for self-categorization than for categorization of others. This difference was significant ($p < .0001$ for the "quality of relationship" dimension, $p < .05$ for the others). Thus, the categorizing activity is more intense when it is aimed at defining the subject him/herself than when it is strictly aimed at others.

4.1.3 The weak weights of the "age" and "sex" dimensions may reflect two very different phenomena: either all subjects categorize weakly on these dimensions, or the subjects who categorize on these dimensions are few in number. To examine this question, we considered the distribution of weights in the individual responses. However, we found it hazardous to interpret the raw values of these weights, because their significance was not uniform across subjects due to large differences in the way they used the response scale. To avoid this difficulty, we transformed raw responses by dividing them by the *SD* of each subject's set of responses. The distributions of these transformed weights are shown in Figure 1.

This figure deserves two comments. First, in categorization of other persons, the "age" and "sex" dimensions were in fact weakly used by most subjects, or even not used at all. In self-categorization, the distributions of weights for these same dimensions are much more dispersed, including a non-negligible proportion of negative values. Though a majority of subjects still use these dimensions in a weakly positive manner, there are two other existing response styles: a moderately positive use of the dimension, and a weakly negative use. This means that some subjects consider themselves as more similar to people older than themselves, or to people of the other sex, than to people of the same age or sex. Though the negative weight values are weak, there are too many of them to deny any psychological meaning to the phenomenon.

4.1.4 Finally, we examined the correlations between the two categorization indices on the same dimension (see Table 2). Our hypothesis was that these correlations would be weak or null. Our first results (left part of the table, self-categorization index in relative value) in fact show almost no correlation. Only on the "quality of relationship" dimension, and for female subjects only, there is a weak, marginally significant correlation ($r = .27$, $p < .10$). All the other correlations are negligible. We nevertheless had some reason to suspect that this calculation was off target. Given that a number of subjects had negative weight values for self-categorization on the "age" and "sex" dimension, the strength of a given dimension of self-categorization should be assessed by the *absolute value* of our categorization index. In this case, the two categorization indices (for self-categorization on one hand, and categorization of other persons on the other) are correlated in female subjects for the "age" dimension ($r = .33$, $p < .05$) and the "quality of relationship" dimension ($r = .26$, $p < .10$).

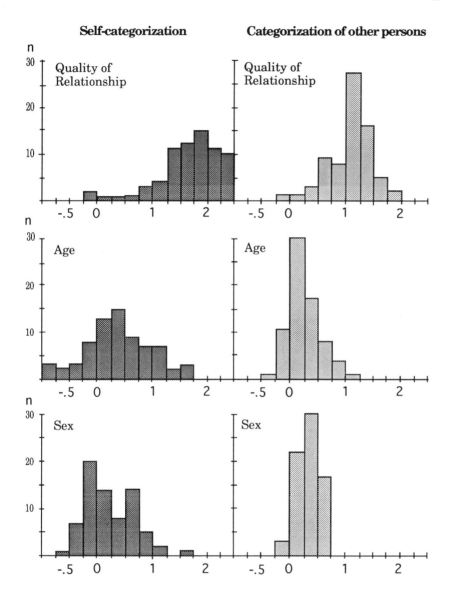

Figure 1. Distribution of weights for each dimension used in categorizing self and other persons (transformed weights).

Table 2
*Correlations between Categorization Indices (Self-Categorization ×
Categorization of Others)*

| Dimension | Self-categorization index | | | |
| | In relative value | | In absolute value | |
	Female Ss	Male Ss	Female Ss	Male Ss
Quality of relationship	.27*	−.02	.26*	−.05
Age	.10	−.05	.33**	.13
Sex	.07	−.13	−.08	.20

* $p < .10$; ** $p < .05$.

4.1.5 This result corresponds relatively well to our expectations. The correlations we observed, though not absolutely null, are weak and scattered. The two sets of judgments similarity between others, and similarity between oneself and an other person – seem to be relatively independent, or to be more precise, their congruence seems to vary among subjects. It is particularly noteworthy that significant correlations appeared exclusively for female subjects. This observation suggests that the usual hypothesis on the consistency of self-perception and the perception of other persons applies to a model of cognitive functioning which may not be universal.

4.2 Is the Self a Prototype?

4.2.1 Each subject produced a large set of responses which can be split into two subsets: judgments of similarity between oneself and other persons on one hand, and similarity judgments between other persons on the other hand. The first eight targets (self excluded) can be ordered in two different ways: according to their perceived similarity to the self, or according to their centrality in the space of inter-target similarities. We examined the correlation between these two hierarchies. In other words, we examined whether it was true that the more one perceives someone as similar to oneself, the more one perceives the same person as similar to people in general. Table 3 gives the distribution of values for the similarity-to-self × centrality correlation. These correlations were computed on each subject's responses, and each one pertains to 8 pairs of values (8 being the number of targets). A correlation of .55 is significant at the .10 level; a correlation of .63 is significant at the .05 level.

Positive correlations are clearly more numerous than negative ones. So, the "self as a prototype" hypothesis is valid as a whole, since this type of psychological functioning is relatively frequent. But correlations are weak or null in a large proportion of subjects; moreover, among the weak correlations, some are negative. If one can indeed take our treatment as descriptive of self-prototypicality, then we can conclude that this kind of functioning is not present in everyone.

Table 3
Distribution of Self-Similarity × Centrality Correlations

$r < -.50$	$r < -.25$	$r < 0$	$r < .25$	$r < .50$	$r < .75$	$.75 < r$
7	8	14	14	8	11	10

4.2.2 Simply observing this heterogeneity could not satisfy us. Trying to go further, we analyzed the response systems of subjects who showed either clearly positive (P group) or clearly negative (N group) correlations between perceived similarity to self and centrality. To this end, we considered only the subjects with non-negligible correlations, i.e. $r > .35$. There are 10 subjects with a correlation lower than −.35 (N group) and 26 with a correlation higher than +.35 (P group). We compared these two groups on the following variables: dimension weights for categorization of other persons; dimension weights for self-categorization; indices of categorization asymmetry on each criterion. The last set of indices pertains to judgments of similarity between others, and is a measure of unequal (or equal) perceived homogeneity within contrasted categories on a given dimension (cf. La Haye & Askevis, 1988). It is computed in the following way:

(mean perceived similarity within one category) − (mean perceived similarity within the other category)

If both categories are perceived as equally homogenous, this index takes on a null value. The differences have been defined so that positive values correspond to greater perceived similarity between persons:
- with whom the subject has a good relationship;
- of the same age as the subject;
- of the same sex as the subject.

Table 4

Mean Weights of the Categorization Dimensions Depending on Groups Defined by the Value of the Self-Similarity × Centrality Correlation

Dimensions	Positive-correlation group	Negative-correlation group	t	p
Categorization of others				
Quality of relationship	1.017	1.309	1.831	.076
Age	0.214	0.205	0.094	*ns*
Sex	0.150	0.013	1.940	.05
Self-categorization				
Quality of relationship	1.799	1.534	1.320	*ns*
Age	0.499	0.431	0.497	*ns*
Sex	0.379	0.264	1.012	*ns*
Categoriz. asymmetry				
Quality of relationship	0.768	−0.647	11.932	< .0001
Age	−0.164	0.172	1.724	.094
Sex	0.001	0.064	0.430	*ns*

Table 4 gives the means of the variables under consideration in the two contrasted groups, and the Student's t-test values for the comparisons between the groups. As for the weights of the categorization dimensions, the groups do not differ very much. We can only note that in the categorization of other persons, the "good vs. not so good relationship" dimension was given a slightly greater weight by subjects in the N group than by subjects in the P group, who in turn give a slightly greater weight to the "sex" dimension. But these differences are really not considerable. The only important difference appears on the categorization asymmetry index, for the "quality of relationship" dimension. This index is clearly negative in the N group, and clearly positive in the P group. This means that the P group subjects (those for whom the self is a prototype) perceive people with whom they have a good relationship as more similar to each other than people with whom they have a less good relationship; the reverse is true for N group subjects.

5. Discussion

This study was designed to examine two questions: Do people categorize themselves and other persons on the same dimensions with the same weights? Is the self a prototype? Our results give no clear-cut answer to either question.

5.1 As for the categorization problem, there are some correlations between the weights of the same dimensions in the two kinds of categorizations, but they are weak, and most importantly, they appear only in female subjects. We do not deem it especially urgent to speculate on why females should be more consistent than males in their use of categorization dimensions. The difference could very well be dependent on some peculiarity in our subject population. The only important point is that consistency in the use of categorization dimensions is not found in everyone. Not only are there individual differences in the weights of some categorization dimensions (as it follows, for example, from the literature on sex-typing), but also, there are differences in the extent to which people are willing to transfer a given dimension from the self-categorization domain to the domain of non-self-centered categorization, and vice-versa. There are people who move from one categorization domain to the other while keeping the same system of judgment, and there are other people who do not proceed in the same way for the two domains. We acknowledge the fact that such a formulation is rather vague. However, it would not be reasonable to draw more precise conclusions from our limited data. Further refinement would need a contribution from personality psychologists.

5.2 On the question of "self as a prototype", individual differences were also found and we managed this time to analyze them in relation to another constructed variable. The self appears to function as a prototype in subjects with positive categorization asymmetry on the "good vs. not so good relationship" dimension, and does not function as a prototype in subjects with negative asymmetry on the same categorization dimension.

The notion of asymmetrical categorization is directly related to the problem of perceived ingroup/outgroup homogeneity. Most studies on this question converge on the "outgroup homogeneity effect". This phenomenon is generally conceived of as a stereotyping effect, i.e. as an over-simplification in the representation of the outgroup; and as such, perceived homogeneity is associated with negative characteristics. But some recent experiments, namely Simon's work (Simon & Brown, 1987; Simon & Pettigrew, 1990), have demonstrated that under certain conditions, the ingroup may be perceived as more homogenous than the outgroup. This perception allows the subject to feel membership within a highly cohesive group with a clearly defined identity. In this case, perceived homogeneity is associated with positive characteristics. In the present study, the notions of similarity and homogeneity are endowed with the same kind of ambiguity. For certain subjects, the greatest similarities are observed between people with whom they have a good relationship, but for other subjects, they occur between people with whom they do not have a good relationship. Notice, however, that even in the last group of subjects, self-other similarity is still a positive characteristic; only the similarities between other persons are associated with negative meanings.

Given the fundamental ambiguity of similarity, there cannot be any straightforward answer to the question: "Is the self a prototype?" The answer is most probably positive in subjects who conceive of similarity as a correlate of a positive social link, not only for their own similarity with others, but also in the way they conceive of similarities between others. But this kind of cognitive-affective functioning is not the only possible one, as we have just seen. Some other subjects make use of similarity in a much more ambiguous way. When judging similarity between themselves and others, good relationships are associated with similarity. On the other hand, when judging similarity between others, bad relationships (with themselves) are associated with judgments of similarity (between others).

These differences generally do not appear in published articles, because the unwritten rules of scientific reports in psychology state that results must be formulated in terms of means. Given that an individual response does not make sense by itself – an assumption with which we could possibly agree – most authors behave as if it were not necessary to look at them, and especially, as if mean results faithfully reflect the psychological processes of every subject, which is a very risky contention. Had we looked only at means, we would have concluded that the self is in fact a prototype (see Table 3, which shows a clearly dominant trend toward positive correlations between similarity to the self and centrality). But a majoritary trend does not reflect universal functioning. Our conclusion will be the same as for the preceding question: in order to better understand how the self-image works in person perception, it seems necessary to take individual differences into account, and each subject's response system should be analyzed in detail.

References

Baxter, T. L., & Goldberg, L. R. (1987). Perceived behavioral consistency underlying trait attributions to oneself and another: An extension of the actor-observer effect. *Personality and Social Psychology Bulletin, 13,* 437-447.

Bond, C. F., & Brockett, D. R. (1987). A social context-personality index theory of memory for acquaintances. *Journal of Personality and Social Psychology, 52,* 1110-1121.

Brewer, M. B., & Lui, L. (1984). Categorization of the elderly by the elderly: Effects of perceiver's category membership. *Personality and Social Psychology Bulletin, 10,* 585-595.

Brewer, M. B., & Lui, L. (1989). The primacy of age and sex in the structure of person categories. *Social Cognition, 7,* 262-274.

Codol, J.-P. (1984). La perception de la similitude interpersonnelle : influence de l'appartenance catégorielle et du point de référence de la comparaison. *L'Année Psychologique, 84,* 43-56.

Codol, J.-P. (1986). Estimation et expression de la ressemblance et de la différence entre pairs. *L'Année Psychologique, 86,* 517-534.

Codol, J.-P. (1987). Comparability and incomparability between oneself and others: Means of differentiation and comparison reference points. *Cahiers de Psychologie Cognitive/European Bulletin of Cognitive Psychology, 7,* 87-105.

Fong, G. T., & Markus, H. (1982). Self-schema and judgments about others. *Social Cognition, 1,* 191-204.

Holyoak, K. J., & Gordon, P. C. (1983). Social reference points. *Journal of Personality and Social Psychology, 44,* 881-887.

Judd, C. M., & Park, B. (1988). Out-group homogeneity: Judgments of variability at the individual and group levels. *Journal of Personality and Social Psychology, 54,* 778-788.

Kelly, C. (1989). Political identity and perceived intragroup homogeneity. *British Journal of Social Psychology, 28,* 239-250.

Kilhstrom, J. F., Cantor, N., Albright, J. S., Chew, B, R,, Klein, S. B., & Niedenthal, P. M. (1988). Information processing and the study of the self. In L. Berkowitz (Ed.), *Advances in experimental social psychology* (Vol. 21, pp. 145-178).New York: Academic Press.

Klein, S. B., & Kihlstrom, J. F. (1986). Elaboration, organization and the self-reference effect in memory. *Journal of Experimental Psychology: General, 115,* 26-38.

Kuiper, N. A., & Rogers, T. B. (1979). Encoding of personal information: Self-other differences. *Journal of Personality and Social Psychology, 37,* 499-514.

La Haye, A. M. de, & Askevis, M. (1988). Asymétrie des catégorisations selon l'évaluation et le pouvoir. *Revue Internationale de Psychologie Sociale, 3-4,* 417-434.

Lewicki, P. (1983). Self-image bias in person perception. *Journal of Personality and Social Psychology, 45,* 384-393.

Lewicki, P. (1984). Self-schema and social information processing. *Journal of Personality and Social Psychology, 47,* 1177-1190.

Linville, P. W., Fisher, G. W., & Salovey P. (1989). Perceived distributions of the characteristics of in-group and out-group members: Empirical evidence and a computer simulation. *Journal of Personality and Social Psychology, 57,* 165-188.

Markus, H., & Smith, J. (1981). The influence of self-schemata on the perception of others. In N. Cantor and J. Kihlstrom (Eds.), *Personality, cognition, and social interaction* (pp. 233-262). Hillsdale, NJ: Erlbaum.

Markus, H., Smith, J., & Moreland, R. L. (1985). Role of the self-concept in the perception of others. *Journal of Personality and Social Psychology, 49,* 1494-1512.

Park, B., & Rothbart, M. (1982). Perception of out-group homogeneity and levels of social categorization. *Journal of Personality and Social Psychology, 42,* 1051-1068.

Prentice, D. A. (1990). Familiarity and differences in self- and other-representations. *Journal of Personality and Social Psychology, 59,* 369-383.

Rogers, T. B., Kuiper, N. A., & Kirker, W. S. (1977). Self-reference and the encoding of personal information. *Journal of Personality and Social Psychology, 35,* 677-688.

Rosch, E. (1978). Principles of categorization. In E. Rosch & B. B. Lloyd (Eds.), *Cognition and categorization* (pp. 27-48). Hillsdale, NJ: Erlbaum.

Sande, G. N., Goethals, G. R., & Radloff, C. E. (1988). Perceiving one's own traits and other's: The multifaceted self. *Journal of Personality and Social Psychology, 54,* 13-20.

Simon, B., & Brown, R. (1987). Perceived out-group homogeneity in minority-majority contexts. *Journal of Personality and Social Psychology, 53,* 703-711.

Simon, B., & Pettigrew, T. F. (1990). Social identity and perceived group homogeneity: Evidence for the ingroup homogeneity effect. *European Journal of Social Psychology, 20,* 269-286.

Srull, T. K., & Gaelick, L. (1983). General principles and individual differences in the self as a habitual reference point: An examination of self-other judgments of similarity. *Social Cognition, 2,* 108-121.

Turner, J. C., Hogg, M. A., Oakes, P. J., Reicher, S. D., & Wetherell, M. S. (1987). *Rediscovering the social group: A self-categorization theory.* Oxford: Basil Blackwell.

Tversky, A. (1977). Features of similarity. *Psychological Review, 84,* 327-352.

THE (SOMEWHAT) ELUSIVE NATURE
OF ASYMMETRIC SELF-OTHER SIMILARITY
JUDGMENTS

Jerzy J. Karylowski

University of North Florida, U.S.A.

Our memories contain an abundance of information about ourselves. Each day brings endless opportunities to gather such information by focusing on our behavior, feelings, and cognitions in a variety of situations. In the case of self, the observed is simply present everywhere the observer happens to be. And the observer is usually eager to both observe and remember. It has been suggested that self functions as a cognitive prototype. In fact, Rogers and his colleagues (Rogers, 1981; Rogers, Kuiper, & Kirker, 1977; Rogers, Rogers, & Kuiper, 1979) proposed that self-knowledge forms a unitary, hierarchically organized structure that "[...] may well be the largest and most rich prototype that we have in our cognitive arsenal."(Rogers, 1981, p. 203). However, a number of other authors have challenged this view and proposed far less radical models in which elements of self-knowledge form smaller scale self-prototypes, or exemplars, that are not necessarily highly interconnected (Cantor & Kihlstrom, 1989; Cantor, Markus, Niedenthal, & Nurius, 1986; Kihlstrom et al. 1988; Markus & Wurf, 1987; Wyer & Srull, 1989, chap. 13).

A central feature of cognitive prototypes is that they are habitually used as points of reference in processing information involving objects that belong to the same or related categories (Holyoak & Mah, 1982;

This research was supported by funds from the University of North Florida Faculty Development Committee and from the Instytut Psychologii Polskiej Akademii Nauk, Warsaw, Poland (project #CPBP 0802). I am indebted to Krystyna Skarzynska, Janusz Reykowski, Jacek Jarymowicz, and Maria Jazwinski for their help at various stages of planning and execution of Experiment 2, to Barbara Dworakowska, Sandy Wood, and Brian Lightsey who worked as research assistants, and to Dave Balota and Mike Strube for their comments on an earlier version of this manuscript.

Rosch, 1975). That is, non-prototypical objects are spontaneously encoded in terms of their similarity to cognitive prototypes. Furthermore, studies show that people perceive greater similarity between a non-prototypical object and a prototype than between a prototype and a non-prototypical object. For instance, Israeli subjects see Mexico as being more similar to the US than the US is to Mexico (Tversky, 1977). In the same vein, people perceive a non-prototypical (non-scalar) melody as more similar to its prototypical (scalar) counterpart than the other way around (Bartlett & Dowling, 1988). Asymmetric judgments of physical distance have also been reported, including judgments of physical distance between people (eg., Codol, 1987; Codol, Jarymowicz, Kaminska-Feldman, & Szuster-Zbrojewicz, 1989; Jarymowicz, 1988; Kaminska-Feldman, 1991) and between non-social targets (eg., Sadalla, Burroughs, & Staplin, 1980).

Perhaps the most widely accepted explanation of what it is about prototypes that causes asymmetric similarity judgments has been proposed by Tversky (1977). According to his contrast model, asymmetric judgments occur as a result of greater articulation of representations of prototypes compared to the representations of ordinary objects. This is based on the assumption that perceived similarity depends on the number of distinct attributes and on the number of attributes in common between the two representations. In judging how similar a prototypical object "P" is to an ordinary object "O" the focus is on the attributes of the object "P". Because of its highly developed cognitive representation this object will have a large number of attributes that are not part of the representation of object "O" (unique attributes of object "P"). On the other hand, in judging how similar object "O" is to object "P" the focus is on object "O" which is described in terms of relatively few attributes. Since its unique attributes are a subset of all attributes of that object, the number of unique attributes will be small. The number of attributes in common between "P" and "O" and between "O" and "P" is, however, always the same regardless of the question form. As a result perceived similarity of object "P" to object "O" is likely to be less than the other way around. Furthermore, the model predicts that the greater the difference in articulation of the two representations (the greater the difference in their prototypicality), the more asymmetric should be similarity judgments involving those representations. While the contrast model does not apply to comparisons involving a single dimension (including judgments of physical distance between non-social objects or even between people) it does apply to a large variety of both social and non-social judgments that explicitly or implicitly involve multidimensional comparisons (however, see Karylowski, 1989, 1990; Karylowski & Skarzynska, 1992, regarding applicability of other models).

In the social domain, the idea of self as a prototype, especially in its more radical variant, which assumes a single, very rich, and well integrated structure (Rogers, 1981; Rogers, Kuiper, & Kirker, 1977; Rogers, Rogers, & Kuiper, 1979), implies that self-other similarity judgments should be highly asymmetric. Empirical evidence for such asymmetric judgments has originally been reported by Holyoak and Gordon (1983), and by Srull and Gaelick (1983). According to those studies, people see others as considerably more similar to themselves than they see themselves as similar to others. For instance, in one study in which subjects were asked to judge similarity between themselves and a friend (Holyoak & Gordon, 1983, Experiment 1) the average difference in responding to "How similar are you to (Friend)...?" and "How similar is (Friend) to you...?" was about .43 on a 9-point scale, or about 5% of the scale range. This result is particularly striking because subjects were asked to select friends that *they knew very well* which, according to the contrast model (Tversky, 1977), should have worked against asymmetric judgments (cf. Srull & Gaelick, Experiment 1).

In contrast to the generally strong results reported in those earlier studies, two recently published papers, based on five different studies, found either no evidence of asymmetric judgments (Karylowski, 1990a), or only a very small effect of about .07 on the 9-point scale, less then 1% of the scale range (Karylowski, 1989). One possibility is that those inconsistent outcomes were due to some subtle aspects of experimental procedures that led to differences in accessibility of self-knowledge. An indirect support for this notion comes from a study by Srull and Gaelick (1983, Experiment 3) in which asymmetric judgments were found for subjects chronically high on private self-consciousness but not for subjects low on that dimension. This suggests that accessibility of self-knowledge might be an important factor determining asymmetric self-other similarity judgments.

In this respect it is relevant to note that subjects in the two experiments by Holyoak and Gordon (1983) in which a high degree of asymmetry was found, were asked to complete the Self-Monitoring Scale (Snyder, 1974) shortly before making similarity judgments. Because completing this scale requires answering a number of questions about one's own psychological characteristics, it is likely to increase accessibility of self-knowledge. In fact, simply being asked to participate in a psychological experiment, especially when participation is not anonymous, is likely to produce some degree of self-focus, thus increasing such accessibility (cf. Wicklund, 1975). Interestingly, in all published studies on asymmetric self-other similarity judgments that produced either negative results (Karylowski, 1990a, Experiments 1 & 2) or very weak results (Karylowski, 1989, Experiments 1, 2, & 3) subjects participated anonymously, and had only very limited contact with the experimenter.

Research shows that in making judgments individuals use only a small fraction of relevant information stored in memory (cf. Higgins, 1989; Wyer & Srull, 1989, chapters 5 & 10). The number of attributes that a person will consider in making similarity judgments will therefore depend not only on how rich the representations of the objects considered are, but also on the accessibility of the attributes contained in the representations. Because priming of self-knowledge, intentional or inadvertent, would increase accessibility of memory stored exemplars of that category (such as trait-related and role-related information about the self) without similarly affecting the other-person category, a strong and reliable asymmetry effect in self-other similarity judgments should be more likely to occur.

Despite the undisputable abundance of self-knowledge, without priming, the effect would not necessarily be expected, unless one assumes that self-knowledge forms a single, highly integrated cognitive structure. However, considerable experimental evidence exists against making such assumption. This evidence comes from recent studies that compared representations of self with representations of other people. For instance, it has been found that, compared to their descriptions of others, in describing themselves subjects use less traits overall (Prentice, 1990), are more likely to use highly specific trait terms, and are less likely to use general trait terms (John, Hampson, & Goldberg, 1991). People are also more likely to endorse both ends of the same trait dimension (eg., to endorse both "introverted" and "extroverted") as self-descriptive than as other-descriptive (Sande, Goethals, & Radloff, 1988), which indicates that self-knowledge is more compartmentalized than our representations of others. In a similar vein, in a series of carefully designed studies which attempted to test interconnectedness between highly self-descriptive characteristics using a modification of the Stroop color-naming technique, no indication of an underlying structure was found (Higgins, Van Hook, & Dorfman, 1988).

Present research

The prediction that the asymmetry effect in self-other similarity judgments depends on accessibility of self-knowledge was recently tested in a series of four experimental studies. Whereas the studies conducted involved additional hypotheses (and additional comparison groups) we will focus here on comparisons relevant to that prediction. Self-knowledge accessibility was manipulated by asking subjects to spend 5-10 minutes thinking of themselves and listing their own characteristics "as they came to mind". This manipulation involved either unobservable characteristics, observable characteristics, or the domain was not specified. Subjects in the control groups were asked to spend the same amount of time thinking of and listing characteristics of their campus, or the priming task was simply omitted. The dependent measure consisted of self-other similarity judgments involving either an acquaintance (same age, younger, or older) or a close friend. The form of the similarity question was manipulated as a between-subject variable with half of the subjects being asked to make judgments of similarity between self and other(s) ("...how similar are you to Person X?") and the other half being asked to make judgments between the other(s) and the self ("....how similar is Person X to you?"). The domain of similarity judgments (observable characteristics, unobservable characteristics, or unspecified) paralleled the domain involved in the priming manipulation.

To minimize *inadvertent* priming of self-knowledge across the experimental conditions, subjects were run in groups in their regular classrooms, were assured of their anonymity and were not asked to sign experimental materials with their names. For the same reason no pre-experimental measures of individual differences were used. Within each study (and also within studies 1 and 2 combined), subjects were assigned to groups randomly. Particulars of the four studies are summarized in Table 1.

Table 1
Samples and procedures

Study	Sample	Other Person(s)	Similarity Domain	Control Priming Task
1*	US Undergraduates $N = 119$	Acquaintance	Unobservable characteristics	Describe campus
2*	US Undergraduates $N = 122$	Acquaintance	Observable characteristics	Describe campus
3	Polish High school students $N = 218$	Two acquaintances (one younger and one older)	Unspecified	None
4	US Undergraduates $N = 112$	Best friend	Unspecified	Describe campus

* Subjects in Study 1 vs. Study I2 were assigned randomly from a combined sample of $N = 241$.

Similarity judgments were analyzed in a meta-analytic manner with the four studies treated as levels of a blocking variable (Rosenthal, 1984). As can be seen in Figure 1 a clear pattern of results emerged. Overall, subjects in the "self primed" condition, but not subjects in the control condition, judged others as being more similar to themselves than they judged themselves to be similar to others.

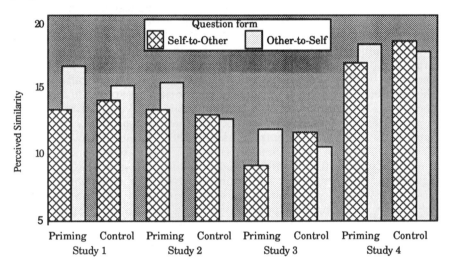

Figure 1. Self-Other Similarity Judgments.

Both the simple effect of the question form in the "self primed" condition and the overall question form × priming interaction were significant $(F(1,316) = 13.30$; $p < .001$ and $F(3,555) = 5.20$; $p < .03$, respectively), but the simple effect of question form in the control condition was not $(F(1,239) < 1)$. No interaction involving the blocking variable approached significance, thus indicating that the effects of priming and question form were consistent across the four studies.

The conclusion that priming was necessary for the asymmetric judgments to occur is consistent with recent studies that have challenged the view of the self as a unitary cognitive structure (Baxter & Goldberg, 1987; Higgins, Van Hook, & Dorfman, 1988; Prentice, 1990; Sande, Goethals, & Radloff, 1988). Those studies suggest that self-knowledge is organized more in terms of multiple *context specific* self-prototypes, or exemplars (Cantor & Kihlstrom, 1989; Cantor, Markus, Niedenthal, & Nurius, 1986; Kihlstrom et al., 1988; Markus & Wurf, 1987; Wyer & Srull, 1989, chap.13) than in terms of a single, chronically accessible, highly powerful prototype, as postulated by Rogers (1981; Rogers, Kuiper, & Kirker, 1977; Rogers, Rogers, & Kuiper, 1979). It seems reasonable to assume that priming of self-knowledge facilitated asymmetric judgments by bringing together information contained in multiple self-prototypes that, without the manipulation, would not have been included in the "working self-concept" (Markus & Wurf, 1987).

At the methodological level, these results suggest that inconsistent findings obtained in previous studies were, at least in part, due to the variations in inadvertent priming of self-knowledge. This underscores the inherent difficulty of the experimental study of the self. Experimental procedures often include more or less subtle cues likely to increase accessibility of self-knowledge, and this may jeopardize generalizability of the results. The problem is particularly critical in studies designed to compare structural and information processing properties of self-representations with such properties of other (social or non-social) representations (see Higgins & Bargh, 1987; Kihlstrom et al., 1988; Sherman, Judd, & Park, 1989, for reviews). This is because any form of inadvertent priming of self-knowledge is likely to give the self unfair advantage over other representations involved in the comparison, thus producing artifactual results. One way to deal with this problem is to incorporate priming manipulation into the experimental design. This was the approach used in the present studies.

References

Bargh, J. A. (1989). Conditional automaticity: Varieties of automatic influence in social perception and cognition. In J. S. Uleman & J. A. Bargh (Eds.), *Unintended thought* (pp. 3-51). New York: Guilford.

Bartlett, J. C., & Dowling, W. J. (1988). Scale structure and similarity of melodies. *Music Perception, 5,* 285-315.

Baxter, T. L., & Goldberg, L. R. (1987). Perceived behavioral consistency underlying trait attributions to oneself and another: An extension of the actor-observer effect. *Personality and Social Psychology Bulletin, 13,* 437-447.

Cantor, N., & Kihlstrom, J. F. (1989). Social intelligence and cognitive assessments of personality. In R. S. Wyer & T. K. Srull (Eds.), *Advances in social cognition: Vol. 2. Social intelligence and cognitive assessments of personality* (pp. 1-59). Hillsdale, NJ: Erlbaum.

Cantor, N., Markus, H., Niedenthal, P., & Nurius, P. (1986). On motivation and the self-concept. In R. M. Sorrentino & E. T. Higgins (Eds.), *Handbook of motivation and cognition: Foundations of social behavior*. New York: Guilford.

Codol, J.-P. (1987). Comparability and incomparability between oneself and others: Means of differentiation and comparison reference points. *Cahiers de Psychologie Cognitive / European Bulletin of Cognitive Psychology, 7*, 87-105.

Codol, J.-P., Jarymowicz, M., Kaminska-Feldman, M., & Szuster-Zbrojewicz, A. (1989). Asymmetry in the estimation of interpersonal distance and identity affirmation. *European Journal of Social Psychology, 19*, 11-22.

Fenigstein, A., & Levine, M. P. (1984). Self-attention, concept activation, and the causal self. *Journal of Experimental Social Psychology, 20*, 231-245.

Higgins E. T. (1989). Knowledge accessibility and activation: Subjectivity and suffering from unconscious sources. In J. S. Uleman & J. A. Bargh (Eds.), *Unintended thought* (pp. 75-123). New York: Guilford.

Higgins, E. T., & Bargh, J. A. (1987). Social cognition and social perception. *Annual Review of Psychology, 38*, 369-425.

Higgins, E. T., Bond, R. N., Klein, R., & Strauman, T. (1986). Self-discrepancies and emotional vulnerability: How magnitude, accessibility, and type of discrepancy influence affect. *Journal of Personality and Social Psychology, 51*, 5-15.

Higgins, E. T., Van Hook, E., & Dorfman, E. (1988). Do self-attributes form a cognitive structure? *Social Cognition, 6*, 177-206.

Holmes, D. S. (1968). Dimensions of projection. *Psychological Bulletin, 69*, 248-268.

Holyoak, K. J., & Gordon, P. C. (1983). Social reference points. *Journal of Personality and Social Psychology, 44*, 881-887.

Holyoak, K. J., & Mah W. A. (1982). Cognitive reference points in judgments of symbolic magnitude. *Cognitive Psychology, 14*, 328-352.

Jarymowicz, M. (1988). Distance perçue entre soi et autrui, et altruisme. *Revue Internationale de Psychologie Sociale, 1*, 275-285.

Kaminska-Feldman, M. (1991). Self-salience and the autocentric versus allocentric asymmetry effect in interpersonal distance rating. *Cahiers de Psychologie Cognitive / European Bulletin of Cognitive Psychology, 11*, 669-678.

Karylowski, J. J. (1989). Trait prototypicality and the asymmetry effect in self-other similarity judgments. *Journal of Social Behavior and Personality, 4*, 581-586.

Karylowski, J. J. (1990). Social reference points and accessibility of trait-related information in self-other similarity judgments. *Journal of Personality and Social Psychology, 58,* 975-983.

Karylowski, J. J. & Skarzynska, K. (1992). Asymmetric self-other similarity judgments depend on priming of self-knowledge. *Social Cognition, 10,* 235-254.

Kihlstrom, J. F., Cantor, N., Albright, J. S., Chew, B. R., Klein, S. B., & Niedenthal, P. M. (1988). Information processing and the study of the self. In L. Berkowitz (Ed.), *Advances in experimental social psychology* (Vol. 21, pp. 145-178). New York: Academic Press.

Marks, G., & Miller, N. (1987). Ten years of research on the false consensus effect: An empirical and theoretical review. *Psychological Bulletin, 102,* 72-90.

Markus, H., & Wurf, E. (1987). The dynamic self-concept: A social psychological perspective. *Annual Review of Psychology, 38,* 299-338.

McGuire, W. J., & McGuire, C. V. (1986). Differences in conceptualizing self versus other people as manifested in contrasting verb types used in natural speech. *Journal of Personality and Social Psychology, 51,* 1135-1143.

Prentice, D. A. (1990). Familiarity and differences in self- and other-representations. *Journal of Personality and Social Psychology, 59,* 369-383.

Rogers, T. B. (1981). A model of the self as an aspect of the human information processing system. In N. Cantor & J. F. Kihlstrom (Eds.), *Personality, cognition, and social interaction* (pp. 193-214). Hillsdale, NJ: Erlbaum.

Rogers, T. B., Kuiper, N. A., & Kirker, W. S. (1977). Self-reference and the encoding of personal information. *Journal of Personality and Social Psychology, 35,* 677-688.

Rogers, T. B., Rogers, P. J., & Kuiper, N. A. (1979). Evidence for the self as a cognitive prototype: The "false alarms effect". *Personality and Social Psychology Bulletin, 5,* 53-56.

Rosch, E. (1975). Cognitive reference points. *Cognitive Psychology, 7,* 532-547.

Sadalla, E. K., Burroughs, W. J., & Staplin, L. J. (1980). Reference points in spatial cognition. *Journal of Experimental Psychology: Human Learning and Memory, 6,* 516-528.

Sande, G. N., Goethals, G. R., & Radloff, C. E. (1988). Perceiving one's own traits and others': The multifaceted self. *Journal of Personality and Social Psychology, 54,* 13-20.

Sherman, S. J., Judd, C. M., & Park, B. (1989). Social cognition. *Annual Review of Psychology, 40,* 281-326.

Snyder, M. (1974). The self-monitoring of expressive behavior. *Journal of Personality and Social Psychology, 30*, 526-537.

Srull, T. K., & Gaelick, L. (1983). General principles and individual differences in the self as a habitual reference point: An examination of self-other judgments of similarity. *Social Cognition, 2*, 108-121.

Tversky, A. (1977). Features of similarity. *Psychological Review, 84*, 327-352.

Wicklund, R. A. (1975). Objective self-awareness. In L. Berkowitz (Ed.), *Advances in experimental social psychology* (Vol. 8, pp. 233-275). New York: Academic Press.

Wyer, R. S., & Srull, T. K. (1989). *Memory and cognition in its social context*. Hillsdale, NJ: Erlbaum.

POINT OF REFERENCE, PROTOTYPICALITY, AND CATEGORIZATION

Riel Vermunt

University of Leiden, The Netherlands

Jan Extra

Royal Netherlands Naval College, The Netherlands

1. Introduction

The asymmetry phenomenon demonstrated and investigated by Codol in various ways can be illustrated by the following example. When a person is asked to indicate the similarity or difference between himself (P) and another (A), then the magnitude of the subjective similarity or difference depends on the point of reference implicated in the phrasing of the question. If the question is: "How similar is A to you?" (P is the point of reference) then the similarity is estimated to be greater than when the question is: "How similar are you to A?" (A is the point of reference). For the degree of difference, A will be seen as less different from P than P from A. This illogical, but apparently quite psychological phenomenon interested Codol so much that he designed and carried out several experiments in order to describe and explain it. Some of Codol's early work (Codol, 1984b, 1984c) seems to have been inspired by the theoretical analysis of perceived similarity proposed by Tversky (1977).

Tversky's explanation is based on information processing and it stresses salience as an explanatory concept. To Tversky, salience is tantamount to number of distinct features. Although Codol never refuted Tversky's approach, and part of his work elaborates on Tversky's views, his prevalent explanatory concept appears to be the affirmation or protection of personal identity (Extra & Vermunt, 1989). We will refer to Tversky's approach as cognitive, and to Codol's as socio-cognitive. In the following we will ignore Codol's apparent appreciation of Tversky's work, and, for the sake of the argument, we will present these approaches as opposing views.

There is little but inferential evidence in favor of the socio-cognitive point of view. Codol assumed that the experience of having to compare oneself to someone else is degrading, whereas the comparing someone else to oneself is upgrading. Although this line of reasoning is plausible (Extra & Vermunt, 1989), there is little experimental evidence to support it. One experimental finding should be noted though, which in general is suggestive of the influence of social factors on the occurrence of asymmetry. Codol (1987) found a reversal of the asymmetry (negative asymmetry) when the subjects' best friends were the other persons in the comparison. Apparently, if the other person is held in high esteem, it is not degrading to accept this person as the point of reference, and if the subject is the point of reference it may seem presumptuous to compare this great person to oneself. In order to get more empirical evidence for Codol's socio-cognitive view, Vermunt, Extra, Rijsman, and De Graaf (1990) conducted an experiment in which the subject was superior, equal or inferior to the average participant in the group. It turned out that in the condition in which the subject was inferior to the average other, the subject judged him/herself as more similar to the other than the other to him/herself.

Codol related asymmetry to the need to differentiate oneself from others. To test this assumption, Codol (1984a) conducted a study in which firemen and undertakers were asked (among other things) to indicate how strong the similarity was between the other members of their own professional group (excluding subject) and within their own group (including subject) as such. Both firemen and undertakers regarded their colleagues as a more homogeneous group than their own group (including subject). A second experiment (Codol, 1984a) in which students were subjects showed a similar result: "other students" (excluding subject) are more homogeneous than "students" in general (including subject).

Tajfel (1984) stated that differentiating is stronger on the intergroup level than on the interpersonal level. It seems logical, therefore, that asymmetry will be stronger on the intergroup level than on the interpersonal level. This assumption is also consistent with Tversky's cognitive point of view. Indicating similarity between an ingroup member and an outgroup member implies the addition of an extra distinctive feature: the out-groupness of the comparison other, as compared to judging the similarity between two ingroup members. We, therefore, predict that asymmetry in comparison of two persons will be stronger if one of them is an outgroup member.

According to Tversky, a less salient object is more similar to a more salient object than vice versa. Tversky demonstrated this in an experiment on comparison of nations. It was found, for instance, that subjects considered North Korea more similar to Red China than Red China to North Korea. Tversky explains this by assuming that in the act of comparing "one naturally focuses on the subject of the comparison. Hence the features of the subject are weighed more heavily than the features of the referent. [...] Consequently, similarity is reduced more by the distinctive features of the subject than by the distinctive features of the referent" (p. 333). Thus, less similarity will be experienced if a salient or prototypical object (possessing a relatively great number of distinctive features) is compared to a less salient object (referent) than if the latter is compared to the former.

Evidence for the applicability of Tversky's theory to the interpersonal domain was reported by Holyoak and Gordon (1983), and by Srull and Gaelick (1983). These researchers investigated the influence of the others' salience on asymmetry. In both instances it was found that the more the others' salience diminished (in terms of known attributes or features), the more asymmetry decreased. In accordance with Tversky we predict greater similarity of a less prototypical person to a more prototypical person than vice versa.

Holyoak and Gordon (1983) and Srull and Gaelick (1983) found stronger asymmetry effects between the self and a stereotype with stereotypes featuring few attributes than with stereotypes featuring many attributes. In an experiment on comparison of stimulus persons, Codol (1984c) varied the degree of prototypicality of the stimulus person. In one of the conditions the prototype and the variant were clearly differentiated, in the other condition they were not. It was found that asymmetry of perceived similarity between the prototype and the variant was greater for the clearly differentiated stimulus persons than for the less clearly differentiated persons. From these studies one can conclude that the number of features the prototype and the variant have in common is strongly related to the magnitude of the asymmetry. We predict, therefore, that the closer the variant is to the prototype the smaller the asymmetry will be.

In the first part of the present experiment subjects indicated similarity between two other stimulus persons, and in the second part subjects indicated similarity between themselves and a stimulus person.

2. Method

2.1 Subjects

One hundred and twelve subjects, all students of the Public Policy Department of Leiden University, participated in this study. Eight students participated in one experimental session. Three subjects did not appear at the experimental session due to illness or lack of time.

2.2 Design

The present study focuses on asymmetry in perceived similarity of two other persons both belonging to the subject's group, or one of them belonging to the subject's ingroup and the other to an outgroup. Ingroup and outgroup were created by a fictitious random assignment of participants to a "yellow" or a "green" group. Subjects invariably ended up in the yellow group. The other persons, B and C, each served as the point of reference for (approximately) half of the subjects. C always was an ingroup member, and B was either an ingroup member or an outgroup member. Also, B's distance to a prototypical other was varied. C was always most similar to the prototype. B was either relatively close to or far from the prototype. The design involving similarity of B and C as the dependent variable was a 2 (point of reference: B or C) × 2 (B ingoup vs. outgroup member) × 2 (B close to vs. far from prototype) between-subjects design.

2.3 Procedure

The experiment was introduced as a study on social skills and interpersonal perception. All information was given on the monitor of an Apple computer. Subjects answered questions by typing a number on the keyboard. The subjects' first task was to fill out 15 items of a test allegedly measuring social skills. After the test, but before the results were announced, subjects were told that the next task would be to indicate how they evaluated themselves as well as others on social skills. It was explained that for technical reasons two groups of four participants were to be formed. Subjects were then asked to type a number (with maximum of 10 digits) and told that participants choosing about the same number of digits were to be assigned to the same group, the other participants being assigned to another group. Subjects always belonged to the yellow group, the others either to the yellow or to the green group. Subjects were also explained that a typical socially skillful person would have given certain answers to 4 (out of 15) particular items. These answers were shown to them.

Then, participants B and C were introduced. C was always a member of the yellow group, the subject's own group. C had 3 out of 4 answers in common with the typical socially skillful person: C was very similar to the prototype. Information about B varied: (1) half of the subjects received information that B was an ingroup member and half were told that B was an outgroup member; (2) half of the subjects received information that B had two answers in common with the typical socially skillful person and half were told that B had one answer in common; (3) half of the subjects were asked to compare B to C (C is referent) and half to compare C to B (B is referent).

After finishing the ratings, the subjects were introduced to the second part of the experiment. They were told that, before receiving information about their test score, they should make a comparison involving themselves and the other member of their own group. Half of the subjects were asked to indicate similarity between C and themselves; the other half was asked to indicate similarity between themselves and C. After the rating, the experiment was finished. Subjects were debriefed and paid.

2.4 Dependent measures

Subjects rated similarity between B and C, as well as between C and themselves, on a 7-point scale ranging from 1 (most similar) to 7 (least similar).

3. Results

For the first part of the experiment the three hypotheses were:
(1) Greater similarity of B to C than of C to B, because C is more prototypical than B (cf. Tversky, 1977);
(2) Greater asymmetry if B is an outgroup member than if B is an ingroup member;
(3) Greater asymmetry if B is far from the prototype than if B is close to the prototype.

We predicted a main effect for reference point (hypothesis 1); an interaction effect of reference point and ingroup/outgroup (hypothesis 2); and an interaction effect of reference point and distance (hypothesis 3). An analysis of variance was carried out with ingroup/outgroup membership of B, distance from B to prototype and point of reference as independent variables and perceived similarity between B and C as the dependent variable. The results revealed a main effect of reference point ($F(1, 101) = 33.89$; $p < .000$) showing that C (assumed to be more prototypical than B) was judged more similar to B (the variant) than B to C ($M = 3.07$ and 4.07, respectively). Also a weak interaction effect of reference point and distance ($F(1,101) = 3.65$; $p < .059$) was found. The unexpected negative asymmetry already manifesting itself in the main effect was stronger when B was far from the prototype. In Table 1, the mean scores of this interaction are presented.

Table 1

Mean Similarity Ratings of the Interaction Between Reference Point and Distance

Distance between B and prototype	Reference Point	
	B	C
Close	3.26	3.93
Far	2.89	4.22

Note. The greater the value the lesser the similarity.

Analysis of variance on the similarity rating between C and the subject as the dependent variable and reference point as the independent variable revealed a significant effect of reference point ($F(1,107) = 6.58$; $p < .02$). The mean similarity score for C-to-subject comparison was 4.15 and for subject-to-C comparison, 4.58. It means that C was more similar to the subject than the subject was to C. These results indicate the occurence of the normal asymmetry effect. The mean similarity score between the subject and C was 4.37, indicating fairly little resemblance between them.

4. Discussion

The results of the present study are rather unexpected. In the first place, there is no interaction effect between reference point and ingroup/outgroup membership on similarity judgments. It was expected that when B was an outgroup member, asymmetry would be stronger than when B was ingroup member. Remember, C was always an ingroup member. When B was an outgroup member an extra feature was added compared to the situation when B was an ingroup member. From Codol's socio-cognitive approach as well as from Tversky's cognitivist approach, the interaction effect could be predicted. The fact that the effect did not occur may be due to the minimal group situation created in the experimental session. The differentiation between in-group and out-group was manipulated very weakly.

In the second place, and more important to the "controversy" between Codol and Tversky, is the finding that the prototypical stimulus person (C) was more similar to the variant (B) than the variant was to the prototype. From Tversky's cognitivist point of view this finding is unexpected. The results are perhaps consistent with Codol's socio-cognitive approach. This approach assumes that not only is the number of distinctive features persons have in common indicative of asymmetry, but so is the quality of the evaluation of the persons: is the other held in high esteem or rejected? The prototype in our study was probably judged far from attractive by the student population from which we selected our subjects. Unfortunately, we did not check this separately, so we cannot be completely certain about our interpretation. However, although we did not directely ask the subjects about the evaluation of stimulus person C, the self-to-C and C-to-self comparison indicates that C, and thus the prototype, was not evaluated positively.

In the literature, some evidence can be found from research based on Tversky's cognitive approach that may support our finding. Srull and Gaelick (1983) found less asymmetry when subjects compared themselves to their parents than when comparing themselves to celebrities like Ronald Reagan, Barbara Walters and Walter Cronkite. The authors consider their findings consistent with Tversky's cognitive model that number of known features (parents being more familiar than celebrities) determines the extent of asymmetry. It appears to us, however, that the mother and the father were more highly valued than the other stimuli, resulting in weaker asymmetry. Holyoak and Gordon (1983) also adhere closely to Tversky's model. They found that, on average, across all stereotypes (preppie, etc.) assymetry occurred when comparing the self to the stereotype and vice versa. However, some of the stereotypes produced stronger asymmetry effects than others. Negative asymmetry (nonsignificant) was even found in a few instances: in cases of more differentiated stereotypes. It cannot be ruled out, however, that the more differentiated stereotypes are also the more valued ones.

One may conclude, therefore, that the value granted to the compared other may be an important explanatory concept for asymmetry. In terms of the socio-cognitive interpretation of judgment asymmetry, a highly valued other decreases the need to differentiate oneself from him or her. On the other hand, if one admires the other person, one may strive to become similar to him or her. It would be worthwhile to further investigate the effects of the socio-cognitive approach initiated by Codol.

The finding that the greater the distance between the compared stimulus person, the stronger the asymmetry, corroborates our assumption. It is in line with both Tversky's and Codol's approaches. The results of our study show that distance also influences reversed asymmetry: reversed asymmetry is stronger for longer distances between the compared stimulus persons and weaker for shorter distances between them.

The present research does not yield convincing empirical evidence entirely in favor of the cognitive approach or the socio-cognitive approach. Asymmetry may partly be explained by referring both to Codol's view that individuals strive for a positive identity, and to Tversky's distinctive features model.

References

Codol, J.-P. (1984a). La perception de la similitude interpersonnelle : influence de l'appartenance catégorielle et du point de référence de la comparaison. *L'Année Psychologique, 84*, 43-56.

Codol, J.-P. (1984b). Quand Dupond ressemble à Dupont plus que Dupont à Dupond : l'asymétrie de la similitude perçue entre des personnes semblables. *Psychologie Française, 29*, 284-290.

Codol, J.-P. (1984c). L'asymétrie de la similitude perçue entre des personnes diversement stéréotypées. *Cahiers de Psychologie Cognitive, 4*, 601-606.

Codol, J.-P. (1987). Comparability and incomparability between oneself and others: Means of differentiation and comparison reference points. *Cahiers de Psychologie Cognitive/European Bulletin of Cognitive Psychology, 7*, 87-105.

Extra, J., & Vermunt, R. (1989). Asymmetrie bij vergelijking tussen personen. In M. Poppe, J. Extra, A. van Knippenberg, G. Kok, & E. Seydel (Eds.), *Fundamentele Sociale Psychologie* (Vol. 3). Tilburg: Tilburg University Press.

Holyoak, K. J., & Gordon, P. C. (1983). Social reference points. *Journal of Personality and Social Psychology, 44*, 882-887.

Srull, T. K., & Gaelick, L. (1983). General principles and individual differences in the self as a habitual reference point: An examination of self-other judgments of similarity. *Social Cognition, 2*, 108-121.

Tajfel, H. (1984). *The social dimension: European developments in social psychology*. Cambridge: Cambridge University Press.

Tversky, A. (1977). Features of similarity. *Psychological Review, 84*, 327-352.

Vermunt, R., Extra, J., Rijsman, J., & De Graaf, S. (1990). Invloed van prestatieverschillen op asymmetrie van waargenomen onderlinge overeenkomst. In J. Extra, A. van Knippenberg, J. van der Pligt & M. Poppe (Eds.), *Fundamentele Sociale Psychologie* (Vol. 4). Tilburg: Tilburg University Press.

PART TWO

COGNITIVE EFFECTS OF THE INTERGROUP STRUCTURE AND REPRESENTATIONS OF SELF-OTHER RELATIONS

INTRODUCTION

Willem Doise

University of Geneva, Switzerland

Social psychologists use a variety of explanatory principles in trying to account for the regularities they observe or produce experimentally. This variety has sometimes been considered as an indication of an intrinsic weakness of social psychology. Various explanatory models are proposed that possess their own internal validity and that have also been proven to be externally valid. But at first sight these diverse models are not linked together; in every journal volume new models or explanations are proposed without apparent concern for theoretical integration with the previous ones. And some of the better models, although very high on validity characteristics, are simply forgotten with research going on in the same problem area.

And indeed, the multiplicity of explanations presented in the various journals of social psychology is not necessarily a sign of intellectual richness. Often one cannot dismiss the thought that this variety is to be explained merely by an exacerbated search for social differentiation among social psychologists themselves. Perhaps such plurality can also serve as a remedy for insufficiencies in available models, but it does not necessarily facilitate the process of accumulation and integration of scientific knowledge.

In fact, the variety of explanations which characterizes contemporary social psychology is not always a mere juxtaposition of unrelated conjectures. Many of them have in common the focus on the study of intraindividual and interindividual processes. Less often they invoke positional differences in a network of societal relations, or bring in general beliefs and values (see Doise, 1980, 1986). But still more important is the fact that the mindful reader often observes interrelationships between explanations when the functioning of a given process is considered to be conditioned by dynamics which are described at another level.

For instance, actualization of such a basic intraindividual process as the search for equilibrium or the reduction of dissonance was viewed by Poitou (1974) as the product of an ideology which promotes the idea of an autonomous and consistent individual. Or, the process of interindividual normalization as studied by Sherif (1935) was shown to depend on aspects of status and intergroup relations (Sampson, 1968). In sum, such examples, as well as many others which have already been reported elsewhere (Doise, 1986; Doise, Deschamps, & Mugny, 1991), reveal that the process of accumulation and integration is nevertheless at work in the collective endeavor of social psychology.

The same process is at work in the contributions of this section. A well-known cognitive process deals with asymmetries in the comparison of similarities and differences according to the characteristics of the reference points (Tversky, 1977). The psychological difference between x and y is not necessarily equal to the difference between y and x, as a prototypical member of a category is usually considered more different from a less prototypical member than the latter is from the former. Several authors in the first section of the book have elaborated upon Codol's (1984, 1987) systematic studies on asymmetry in judgments of resemblance and difference between the self and others.

In this section three contributions deal with the theme of asymmetries in the judgment of similarity and difference as a function of different social reference points. In her contribution, **Serino** analyzes differences in the cognitive characteristics of reference frames that are actualized in judgments of similarity and difference involving the self. The starting points in the comparison process can be category-based or person-based cognitions. Her own previous research (Serino, 1988) has suggested that self/ingroup and self/outgroup comparisons may involve different reference points: the group may be the reference point in the first case and the self in the second. Such distinctions not only enrich the initial conjectures of Tversky but also question Turner's (1987) conception of an opposition between the personal and the social pole.

Mailloux, Massonnat, and Serino situate the analysis of asymmetries in similarity and difference judgments in the context of relationships between professional groups of differing status. In the same vein, they link these specific comparison studies to those intergroup studies that have dealt with asymmetric and hierarchical relationships. According to their groups' position in relationships of dominance, members should accentuate similarities or differences with other groups. Overall this effect of status (accentuation of similarities with higher status groups and of differences with lower status groups) seems more important than the effect of inverting the reference points in the comparison process.

Comparisons involving the relationships between autochthonous French and immigrants from Magrab in France were studied by **Vinsonneau**. The Gulf War crisis at the start of 1991 prevented this researcher from investigating the same comparisons in North African countries. That incident in itself is an illustration of the objective differences which characterize groups occupying different positions in a network of complex societal relationships. Her study confirms the variability of the comparison processes in groups of different status and culture. These processes are supposed to be linked to the minority position of immigrants from Magrab, but they can also be related to cultural differences in identification with membership groups.

Basically the three aforementioned contributions depart from Tversky's comparison model and show how it functions differently according to the positions that given reference points occupy in a network of intergroup relations. Two other contributions explicitly refer to Tajfel's (1981) categorization model. From this model, **Clémence** draws the assumption that between-category differentiation is inversely related to within-category differentiation and opposes it to Deschamps' (1984) covariation model, which implies that greater between-group differentiation can accompany an increase in within-group differentiation. Some results do indeed support the covariation model, but it should be mentioned that the self was explicitly involved in the procedure whereas in most of Tajfel's experiments this was not the case. Paradoxically Tajfel theorized on the importance of the categorization process for enhancing positive aspects of the self but he did not empirically study attitudes and behaviors toward the self in his intergroup experiments.

Oriol has also focused on the study of immigrants' identity, as Vinsonneau has done. But his theorizing is more directly related to Tajfel's model, and he draws implications from that model for Portuguese youngsters, who are sons or daughters of emigrants to France, but half of them living with their parents in France and the other half living with relatives or friends or in institutions in Portugal. For the former group, relationships with the French people are certainly different from those of the latter. The difference is reflected in attitude structures toward the Portuguese community. More specifically, individuals of the sample settled in France manifest combined loyalties toward the Portuguese and French communities, often integrating new attributes in their self-definition. However, this group effects comparisons with other Portuguese who remain in the home country as well as with the French.

Oriol judges such comparison strategies to be far more complex than the ones usually studied in experimental settings.

If one extrapolates Oriol's postulates, it is no longer sufficient to know an individual's category membership in order to deduct the direction and content of the comparison processes linked to that membership, or in order to know the attributes an individual ascribes to himself. **Leyens, Yzerbyt, and Bellour** approach the categorization problem from the other end: how can we safely decide on an individual's group membership when we are informed that he/she possesses some attributes linked to that membership? This question is related to the more general concern about conditions that lead people to make use of group or category membership in drawing conclusions about individuals (see Leyens, Yzerbyt, & Schadron, 1992). One important finding is that subjects are cautious in deciding that someone who is unknown to them belongs to their own group since ingroup overexclusion would serve the need to maintain a positive image of the ingroup, whose motive is a basic component of Tajfel's social categorization theory (see Tajfel, 1972, for a previous formulation of an overinclusion and overexclusion hypotheses).

Let me conclude this short presentation of the contributions to this section by adding that they were chosen by the editors for their relevance to the study of the self in a social cognitive perspective, not to illustrate a more general conception of theorizing in social psychology. The informed reader will acknowledge their relevance for the theme of the book.

In this introduction however my concern was more general, as I felt obliged, as it were, to highlight a common characteristic of the six contributions. The authors do not limit themselves to describing a sociopsychological process, but in some way or another they analyze social conditions that modify the functioning of such a process in important ways. In doing so they remind us that no description of a given sociopsychological process exhaustively enumerates all conditions necessary for its analysis. A more exhaustive understanding of a given process therefore requires linking the analysis of its functioning with the analysis of dynamics which are not described by the process.

According to McGuire (1986, pp. 99-100), a convergent style is what characterized research on attitude change during the fifties when teams of social psychologists studying processes of attitude change casted "[...] a wide theoretical net to ensnare as many relevant independent variables as possible, bringing a wide variety of explanatory notions convergently to bear on the phenomenon to be explained." In the sixties style of research programs changed and diverged: "The divergent hypothesis-generating strategy of taking a theory, rather than an observed phenomenon, as the point of departure and using this theory to account for a small amount of variance in each of many phenomena largely determines the divergent stylist's characteristic hypothesis-testing strategy, including use of simple designs with few independent variables which are carefully manipulated in elaborately contrived situations, while the dependent variable is often measured on a crude dichotomous scale."

The experimental paradigms of Tversky or Tajfel are typical divergent paradigms but the different ways the contributors to this section make use of them are convergent. Each contribution integrates different theoretical approaches and practices a more accumulative science which transforms juxtaposed heterogeneous explanations into pluralistic theoretical constructions.

References

Codol, J.-P. (1984). Quand Dupond ressemble à Dupont plus que Dupont à Dupond. *Psychologie Française, 29,* 284-290.

Codol, J.-P. (1987). Comparability and incomparability between oneself and others: Means of differentiation and comparison reference points. *Cahiers de Psychologie Cognitive/European Bulletin of Cognitive Psychology, 7,* 87-105.

Deschamps, J.-C. (1984). Identité sociale et différentiations catégorielles. *Cahiers de Psychologie Cognitive, 4,* 449-474.

Doise, W. (1986). *Levels of explanation in social psychology.* Cambridge: Cambridge University Press.

Doise, W., Deschamps J.-C. & Mugny, G. (1991). *Psychologie sociale expérimentale* (2nd ed.). Paris : Armand Colin.

Leyens, J.-P., Yzerbyt, V. Y., & Schadron, G. (1992). A social judgeability approach to stereotypes. In W. Stroebe & M. Hewstone (Eds.), *European Review of Social Psychology, 3,* 91-120.

McGuire, W. J. (1986). The vicissitudes of attitudes and similar representational constructs in twentieth century psychology. *European Journal of Social Psychology, 16,* 89-130.

Poitou, J.-P. (1974). *La dissonance cognitive.* Paris : Armand Colin.

Sampson, S. F. (1968). *Crisis in the cloisters: A sociological analysis.* Ph.D. thesis, Cornell University.

Serino, C. (1988). Stratégies et structure de la comparaison sociale : quelques aspects de l'asymétrie Soi/Autrui dans les relations entre groupes. *Cahiers de Psychologie Cognitive/European Bulletin of Cognitive Psychology, 8,* 627-648.

Sherif, M. (1935). A study of some social factors in perception. *Archives of Psychology,* No. 187.

Tajfel, H. (1972). La catégorisation sociale. In S. Moscovici (Ed.), *Introduction à la psychologie sociale* (Vol. 1, p. 272-302). Paris : Larousse.

Tajfel, H. (1981). *Human groups and social categories*. Cambridge: Cambridge University Press.

Turner, J. C., Hogg, M. A., Oakes, P. J., Reicher, S. D., & Wetherell, M. S. (1987). *Rediscovering the social group: A self-categorization theory*. Oxford: Basil Blackwell.

Tversky, A. (1977). Features of similarity. *Psychological Review, 84*, 327-352.

INFORMATION PROCESSING AND SELF-OTHERS COMPARISON

SOCIAL-COGNITIVE EXTENSIONS OF A NON-METRICAL APPROACH TO SIMILARITY

Carmencita Serino

University of Napoli, Italy

1. The Cognitive Analysis of Similarity Relationships

According to Tversky (1977), similarity and difference between two objects cannot always be translated into simple ratings of proximity/distance between points along a straight line; nor do comparisons usually made in everyday life appear to conform to such axioms as symmetry and transitivity. Comparison of two objects may, in fact, be a global process wherein a number of items are simultaneously taken into account. This is done by means of a "matching process", focusing on several (common and distinctive) features of the objects to be compared. In general, one of the two objects is more salient, more *prototypical* than the other. For this reason, a comparison may have a specific direction: thus, when we say that "A is similar to B", A and B take different roles (B is the *referent,* the comparison model, whilst A is the comparison *subject,* i.e., a term which is compared to that model and evaluated in reference to it). Attention may spontaneously focus on the comparison subject: its unique features carry a special weight (Houston, Sherman, & Baker, 1989) and thereby reduce similarity more than the distinctive features of the referent do (Tversky, 1977). In other words, the subject's condition is variable, whilst the model holds a more stable position in the comparison context. In each feature, we can distinguish two main components (*intensity* and *diagnostic value*): when comparing two objects, their relevant features are weighted according to the degree of salience of these components (Tversky, 1977). Tversky suggests that these two components can hardly be separated from each other, as they are complementary aspects of any matching process. They highlight the "dynamic interplay between similarity and classification" (Tversky, 1977, p. 344): similarity can determine the way in which objects are classified, but it also depends on that classification. These two faces of similarity are assumed to be both present and tightly intertwined in any comparison process.

Yet, when considering the similarity-classification interplay, two distinct ways of yielding similarity relationships might be pointed out. Look at the following instances:

(a) In everyday speech, some similarity relationships are spontaneously introduced, wherein the comparison meaning and its verbal form (i.e., its direction) are closely interdependent. Some expressions (such as, for instance, a metaphor: see Tversky, 1977) are aimed solely at showing an analogy, the conformity to a model. The focus is on the comparison subject, but the features taken into account are mainly the common ones, which allow the "subject" to be defined as a (better or worse) variant of the prototype. Differences in the salience of the two terms are mostly dependent on the different *intensities* of the features common to the variant and prototype: the distinctive features of the variant are just non-pertinent, interfering items, which shed light on its weakness, on its peripheral position. From the beginning, the objects under consideration are interdependent in this kind of relationship: the prototypical object is representative, and the variant is (more or less) conforming, in a shared frame of reference.

(b) In other cases, comparison looks like a task. Subjects are presented with external stimuli whose relation is yet to be determined. This condition, also existing in everyday life, frequently occurs in experimental research inspired by Tversky's model. In these cases, the comparison direction is manipulated, so that each object alternately takes on the roles of comparison subject and comparison referent. Due to the "focus on subject" effect, and to the different salience of the two terms, asymmetry phenomena can be observed. Perceived similarity may vary, in fact, according to the comparison direction, so that the variant's similarity to the prototype is judged to be greater than the prototype's similarity to the variant. It is worth noting that, in the latter condition, subjects are presented with an unusual relationship, wherein an anomalous variant (the more salient term) is compared to an unlikely model. This may be an additional explanation of the decrease in similarity. This explanation (which is consistent, however, with the "focus on subject" effect) emphasizes the close connection between similarity and classification. In those atypical comparisons where the prototype is judged in reference to the variant, respondents may become uncertain about the type of classification, or it may turn out to be an ambiguous and inadequate one. The pertinence of the relationship itself might be questioned in this case. Distinctive features are brought to the foreground, and the comparison quality may change. As we mentioned above, when common features are emphasized, comparison is likely to give rise to their (differential) intensity. By contrast, distinctive features can hardly be compared with each other in the same way. Distinctive features are conceptually independent of each other (Serino, 1988a, b). It is just their presence/absence that is likely to be taken into account: this gives rise to the categorical significance of the features, to their *diagnostic value* (which refers mainly to the kind of classification they introduce and into which they fit).

Focus on common vs. distinctive features has become an important item in cognitive research on similarity. It has already been argued that common and distinctive features carry a different weight in different conditions. As Gati and Tversky (1984) showed, this choice may depend, for instance, on the conceptual vs. perceptual nature of the stimuli to be compared. However, this distinction also elucidates a more general issue, pointed out by the present discussion: the comparison may be underlain by different aims, and there may be different ways of comparing two objects, depending on whether the search for similarity or the impact of differences is in the foreground. The importance of goals in cognitive processes such as impression formation has been emphasized in several studies (Trzebinski & Richards, 1986; Brewer, 1988). Yet, the consequences of processing information under different comparison conditions (such as the ones described above) have been barely investigated. One of these consequences might be, for instance, the different focus on *feature intensity* vs. *feature diagnostic value,* which we referred to above.

Some of the findings of cognitive research seem to support this idea. When focusing on common features, a considerably smaller number of relevant dimensions is in fact needed. As Prinz and Sheerer-Neumann (1974) demonstrated, the number of relevant dimensions affects the classification task. Dimensional discrimination is only possible when a limited number of dimensions are considered. When there are more than two or three, dimensional discrimination is replaced by a feature detection strategy. Feature intensity is then disregarded, while the discriminating features are taken into account only in terms of their presence: their classificatory significance is mostly emphasized in this case. Thus, the *search for similarity* condition and the *impact of differences* condition may lead to different modes of comparison. When the search for similarity is emphasized, the compared objects are assumed to belong to the same category (wherein they are likely to take on a more or less central position). From the beginning, a common category is involved, at least implicitly. In this case, then, the shared, categorical features (which are expressed in an "exemplar" manner by the prototypical term) are a sort of starting point for similarity judgment. Selective attention towards congruent information is likely to characterize this comparison process.

As noted above, however, the frame of reference is not always so clear. The unique features of each object are then emphasized, and special attention is paid to inconsistent information: respondents have only to decide whether a relationship between the two objects exists, whether they can fit into a common class, and, consequently, whether the similarity judgment makes sense.

Indeed, a crucial question involved in this discussion concerns the relationship between categorical (top-down) information and stimulus-related (bottom-up) information.

Fiske and Pavelchak (1986), for instance, pointed out two different modes of information processing, depending on whether or not the stimulus properties are congruent with an available category. In her analysis of person perception, Brewer (1988) ascribes these different routes to a "dual model", wherein the route chosen depends mainly on the perceiver's purposes and goals. According to her "the same social information can be processed in a top-down manner (resulting in category-based cognitions) or in a bottom-up fashion, that results in person-based representations" (Brewer, 1988, p. 4). Which route is taken may affect the way information is processed and integrated with prior knowledge.

Depending on the perceiver's goals, the same information can be processed in a *top-down* (depersonalized) manner or in a *bottom-up* (personalized) one. Thus, personalization refers to a different kind of cognitive structure in which the individual becomes the basis for organization of all relevant information (Brewer, 1988). This would occur whenever the stimulus is personally relevant and self-involving. In Brewer's view, then, self/other comparison and interpersonal similarity give rise to person-based ("bottom-up") perception.

2. Self/Other Asymmetry and Modes of Interpersonal Comparison

A great deal of research has centered on the analysis of cognitive processes involved in self/other comparison. Some of the studies highlight the asymmetrical structure of this comparison. Starting from Tversky's seminal research, several authors attempted to determine whether (and under what conditions) the self is a major reference point of interpersonal comparison (Codol, 1984; Holyoak & Gordon, 1983; Srull & Gaelick, 1983).[1] In a study, Holyoak and Gordon (1983) focused on social objects such as the self and a number of current stereotypes. According to them, the self acts as a habitual reference point only when the comparison involves social stereotypes about which little is known. Subjects rated similarity between themselves and 9 different stereotypes. Later, they were asked to list attributes describing each stereotype. The authors noticed that the number of listed attributes (i.e., the amount of available information) varied across different stereotypes, and they argued that stereotypes about which much is known are at least as good as reference points as the self. When considering this study, our impression is that even the self/others comparison can be performed in a depersonalized manner. Indeed, this occurs because subjects presented with a number of social stereotypes are led to favor categorical information. We think, however, that the depersonalized character of these comparisons may depend even more on the *function* assigned to the social categories in this experiment. As a matter of fact, the "social reference points" described by Holyoak and Gordon are more similar to abstract concepts than to the social entities which are involved when people perform meaningful comparisons in their everyday life. Nor do we know whether the attributes describing each stereotype were also features of a matching process involving the self: because of the high number of stimuli, sujects listing attributes may first have attempted to differentiate the 9 stereotypes from each other. As a result of the special stress on information quantity, the descriptive nature of the classification may be enhanced, while respondents' personal involvement may be markedly reduced.

However, in social reality, categories usually perform quite a different function. As Zavalloni (1983) argued, category membership may be a significant component of personal identity. She showed that, by introducing alternative stimuli such as "We" or "They", different representations of one's own group were elicited. Her findings may suggest that a bottom-up, personalized representation arises when the former stimulus ("We") is employed, by contrast, a top-down, depersonalized representation may be elicited by the latter stimulus ("They"). On the other hand, the "Me/We reversibility" put forward by this research also suggests that, in some cases, categorical and person-based information are tightly intertwined.

Codol's experiments on similarity and difference between oneself and another clearly highlight some aspects of this close interdependence between different kinds of information. In his studies on the "superior

---

[1] Some of the most recent European contributions in this field, deeply inspired by Codol's work, are gathered in a volume edited by Arcuri & Serino (1992).

conformity of self " behavior (Codol, 1975), an interesting phenomenon was observed. The subjects of those experiments, set in a highly normative situation, tended to present themselves as conforming better than the others to the shared norms. Actually, they based their self-distinctiveness on the claim for similarity, considered as a value. In this light, we can outline the social-cognitive side of prototypicality. This phenomenon in fact shows that there is a dynamic, genetic relationship linking personal to social identity: it is only by starting from some degree of conformity, deemed to be positive, that it becomes possible to develop the idea of personal distinctiveness. Indeed, subjects showing "superconforming behavior" make self/others comparisons in a frame of similarity: they are compared not only to other group members, but also to a general norm. In this case, comparison may be based on common characteristics, shared (to a different extent) by oneself and by others.

On the other hand, when a common category is not available, we are faced with more abstract interpersonal conditions. Codol (1987, 1988) showed a self-centered assimilation effect in this kind of comparison, wherein subjects are just individuals opposed to other individuals. It is no longer the search for similarity, but the impact of differences that seems to be stressed in this case.[2] Asymmetry, in this condition, might disclose the "derivative face" of similarity: this can be assessed only after an acceptable common classification has been found, the judgment depending on what classification is adopted.

The more salient term (which is likely to be the self, at least in this very general context) provides the basic outlines for classifying. Distinctive features of the self, then, carry a special importance under these conditions. Their simple presence/absence is the main focus, while dimensional discrimination turns out to be somehow irrelevant.

Research on intergroup relations also demonstrated that ingroup members are perceived as varying along specific dimensions more than the members of an outgroup do (Park & Rothbart, 1982): actually, it seems that "in-groupers" are compared in terms of different intensities of the same features, while "out-groupers" are not. Consistent with Brewer's (1988) arguments, this may lead to the conclusion that, in comparisons based on a fundamental, accepted similarity, greater attention is paid to congruent information. By contrast, when categorical membership is less salient, and individuals' distinctive traits are the main focus, attention towards inconsistent information is likely to be enhanced.

A study by the present author (Serino, 1988b, c) centered on the

---

[2] Notice that when subjects were confronted to their own "best friend" (i.e., when the special, warm quality of the self/other relationship was emphasized) the comparison direction changed: the other, rather than the self, acted as the reference point (Codol, 1987).

cognitive structure of self/others comparison in an intergroup context. Subjects belonging to a socially "dominant" group (Northern Italians) and to a socially "dominated" one (Southern Italians) performed self/others comparisons where the others were represented by either ingroup members or outgroup members; the comparison reference point (self or others) varied. Some particular asymmetry effects were observed, as well as a clear difference between northern and southern subjects. Comparisons performed by the Northerners were more asymmetrical, aiming at stressing the respondents' similarity to the dominant ingroup. The Northerners, however, also emphasized their self-distinctiveness significantly more than the Southerners did, showing that a complex process of intra-categorical assimilation and intra-categorical differentiation was likely to occur in comparisons with their own (highly evaluated) identity group (Serino, 1990; Serino, 1992). In any case, when asymmetry occurred, the self/ingroup comparison and the self/outgroup comparison tended to take different directions. Only in the self/outgroup condition, in fact, subjects appeared as conforming to the expected asymmetry effect, showing a slight tendency to choose the self as the reference point in similarity judgments. By contrast, in comparisons with their own group, the reference point was the group, rather than the self. Starting from Tversky's model, it is possible to represent these different self/others conditions in a manner which highlights their different structure (Serino, 1992). As a matter of fact, the self/ingroup condition is characterized by a wide range of common features, while, when the self/others difference is emphasized (as was the case in comparisons with the southern out-groupers), shared characteristics are much fewer in number and probably less salient. Thus, when the self/other similarity is activated, we may also be dealing with a specific kind of *particularization:* this would be based on dimensional discrimination about some crucial categorical caracteristics (shared to a different extent by oneself and by others). On the other hand, a *generalization* process seems to be required when the self and the other person are perceived as being quite different. In this case, in fact, "similarity" can only be assessed by shifting to a very general and inclusive category, wherein people may at least share the fact of being "individuals", endowed with their own personality. In this sense, personal traits, which are usually considered as the most specific and concrete identity expressions, may just underlie the interpersonal comparison in these extremely generalized conditions.

All things considered, social comparison seems to fit quite well into our previous distinction of two different kinds of similarity judgment. These two ways of comparing the self and others can be described by the following scheme:

Frame of self/other similarity	_Impact of self/other difference_
Focus on common features	Focus on distinctive features
Dimensional discrimination	Presence/absence
Different intensity	Different diagnostic value
Particularization	Generalization
Congruent information	Inconsistent information
Superior conformity of the self (Codol, 1975).	Self-centered asymmetry (Codol, 1988).

According to our distinction, categorical information could also take a markedly personalized character. In our opinion, the difference between personalized and depersonalized routes would be better underlined by referring to the different components of knowledge (Beauvois, 1990), that is by distinguishing between the descriptive and evaluative functions of cognition. Notice for instance that, consistent with Brewer's model, Peeters' analysis of relational information processing (Peeters, 1983; 1992) described two different ways of thinking which would give rise, respectively, to warm, subjectivistic, personalized views (self/others anchored thinking), and to cold, objectivistic, depersonalized ones (third-person anchored thinking). Unlike Brewer's general assumption, however, Peeters suggests that "at least in person perception subjects are biased towards the S-O program" (Peeters, 1992, p. 103).

In this view, Brewer's idea that "perception of social objects does not differ from non-social perception in either structure or process" (Brewer, 1988, p. 4) should be more deeply discussed. As we mentioned above, this author suggests that the differences in the perceiver's goals and purposes are the major discriminating aspect of social vs. non-social information processing. Goals and purposes, however, quite regularly take a different weight and a different meaning in the two domains. In general, classification of social reality is not aimed at yielding merely descriptive typologies: its primary function deals with evaluation. A dynamic interplay between categorical and person-based information is likely to take place under these conditions. For this reason, the assumption that "category-based processing of person information produces little difference between social and non-social cognition" (Brewer, 1988, p. 22) could be questioned. Particularization, which we referred to above, is just an exemple of this close connection between category-based and person-based processes. According to Brewer, particularization (Billig, 1985) simply illustrates the individuating level of classification. Of course, particularization still refers to a category-based process, even when it deals directly with just one individual (Brewer, 1988). Nonetheless,

Billig's analysis also highlights the specificity of social categories and of the way they are produced (Serino, 1990).[3]

In Billig's example, the category of "religious Christian" was split as a function of discrimination between black and white people. This distinction was aimed at introducing a sort of opposition between religiousness based on superstition (attached to black Christianity) and religiousness based on doctrinal considerations (granted to the white Christians). Thus, this exemple can illustrate the shifting from one wide category (superordinate level) to a less abstract and inclusive level of categorization. Nevertheless, we are also dealing, here, with a basic distinction between superstitious people and deeply religious ones, between a primitive lay religiousness and a real, mature one. Finally, this particularizing principle does not just specify two sub-categories, by means of a merely horizontal analysis of their distinctive features. It yields an evaluative discrimination which locates the new ingroup at the top of a quite general hierarchy: that opposing *true* religiousness to superstition. This new classification might be even wider than the one from which the whole process had originated ("Christianity"). Reference to a value system, which is a crucial component of social categorization, entails both particularization and generalization, as two interrelated aspects of categorizing. Some particular characteristics of social taxonomies, pointed out by Cantor and Mischel (1979), could be explained in this respect. As it is well known, Cantor and Mischel's analysis was aimed at highlighting some essential analogies between classification systems in social vs. non-social domains. Nonetheless, it also ended up underlining the specificity of social taxonomies (Capozza & Nanni, 1986; Serino, 1990).

These authors, for instance, found that differentiation between social categories is mainly based on incompatibility, i.e. on a bipolar opposition rather than on a typological approach. Thus, their observations seem to support the idea that taxonomies in the social domain have an essentially evaluative structure.[4] Emphasis on evaluative knowledge could also

---

[3] From this point of view, we believe that particularization is not opposite to categorization, but represents its most dynamic aspect (Serino, 1990; Turner, 1988).

[4] Of course, under some conditions, a descriptive orientation may be prevailing even in social knowledge. However, description is often imbued with evaluative judgments in these cases. Respondents quite spontaneously take a position and express their preferences, as shown in a study by Cantor, Mischel, and Hood (mentioned by Cantor & Mischel, 1979). When asked to describe the "typical" RP person, subjects answered this would be "male, rather overwhelming and consequently quite unpleasant". In the construction of social categories, the most typical traits seem to be those characterized by a clearly positive or negative value.

explain another important aspect of social taxonomies, highlighted by Cantor and Mischel as well. They noticed that at least in the person domain "it seems likely that what is the middle level and what is superordinate and subordinate is not immutable: [...] level may depend on the context, the purpose, and the frame of reference one adopts" (Cantor & Mischel, 1979, p. 16). Our analysis of particularization could explain why different levels of abstraction are interchangeable with each other in categorical differentiation processes which are mainly based on values (see also Serino, 1990).

3. Self/Other Categorization and the Personal-Social Continuum

As the above analysis of particularization suggests, a basic distinction between top-down and bottom-up routes should also be introduced as far as categorization itself is concerned (Doise, 1988). In this view, however, they would be complementary: the dynamic interplay between category-based and person-based information is an essential condition for the production of new categories, a process which is particularly rich and intense in social categorization (Serino, 1988a). Tajfel himself was aware of this aspect, although as Doise (1988) remarked, his analysis centered mainly on the deductive (top-down) face of categorization.

As we argued elsewhere (Serino, 1990), this might be due to Tajfel's view of similarity (an essentially "metrical" one). Indeed, Tajfel (Wilkes & Tajfel, 1966) managed to show that proximity (distance) along a physical dimension leads to a similarity (difference) judgment. Later, most of his research focused on conditions wherein a specific dimension was introduced, and the consequences of this *a priori*-induced categorization were observed (Tajfel, 1981). However, this procedure cannot explain how similarity judgments are obtained whenever a linear dimension is not initially provided as a yardstick. Under these conditions (which are also the most frequent ones in everyday life), comparison may be based on a feature matching process according to Tversky's suggestions. This means, however, that categories are conceived as fuzzy sets (Rosch, 1975), rather than as *all-or-nothing* structures. In this light, similarity and difference may both appear as concomitant judgments, rather than as mutually exclusive alternatives (Serino, 1988a, 1990).

The distinction between top-down and bottom-up processes could be related to the analysis of relationships between social and personal identity. Not surprisingly, this relationship was described by Tajfel in terms of a *personal-social continuum* within his Social Identity Theory (Tajfel & Turner, 1979). In a more recent analysis of the individual/group interplay, Turner (1987) reconsidered the assumptions of that theory, attempting to extend, and also modify, it with respect to certain important aspects. In his opinion, "all social comparison with the others depends upon the categorization of the others as part of a self-category at some level of abstraction" (Turner, 1987, p. 48). Actually, Turner (also overcoming the strictly motivational orientation underlying their previous assumptions) integrates his view with some important issues of the prototypicality theory (Rosch, 1975), and seems to meet Brewer's distinction of top-down and bottom-up processes.[5]

Yet, Turner also confirms the basic assumption that self/others comparisons take place along an ideal personal-social continuum. He claims there is a "functional antagonism between the salience of one level of self-categorization and other levels", assuming that "there tends to be an inverse relationship between the salience of the personal and of the social levels" (Turner, 1987, p. 49).

In our opinion, this way of representing the personal-social interplay is not always suitable (Serino, 1988b; 1990). We think it is not sufficient to postulate a "midpoint of this continuum, where self-perception is likely to be located much of the time " (Turner, 1987, p. 50). In Turner's view, the personal pole and the social one still appear essentially as inversely related alternatives and juxtaposed concepts. As we showed above, a number of self/others comparisons do not seem to be suitably represented in that way. Comparisons with the members of an ingroup and of an outgroup, for instance, may appear somewhat puzzling from the continuum point of view: in fact, either they are merely translated into the opposition between the two groups, or they are located at the same ("interpersonal") level of categorization, appearing as two, more or less equivalent forms of the same comparison between individuals. Nevertheless, there are other possible processes, which may be underlain by special forms of particularization and generalization like the ones we referred to above. These forms seem to show that categorical features may be at the basis of personal identity, and that, on the other hand, quite specific and "idiosyncratic" individual traits may be invoked in the most general and abstract comparison conditions.

---

[5] See for instance Brewer (1988, p. 23): "The level of abstraction at which new information is initially encoded is also expected to be different for category-based and person-based processing".

Concluding Remarks

In conclusion, we think that the unsolved "metrical bias" involved in the continuum idea deals with the difficulty of treating the self/other similarity and difference *simultaneously*. This makes it impossible to think of interpersonal and intergroup comparisons as co-occurrent, interdependent and covariant judgments (Serino, 1990). Yet, experimental social research provides an increasing amount of evidence which can hardly be reduced to the classical, rigid connection of intra-categorical assimilation and inter-categorical differentiation. Further cognitive strategies and different ways of articulating interindividual and intergroup comparisons with each other seem to be possible (Clémence & Doise, in press; Deschamps, 1982a; Monteil, 1992; Serino, 1988b, 1992). They may be satisfactorily explained only in the frame of a non-metrical view on similarity and of a more dynamic connection between different sources of social knowledge. From this point of view, Brewer's suggestions are very insightful, as they show that differences in the processing of social information do not just depend on content: the same knowledge can take on a personalized or a depersonalized quality, according to the perceiver's goals, personal relevance and self-involvement. In that light, the difference between personal and social identity could hardly be reduced to a distinction between personality traits and categorical characteristics. Moreover, we should also remember that, in general, perceivers are not isolated individuals, and that their goals and purposes are not the result of merely individual motivational orientations. Thus, we could usefully focus on the social conditions leading to top-down or bottom-up processes, to depersonalized or personalized information, and to the different ways of comparing (*search for similarity* or *impact of differences*) described above. Research on "dominant" and "dominated" social groups, for instance, may provide some fruitful insights in that direction. Even personal identity as it is defined by Turner can be conceived solely as a social issue: a *vacuum*, wherein individuals are just described in terms of their idiosyncratic traits and personal features, is in fact a social condition as well (Deschamps, 1982b; Lorenzi-Cioldi, 1988). We believe these questions are of central concern when dealing with a social-cognitive level of analysis, and attempting to develop a closer connection between mental and social processes.

References

Arcuri, L., & Serino, C. (1992). *Asymmetry phenomena in interpersonal comparison: Cognitive and social issues.* Napoli: Liguori.

Beauvois, J.-L. (1990). L'acceptabilité sociale et la connaissance évaluative. *Connexions*, No. 56, 7-16.

Billig, M. (1985). Prejudice, categorization and particularization: From a perceptual to a rhetorical approach. *European Journal of Social Psychology, 15*, 79-103.

Brewer, M. B. (1988). A dual process model of impression formation. In T. K. Srull & R. S. Wyer (Eds.), *Advances in social cognition* (Vol. 1, pp. 1-36). Hillsdale, NJ: Erlbaum.

Cantor, N., & Mischel, W. (1979). Prototypes in person perception. In L. Berkowitz (Ed.), *Advances in experimental social psychology* (Vol. 12, pp. 3-52). New York: Academic Press.

Capozza, D., & Nanni, R. (1986). Differentiation processes for social stimuli with different degrees of category representativeness. *European Journal of Social Psychology, 16*, 399-412.

Clémence, A. & Doise, W. (in press). Catégorisation sociale et comportement de discrimination dans une tache d'allocation d'argent à soi et aux membres de l'intra- et du hors-groupe. In J.-L. Beauvois, R. V. Joule & J.-M. Monteil (Eds.), *Perspectives cognitives et conduites sociales* (Vol. 4). Cousset : DelVal.

Codol, J.-P. (1975). On the so-called "superior conformity of the self" behavior: Twenty experimental investigations. *European Journal of Social Psychology, 5*, 457-501.

Codol J.-P. (1984). La perception de la similitude interpersonnelle: influence de l'appartenance catégorielle et du point de référence de la comparaison. *L'Année Psychologique, 84*, 43-56.

Codol, J.-P. (1987). Comparability and incomparability between oneself and others: Means of differentiation and comparison reference points. *Cahiers de Psychologie Cognitive/European Bulletin of Cognitive Psychology, 7*, 87-105.

Codol, J.-P. (1988). Studies on the self-centered assimilation processes. In J.-P. Caverni, J.-M. Fabre, & M. Gonzalez (Eds.), *Cognitive biases* (pp. 387-401). Amsterdam: North-Holland.

Deschamps, J.-C. (1982a). Différenciations entre soi et autrui et entre groupes. Recherches sur la "covariation" entre les différenciations inter-individuelles et inter-groupes. In J.-P. Codol & J.-P. Leyens (Eds.), *Cognitive analysis of social behavior* (pp. 247-266). The Hague: Nijhoff.

Deschamps, J.-C. (1982b). Social Identity and relations of power between groups. In H. Tajfel (Ed.), *Social identity and intergroup relations* (pp. 203-217). Cambridge: Cambridge University Press.

Doise, W. (1988). Individual and social identities in intergroup relations. *European Journal of Social Psychology, 18,* 99-111.

Fiske, S. T., & Pavelchak, M. A. (1986). Category-based versus piecemeal-based affective responses: Developments in schema-triggered affect. In R. M. Sorrentino & E. T. Higgins (Eds.), *Handbook of motivation and cognition: Foundations of social behavior* (Vol. 1, pp. 167-203). New York: Guilford Press.

Gati, I., & Tversky, A. (1984). Weighting common and distinctive features in perceptual and conceptual judgments. *Cognitive Psychology, 16,* 341-370.

Holyoak, K. J., & Gordon, P. C. (1983). Social reference points. *Journal of Personality and Social Psychology, 44,* 881-887.

Houston, D. A., Sherman, S. J., & Baker S. M. (1989). The influence of unique features and direction of comparison on preferences. *Journal of Experimental Social Psychology, 25,* 121-141.

Lorenzi-Cioldi, F. (1988). *Individus dominants et groupes dominés. Images masculines et féminines.* Grenoble : Presses Universitaires de Grenoble.

Monteil, J.-M. (1992). Intergroup differentiation and individuation: The effect of social deprivation. *Cahiers de Psychologie Cognitive/European Bulletin of Cognitive Psychology, 12,* 189-203.

Park B., & Rothbart, M. (1982). Perception of out-group homogeneity and levels of social categorization: Memory for subordinate attributes of in-group and out-group members. *Journal of Personality and Social Psychology , 42,* 1051-1068.

Peeters, G. (1983). Relational and informational patterns in social cognition. In W. Doise & S. Moscovici (Eds.), *Current issues in European social psychology.* Cambridge: Cambridge University Press.

Peeters, G. (1992). Asymmetry in self-other comparison, identity, and relational information processing: A study on the assessment of similarity and difference. In L. Arcuri & C. Serino (Eds.), *Asymmetry phenomena in interpersonal comparison: Cognitive and social issues* (pp. 101-114). Napoli: Liguori.

Prinz, W., & Scheerer-Neumann, G. (1974). Component processes in multiattribute stimulus classification. *Psychological Research, 37,* 25-50.

Rosch, E. (1975). Cognitive representations of semantic categories. *Journal of Experimental Psychology: General, 104,* 192-233.

Serino, C. (1988a). Biases egocentrici e fenomeni di asimmetria nei confronti Sè/Altro. *Giornale Italiano di Psicologia*, *15*, 213-233.

Serino, C. (1988b). Cognitive biases in assessing similarity and difference between oneself and others: an intergroup perspective. In *Proceedings of the CREPCO European Conference on Cognitive Biases* (pp. C1-C13). Aix-en-Provence: Université de Provence.

Serino, C. (1988c). Stratégies et structure de la comparaison sociale: Quelques aspects de l'asymétrie Soi/Autrui dans les relations entre groupes. *Cahiers de Psychologie Cognitive/European Bulletin of Cognitive Psychology*, *8*, 627-648.

Serino, C. (1990). La comparaison sociale et la structure des systèmes catégoriels: quelques réflexions sur la prototypicalité du soi. *Les Cahiers Internationaux de Psychologie Sociale*, *2* (6), 73-96.

Serino, C. (1992). From the asymmetry phenomena to the prototypicality of self: Studies on the structure of social categories. In L. Arcuri & C. Serino (Eds.), *Asymmetry Phenomena in interpersonal comparison: Cognitive and social issues* (pp. 47-60). Napoli: Liguori.

Srull, T., & Gaelick, L. (1983). General principles and individual differences in the self as a habitual reference point: An examination of self-other judgments of similarity. *Social Cognition*, *2*, 108-121.

Tajfel, H. (1981). *Human groups and social categories*. Cambridge: Cambridge University Press.

Tajfel, H., & Turner, J. C. (1979). An integrative theory of intergroup conflict. In W. G. Austin & S. Worchel (Eds.), *The social psychology of intergroup relations* (pp. 33-47). Monterey: Brooks/Cole.

Trzebinski, J., & Richards, K. (1986). The role of goal categories in person impression. *Journal of Experimental Social Psychology*, *22*, 216-227.

Turner, J. C. (1988). Comments on Doise's individual and social identities in intergroup relations. *European Journal of Social Psychology*, *18*, 113-116.

Turner, J. C., Hogg, M. A., Oakes, P. J., Reicher, S. D., & Wetherell, M. S. (1987). *Rediscovering the social group: A self-categorization theory*. Oxford: Basil Blackwell.

Tversky, A. (1977). Features of similarity. *Psychological Review*, *84*, 327-352.

Wilkes, A. & Tajfel, H. (1966). Types de classification et importance du contraste relatif. *Bulletin du C.E.R.P.*, *15*, 77-81.

Zavalloni, M. (1983). Ego-ecology: The study of the interaction between social and personal identities. In A. Jacobson-Widdings (Ed.), *Identity: personal and socio-cultural*. Stockholm: Almqvist & Wicksell International.

SOCIAL COMPARISON
AND CATEGORICAL DIFFERENTIATION

THE EFFECTS OF GROUP STATUS
AND REFERENCE POINT ON COGNITIVE ACTIVITY

Françoise Mailloux and Jean Massonnat
University of Provence, Aix-en-Provence, France

Carmencita Serino
University of Napoli, Italy

Within established and stable groups, intergroup and interpersonal relations, along with the affirmation of values, the pursuit of goals, and the accomplishment of actions, contribute to the construction and renewal, by the social agents, of a group or collective identity (Doise, 1988). In the study of intergroup relations, our focus here, two major processes are stressed: social comparison and categorical differentiation (Brown, 1988; Tajfel, 1982). Social comparison involves the estimation of similarities and differences between individuals, between groups, and within a group. Categorical differentiation concerns the dynamics of interacting group relations, whether occasional or regular, cooperative or competitive, sporadic or throughout their history. Two factors which affect social comparison are differences in status attributed initially or in the course of goal pursuit, and the nature of the relations between the groups (independence, agonism or antagonism, etc.) (Worchel & Austin, 1986).

The comparison activity contributes in an ongoing manner to specifying the identity of individuals and groups. But how does the system of relations maintained among established groups influence the cognitive activity of most of their members? In the present article, the term sociocognitive processes refers to those processes carried out by separate individuals to process information about the activity of the group. These processes are strongly marked by the social position of the groups and the dynamics of their past social relations. The objective of this study goes beyond simply proving the existence of a link between an individual's cognitive activity and his/her long-lasting membership in a professional group at some point in time. It also attempts to describe the effects of categorical differentiation on the way subjects process information in an intergroup comparison, and in particular, whether a change in comparison reference point influences the comparison.

1. Category Membership, Categorical Differentiation and Intergroup Relations

Rabbie and Horowitz (1969) showed that simply belonging to one, rather than the other, of two groups with a common situation is sufficient to create discrimination in person or group perception. Such discrimination even affects behavior, as demonstrated, for instance, in experiments where the amount of competition in a game or work environment is varied (Wilson, Chan, & Kayatani, 1965). The extent of such discrimination also depends on whether a task is performed in the presence of a friendly group or a hostile group: when two parallel subgroups with an equivalent sociometric status perform the same task, the discrimination effect is stronger when the hostile group is present. In another perspective, Sachdev and Bourhis (1991), working from the Tajfel and Turner paradigm, studied the effect of positional variables (status, power) on intergroup behavior and perception. They showed that these variables, taken both separately and jointly, affected the number of points given to the creative work done by individuals in one's own group or another. Positional variables were also found to affect subjects' perception of the situation. High-status groups, and groups with a great deal of power over their own actions, were more discriminating and less egalitarian in their scoring across groups. Minority, low-status, no-power groups, on the other hand, discriminated less against others and had more egalitarian attitudes. The structuring effect of this interaction system has been clearly demonstrated. But the fact that this effect also depends on the relationship between the long-term goals and the short-term activities of the groups involved (Sherif & Sherif, 1979) has often been neglected. These activities exert their control by means of the representations they induce in each group (Doise, 1984). As part of the discimination process, a perceived or ascribed difference which extends over a period of time becomes the basis for categorical or group differentiation according to status. Consequently, it helps each group incorporate, or not, that specificity into its identity (Sainsaulieu, 1985). The type of interaction that is established between groups can thus create a comparison or categorization style. What is known about this phenomenon in the socio-professional world?

Tajfel (1972, p. 299) contended that "the distinct meaning attributed by social identity in the social categorization framework has an infinitely greater effect in real social situations". To validate their experimental studies, Sachdev and Bourhis (1991) are now planning to extend their work to majority and minority groups of different cultures with past histories involving confrontations and collaborations. For the present study, this perspective guided our choice of three professional groups, all from the same field: social work. The normal socio-professional life of each of the groups is such that, in addition to their common educational background, they acquire shared experiences and objectives which regularly promote intragroup solidarity, and occasionally, intergroup solidarity. The groups under study have alternated between cooperative and competitive action, depending on the field work done and the point in time. But, as Beauvois and Deschamps (1990) remind us, intergroup differentiation can only exist if the groups share the same set of values and symbols. As common ground, our professional groups have necessarily all been led to reflect upon the field of social work and to cooperate with each other in both their day-to-day functions and in projects of a broader scope. But their past experience differentiates them by the fact that legislation has attributed specific roles to each group. The permanence of this situation has transformed these differences into status levels. Group members estimating the degree of intergroup proximity must evaluate the other groups and situate themselves with respect to those groups. In doing so, the group that will be considered the "closest" will no doubt be the most similar one (perhaps even the one to be imitated), but above all, it will be the group which grants one's own group the most recognition. The group considered the "farthest away" will be the one perceived as different, or even indifferent. Another factor affecting this estimation is the amount of recognition attributed to each group by the entire set of groups, based on their work experience and representations of each other. The question that arises, then, is whether or not the cognitive comparison activity is determined by the status of each group in the professional field, and to what extent that status plays a part.

2. Intergroup Relations and Sociocognitive Processes

Categorical differentiation does not only structure the interaction among social agents. It also plays a part in "the processes of social transformation and elaboration of reality" (Beauvois & Deschamps, 1990, *our translation*). This means that the cognitive activity involved in the simple estimation of similarity or difference can be explained from two standpoints. The first is the cognitive approach to the objects. This approach examines the effects of the asymmetric and probabilistic structure of the categorical comparison and inclusion processes (Rosch, 1975; Rosch & Lloyd, 1978; Tversky & Gati, 1978). Here, the emphasis is placed on the role of the primary referent, played by certain salient category members. The second is the study of the impact of intergroup relations (Doise, 1976; Deschamps, 1982; Messick & Mackie, 1989; Sachdev & Bourhis, 1991). In this approach, the emphasis is placed on the valorizing aspect of group status, and on the evaluative activity of group members.

These contentions support the assumption that the cognitive organization of social reality into classes or schemas for analysis is the result of sociocognitive processes which depend on the social interaction of social actors (Beauvois, 1984). Basic operations or thought categories are required for analyzing objects, but since social workers are members of a group, they must coordinate those operations and categories with each other in order to solve group problems and maintain or modify the group (Le Poultier, 1990). Here, the subject is a social agent who habitually processes cases not so much according to the description of the case produced by an outside party, but rather according to the value granted to the social actions to be taken (Echebarria Echabe, 1990). Moreover, when one of the terms being compared is the group making the comparison, the intergroup comparison leads the members of that group to attempt to establish a favorable group identity by maintaining or changing the group's status and characteristics. This means that the position of the cognitive operator in the intergroup network has a greater effect on cognitive structures than the actual information available on the case. One question remains unanswered: Is intergroup comparison sensitive to changes in the way the problem is presented?

It is known that the point of reference used by a subject to make an interindividual comparison introduces an estimation bias (Codol, 1984, 1987). In this case, it looks as if the meaning of the question posed changes according to whether or not the subject serves as the reference point. But Serino (1988a, 1988b) showed that such asymmetry phenomena in self/others comparison takes on a particular form when hierarchical social categories are being compared. This suggests the potential value of relating these phenomena to those observed in comparisons between real groups.

Furthermore, depending on the social context in which the comparison takes place, the meanings attributed to the notions of similarity and difference are not univocal. In the light of the overall results obtained by Codol, Serino (1988c, 1990) raised the question of whether the refinement of the concepts "similarity" and "difference" depends on the context and reference point of the comparison. She believes that similarity encompasses "representativity" (being a representative member of a group, i.e. just like the other members) and "conformity" (adhering to group norms). Difference is thought to refer to two notions, "innovation" (a desirable characteristic) and "marginality" (a rejected or barely tolerated form of deviance). Serino found that in interpersonal comparison, there is a tendency on the part of individuals to affirm both their own representativity (others resemble me) and their own specificity (I am different from others). These meanings, and others, are constructed through the ongoing efforts of each group to attain optimal social visibility (Lemaine, Kasterstein, & Personnaz, 1978; Tajfel, 1978). Our idea is to use these notions to study the comparison of professional groups, while varying the comparison reference point. The question to determine, in the currently evolving field of social work in France, is which characteristic is more highly valued, conformity or originality.

3. Method

3.1 Subjects

Subjects were selected from three categories of social work (n = 29 per group), each category with a different administrative status: so-called "social assistants" (social workers per se: SA), "counselors" (advisors in social, home, and family economics: CO), and "educators" (instructors and activity leaders working directly in the field: ED). All three groups work in the same geographical area and continuously deal with the same cases or files, either in cooperation or competition with the other groups. Certain functions are handled by all three groups. The three professions can be considered functionally interdependent in that they provide aid to populations having difficulty, some being marginal groups, in an attempt to ensure their reinsertion into the society at an acceptable social position. The three professions differ, however, in composition (sex and socioeconomic background of its members), date of creation of the profession, and type of schooling required. Social assistants have existed for nearly a century and have always received three years of post-secondary education in social work. The profession of educator was created in France in 1940 and now requires three years of vocational training after high school; educators form the only predominantly male group, and are the only ones trained on-the-job. The counseling profession began in 1973. Counselors must obtain a two-year "superior technician's" degree and then go on to one year of technical training in counseling (for a total of 3 years of post-secondary education). A fourth group, called family workers, was proposed as a possible choice. This group's responses were not included in the analysis due to the small number of subjects.

3.2 Materials and Procedure

The subjects filled out a questionnaire at their work place. The three main aspects treated on the questionnaire were intergroup distance, point of reference, and group status.

3.2.1 Estimation of Intergroup Distance.

On the basis of their personal conception of social work, subjects were asked to indicate, among the three groups proposed (excluding their own), which one they felt was the "closest" (C) to their own group, and which one was the "farthest" (F). The social distance measure was the inverse of the proximity of the subject's own group (from 1 = not very close to 7 = very close) to groups C and F. Subjects were asked to justify their answers in writing so that their comprehension of the concept could be verified.

3.2.2 Intergroup Comparison as a Function of Reference Point.

Each person compared his/her own group with the two groups designated as C and F. Four comparison criteria were used, two as dimensions of similarity (representativity and conformity) and two as dimensions of difference (innovativeness and marginality). The subject was not informed in any way of this two-way partition. Two versions of the questionnaire were generated, depending on the comparison reference point. Subjects were asked to compare their own group with the close group along the similarity dimensions, and with the far group along the difference dimensions. The first version of the instructions for the representativity dimension was: "Now you are going to compare your category with the category closest to yours [...]. Answer the following question by marking an 'x' on the response scale: How representative of social work in general is my category as compared to the closest category?" The other version was: "How representative [...] is the closest category as compared to my category?". The response scale ranged from 1 (my group is less representative than the close group) to 6 (my group is more representative...). Ratings 3 and 4 indicated group similarity.

3.2.3 Ranking the Groups by Status.

The criterion chosen for this assessment, which was done last, was how well the professional group satisfies the demands of its clients. It was based on the daily evaluation of the actions of each group. The subjects were asked to classify the three groups under study on a rating scale ranging from 1 (lowest client satisfaction) to 4 (highest client satisfaction). The mean rating obtained for each group, all 87 subjects pooled, was used to determine an *a posteriori* status level on the basis of social recognition. The mean rank assigned to each group could range from 4 (high status) to 1 (low status).

4. Hypotheses

It was hypothesized that a subject's membership in a group and the status of that group affect the subject's cognitive comparison behavior.

Hypothesis 1: The ideas put forward by Deschamps (1979, 1982, 1984) and Deschamps and Personnaz (1979) concerning relations of dominance between a dominant group and a dominated group can account in part for the mechanisms underlying their comparison. On this basis, it can be hypothesized for our experiment that the status of the designating group will affect which groups are designated as C and F. The members of the high status group (social assistants) should choose a group with an intermediate status as the close group, and a group with a low status as the far group. The members of the low status group (educators) should choose a high status group as the close group and an intermediate group as the far group.

Hypothesis 2: The members of the high status group should consider themselves to be globally less similar to the close group, and more different from the far group. For the members of the low status group, the opposite should be true. The remaining question is whether all dimensions of similarity and difference give rise to this same phenomenon.

Hypothesis 3: The change in comparison reference point should produce the same effects as those observed in prior research on interindividual and categorical comparisons, i.e. reference to the other group should increase the search for specificity.

5. Results

The subjects' justifications of their choice of groups C and F were classified by thematic content. Due to the low volume of this qualitative data, they will be analyzed in the discussion. The quantitative data were processed by analysis of variance on the three groups, which were balanced with respect to the controlled factors ($N - 22 \times 3 - 66$). The number of subjects per group was reduced from 29 to 22 in order to include an equal number of questionnaires for each point of reference. The initial number of subjects was only used to classify the groups by status ($N = 29 \times 3 = 87$).

5.1 Attribution of a Status Level to each Group

The ranks assigned by each group to itself and to the other groups were biased by intragroup favoritism and sociocentrism (Table 1). All three groups stated that they satisfied their clients' needs better than the others. This effect is due either to the need to valorize one's own work, and oneself in general, and/or to the subjects' exclusive reference to the specific actions of their own group. Note however that the group with the longest history (the social assistants) was the occasion of the most homogeneous estimations (SD = .39 to .88), whereas the attitudes of the youngest group (the counselors) were less stable (SD = .62 to 1.17). The estimations of all subjects pooled defined the following group hierarchy, in decreasing order of status: social assistants, counselors, educators. The only status difference which was significant separated the first group from the other two, but the order (hereafter denoted SA+, CO=, ED−) will be retained in the analysis of the status effect.

Table 1

Mean Rank and Standard Deviation for the Status Assigned by Each Group to the Other Groups

	Judging Group							
	SA n=29		CO n=29		ED n=29		All Groups N=87	
Judged Gr.	M	SD	M	SD	M	SD	M	SD
SA	3.71	0.39	3.4	0.88	3.4	0.82	3.51	0.78
CO	2.57	1.17	3.56	0.62	2.71	1.08	2.89	1.05
ED	2.74	0.75	2.42	1.02	2.88	1.09	2.70	1.00

Note. SA: Social Assistants; CO: Counselors; ED: Educators.

5.2 Effects of Status on the Choice of Groups C and F (H1)

Relating each group's status to its choice of groups C and F gave us the following:

(a) For the close group, intermediate and low status groups were designated in equal proportions by the members of the high status group, whereas members of the other two groups overwhelmingly chose the high status group (χ^2 = 64.71; p < .001);

(b) for the far group, this difference disappeared: all subjects, regardless of their group's status, chose a low status group.

These results are only consistent with predictions for the low status group. The intermediate group (CO=) responded like the low status group:

Do the counselors perceive themselves as minority group members? The working traditions and relations between SA+ and ED– took precedence here over group status, which is inconsistent with our predictions.

5.3 Sociocognitive Processes Involved in the Comparison

An analysis of variance was computed, this time for the 6 groups of 11 subjects obtained by crossing the reference point (P) and professional group (G) variables. Subjects estimated their own group's similarity or difference (E) along two dimensions (D) in each case. The analysis design was S11<P2*G3>*E2<D2>. The dependent variables ranged from 1 to 6: "my category is less ... than ..." (1 to 3); "my category is as much ... as ..." (3 to 4); "my category is more ... than ..." (4 to 6).
The following results were obtained.

5.3.1 Effect of Categorical Differentiation (Status) on the Subject's Estimates of Similarity and Difference (H2)

The cognitive activity involved in the comparison varied with group status. In this perspective, the G×E interaction is interesting ($F(2,60) = 12.60$; $p < .0005$). It does coincide with our predictions, but the corresponding graphs (Fig. 1) show, unexpectedly, that the curves are located in the middle or upper part of the response scale. This phenomenon leads us to propose the following interpretation, which is a little different from our predictions:

(a) In the close-group/similarity comparison, subjects in the high status group (SA+) felt they were similar to the close group. Subjects in the other groups (CO=, ED–), however, marked their specificity by stating they were more representative and conforming than their close groups;

(b) in the far-group/difference comparison, the opposite was true. The SA+ stated they were different from the far group, whereas in the other groups subjects said they were similar to the far group.

Thus, the SA+ accepted their similarity to the close group and asserted their difference from the far group, hence assuming their high status role. The other two groups acted accordingly, claiming they were barely more representative but more conforming than the close groups and similar to the far groups for distinctiveness. These attitudes correspond to the strive for better status. Cognitively speaking, this is the behavior of a minority group.

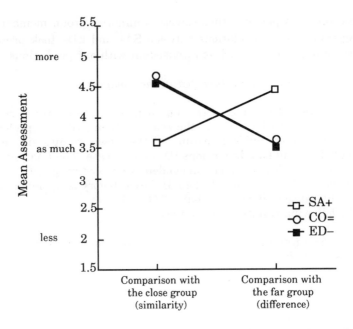

Figure 1. Comparisons with the close group and the far group, by professional group (*N*= 66).

Group status also influenced the estimates made for each of the dimensions of similarity and difference taken separately by its members (see Fig. 2). In the above analysis of variance, E2<D2> was replaced by D4 (each subject answered four questions). This yielded a G×D interaction ($F(6,80) = 5.3$; $p < .005$). The high status group subjects (SA+) said they were similar to the close group in both representativity and conformity, and that they were as innovative but strongly more marginal than the far group. The other two groups' comparisons depended on the dimension being considered. Subjects in the intermediate group (CO=) deemed themselves to be just as representative but more conforming than the close group, and as innovative and marginal as the far group. The low status subjects (ED−) claimed to be more representative and slightly more conformist than the close group, but slightly less innovative and more marginal than the far group. The perception of group difference by subjects in the CO= group (the youngest profession, striving to make its place in the field of social work) seems to be out of touch with reality. This may stem from the fact that these individuals judged themselves in reference to newer rules in the field of social work. The ED− group subjects, which belong to an older profession, perceived themselves as well within the norms of social work. The predominant overall attitude towards the far group was that it is not marginal, while the norm in all three professions was to consider oneself to be more marginal than in actuality.

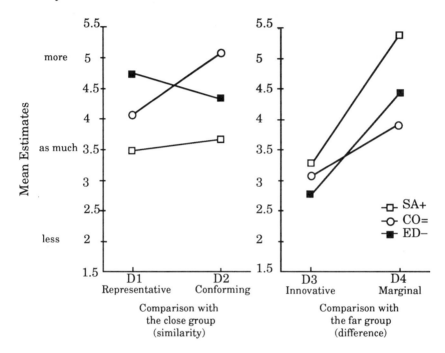

Figure 2 . Comparisons with the close group and the far group, by group and comparison dimension (the differences between SA+ and ED– for the dimension "representative" and between SA+ and CO= for the dimensions "conforming" and "marginal" are significant at $p < .01$).

As a whole, these results indicate that, among individuals in the social work professions, the two similarity characteristics belong to the same universe of concepts and values. In contrast, innovation and marginality are two highly distinct dimensions of difference. Our initial idea was that uniqueness may be close to marginality, but this assumption did not take into account the fact that social work creates a subculture that grants marginality a stronger, more valued meaning than just "being different".

5.3.2 Effect of Comparison Reference Point (H3). In the above analysis of variance, the factor P was not significant, nor was the P×E interaction ($F(1,60) = 2.0$, *ns*). This weakens our hypothesis. The change in reference point only produced a slight difference in the estimations of intergroup similarity and difference. With one's own group as the reference point (when the question was "Category X is like mine"), the close group is slightly more representative and conforming than one's own group. For the difference comparison along the innovation dimension, the tendency was reversed: subjects deemed their own group to be less innovative. For marginality, however, they felt they were more so than the far group.

6. Discussion

Long-lasting membership in a professional group, and the accompanying intergroup differentiation, build the foundation for group identity and for the cognitive structures used by group members to represent their socio-professional life. All cognitive comparisons are linked to the respective statuses of the group making the comparison and the group being compared. In other words, the amount of recognition granted to a group, in conjunction with the recognition it grants other groups, determines to a large extent the degree of intergroup similarity and difference perceived. Categorical differentiation in natural groups amplifies the outcome of this comparison process, which can only be understood by reintroducing into current cognitive theories the notion of reference to conventions and traditions that are established in the course of a group's history.

Note that our experimental set-up allowed the subjects to express fine nuances in status, which they indeed did. But the real actions of these groups indicate in fact that their attitudes towards group status is based on a dichotomy. This simplified representation limits their cognitive flexibility in the way the socio-professional world is construed.

The idea that the physical distance between individuals gives rise to the estimation of a psychosocial distance, measured on a different scale, is well illustrated by Codol's work (1985). But when the problem is posed directly in terms of psychosocial distance, it becomes necessary to better define the notion, namely, by determining its associated meanings. Some answers to this question might be found in the written justifications our subjects gave in this experiment to explain their choice of the close and far groups. There was a varying number of arguments across subjects and themes, so the percentages given here are non-cumulative. Intergroup proximity was associated with ideas of similarity and complementarity.

The "closeness" described by 45.3% of the subjects involved common conceptions, objectives, and evaluation criteria. Also mentioned were joint meetings and encounters in the field (24.2%), and similar backgrounds (12.1%). "Farness" was associated with difference, usually in connection with a lack of commonality. The differences noted by the subjects pertained to criteria for taking social action, modes of operation, etc. The discrepancies (differences qualified as lacking in the other groups) dealt with work methods (45%), team meetings (30%), overall view of social work (13.3%), and direct contacts in the field (10%). These results confirm our initial assumption that the close group would be a similar group and the far group, a different group. But behind this surface symmetry, there is dissymmetry in content. Proximity was associated with similarity in conceptions, values, and objectives, whereas remoteness was tied to a difference in working modes. Hence, similarity pertains to ideas, difference to actions. These results suggest that judgment biases may reflect a basic asymmetry in the meanings subjects attribute to the opposing concepts they are forced to assess. The analysis of the subjects' justifications could also by applied to the study of similarity and difference in the social context, for it is true that the connotations of words depend on the history of the groups. This, in conjunction with the exploration of the values linked to required or optional criteria, could be used in Serino's perspective (1990) to reexamine the interrelationships between intragroup and intergroup phenomena.

References

Beauvois, J.-L. (1984). Sujet de la connaissance et sujet de l'action : pour un néocognitivisme en psychologie sociale. *Cahiers de Psychologie Cognitive, 4,* 385-400.

Beauvois, J.-L. & Deschamps J.-C. (1990). Vers la cognition sociale. In R. Ghiglione, C. Bonnet & J. F. Richard (Eds.), *Traité de psychologie cognitive: Vol. 3, Cognition, représentation, communication* (p. 3 110). Paris : Dunod.

Brown, R. J. (1988). *Group processes: Dynamics within and between groups.* Oxford: Basil Blackwell.

Codol, J.-P. (1975). On the so-called "superior conformity of the self " behavior: Twenty experimental investigations. *European Journal of Social Psychology, 5,* 457-501.

Codol, J.-P. (1984). La perception de la similitude interpersonnelle : influence de l'appartenance catégorielle et du point de référence de la comparaison. *L'Année Psychologique, 84 ,* 43-56.

Codol, J.-P. (1985). L'estimation des distances physiques entre personnes : suis-je aussi loin de vous que vous l'êtes de moi? *L'Année Psychologique, 85,* 517-534.

Codol, J.-P. (1987). Comparability and incomparability between oneself and others: Means of differentiation and comparison reference points. *Cahiers de Psychologie Cognitive/European Bulletin of Cognitive Psychology, 7,* 87-105.

Deschamps, J.-C. (1979). Différenciation catégorielle et différenciation de soi par rapport à autrui. *Recherches en Psychologie Sociale, 3,* 29-38.

Deschamps, J.-C. (1982). Social identity and relations of power between groups. In H. Tajfel (Ed.), *Social identity and intergroup relations* (pp. 203-217). Cambridge: Cambridge University Press.

Deschamps, J.-C. (1984). Identité sociale et différenciations catégorielles. *Cahiers de Psychologie Cognitive, 4,* 449-479.

Deschamps, J.-C. & Personnaz, B. (1979). Etude entre groupes "dominants" et "dominés" : importance de la présence du hors groupe dans les discriminations évaluatives et comportementales. *Information sur les Sciences Sociales, 18 ,* 269-305.

Doise, W. (1972). Relations et représentations intergroupes.In S. Moscovici (Ed.), *Introduction à la psychologie sociale* (Vol. 2, p. 194-213). Paris : Larousse.

Doise, W. (1976). *L'articulation psychosociologique et les relations entre groupes.* Bruxelles : De Boeck.

Doise, W. (1984). Les relations entre groupes. In S. Moscovici (Ed.), *Psychologie sociale* (p. 253-274). Paris : Presses Universitaires de France.

Doise, W. (1988). Individual and social identities in intergroup relations. *European Journal of Social Psychology, 18,* 99-111.

Echebarria Echabe, A. (1990). The minimal group paradigm: Status and values. *Revue Internationale de Psychologie Sociale, 3,* 559-574.

Harvey, O. J. (1956). An experimental investigation of negative and positive relations between small groups through judgmental indices. *Sociometry, 19,* 201-209.

Lemaine, G., Kasterstein, J., & Personnaz, B. (1978). Social differentiation. In H. Tajfel (Ed.), *Differentiation between social groups* (pp. 182-190). London: Academic Press.

Le Poultier, F. (1990). *Recherches évaluatives dans le travail social.* Grenoble: Presses Universitaires de Grenoble.

Messick, D. M., & Mackie, D. M. (1989). Intergroup relations. *Annual Review of Psychology, 40,* 45-81.

Rabbie, J. M., & Horwitz, M. (1969). The arousal of ingroup-outgroup bias by a chance win or loss. *Journal of Personality and Social Psychology, 13,* 269-277.

Rosch, E. (1975). Cognitive representations of semantic categories. *Journal of Experimental Psychology: General, 104,* 192-233.

Rosch, E., & Lloyd, B. B. (Eds.) (1978). *Cognition and categorization.* Hillsdale, NJ: Erlbaum.

Sachdev, I., & Bourhis, R. Y. (1991). Power and status differentials in minority and majority group relations. *European Journal of Social Psychology, 21,* 1-24.

Sainsaulieu, R. (1985). *L'identité au travail.* Paris : Presses de la Fondation Nationale des Sciences Politiques.

Serino, C. (1988a, March). *Asymétrie objective et asymétrie subjective: stratégies et structure de la comparaison soi-autrui dans un contexte intergroupes.* Paper presented at the Colloque européen : Construction et fonctionnement de l'identité, Aix-en-Provence, France.

Serino, C. (1988b). Cognitive biases in assessing similarity and difference between oneself and others: an intergroup perspective. In *Proceedings of the CREPCO European Conference on Cognitive biases* (pp. C1-C13). Aix-en-Provence: Université de Provence.

Serino, C. (1988c). Stratégies et structure de la comparaison sociale : quelques aspects de l'asymétrie Soi/Autrui dans les relations entre groupes. *Cahiers de Psychologie Cognitive / European Bulletin of Cognitive Psychology,* 8, 627-648.

Serino, C. (1992). From the asymmetry phenomena to the prototypicality of self: Studies on the structure of social categories. In L. Arcuri, & C. Serino (Eds.), *Asymmetry phenomena in interpersonal comparison: Cognitive and social issues* (pp. 47-60). Napoli: Liguori.

Sherif, M., & Sherif, C. (1979). Les relations intra et intergroupes : analyse expérimentale. In W. Doise (Ed.), *Expériences entre groupes.* Paris : Mouton.

Tajfel, H. (1972). La catégorisation sociale. In S. Moscovici (Ed.), *Introduction à la psychologie sociale* (Vol. 1, p. 272-302). Paris : Larousse.

Tajfel, H. (Ed.) (1978). *Differentiation between social groups: Studies in the social psychology of intergroup relations.* London: Academic Press.

Tajfel, H. (1982). Social psychology of intergroup relations. *Annual Review of Psychology, 33,* 1-39.

Tversky A., & Gati, I. (1978). Studies of similarity. In E. Rosch & B. B. Lloyd (Eds.), *Cognition and categorization.* Hillsdale, NJ: Erlbaum.

Wilson, W., Chun, N. S., & Kayatani, M. (1965). Projection, attraction and strategy choices in intergroup competition. *Journal of Personality and Social Psychology, 2* , 432-435.

Worchel, S., & Austin, W. G. (Eds.) (1986). *Psychology of intergroup relations* (2nd ed.).Chicago: Nelson-Hall.

SELF-PROTOTYPICALITY, INTERGROUP RELATIONS, AND SOCIOCULTURAL VARIATIONS

Geneviève Vinsonneau[1]
René Descartes University, Paris, France

In an attempt to understand the phenomena at play in the quest for social similarity and differentiation, Codol (1979, 1984, 1986) gathered empirical data showing that while individuals readily consider that others resemble them, they do not feel they resemble others to as great an extent. They simultaneously consider themselves to differ more from others than others do from them.

Thus, the reference point individuals use to make interpersonal comparisons largely determines how they estimate similarity and difference.

Relating these observations to Tajfel's (Tajfel et al., 1971; Turner, 1975) categorization model, Codol concluded that when the comparison reference point is the self, individuals give higher estimates for self/others similarity than when the reference point is another person, because of their sense of categorical membership: individuals readily agree that others belong to their own category, but are reluctant to accept that they belong to the same category as others. In other words, each individual acts as if he or she was a prototype.

Isn't this type of self-centering schema a mishap of identity construction, resulting from factual and situational variables such as membership in a given social structure or culture, with its incumbent norms? The present study is an attempt to provide some answers to this question, previously raised by well-known studies (Deschamps & Personnaz, 1979; Lemaine, 1966; Mummendey & Schreiber, 1983; Serino, 1988). It deals with the effects of the coexistence of French and Maghrebian populations in France, and the relations between them.

Subjects were asked to estimate the degree of similarity or difference between (i) themselves and other members of their own group, (ii) themselves and members of the foreign group, or (iii) the two groups. This procedure was used to detect the effects of the norms in the subjects'

---

[1] With contributions from A. Arich, B. Becker, and C. Beuzit.

culture of origin: for the French, raised in a culture where individualism is a primary value, the utilization of the self as a prototype is expected to be more prevalent than in the Maghrebian culture, where "traditional" (i.e. group-oriented) values generally take precedence over individually-oriented ones.[2]

The main objective of the present study was to show how certain cognitive mechanisms which are considered to be fundamental in fact depend on the norms in effect in the culture in which the social actor was raised, and on the position of the actor's group in the society as a whole.

1. Method

Data was collected in the field from 240 male workers (120 French, 120 Maghrebis).[3] Each subject was asked to answer one question corresponding to one of the conditions in the experimental design, which included four factors: (1) the terms of the comparison (subjects were asked to compare themselves with the members of their own group *or* the foreign group, *or* to compare the two groups); (2) the comparison reference point (oneself *or* the group when the self was involved, one of the two groups for the between-group comparison); (3) the type of comparison (assessment of similarity *or* difference); and (4) the cultural origin of the subjects (French *or* Maghrebian). Twelve different questions were generated accordingly, and assigned to 24 independent groups of 10 subjects (12 French and 12 Maghrebian groups).

Thus, the question asked subjects to estimate the degree of similarity or difference between themselves and one of the groups, or between the two groups. Subjects answered on a 7-point scale ranging from "not at all" to "completely" by marking an × next to the statement which best described their estimation of the degree of similarity or difference.[4]

---

[2] This study was initially planned to compare the results obtained for two equivalent populations of Maghrebis, one living in the Maghreb and the other living in France following emigration. This would have made it possible to examine how the self-centering phenomenon changes in individuals subjected to acculturation and to non-egalitarian intergroup relations. However, the Gulf War broke out at the end of 1990 when we were collecting the data in the Maghreb. This disrupted the system of symbolic relations between the French and the Muslim Maghrebis, and all research projects were immediately interrupted. Thus, the present study only deals with data collected among the French and Maghrebis living in France.

[3] It was of course inconceivable to mix the two sexes. A female study could not be conducted due to the norms governing group life in the Maghrebian culture.

[4] The questions were as follows:
"How similar/different do you feel ... are to/from ...?"
"How similar/different do you feel you personally are to/from ...?"
"How similar/different do you feel .... are to/from you personally?"

Due to the fact that part of the experimental population was unfamiliar with the French language, especially the written language, questionnaires could not be simply handed out to the subjects. For the Maghrebis, the experimenter conducted an oral interview in the language they preferred, explaining how they were supposed to answer. Since the question was a forced-choice one, the subjects were given the opportunity to speak freely and explain their point of view or add further information; in this case, the experimenter marked down the appropriate answer.

2. Results

The data was processed using the Var3 analysis of variance program (Lebeaux, Lépine & Rouanet, 1986). Table 1 summarizes the observed means and standard deviations.

Table 1

Means and Standard deviations of Perceived Similarity and Difference for French and Maghrebian Subjects in Each Experimental Condition

Subjects and compar. mode	Self/Ingroup Comparison Reference point		Self/Outgroup Comparison Reference point		Ingroup/Outgroup Comparison Reference point	
	Self	Ingroup	Self	Outgroup	Ingroup	Outgroup
French subjects (n= 120)						
Similarity	4.80	3.70	2.90	3.30	2.90	3.50
	1.81	*0.67*	*2.51*	*1.70*	*0.99*	*2.12*
Difference	2.20	2.90	4.80	4.30	4.70	4.50
	1.23	*1.52*	*2.25*	*1.57*	*1.06*	*1.51*
Maghreb. subj. (n=120)						
Similarity	4.90	5.60	1.20	1.70	1.20	2.20
	0.57	*0.71*	*0.42*	*0.48*	*0.42*	*2.30*
Difference	1.60	1.70	5.80	4.10	4.60	6.80
	0.84	*1.89*	*0.92*	*1.60*	*2.12*	*0.63*

Note. Standard deviations are in italics.

158

2.1 Comparisons between Oneself and the Ingroup

Figure 1 shows that when the subjects compared themselves with the other members of their own group, the French response pattern in relation to the reference point tended to be consistent with Codol's (1984, 1986) findings for both similarity and difference estimation (although the effects were not significant). In other words, the French subjects had a tendency, on the one hand, to consider the French in general to be more like themselves than they are like the French, and on the other, to consider the French in general to be less different from themselves than they are from the French.

In the experimental condition where the self was the comparison reference point, the French and Maghrebian estimations for self/ingroup similarity were identical and above the midpoint of the scale. In contrast, when the ingroup was the point of reference, the responses of the two populations differed significantly ($F(1,38) = 9.15$; $p < .01$), with the Maghrebis exhibiting a tendency (ns) to perceive more similarity than in the other experimental condition, and the French exhibiting the opposite tendency (ns), i.e. perception of less similarity (Fig. 1a).

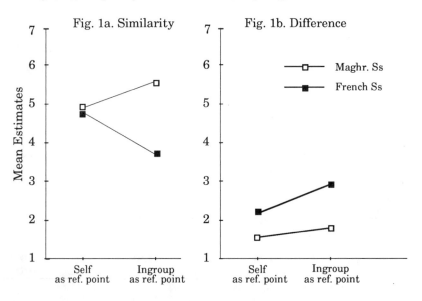

Figure 1. Mean estimates of self/ingroup similarity and difference by reference point for French and Maghrebian subjects.

While the French response pattern tended to be consistent with Codol's observations, the one of the Maghrebian population was not. Accordingly, in comparisons of oneself with other members of one's own cultural group, the interaction between cultural origin and comparison reference point was significant $(F(3,36) = 8.04; p < .01)$.

In the situation involving comparison with other Maghrebis, the Maghrebian subjects felt they were more similar to others than others were to them. Thus, the self did not act as a prototype in the sense observed by Codol for western cultures (where subjects accentuate perceived similarity between themselves and others when the self is the reference point). On the contrary, for the Maghrebian subjects, the self tended to be assimilated with the group.

For the estimates of difference between the self and the ingroup (Fig.1b), the point of reference did not have a significant effect whatever the subjects' cultural origin. Thus, these results are not entirely consistent with Codol's previous research which demonstrates the constant concern in western cultures to differentiate oneself from others.

2.2 Comparisons between Oneself and the Outgroup

Figure 2a shows that when the subjects were required to compare themselves with members of the foreign group, the responses of the two populations differed $(F(1,38) = 7.8; p < .01)$, regardless of the reference point: the French perceived more similarity between themselves and the Maghrebis than the Maghrebis did between themselves and the French.

Figure 2a also shows that the comparison reference point had a significant effect for the Maghrebis, who perceived more similarity when the French population was the reference point $(F(1,18) = 4.98; p < .05)$. The French exhibited a similar tendency to perceive more similarity when the self was compared to the outgroup, but not to a significant extent.

Whatever the case may be, the Maghrebis feel they are less like the French than the French feel they are like the Maghrebis. For these immigrants, this phenomenon can be easily understood as the expression of the desire for social differentiation frequently found in minority groups. In contrast, the response pattern of the French can be explained as the concern for "fair play" stemming from the French norms of tolerance and open-mindedness.

Some slightly unfamiliar results, however, can be seen in Figure 2b. In western cultures, a greater perceived difference is ordinarily observed between oneself and others when the other population is the comparison reference point. In other words, subjects are generally inclined to consider others to be hardly different from themselves, while considering themselves to be different from others. In the present study this reference-point effect was not obtained for the French. For both reference points, the French estimated a substantial degree of difference between themselves and the Maghrebis. For the Maghrebian subjects, the perceived differences were significantly greater in the condition where the comparison reference point was the self ($F(1,18) = 9.00$; $p < .01$).

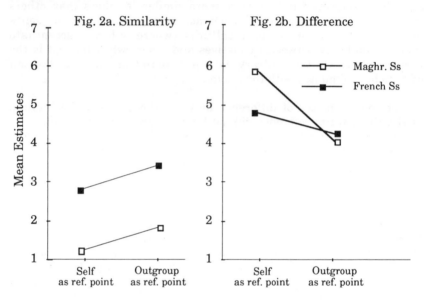

Figure 2. Mean estimates of self/outgroup similarity and difference by reference point for French and Maghrebian subjects.

This difference once again indicates the reversal of the mechanisms known to exist in western cultures. It means that for Maghrebis, the group rather than the self functions as the prototype, whether the group in question is one's own group of membership (comparison with the ingroup) or the foreign group (comparison with the outgroup).

This phenomenon can also be viewed as the manifestation of the desire for conformity with, and assimilation into, a highly-envied majority group.

The self/outgroup estimates of both similarity and difference obtained here for the Maghrebis are not easy to interpret. The results for the French population can be interpreted in terms of French indifference towards the direction of the comparison, or of their feeling that such a comparison is in fact irrelevant.

2.3 Comparison between the Ingroup and the Outgroup

Figure 3 shows that for the French, the estimates did not vary much more by reference point in the group comparisons than they did in the preceding self/outgroup comparisons. In contrast, the responses of the Maghrebis making the same comparisons again varied significantly.

For the comparisons between their own group and the foreign group, the two populations responded differently, as found above for the self/outgroup comparisons. The Maghrebis perceived less similarity between the two groups than the French did ($F(1,38) = 9.40$; $p < .01$), regardless of the reference point.

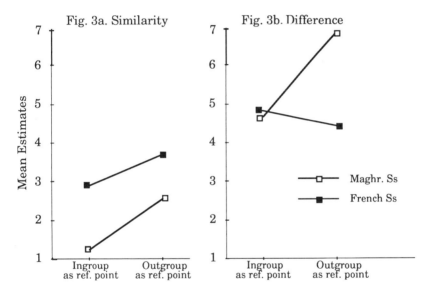

Figure 3. Mean estimates of ingroup/outgroup similarity and difference by reference point for French and Maghrebian subjects.

In one respect, the two populations manifested similar attitudes: whether they were comparing individuals from the foreign group with themselves (Fig. 2a) or with the members of their own group (Fig. 3a), the degree of perceived similarity was always greater when the foreign group was the reference point. This phenomenon is the reversal of what has been previously observed in studies on western cultures.

However, when the subjects were not personally involved in the comparison, and when the degree of difference between their own group and the foreign group was being assessed (Fig. 3b), the Maghrebis responded differently, this time in accordance with the well-known pattern, i.e., when the members of their own group were compared to the French, the magnitude of the perceived difference between the two parties was the greatest, and above the midpoint of the scale. The change in point of reference led to a significant variation in the perceived difference $(F(1,18) = 11.5; p < .01)$, an effect which did not occur for the French.

The two populations responded similarly in their estimates of the difference between their own group and the foreign group when the former was the point of reference, but no longer did so when the foreign group played that role: whether French or Maghrebian, the subjects felt that the members of the foreign group clearly differed from the members of their own group. But for the Maghrebis, the difference increased when the comparison reference point changed, in which case they felt the Maghrebis were completely different from the French $(F (1,18) = 9.98; p < .01)$. Under the same circumstances, the French considered that their own group differed a little less from the Maghrebis than the Maghrebis differed from their own group.

It looks as though strong group identification in the Maghrebian culture leads its members to manifest the classical response pattern of Westerners during intergroup comparison. The French do not do this, perhaps out of a concern for "fair play" (van Knippenberg & Ellemers, 1990) or more probably out of a feeling of indifference. Compared to the Maghrebis, the French indeed occupy the favored social position in France, and thus need not be concerned about emphasizing their differences in order to obtain social recognition.

3. Discussion

In the present study, the behavior of the Maghrebis can thus be viewed as a differentiating behavior which individuals – who are aware of the unfavorable social position their group occupies – use to generate a positive identity.

For the French population, this study confirms the well-known tendency towards self-centered assimilation in self/others comparison with members of their own culture.

In contrast, the Maghrebis appear to be group-centered, taking the group as the reference point in self/others comparison, regardless of whether the group in question is foreign or not.

For similarity estimation by both populations, the response patterns obtained for own group/foreign group comparison were comparable to those obtained for self/foreign group comparison, as if the subjects identified with their own group members whenever they were not personally involved in the comparison. But the Maghrebis' similarity estimates were lower than the French ones. The Maghrebis, being in an unfavorable position in French society, manifest this behavior as an affirmation, by differentiation, of their threatened social identity.

The estimates of difference obtained here revealed more complex behaviors. When the Maghrebis were identifying with their own cultural group, their estimations reflected a need for differentiation, a tendency which did not emerge when they compared themselves individually to the French. It can be concluded from this data that when the comparison process personally involves the Maghrebian immigrant, the desire to be assimilated into the dominant group prevails, while the intergroup situation created by the comparison of the two groups abruptly evokes the need for a unique social identity. They attempt to achieve this identity through mechanisms of assimilation into the ingroup. Recourse to these mechanisms is considered as legitimate under these circumstances, since such mechanisms operate to the benefit of the group and not the individual.

To conclude, we can only regret the lack of available data for comparing the respective attitudes of the Maghrebis living in France and in the Maghreb. This comparison would have allowed us to separate cultural effects *per se* from those stemming from membership in a group which occupies a disadvantageous social position. At this point in our research, these two sources of variation cannot be disassociated.

The impact of underlying sociocultural structures on the destiny of individuals nevertheless appears evident. Our analysis demonstrates the need in research on cognitive processes to re-insert all operations under study into the context which makes them meaningful and from which they cannot be separated (Bruner, 1991).

References

Bruner, J. (1991). *Car la culture donne forme à l'esprit. De la révolution cognitive à la psychologie culturelle*. Paris : ESHEL.

Codol, J.-P. (1979). *Semblables et différents. Recherches sur la quête de la similitude et de la différenciation sociale*. Unpublished doctoral thesis, University of Provence, Aix-en-Provence, France.

Codol, J.-P. (1984). La perception de la similitude interpersonnelle : influence de l'appartenance catégorielle et du point de référence de la comparaison. *L'Année Psychologique, 84,* 43-56.

Codol, J.-P. (1986). Estimations et expressions de la ressemblance et de la différence entre pairs. *L'Année Psychologique, 86,* 527-550.

Deschamps, J.-C. & Personnaz, B. (1979). Etude entre groupes "dominants" et "dominés" : importance de la présence du hors-groupe dans les discriminations évaluatives et comportementales. *Informations sur les Sciences Sociales, 18,* 269-305.

Lebeaux, M.-O., Lépine D. & Rouanet, H. (1976). *Introduction au programme Var3.* Paris : Groupe Mathématiques et Psychologie.

Lemaine, G. (1966). Inégalité, comparaison et incomparabilité : esquisse d'une théorie de l'originalité sociale. *Bulletin de Psychologie, 20,* 24-31.

Mummendey, A., & Schreiber, H. J. (1983). Better or just different? Positive social identity by discrimination against, or by differentiation from outgroups. *European Journal of Social Psychology, 13,* 389-397.

Serino, C. (1988). Stratégies et structure de la comparaison sociale : quelques aspects de l'asymétrie Soi/Autrui dans les relations entre groupes. *Cahiers de Psychologie Cognitive / European Bulletin of Cognitive Psychology, 8,* 627-648.

Tajfel, H., Billig, M. G., Bundy, R. P., & Flament, C. (1971). Social categorization and intergroup behaviour. *European Journal of Social Psychology, 1,* 149-177.

Turner, J. C. (1975). Social comparison and social identity: Some prospects for intergroup behavior. *European Journal of Social Psychology, 5,* 5-34.

van Knippenberg, A., & Ellemers, N. (1990). Social identity and intergroup differentiation processes. In W. Stroebe & M. Hewstone (Eds.), *European Review of Social Psychology* (Vol. 1, pp. 137-169). New York: Wiley.

LEVELS OF CATEGORIZATION
AND DIFFERENTIATION
BETWEEN AND WITHIN CATEGORIES

Alain Clémence

University of Geneva, Switzerland

The application of categorization in the field of intergroup relations has considerably renewed the psychosocial approach to identity (cf. Doise, 1979; Tajfel, 1982; Tajfel & Turner, 1986). Following Tajfel's work, a systematic presentation of the propositions stemming from this approach was developed by Turner and his colleagues (Turner, Hogg, Oakes, Reicher, & Wetherell, 1987) in a self-categorization theory. From their point of view, an individual's identity depends on the level of comparison activated by the social context. For instance, when this context makes group boundaries salient (Oakes, 1987), it is category membership which becomes psychologically determinant for the definition of the subjects, who then tend to accentuate intra-category similarities and inter-categories differences. If the situation leads to a weakening of this intermediate comparison level by increasingly involving the subjects in an inter-individual or subordinate comparison, intra-category similarities and inter-categories differences diminish. According to Doise (1976), this process operates simultaneously on behaviorial and cognitive aspects.

These propositions are supported by the results of numerous studies (e.g. Doise, Deschamps, & Meyer, 1978; Arcuri, 1982; Brown & Smith, 1989). Some studies have nevertheless suggested that social categorization does not always lead to the accentuation of intra-category similarities (e.g. Deschamps & Lorenzi-Cioldi, 1981; Capozza & Nanni, 1986). Moreover, a series of studies supported the hypothesis of a more homogeneous perception of the outgroup than of the ingroup (Linville & Jones, 1980; Park & Rothbart, 1982). Other results have contradicted this hypothesis (Stephan, 1977; Simon & Brown, 1987). Homogenization of the outgroup seems to be modulated by the type of measures and dimensions used (Judd & Park, 1988; Linville, Fischer, & Salovey, 1989). Various authors have recently explained this process and some of its variations in the context of the self-categorization theory (Marques, Yzerbit, & Leyens, 1988; Simon & Pettigrew, 1990).

In general, the vast majority of these studies explored only the deductive effects of social categorization and often ignored the self, which is reduced to one member among others of an ingroup. The interest of an approach such as Codol's (1982) lies precisely in the attention paid to the self in the structuring of social relations. Here, the self acquires a status as a full fledged category, a determinant category in the comparison with the other, whether as a point of reference for this comparison or not (Codol, 1984). It is also by stressing the differentiation between the self and others that Deschamps proposed a model of the covariation of similarities and differences, defending the idea that accentuating individualization could entail an increase in intergroup differentiation and, inversely, that an increase in inter-category salience could induce stronger discrimination between the self and the ingroup (Deschamps, 1982; 1984). The model is derived from the idea that inter-category differentiation entails intra-category tension and a greater visibility of individuals (in particular of the ingroup). This effect should be stronger when the subjects are characterized by a high social status and are individually identified. Lorenzi-Cioldi (1988) related results of several experiments focusing on the asymmetry of inter-sex relations which go in that direction.

By privileging the deductive aspect of social categorization, one is led to deal with intergroup relations according to a prototypical definition of their members and attributes. So it is hardly surprising that self-categorization theorists should explicitly adopt Rosch's principles of categorization (1978) as well as those of many other authors working on intergroup relations (e.g. Wilder, 1981). Therefore, empirical works on intra- and inter-category relations more often than not evoke either groups in general or anonymous and prototypical members of groups. When the subjects' judgments or behaviors can be deduced only from the superposing, albeit minimal, of an attribute specific to one category, they correspond most frequently to social categorization hypotheses. However, Smith and Zarate (1990) found that subjects could build categories on the basis of the similarity between particular exemplars and not on common traits specific to the members of a category. In another field, Judd and Park (1988) related results which indicate that the homogenization of the outgroup manifests itself mainly when perception is focused on the category itself and not on the exemplars composing it.

One of the objectives of the present study was to compare the deductive and inductive aspects of social categorization for the same subjects by exploring, on the one hand, the intra- and inter-category differences when the categories are evoked in a general (and therefore prototypical) way and, on the other hand, the differences between the exemplars of each category chosen by the subjects, the self being included in this last comparison. The general hypothesis was that the self-categorization model makes it possible to account for the deductive aspect of social categorization and that the covariation model makes it possible to account for its inductive aspect.

More precisely, we hypothesized that the subjects' judgments on "prototypical" targets would be consistent with the propositions of self-categorization; the intra-category differences should be smaller and the inter-category differences greater when the judgments bear on the characteristic attributes of the categories in question, and vice versa when the attributes define the individuals as such. Much more homogenization of the outgroup than of the ingroup was also predicted.

To tackle the inductive aspect of categorization, the subjects themselves need to define the criteria for comparison. It therefore seemed relevant to use a modified version of Codol's (1985) idea on the estimation of distances between targets. The subjects were invited here to place the targets, rather than assess the distances between them. To test the effects of social categorization, we compared the distances set by the subject between exemplars of the ingroup only (distinguishing between two sub-categories) with those set between exemplars of two different categories. The intra- and inter-category distances should be consistent with the model of covariation between similarities and differences. So we predicted that the intra- and inter-category distances would be directly proportional and that social categorization would not lead to shorter intra-category distances (in particular between the self and others) and longer inter-categories distances. Moreover, we predicted more homogeneity of the ingroup than of the outgroup from the fact that exemplars composing the latter should appear as a vaguer entity than exemplars of the ingroup (Simon & Brown, 1989).

These different effects were compared in two categorization conditions, one where the presence of the two categories was introduced immediately and the second where it was introduced after a series of tasks concerning only the ingroup. This manipulation was intended to test the effects of categorization on the perception of the ingroup. In the self-categorization model, prior identification with an ingroup should accentuate inter-category differences and intra-category similarities (as well as the distances between the ingroup's sub-categories) more than in the situation where categorization was deferred (cf. Turner, 1975). According to the covariation model, immediate introduction of categorization should accentuate intra-category tension and therefore increase the differences and the distances between ingroup members (as well as the distances between the ingroup's sub-categories). Finally, we predicted that the males would distinguish more between themselves and other ingroup members and that, more than the females, their reactions would be more consistent with the predictions of covariation theory than of self-categorization theory.

1. Experiment

1.1 Subjects

The 78 subjects (41 females and 37 males) were aged 16 to 18. They were full-time students from three different grades at a Geneva school of commerce. They were different from another category of students at this establishment (commercial apprentices) who were being trained partly at school and partly in a firm. Eight subjects were eliminated from the analyses because of incomplete data.

1.2 Procedure and Material

The subjects filled in two questionnaires which were given to them in a school classroom. One included measures concerning only the ingroup ("full-time students"), and the other repeated the same measures for the outgroup ("commercial apprentices") and for both categories together. The distribution order of the questionnaires was alternated so that categorization was either introduced immediately (before order) or deferred (after order).

Three sets of measures were carried out. The subjects had to indicate the degree of similarity between ingroup members on one of the questionnaires, and between outgroup members and both ingroup and outgroup members in another questionnaire. Six attributes (musical tastes, academic achievement, open-mindedness, professional future, interest in training, and friendliness) were rated on a 7-point scale (1: very different and 7: very similar).

On the first questionnaire the subjects wrote down the degree of importance they attributed to each characteristic on a 7-point scale (1: little and 7: much).

The second measure was an indication of the distance perceived between a given number of ingroup members, the self included (on one of the questionnaires) and of members of both categories, the self included (in another questionnaire). The task was presented as follows when the measure dealt with the distance between ingroup members (intra-category context):

> "One way to indicate extent to which two people have a close relationship is to represent them by two circles. When these two circles are close to one another it will be understood that the two

people are close to one another; when they are far from each other, this will mean that the two people are not close or have a bad relationship. Think of ten people who, like yourself, are full-time students at the Higher School of Commerce. Please represent these ten full-time students and yourself in the picture below using circles. Represent each person by one circle; in the circle which corresponds to you, write ME. You may place these circles as you like. What matters is to show with these circles how you see these ten people and yourself, those you think are close to each other, those you think are far, etc."

When members of both categories were evoked (inter-category context), the instructions were changed to the following:

"...Think of five people who, like yourself, are full-time students at the Higher School of Commerce and of five people who are commercial apprentices. Please represent these ten people and yourself in the picture below using circles. Write S in the circles corresponding to full-time students, A in those corresponding to apprentices and ME in the circle corresponding to yourself..."

The subjects drew the circles inside a 14-centimeter-sided square.

At the end of the second questionnaire, whatever the order, the subjects were invited to distribute a sum of money ranging from 0 to 100 Swiss Francs to each of the five members of the ingroup, to each of the five members of the outgroup, and to themselves. This measure will not be discussed here.

1.3 Method

The data was processed in a multivariate analysis of variance (MANOVA procedure by SPSSX) with the order and sex as sources of inter-subject variation, the degree of training as a source of covariation, and the target of the comparison (category, sub-category, exemplar) as repeated measures. To clarify the presentation of the results, different analyses were carried out.

For the measures of differences, two analyses were carried out. The first used the attributes and the intra- and inter-category targets as repeated measures. The second used the attributes and the ingroup and outgroup targets as repeated measures. The importance attributed to the characteristics was introduced as a source of covariation.

To process the data relating to the spatial representations of the category exemplars (measures of distance), the euclidian distance between each pair of exemplars was calculated. The measures thus obtained can be input into a multidimensional analysis, which is particularly appropriate for separately processing the data of each context (ingroup member data and two-category member data). The results obtained by following this procedure are presented elsewhere (Clémence & Lorenzi-Cioldi, 1991). To compare the data of the two contexts, it was necessary to rely on another method. The exemplars of each category were arranged in order and numbered according to their distance from the self target. When the task evoked only exemplars of the ingroup (intra-category context), we distinguished two sub-categories, the close category (the five members closest to the self) and the far category (the five members farthest from the self). These two sub-categories were compared to the ingroup and the outgroup represented in the inter-category context.

Four analyses of variance were carried out, two considering only exemplars of the categories and two including the self. The analyses dealt with two repeated measures: distance between the two contexts (intra- vs. inter-category context) and distance between targets (intra- vs. inter-category comparison, on the one hand, and ingroup vs. outgroup, on the other).

2. Results

2.1 Inter-Category Differences
The multivariate analysis of variance revealed two important effects of the repeated measures: a simple effect of the type of attribute ($F(5,65) = 5.82$; $p < .001$), and an interaction between the comparison (intra- vs. inter-category) and the type of attribute ($F(5,70) = 14.24$; $p < .001$). Apart from the fact that the level of intra- and inter-category differentiation varied according to the type of attribute (see Table 1), the similarities perceived within the ingroup were weaker than those between the categories when the attributes described personality traits (friendliness: $t(77) = -5.43$; $p < .001$; musical tastes: $t(77) = -5.06$; $p < .001$) and stronger when they concerned the categories' immediate (school) existence (professional future: $t(77) = 3.04$; $p < .001$). On the whole, there was greater differentiation between the members of the ingroup than between those of both categories (simple effect of comparison: $F(1,74) = 5.12$; $p < .03$). Despite this observation, the results are coherent with the self-categorization model in that they showed accentuation of inter-category differences and, though less clearly, of intra-category similarities, when the comparison dealt with a dimension specific to the division between categories, and reduction when the dimension was more concerned with defining the individuals as persons than as members of a category.

Table 1

Average Intra- and Inter-Category Similarities on Attributes

	Similarities		
	Intra-category		Inter-category
Attributes	In	Out	In/Out
Friendliness	3.68	4.10	5.00
Musical tastes	3.22	3.72	4.38
Open-mindedness	3.30	4.12	3.48
Academic achievement	2.83	3.78	3.19
Training interest	4.03	3.90	3.90
Professional future	3.77	4.77	2.96

Note. Scale: 1= very different to 7= very similar.

The comparison-by-type of attribute interaction was modulated by the the comparison order ($F(5,70) = 2.44$; $p < .05$). When social categorization was introduced before the comparison between members of the ingroup, inter-category similarities were stronger for the "personality" attributes than in the after-order condition (contrast comparison: friendliness: $t(74) = -3.16$; $p < .005$ and musical tastes: $t(74) = -3.07$; $p < .005$). The before-order condition produced more differentiation at the intra-category than at the inter-category level for the "personality" dimension, while the opposite was observed for the after-order condition as Table 2 shows. These results were reversed for the "category" dimension.

Table 2

Intra- and Inter-Category Similarities According to the Presentation Order of the Categorization for the Attributes "Friendliness" and "Professional Future"

	After order $n = 39$		Before order $n = 39$	
Attributes	Intra	Inter	Intra	Inter
Friendliness	3.70 [a]	4.36 [a]	3.66 [b]	5.64 [b]
Professional future	3.72 [c]	2.80 [c]	3.82 [d]	3.13 [d]

Note. Means with same superscripts differ at $p < .05$ (b, c) and $p < .08$ (a, d).

These results are consistent with the predictions derived from a model of covariation. The initial salience of categorization accentuates the similarity between members of opposite categories for a personal dimension, while the initial salience of the intra-category comparison accentuates inter-category differentiation for a common dimension.

2.2 Intra-Category Differences

As Table 1 shows, the outgroup was more homogeneous than the ingroup ($F(1,75) = 29.64$; $p < .001$). Moreover, there was an interaction effect between order and type of attribute ($F(5,70) = 2.54$; $p < .04$), which is explained by the fact that the difference between both categories is significant for all attributes ($t(77) > 2.10$; $p < .04$) except for "interest in training" where this insignificant difference was reversed.

Sex group membership interacted significantly with the difference in homogeneity perceived between the two categories ($F(1,70) = 4.37$; $p < .04$) and with the type of attribute ($F(5,65) = 2.56$; $p < .04$). This last effect is due to the greater differentiation between the members of the ingroup on "personality" attributes made by the females than the males (contrast comparison: open-mindedness: $t(74) = 2.68$; $p < .01$ and friendliness: $t(74) = 2.69$; $p < .01$). The first interaction effect (sex-by-target) is explained by the stronger homogenization of the outgroup compared to the ingroup observed among the females than among the males. Indeed, the males differentiated significantly more between the members of the ingroup than between those of the outgroup for just one attribute (academic achievement: $t(36) = 3.38$; $p < .002$), whereas the females did it systematically (all the differences except the attribute "interest in training" were significant at $p < .02$: all $t(40) > 2.60$).

2.3 Inter-Category Distances

The distances between the exemplars of the two different categories were much greater than those between exemplars of the ingroup ($F(1,74) = 197.50$; $p < .001$). The context-by-comparison between categories interaction was highly significant ($F(1,74) = 7.16$; $p < .01$). Table 3 shows that inter-category distances were greater between the close and far sub-categories (CF) than between the ingroup and outgroup (IO). It also shows that the exemplars of the ingroup (II) were farther from one another than the close exemplars (CC).

Table 3

Means of Distances between and within Categories According to the Context of Comparison

	Context of comparison	
	Intra	Inter
Distances		
Within (CC/II)	1.81 ac	2.03 bc
Between (CF/IO)	4.92 ad	4.17 bd

Note. CC: distances between close exemplars (Intra); II: distances between ingroup exemplars (Inter); CF: distances between close and far sub-categories (Intra); IO: distances between ingroup and outgroup (Inter).
Means with same superscripts differ at $p < .05$ (a,b,d) and $p < .07$ (c).

While this result clearly supports the fact that the subjects used the exemplars' group membership to place them in the inter-category context, it would also seem that the presence of another category did not lead to an accentuation of the proximities between the exemplars of the ingroup (distance CC < II). Moreover, it was observed that the distance between the sub-categories (CF) was greater than the distance between the two induced categories (IO). It should also be noted that the correlations between the distances within and between the different categories were systematically positive.

2.4 Intra-Category Distances

The multivariate analysis of variance revealed a simple effect of the comparison between intra-category distances ($F(1,74) = 59.25$; $p < .001$), indicating a tendency toward greater homogeneity of the ingroup than of the outgroup. This effect was stronger between the two ingroup sub-categories than between the ingroup and the outgroup (since the exemplars were ordered, this result is perfectly logical after all), as the interaction between context and comparison between targets indicated ($F(1,74) = 16.38$; $p < .001$). But it was significant in both cases ($t(77) = -8.22$; $p < .001$ and $t(77) = -3.82$; $p < .001$, respectively). Sex group membership modulated the difference between the two categories (sex-by-comparison interaction: $F(1,74) = 5.53$; $p < .025$): the males drew equal distances between the exemplars of the ingroup and the outgroup in the inter-category context (see Table 4), unlike the females.

Table 4

Means of Distances within Categories According to Sex Group Membership and Context of Comparison

	Context of comparison			
	Intra	Inter	Intra	Inter
Distances	Females		Males	
Close/In (CC/II)	1.81 [a]	1.80 [b]	1.82 [c]	2.30
Far/Out (FF/OO)	3.81 [a]	2.94 [b]	3.42 [c]	2.55

Note. CC: distances between the close exemplars (Intra); II: distances between the ingroup-exemplars (Inter); FF: distances between the far exemplars (Intra); OO: distances between the outgroup exemplars (inter).
Means with same superscripts differ at $p < .001$.

The correlations (significantly positive) are the greatest between the two sub-categories for the females and between the ingroup and the outgroup for the males.

As a whole, these results confirm the predictions derived from the covariation model.

2.5 Distances between the Self and Others (Inter-Category Comparison)

The comparison here involved the self and the first 4 exemplars of the close and ingroup categories, and these same exemplars and the corresponding exemplars of the far and outgroup categories.

Multivariate analysis of the variance indicated both a strong effect of the inter-category comparison ($F(1,74) = 28.48$; $p < .001$) and an interaction between the context and the inter-category comparison ($F(1,74) = 12.34$; $p < .001$). These effects are comparable to those previously observed, as shown in Table 5. Apart from the very distinct inter-category separation, whether at the level of the induced categories (IO) or at the level of the ingroup sub-categories (CF), the distance between the self and others increase (SI > SC) and inter-category distances decrease (CF > IO) as we go from the intra-category to the inter-category context. All correlations are significantly positive and indicate that all the distances covary in direct proportion.

Table 5

Means of Distances between the Self and Ingroup and between Categories According to the Context of Comparison

	Context of comparison	
Distances	Intra	Inter
Self-In (SC/SI)	1.61 [ac]	1.95 [bc]
Between (CF/IO)	4.54 [ad]	3.86 [bd]

Note. SC: distances between the self and the close exemplars (Intra); SI: distances between the self and the ingroup exemplars (Inter); CF: distances between the close and far sub-categories (Intra); IO: distances between ingroup and outgroup (Inter). Means with same superscripts differ at $p < .001$ (a,b,c) and $p < .05$ (d).

The inter-category comparison interacted with the sex ($F(1,74) = 4.16$; $p < .05$) and was modulated by an interaction between the order and the sex ($F(1,74) = 5.93$; $p < .02$). The sex effect can be explained by the greater distance that the males drew between the self and the ingroup (2.22 vs. 1.70 for the females; contrast comparison: $t(74) = 2.23$; $p < .03$) and more generally between the self and the subordinate or induced ingroup categories (1.98 (males) vs. 1.59 (females); $t(74) = 1.98$; $p < .055$). To deal with the order-by-sex interaction, let us consider the means in Table 6.

Table 6

Means of Distances between the Self and the Ingroup and between Categories According to Sex and Order of Presentation

	Order of presentation			
	After $n = 23$	Before $n = 18$	After $n = 16$	Before $n = 21$
Distances	Females		Males	
Self-Close (SC)	1.47	1.51 [b]	1.95	1.58 [c]
Self-In (SI)	1.62	1.80 [b]	2.21	2.23 [c]
Close-Far (CF)	5.18 [a]	4.17	4.13	4.47
In-Out (IO)	4.16 [a]	3.51	3.75	3.91

Note. All the t's of the inter-category comparisons (SC-CF and SI-IO) were significant at $p < .001$; means with same superscripts differ at $p < .01$ (c) and $p < .09$ (a,b).

In the after-order condition, the distances between the self and others were greater among the males than among the females ($t(74) = 1.90$;

$p < .065)$. In the before-order condition, the males showed the greatest gap between the self and close category (SC) distances and the self and ingroup (SI) distances.

2.6 Distances between the Self and Others (Intra-Category Comparison)

Overall, the distances between the self and others (close or ingroup) were slightly greater than the distances between the exemplars of these categories ($F(1,74) = 3.33$; $p < .075$). This gap was modulated only by an interaction between the order and the sex ($F(1,74) = 4.27$; $p < .05$), and to a smaller extent by sex group membership ($F(1,74) = 3.69$; $p < .06$). As already previously noted but with another index, the males differentiated the self and the exemplars of the ingroup more than the females (contrast comparison: $t(74) = 2.25$; $p < .03$). Moreover, the males of the before-order condition distinguished the exemplars of the ingroup more than the other groups of subjects (all $t > 2.13$; $p < .04$). For the males in the after-order condition, the distances between the self and others, and in particular between the self and the ingroup, were the farthest removed from the distances between exemplars of the same category (Self-In: 2.59 and In-In: 1.82; $t(15) = 2.09$; $p < .055$).

The results concerning the distances set between the self and others also confirm the predictions derived from the covariation model.

3. Discussion

These results clearly verify our hypotheses. The self-categorization model can be used to account for the intra- and inter-category differentiations when the judgments bore on general, "prototypical", targets, i.e. when the deductive aspect of the categorization was activated. However, a procedure which also activated the inductive aspect of categorization by leading the subjects to class particular exemplars of the categories produced more complex results. It appeared *inter alia* that the intra- and inter-category differentiations, which were approached through the distance perceived between group members, were positively correlated and that the explicit imposition of categorization tended to accentuate intra-category distances and inter-category proximities. This last result must be confirmed by other studies, because the procedure used did not make it possible to verify that the exemplars placed by the subjects in the inter-category context corresponded to the exemplars that were closest to the self in the intra-category context.

Moreover, we observed that the self was farther away from the ingroup exemplars when faced with another category than analogous exemplars compared with other ingroup members. This result was more clear-cut among the males than females. In general, it is also possible to conclude that the immediate introduction of categorization accentuated intra-category differentiations, while focusing first on ingroup members increased inter-category distinctions. Such observations are coherent with the covariation model. They confirm the results previously obtained in the analysis of the distances in the inter-category context of two experiments, results which showed that the deferred introduction of categorization increased the concomitant use of the intra- and inter-category levels to differentiate the exemplars of the categories (Clémence & Lorenzi-Cioldi, 1991).

It should nevertheless be stressed that this study is necessarily an exploratory one. Apart from the fact that the procedure requires some improvement, more systematic studies should be conducted to clarify issues like the organizing function of the self in intra- and inter-category differentiations, and the characteristics of the exemplars chosen by the subjects.

References

Arcuri, L. (1982). Three patterns of social categorization in attribution memory. *European Journal of Social Psychology, 12*, 271-282.

Brown, R., & Smith, A. (1989). Perception of and by minority groups: The case of women in academia. *European Journal of Social Psychology, 19*, 61-75.

Capozza, D., & Nanni, R. (1986). Differentiation processes for social stimuli with different degrees of category representativeness. *European Journal of Social Psychology, 16*, 399-412.

Clémence, A. & Lorenzi-Cioldi, F. (1991). Catégorisation sociale et homogénéité des catégories. *Les Cahiers Internationaux de Psychologie Sociale, 3* (9-10), 31-47.

Codol, J.-P. (1982). Differentiating and non-differentiating behavior: An approach to the sense of identity. In J.-P. Codol & J.-P. Leyens (Eds.), *Cognitive analysis of social behavior* (pp. 267-291), The Hague: Nijhoff.

Codol, J.-P. (1984). La perception de la similitude interpersonnelle: influence de l'appartenance catégorielle et du point de référence de la comparaison. *L'Année Psychologique, 84*, 43-56.

Codol, J.-P. (1985). L'estimation des distances physiques entre personnes: suis-je aussi loin de vous que vous l'êtes de moi? *L'Année Psychologique, 85*, 517-534.

Deschamps, J.-C. (1982). Différenciations entre soi et autrui et entre groupes : recherches sur la "covariation" entre les différenciations inter-individuelles et inter-groupes. In J.-P. Codol & J.-P. Leyens (Eds.), *Cognitive analysis of social behavior* (pp. 247-266). The Hague: Nijhoff.

Deschamps, J.-C. (1984). Identité sociale et différenciations catégorielles. *Cahiers de Psychologie Cognitive, 4,* 449-474.

Deschamps, J.-C. & Lorenzi-Cioldi, F. (1981). "Egocentrisme" et "sociocentrisme" dans les relations entre groupes. *Revue Suisse de Psychologie Pure et Appliquée, 40,* 108-131.

Doise, W. (1976). *L'articulation psychosociologique et les relations entre groupes.* Bruxelles: De Boeck.

Doise, W. (1979). *Expériences entre groupes.* Paris: Mouton.

Doise, W., Deschamps, J.-C., & Meyer, G. (1978). The accentuation of intra-category similarities. In H. Tajfel (Ed.), *Differentiation between social groups* (pp. 159-168). London: Academic Press.

Judd, C. M., & Park, B. (1988). Out-group homogeneity: Judgments of variability at the individual and group levels. *Journal of Personality and Social Psychology, 54,* 778-788.

Linville, P. W., Fischer, G. W., & Salovey, P. (1989). Perceived distributions of the characteristics of in-group and out-group members: Empirical evidence and a computer simulation. *Journal of Personality and Social Psychology, 57,* 165-188.

Linville, P. W., & Jones, E. E. (1980). Polarized appraisals of out-group members. *Journal of Personality and Social Psychology, 38,* 689-703.

Lorenzi-Cioldi, F. (1988). *Individus dominants et groupes dominés. Images masculines et féminines.* Grenoble : Presses Universitaires de Grenoble.

Marques, J. M., Yzerbyt, V. Y., & Leyens, J.-P. (1988). The "black sheep effect": Extremity of judgment towards ingroup members as a function of group identification. *European Journal of Social Psychology, 18,* 1-16.

Oakes, P. J. (1987). The salience of social categories. In J. Turner, M. A. Hogg, P. J. Oakes, S. D. Reicher, & M. S. Wetherell (Eds.), *Rediscovering the social group: A self-categorization theory* (pp. 117-141). Oxford: Basil Blackwell.

Park, B., & Rothbart, M. (1982). Perception of out-group homogeneity and levels of social categorization: Memory for the subordinate attributes of in-group and out-group members. *Journal of Personality and Social Psychology, 42,* 1051-1068.

Rosch, E. (1978). Principles of categorization. In E. Rosch & B. B. Lloyd (Eds.), *Cognition and categorization* (pp. 28-48). Hillsdale, NJ: Erlbaum.

Simon, B., & Brown, R. (1987). Perceived intragroup homogeneity in minority-majority contexts. *Journal of Personality and Social Psychology, 53*, 703-711.

Simon, B., & Pettigrew, T. F. (1990). Social identity and perceived intragroup homogeneity: Evidence for the ingroup homogeneity effect. *European Journal of Social Psychology, 20*, 269-286.

Smith, E. R., & Zarate, M. A. (1990). Exemplar and prototype use in social categorization. *Social Cognition, 8*, 243-262.

Stephan, W. G. (1977). Cognitive differentiation in intergroup perception. *Sociometry, 40*, 40-58.

Tajfel, H. (1982). *Social identity and intergroup relations.* Cambridge: Cambridge University Press & Paris: Maison des Sciences de l'Homme.

Tajfel, H., & Turner, J. C. (1986). The social identity theory of intergroup behaviour. In S. Worchel & W. G. Austin (Eds.), *Psychology of intergroup relations* (pp. 7-24). Chicago: Nelson-Hall.

Turner, J. C. (1975). Social comparison and social identity: Some prospects for intergroup behaviour. *European Journal of Social Psychology, 5*, 5-34.

Turner, J. C., Hogg, M. A., Oakes, P. J., Reicher, S. D., & Wetherell, M. S. (1987). *Rediscovering the social group: A self-categorization theory.* Oxford: Basil Blackwell.

Wilder, D. A. (1981). Perceiving persons as a group: Categorization and intergroup relations. In D. L. Hamilton (Ed.), *Cognitive processes in stereotyping and intergroup behavior* (pp. 213-257). Hillsdale, NJ: Erlbaum.

VALORIZATION AND DEVALORIZATION
OF GROUP MEMBERSHIP

SITUATIONAL AND STRUCTURAL PROCESSES

Michel Oriol

University of Nice, France

1. How Migration Studies May Lead to Question some Social Comparison Processes

In order to make use of comparative observations about the processes of categorization in relation with group membership, let us stress the relevance and importance of migratory phenomena, especially when they produce large national and/or cultural groups living in a diaspora situation. Let us take two samples of subjects sharing the same national/cultural origin, everything being equated in other respects. Individuals in the first sample are settled more or less stably in the home country, but have significant familial or personal motivations for comparing themselves to those settled abroad, among whom we shall recruit the second sample. At least two potentially correlated sets of differences can be investigated :

(1) What are the differences between the two groups in regards to the definitions and evaluations of traits considered relevant for assessing the specificity of the national/cultural group?

(2) What are the differences between the two groups when their members must assume or deny their original national/cultural membership?

2. Henri Tajfel Recalled and Revisited

Basic assumptions drawn from Tajfel and his disciples (Tajfel, Jahoda, Nemeth, Rim, & Johnson, 1972) lead us to expect the following answers to these questions:

(1) In the home country, the salience of traits commonly used to refer to the national/cultural group should be quite strong (Tversky, 1977). Then the conformity of the self and its specificity, both as defined by Codol (1975), should fit adequately and easily. On the contrary, in the immigrant situation, the traits commonly used to refer to the host group, which is at the same time a dominant group, should have a much higher degree of salience. Then, it is highly probable that, for immigrants, a process of devalorization of the traits used to refer to the group of origin will be observed.

(2) In the home country, whatever the role and importance of imagined references to people abroad, the desire (and a fortiori the plan to change one's group membership) should be highly improbable because of pressure to conform. In contrast, in the emigration country, strategies of social mobility or social change – as defined by Tajfel (1981) when he opposed the individual aspect of the former to the collective aspect of the latter – can be expected to be widespread. According to the degree of social stability and the legitimacy of the domination exerted by the host group, these strategies may lead immigrants to desire to identify with the host group (if the domination is not challenged) and then perhaps to strengthen their original group membership if the symbolic power of the dominant group is perceived as decaying. In the latter case, we would observe a reversal of stigmas, i.e. the valorization of traits previously marked with a pejorative connotation.

Such statements have been more or less thoroughly validated by experiments carried out by Tajfel and his disciples (1978).

Field research could complete and potentially revise these experimental propositions in two main respects:
– Tajfel's assumptions imply the more or less constant, clear-cut distinction between ingroup and outgroup. What happens, then, to the processes of valorization and devalorization whenever subjects belong to several groups, make use of *"bilateral affiliations"* (Catani, 1983)?
– These assumptions imply that the processes of valorization and devalorization occur in relation to possible changes in the valence of certain traits. But when you study field situations, which are distant in both space and time, you may observe that the repertory of comparative traits changes not only in terms of value, but also in terms of relevance. On both sides, the comparison between two (or more) groups may bear on very different fields of activities (i.e. culture and morality on one side, economy and efficiency on the other).

If our questions about Tajfel's theory are legitimate ones, they may lead us to define the problem of social identity in more complex terms: this problem deals not only with judgements made in relation to a given membership, but also, more basically, with the very meaning of *"belongingness"*. This leaves us with the difficult task of accounting for the paradoxical aspects of diasporic groups: their members may share a deep sense of unity and value, but make use of very different sets of relevant meanings for assuming collective differentiation in very diverse situations.

3. Method

The population studied by the multinational research team comprised two groups of male and female adolescents and young adults, between 16 and 20 years old, who were from the geographical area, the department of Guarda, in central Portugal (Beira alta). One hundred of them were observed and interviewed in the city of Guarda or its surroundings. They were sons or daughters of emigrants, left behind by their parents in the care of relatives, friends, or religious and educational institutions. Among the 100 subjects studied in France, 50 had settled in the area of Pau, 50 in the northern suburbs of Paris (Saint-Denis, Villetaneuse). The rationale for this "area sampling" was the possibility of comparing the effects of duration of stay and proximity of the country of origin, the people in Pau having settled several years before those in the Paris area and living much closer to the Guarda district.

Semi-directive questionnaires were filled out in either Portuguese or French according to the subject's choice. They dealt with behaviors, attitudes and opinions concerning the various possible dimensions (political, cultural, linguistic, economic) used to express national/cultural identity, either Portuguese or French. Pre-enquiry analysis of data pointed out the importance of answers dealing with what we proposed to call "decision of belonging". This expression refers to whatever the subjects may express (in terms of future) about their possible commitment to the Portuguese and/or French community: did they care to contribute to the unity of either group by their choice of language (linguistic community), work place and partnership (economic community), marriage (intermarried community), political participation (political community), general interest and solidarity (undefined community, a category which was not initially foreseen, but proved relevant in our subjects' answers)?

The age chosen for sampling made this topic especially pertinant. The validity of answers was checked by intense observation of the subjects' daily life, ceremonies (such as marriages), religious activities, participation in social activities, etc.

Specific items were used to assess the youths' attitudes towards sexual permissiveness, in order to test the common sociological assumption that there is a close correlation between a change in reference group and a change in moral patterns (generally moving from traditional ones to modern ones).

The data collected were processed by a factorial analysis of correspondence (Benzécri, 1973).

4. Themes and Variations Concerning National/Cultural Identities

4.1 The data processing (first with a very high number of variables, N = 202) shows that the distribution of responses in the two groups (in Portugal and in France) is analogous. The two principal axes defined by the factorial analysis[1] correspond to two very similar sets of variables: the first determined by the distribution of responses dealing with national identity (from the exclusive choice of Portugal to the exclusive choice of France), the second, by responses referring to attitudes towards modernism (in both the sexual and political realms).

A first statement is verified: as the two axes are almost orthogonal, one may assume that the polarization of national identity is not correlated with orientations towards traditional or modern values.

4.2 If only the variables related to "decisions of belonging" are taken into account, factorial analysis of correspondence shows a "Guttman" effect in the sample of youths settled in France (see Fig. 1 and Table 1).

Responses and subjects are distributed along a hierarchic scale (the reproductibility coefficient being 0.89) from the choice of belonging to economic and linguistic Portuguese communities (closely correlated), to the choice of belonging to the intermarried Portuguese community, to the political Portuguese community, and ending on complete absorption into the French community.

---

[1] The percentage of variance accounted for by these axes may be considered as small (11.6 and 5.3 for the sample settled in France; 6.3 and 5.9 in Portugal). But the very large number of variables treated could hardly allow for the production of a highly structured pattern distribution.

184

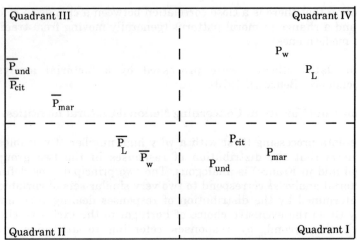

P: approval of belonging to Portuguese community; $\overline{P}$: denial of belonging to Portuguese community; w: economic community; L: linguistic community; mar: intermarried community; cit: political community; und: undefined community.

Figure 1. Factorial analysis of variables related to decisions of belonging for the sample settled in France (simplified presentation).

Table 1
Guttmann Scale Inferred from Figure 1 (simplified presentation)

Class I	Approval of belonging to economic and/or linguistic Portuguese community	P_W and/or P_L
Class II	Approval of belonging to intermarried Portuguese community	P_{mar}
Class III	Approval of belonging to political Portuguese community	P_{cit}
Class IV	Approval of belonging to undefined Portuguese community	P_{und}
Class V	Denial of belonging to any dimension of Portuguese community (exclusive belonging to French community)	$\overline{P}$

The responses of the sample settled in Portugal did not exhibit such a beautifully structured pattern. The diagram produced by the factorial analysis may, however, be divided into four quadrants (see Fig. 2), which can be characterized in the following terms (moving clockwise from the lower right quadrant):

Quadrant I. Variables and subjects representing priority given to local identity in regard to national identity

Quadrant II. Variables and subjects representing combination of national (Portuguese) identification, somewhat ambivalent, with the assessment of "modern values"

Quadrant III. Variables and subjects representing prospective combination between French and Portuguese identities (for instance, the plan to teach French in Portugal)

Quadrant IV. Variables and subjects representing combination between Portuguese identity and a cosmopolitan spirit (for instance, the denial of relevance of national identities in the area of love and marriage).

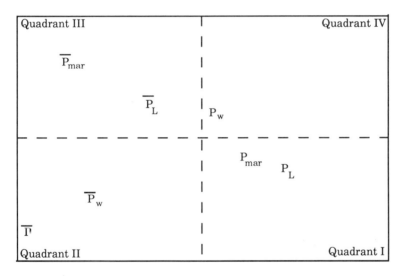

Figure 2. Factorial analysis of variables related to decisions of belonging for the sample settled in Portugal (simplified presentation).

4.3 However this cosmopolitan option is rather exceptional in both samples. It refers to a commonplace saying – that love has neither rule nor territory – which is popular in a part of the Guarda sample wishing to live without religious, moral or military obligations.

But as a whole, reference to a national group remains for a large majority a relevant matter of concern and choice.

4.4 However, especially in the sample settled in France, such a choice is commonly oriented towards a combination of loyalties (among the youths living in Pau or near Paris, only 7 out of 100 wish to belong exclusively to the Portuguese community, 20 out of 100 to the French community).

5. Self-Esteem and Combined Affiliation

This brings us to the question raised earlier: How do these people manage to combine self-esteem and valorization of group reference if membership is no longer exclusive and may correspond to very diverse forms of affiliation ?

5.1 Note first that the selection of traits considered as relevant for group differentiation is related to the orientation of the decision of belonging. In the sample settled in France, the responses to the question "What traits distinguish the French from the Portuguese the most" refers to moral virtues (thriftiness, earnestness) for subjects oriented towards exclusive belonging to Portugal, but to much more superficial traits (look, clothes) for subjects typical of the opposite class on the Guttman scale.

Such a result may be viewed as a confirmation of the experimental conclusions drawn by Lemaine, according to whom fields of comparison between groups are chosen according to strategies of optimization of self-esteem (Lemaine, 1974). One may however add to Lemaine's interpretation the hypothesis that such choices are also related to strategies of "social change": people resisting the possible change in identity place priority on deeply internalized values, people oriented towards such a change consider more superficial and therefore more mobile traits as differentially relevant.

5.2 Therefore, relevant frames or themes used for group comparisons are much more diverse than those commonly used in experimental studies. For members of a given group, they may vary according to their specific situations. For instance, for promoting their self-esteem, young Portuguese settled in France may use a comparison with Portuguese living in Portugal rather than with French (they commonly think that they are much more hard working). Is this an ingroup or outgroup comparison?

The group image appears to the built by cognitive strategies, depending on the subjects' degree of commitment to that image. The notion of "Portuguese mentality" means a completely different thing to a girl or boy living at Guarda and assuming her or his national membership positively and for a girl or boy living near Paris and sharing the same positive assumption: the former will oppose the moral virtues of his national fellows to the frivolity of the French, and the latter will attribute a high ability to adjust to his national fellows.

Some assumptions by experimental psychologists may help to interpret these data. Serino (1990) formulated her criticism of Tajfel's theory by saying that he "explored the deductive phase rather than the inductive steps of the process of comparison and categorization" (our translation). According to Rabbie and Horwitz (1988), " Belonging to the group is more important than likeness between members of ingroup and outgroup ".

But all these assumptions cannot account for the fact that considerable situational variations of categorization do not prevent people who are geographically and socially very distant from each other from thinking that they share the same basic membership.

The following interpretation is conceivable (Oriol, 1988). First, the conviction that some sort of a collective mentality does exist may be induced by the potential anticipation of expected solidarity and complicity rather than by a well defined prototypicality of the representations. Explanatory use of the implicit theory of personality may then be irrelevant.

Secondly, the shared behaviors aimed at the objectivization of marks of membership may be more important than the subjective valorization of such and such a psychological trait which is represented as collective. Our Portuguese subjects (especially those dedicated to remain so) had no trouble assuming their belonging to a people who suffers from a process of historical decay, provided they could state this membership in the practice of shared mourning, as is the case in fado songs. But it is difficult to submit statements about death to experimental validation...

More generally, we are led by our observations to think that attribution of personological traits (as commonly used in experimental designs) is neither exclusive nor even predominant in the comparative process of self-esteem production in intergroup relations. On the Guttman scale we mentioned earlier, differential items between ordinal classes refer to expected or wished for behavior (language practice, returning to home country, marrying a national fellow, ...). Attribution of traits does

188

not play such a differential role: as exposed earlier, one may wish to remain a loyal Portuguese in assuming both traditional attributes (such as earnestness, thriftiness) and modern ones (being individualistic, liking permissive education and behavior).

6. Conclusion

This leads us to contend that the theory of collective identity production suffers commonly in contemporary social psychology from a lack of complexity.

(1) Is it possible when in building such a theory to avoid taking into account the kind of symbolic resources which are used by the subjects when they define themselves? Is it not necessary to explore the schematic adjustment to variable situations along specific dimensions such as language, territory, history, culture, etc?

(2) To what extent is membership a mere product of cognitive psycho-sociological processes? Isn't it also, at least partially, a variable which conditions how cognitive processes function? Wouldn't it be relevant to apply the theory of commitment to such an interrogation ?

References

Benzécri, J.-P. (1973). *L'analyse des données: Vol. 2, L'analyse des correspondances.* Paris : Dunod.
Catani, M. (1983). L'identité et les choix relatifs aux systèmes de valeur. *Peuples Méditerranéens/Mediterranean Peoples*, No. 24, 117-126.
Codol, J.-P. (1975). On the so-called "superior conformity of the self " behavior: Twenty experimental investigations. *European Journal of Social Psychology, 5,* 457-501.
Lemaine, G. (1974). Social differentiation and social originality. *European Journal of Social Psychology, 4,* 12-17.
Oriol, M. (1988). Un processus paradoxal : la production dialectique d'une identité substantielle. *Sociologie du Sud-Est,* No. 55-58, 17-25.
Rabbie, J. M., & Horwitz M. (1988). Categories versus groups as explanatory concepts in intergroup relations. *European Journal of Social Psychology, 18,* 117-123.
Serino, C. (1990). La comparaison sociale et la structure des systèmes catégoriels : quelques réflexions sur la prototypicalité du soi. *Les Cahiers Internationaux de Psychologie Sociale, 2*(6), 73-96.
Tajfel, H. (Ed.) (1978). *Differentiation between social groups: Studies in the social psychology of intergroup relations.* London: Academic Press.

Tajfel, H. (1981). *Human groups and social categories.* Cambridge: Cambridge University Press.

Tajfel, H., Jahoda, G., Nemeth, C., Rim, Y., & Johnson, N. B. (1972). Devaluation by children of their own national or ethnic group: Two case studies. *British Journal of Social and Clinical Psychology, 11.* 235-243.

Tversky, A. (1977). Features of similarity. *Psychological Review, 84,* 327-352.

SOCIAL JUDGEABILITY AND MOTIVATION

THE INGROUP OVEREXCLUSION EFFECT

Jacques-Philippe Leyens, Vincent Yzerbyt, and Fanny Bellour
Catholic University of Louvain, Belgium

Assuredly, sociability is a search for a blend of similarity with, and differences from, others. As social beings, we cannot afford to be completely different from our fellows; as persons, however, we cannot endure to be totally similar to them (Leyens, 1983). Some societies will insist more on similarities, others on differences (Markus & Kitayama, 1991). The same principle will also manifest itself in the fact that some societies will value conformism more than others (Berry, 1967), or that behaviors will be explained by individual personality traits in some cultures and by social roles in other cultures (Miller, 1984; Cousins, 1989).

In twenty ingenious studies, Codol (1975) found that, in our occidental culture, we treasure differences more than similarities, although we consider both dimensions as essential (the PIP effect). This led him to regard the self as some kind of prototype.

Such a conception is fundamental for social psychology, and it is no wonder that it can be linked to other streams of research such as Tesser's self-evaluation maintenance model (1988), and Swann's concern for self-verification and self-promotion (1990). Serino (1988) has also applied Codol's paradigm to groups rather than individuals.

In this chapter, we would like to introduce still another line of research related to Codol's work. After all, Codol was interested in social perception, where the self is the privileged object, the point of reference from which similarities and differences are evaluated. The entire contemporary problem of social perception is the "fit" between categories and individual information (Higgins & Bargh, 1987; Leyens & Dardenne, in press; Schadron & Yzerbyt, 1991, in press). Whereas establishing an adequate fit has usually been considered similar to an intellectual problem-solving task involving only cognitive and motivational factors, we have insisted upon another dimension which we call social judgeability. By this we mean that social judgments also depend upon social rules and values which provide or do not provide the conditions under which one feels entitled to make a judgment. One aspect of social judgeability that is necessary to solve the problem of fit is the amount of information needed to express a judgment. While this amount may be objective, it may also be subjective, giving the impression that one is entitled to judge (Leyens, Yzerbyt, & Schadron, 1992; Schadron, 1991; Yzerbyt, 1990).

1. Prejudice and Accuracy in Social Perception: A Reinterpretation

As we hope to show, the amount of information needed to make a social judgment is linked to the perception of differences and similarities between ourselves and others, between our group and the other group. Our point of departure has been the classic research on the accuracy of anti-Semitic subjects in detecting Jewish faces. These studies are an upshot of the Second World War when some social psychologists wondered whether the success of informing was the consequence of anti-Semites being particularly good at detecting Jewish cues.

The paradigm of these studies consisted of presenting anti-Semitic as well as unprejudiced subjects with a set of pictures, usually half of them of Jews, and the other half representing Caucasian persons. The task of the subjects was to distribute these pictures into two piles, one Jewish and one non-Jewish. In general, it was shown that anti-Semitic subjects were better judges than unprejudiced participants in these experiments. In some cases, though, there were no differences between the two samples. More important for our concern is that, in almost all cases, anti-Semitic persons placed significantly more pictures in the Jewish pile than unprejudiced people did (Tajfel, 1969).

Allport and Kramer (1946; see also Lindzey & Rogolsky, 1950) reported an instance of a study showing both findings. Their students filled in a long questionnaire aimed at measuring prejudice. In addition, the authors confronted a subgroup of 223 subjects with twenty slides showing the photograph of a male college student. After a 15-second exposure, subjects were simply to tell whether the picture was of a Jew or non-Jew or whether they did not know. Unknown to the subjects, the pictures comprised an equal number of Jews and non-Jews. Also, the faces varied widely and the order of presentation was random. Results show that subjects with higher prejudice scores judged more faces to be Jewish than did subjects with lower scores. They were also better able to identify Jewish and non-Jewish faces than subjects with lower scores.

Carter (1948) questioned and greatly qualified Allport and Kramer's conclusions. This author distinguished between second-generation non-

Jewish Mediterraneans, non-Jewish North-Europeans, and European Jews and presented 15 slides of each group. Whereas half of the subjects were asked to tell which of the above three labels applied to each of the 45 pictures, the remaining subjects had to judge whether the picture was of a Jewish or a non-Jewish person. Her data indicated a weak relationship between the degree of prejudice and the number of slides classified as Jewish when a twofold classification was required. This relationship was not significant however when people were confronted with a threefold classification. More crucially, Carter (1948) found no evidence of higher accuracy for prejudiced as opposed to unprejudiced subjects. Subsequent work by Elliott and Wittenberg (1955) showed that persons high in anti-Semitism were more accurate only when the sample comprised a high proportion of Jewish photographs. These authors argued that the positive link between prejudice and accuracy may be the result of the tendency of prejudiced individuals to label more photographs as Jewish than do non-prejudiced persons.

In order to better estimate the impact of the response bias on recognition accuracy, Pulos and Spilka (1961) performed an analysis of covariance to eliminate the effect of the number of photographs identified as Jewish on the number of correct identifications of Jews. Their data revealed that the significant difference in accuracy between prejudiced and unprejudiced people existed even when the number of Jewish identifications of non-Jews was controlled. As pointed out by Himmelfarb (1966), however, Pulos and Spilka's (1961) data are not well suited for an analysis of covariance. Himmelfarb (1966) proposed to rely instead on experimental procedures to control for response bias. In his first study using the classic paradigm, Himmelfarb was able to replicate Allport and Kramer's findings. In his second experiment, subjects were confronted with a forced-choice presentation of the photographs. This time, the relationship between prejudice and accuracy vanished (for other experimental methods leading to similar conclusions, see Scodel & Austrin, 1957; for a study about recognition of Jewish and non-Jewish names, see Secord & Saumer, 1960).

To sum up, there are two competing explanations. One is derived from the New Look approach and attributes the differential accuracy results to perceptual vigilance (Bruner, Goodnow, & Austin, 1956). According to Allport and Kramer (1946, p. 37), "people prejudiced against any minority group are sensitized to the visible signs of identity of members of such group". In other words, prejudiced subjects are particularly vigilant in detecting the cues betraying the threatening group (Dorfman, Keeve, & Saslow, 1971). The second explanation refers to an artifact in the data: better accuracy is obtained by the prejudiced subjects because they simply put more pictures in the outgroup pile, thereby decreasing their chances to miss a Jew (Quanty, Keats, & Harkins, 1975). Our reinterpretation of these data is that the prejudiced subjects put a greater number of pictures in the Jewish pile than the unprejudiced individuals did because they needed more information before accepting the faces in their group. There is thus no peculiar vigilance against the outgroup but special caution in favor of the ingroup. Our hypothesis is therefore that, in case of confrontation with a threatening group, people need more information to accept a person in their ingroup than they need to put someone in an outgroup. We have called this tendency the overexclusion of the ingroup (Leyens & Yzerbyt, 1992).

Technically speaking, the ingroup overexclusion effect is rather simple to describe. It corresponds to people's tendency to reject ingroup members who are not totally in line with the requirements for ingroup membership. As far as ingroup membership is concerned, people thus would seem to be close to adopting a classic view of categories: any potential ingroup member must have more than a fair number of ingroup characteristics before acceptance takes place. Such a strategy runs counter to what is expected on the basis of the more recent approaches on inter- and intra-category relationships.

2. Protecting Social Identity

From an intergroup perspective, the effect is somewhat at odds with a simplistic interpretation of Social Identity Theory (SIT) which claims that a fundamental ethnocentric bias is at the heart of people's behaviors and evaluations (Wilder, 1981). Several predictions follow if one adopts this view in the context of decision making about group membership. Most relevant for the present purpose is that people should tend to accept as a group member a target person who displays positive characteristics.

In our opinion, this simple-minded view of SIT is alien to the more dynamic perspective about social identity proposed by Tajfel (1978) and his co-workers (Turner, 1978). People seem able stand outgroup superiority, and recent work by Mummendey and her colleagues (Mummendey & Schreiber, 1983; Mummendey & Simon, 1989) illustrates how ingroup members go as far as displaying outgroup favoritism when the dimensions at stake are irrelevant for the ingroup identity.

Along the same lines, we carried out a research program on the so-called "black sheep effect" (Marques, Yzerbyt, & Leyens, 1988; Marques & Yzerbyt, 1988). Black sheeps are undesirable ingroup members. Merely because of their membership, black sheeps should benefit from ingroup bias, at least if this bias applies blindly. But as Marques (1990, p. 133) put it, "One way to protect social identity may be by developing and promulgating negative attitudes towards ingroup members seen to deviate from ingroup normative standards. Such deviants can, after all, be considered to represent a threat to positive ingroup distinctiveness".

As we see it, a great many strategies aiming at identity maintenance and intergroup discrimination are non-obvious, and future work on social identity will most likely report on them at an increasing rate (Haslam, McGarty, Oakes, & Turner, 1992). The ingroup overexclusion effect is one of these strategies. When people have to make a decision about group membership, they will be quite cautious in attributing the ingroup label. In our opinion, a study by Pettigrew, Allport, and Barnett (1958) can easily be interpreted along these lines.

These authors worked in South Africa with five samples of subjects: Afrikaners, English-speaking Europeans, Mulattoes, Indians, and Black Africans. Each subject was exposed to a brief (2 sec.) stereoscopic presentation of 2 racial photographs, with all possible combinations for each eye. Subjects had to tell which race they had seen; there were 4 judgments per subject and per combination. The authors reported that the White South Africans, especially the Afrikaners, tended to see the racially mixed presentations as either pure European or full-blooded African; they did so more than the other races did. When inspecting their data with our hypothesis in mind, other and more pronounced findings are apparent. We will restrict our report to the data pertaining to the Whites and the Indians because these persons are less prone to consider social mobility in terms of their race and therefore their misidentifications in the judgments of races are less likely to be due to social mobility strategies (Tajfel & Turner, 1986; Clark & Clark, 1947).

Whereas 100% of the Afrikaners and 93% of the English-speaking Whites saw a European when faced with 2 European faces, 87.5% of the Indians saw an Indian when there were 2 Indian faces. Also, Whites and Indians were equally accurate for other races. The results were quite different when the faces were racially mixed: in these cases, 40% of the Afrikaners and 37% of the English-speaking Whites saw a European while 63% of the Indians saw someone of their own race. In other words, members of the White minority less easily saw someone of their own race than do the Indians when the stimuli were ambiguous; this was not the case when the stimuli were clearly recognizable. If we consider only the mixture of European-Indian faces, the percentages of recognition of one's race were 54, 46, and 74 for the Afrikaners, the English-speaking Whites, and the Indians, respectively. Obviously, these results are more in line with an ingroup overexclusion hypothesis than with a perceptual vigilance hypothesis, provided that the importance of race is of more concern for the Whites than for the Indians. Pettigrew, Allport, and Barnett (1958) report no data in support of the last assumption but it is clearly implicit in their paper.

The difference between White and Indian people in Pettigrew, Allport, and Barnett's (1958) study takes on even more significance in the light of the recent work by Zebrowitz (1991). This author presented faces of U.S. White, U.S. Black, and Korean students to subjects from the three racial groups and found that target persons were rated similarly on various personality traits both by subjects of their own and of another race and that subjects equally differentiated targets of their own and of another race.

Zebrowitz' (1991) findings run counter to the belief, widely spread both among lay people and scholars, that members of other race groups are quite difficult to distinguish one from another. The famous adage "They all look alike" encountered in folk psychology indeed finds substantial support in social psychology research (for a review, see Shapiro & Penrod, 1986). Above and beyond facial recognition, social judgment research indicates that outgroup members are perceived to be more homogeneous than ingroup members (for a review, see Linville, Salovey, & Fischer, 1986). Still, according to Zebrowitz (1991, p. 4), perceivers will detect similarities and differences in the appearance of members of another race when judgments take place in a context fostering attention to individual targets. In other words, when people are motivated to process information in terms of the unique features of the persons rather than in terms of their group membership, outgroup homogeneity will not be obtained (Fiske & Neuberg, 1990; Judd & Park, 1988).

Clearly, then, the ability to discriminate other people's faces in particular and other people's personality characteristics in general, especially when confronted with a target from another social category, seems to depend on motivational factors more than was previously suspected. This means that the difference observed by Pettigrew, Allport, and Barnett (1958) between White and Indian subjects may well be motivational in nature. Whites may have had particular reasons that led them to avoid identifying the mixed-race stimuli as their own race targets.

Along these lines, Jarymowicz (1991) reports a study which is relevant for our purpose. In that experiment, Polish subjects who thought of themselves in terms of categories (i.e. they did not make a strong distinction between "I" and "WE") believed they could more easily identify members of clearly distinct groups such as Italians and Gypsies than did subjects who considered themselves as unique persons. The former more than the latter also pinpointed external features (e.g. physical appearance) as cues for identifying the so-called distinctive groups. In other words, those people who view themselves as specific individuals do the same with members of other groups and are unsure that they could pick them out; those people who reason in terms of social categories, in contrast, see themselves as better able to detect members of other social categories, and that cues to do so are available.

3. Two Tests of the Ingroup Overexclusion Effect

Up to now, we have restricted ourselves to a reinterpretation of existing data. In order to more precisely test their ingroup overexclusion hypothesis, Leyens and Yzerbyt (1992) took advantage of the linguistic situation in Belgium. They asked French-speaking Belgians (called Walloons)[1] to provide them with positive and negative stereotypical personality traits for Walloons and for Flemish people. Those traits which clearly identified a community were discarded (e.g. "flamingant"). A total of 53 traits remained. Pilot work revealed that traits in each valence (positive vs. negative) -by-group (Walloon vs. Flemish) combination were equally polarized. The experiment itself built upon earlier work by Yzerbyt and Leyens (1991; Fiske, 1980; Peeters & Czapinski, 1990; Skowronski & Carlston, 1989) and was presented as a study about the ability to make decisions about linguistic belongingness on the basis of a minimal amount of information about personality traits. Walloon subjects were warned that they would see one trait at a time, and that there was a maximum of 10 traits per profile, but they were encouraged to decide as soon as possible whether the target, described by the traits, was a Walloon. Each subject was confronted with 4 profiles for each of the four cells of the design: positive Walloon, negative Walloon, positive Flemish, negative Flemish. Three types of data were recorded: the type of decision, the confidence in the decision and the number of items necessary to make the decision.

As one could easily imagine, most rejections occurred for the negative Flemish and the least for the positive Walloons. These data concur with the classical findings of ingroup favoritism (Brewer, 1979; Hogg & Abrams, 1988; Mullen, Brown, & Smith, 1992; Turner, Hogg, Oakes, Reicher, & Wetherell, 1987). Interestingly, the subjects also tended to report less often that the target was a Walloon than a Flemish. Finally, the information needed to make a decision was influenced by both its positivity and its relation to the linguistic groups. More information was asked when the traits were positive than negative, and when they concerned Walloon targets than when they supposedly described Flemish persons. In other words, more information was necessary for the positive ingrouper. This result is completely consistent with our hypothesis.

---

[1] Except for a minority of German speakers, Belgium is especially made up of two communities; one speaks Flemish and the other one, French. Most of this second community is composed of Walloons who live in the South.

Linville and her collaborators defended the idea that people have a more complex representation of their ingroup than of the outgroup (Linville, 1982; Linville & Jones, 1980). According to Linville, we are more familiar with individuals in our own group than with members of other groups and therefore we should have a more fine-grained, complex view of the former than the latter. If the stereotypes that we gathered reflect a difference in complexity, they could explain why we needed more information for the ingroup. Fortunately, this was not the case; a factorial correspondence analysis was conducted on the material and did not show a difference between the linguistic communities.

Now, there are two other related problems with the above study. Remember that we asked our Walloon subjects to decide whether the target was a Walloon or not. We did not ask Flemish subjects to do the same nor did we ask our Walloon subjects to decide whether the targets were Flemish. One way to interpret our data has nothing to do with group relationships and is strictly linked to the nature of the information. Indeed, to the extent that subjects were asked whether the targets were Walloons, the Walloon targets confirmed the hypothesis whereas the Flemish targets disconfirmed that hypothesis. One could then say that ingroup overexclusion is simply due to the positivity and confirming status of the information, two variables which have been shown to have less informational weight (Yzerbyt & Leyens, 1991).

One way to test that hypothesis with the same paradigm would have been to ask the Walloon subjects whether the targets were Flemish. Had we still obtained the same results, one could have argued that the confirming status of the information was not responsible for the effect. However, we had good reasons to believe that such a manipulation would have been misleading for a test of the confirming status of the information, given that people tend to take their ingroup (or themselves) as the reference point (Codol, 1987): in our situation, to be Flemish is not to be a Walloon. Thus, to change the wording of the question would not have been a fair test of the criticism.

Another way to verify the specific group status – motivational status – of the information would have been to measure the anti-Flemish feelings of our subjects. If there is an exclusion of the ingroup because of the threatening outgroup, the effect should manifest itself more among anti-Flemish than among unprejudiced subjects. Unfortunately, we did not have those data. The only hint in that direction is that there was a correlation between rejecting a negative Flemish and accepting a positive Walloon.

To answer these criticisms, we planned another experiment where we again took advantage of the Belgian situation. We were even inspired by a historical event in the Flemish tradition. In the Middle Ages, the

Flemish rebelled against the French, and one morning in Bruges, they tried to spot the French spies by asking every unknown person to pronounce the Flemish words: Schild en Vriend. Those who did not succeed in pronouncing correctly were killed by receiving a "goeddendag" blow.[2]

For this experiment, we taped easy or difficult sentences read in French or in Flemish by Walloon and Flemish subjects. The tapes were played with some background noise to real Walloon and Flemish subjects, whose feelings toward the other linguistic community had been measured. The main dependent variables were the decisions and the time taken to express the decision for each sentence. Half of the subjects received the instructions to decide whether the speaker was a Walloon; the other half had to decide whether these same speakers were Flemish.

Only part of the data (for the Walloon subjects) are available at this moment, but they already confirm some of the previous findings and answer some of the criticisms. The Walloon judges showed the same results for the Flemish targets, independently of the fact that they read French or Flemish sentences, and independently of the direction of the question. They were correct about 8.5 times out of 10. This did not occur for the ingroup targets: the judges were somewhat more correct for the Walloons who pronounced French sentences but they were less correct for the Flemish sentences read by Walloons. This is true regardless of the wording of the question. These data do not support a simple confirmation hypothesis. Moreover, the time to decide for an ingrouper who speaks another language was much longer than in the other conditions which did not differ from each other. In sum, when the stimulus is difficult – ambiguous – for the ingroup, but not for the outgroup, subjects need more time to decide and make more "errors", that is, reject members of the ingroup.

As can be seen, people confronted with a decision about group membership behave more carefully when the candidate is a potential ingroup member than when the target is (unknown to the judges) a member of the outgroup. The ingroup overexclusion hypothesis thus seems quite well supported. People are indeed more concerned with falsely labeling a person as an ingroup member than with correctly identifying outgroup members.

---

[2] "Goeden dag" meant "good morning": this is what your head implied when hit by this weapon.

4. Differences Weigh more than Similarities

We also applied the information-search paradigm to some questions which are more precisely related to Codol's work. If differences are indeed valued more than similarities, people should need more information to make a decision when the comparison target looks similar than when the comparison target seems dissimilar. We designed an experiment to address this specific issue.

The experiment comprised two distinct parts. In the first part, subjects were taken into the laboratory one at a time and presented with the general goal of the experiment which allegedly was to uncover how well traits can help define people from certain age groups. The task of the subjects was simply to indicate which traits were important to them, that is, which traits made it possible to know quite a bit about the kind of person they were. Each of the 66 traits appeared on a computer screen and subjects were to push one of two keys depending on whether or not they thought the trait was important to them and made it possible to describe themselves. A third key was available to indicate that subjects were not really able to tell whether the trait defined themselves or not. This possibility of giving an intermediate answer was added for three reasons. First, some traits are neither important in describing subjects nor really regarded as totally alien to what they are. Potentially, every trait can be understood as providing some information relevant to the description of a person. The possibility of avoiding a clear-cut answer on ambiguous traits was designed to put subjects more at ease with their decisions for important or self- descriptive and non-important or non-self-descriptive traits. Secondly, and despite heavy pretest work, some traits were simply not very well understood by a few subjects and the best way out of this problem was to keep these traits out of the sets aimed at suggesting similarity or dissimilarity. Finally, this setup allowed us to construct a few ambiguous sets of traits thereby increasing the realism during the second part of the experiment.

A computer program was designed to use the subjects answers to the 66 traits in order to define a series of 15 personality profiles. Traits which had been deemed self-descriptive and important were used to create 6 "similar" profiles of 10 traits each. Traits which were seen as non-self-descriptive served to prepare 6 "dissimilar" profiles of 10 traits each. Finally, the ambiguous traits were used to set up 3 profiles of 10 traits each. Interestingly, the procedure allowed us to build upon each subject's answers in order to prepare a unique series of profiles.

In the second part of the experiment, subjects were warned that the computer screen would display the personality profiles of 15 people, one trait at a time, up to a maximum of 10 traits per profile. Depending on the condition, their task was to indicate as soon as possible but with a high degree of confidence whether they were similar or not to the target person versus whether the target person was similar or not to them. This difference in the task was introduced in the light of the fact that Codol repeatedly found asymmetry in judgments of difference and similarity depending on the point of reference. For each of the first 9 traits of a given profile, subjects could either make a decision or ask for further information, i.e. another trait. Upon presentation of the last trait, a decision was forced to respond. Leaving the ambiguous profiles aside, each subject provided three dependent measures for each of the 12 experimental profiles: the final decision of similarity or dissimilarity, the number of traits used to make a decision, and the level of confidence. Because the six similar profiles on the one hand and the six dissimilar profiles on the other hand were but replications of each other, their results were averaged.

Before the other dependent variables are examined, it is crucial to make sure that our subjects made their decision with the same level of confidence in the various experimental conditions. This is indeed what happened. Neither the point of reference used in the question displayed on the screen nor the similarity of the target influenced directly (or via an interaction) the level of confidence expressed by the subjects. In general, our subjects displayed a very high degree of confidence, $M = 7.16$. This allowed us to proceed to the analysis of the decisions and the number of traits requested by our subjects.

As far as the decisions are concerned, we predicted that subjects would discard dissimilar targets while retaining similar targets. The expected difference between the two kinds of targets came out highly significant, as our subjects rejected an average of 88% of the dissimilar targets while they accepted an average of 95% of the similar targets, $F(1,27) = 133.33, p < .0001$.

The central prediction of our experiment was that subjects would make decisions on the basis of a larger number of traits if a profile tended to be similar to the subject than if the profile depicted a dissimilar target. Our data provide strong support for this conjecture. As it turned out, subjects requested as much as 4.04 traits to make a decision about a similar target while they only needed an average of 3.14 traits when the target was dissimilar, $F(1,27) = 6.67, p < .02$.

Interestingly, the interaction did not come out significant, $F(1,27) < 1$. In other words, the wording of the question did not make a difference, as it did not in the ingroup overexclusion experiments. Obviously, Codol's paradigm and ours tap different processes. It remains that we always asked a question concerning similarity, and that subjects needed more information when they were the point of reference ($M = 3.83$) than when the target served as the reference (M = 3.45). This latter result is completely in line with Codol's findings.

As a whole, these results are consistent with the idea that information about differences is valued more than information about similarities (Leyens, 1990). As a consequence, people need less information to make a decision about others and themselves when the two tend to differ than when there is a similarity. Our data reveal that this phenomenon took place despite the fact that people felt equally confident about their decisions in these two situations. A most important feature of the above experiment is that each subject was confronted to a unique set of targets. This set was prepared on the basis of self-descriptive information provided by each subject a couple of minutes earlier.

5. Conclusions

In this chapter, we have attempted to show the importance of the social judgeability approach to stereotypes. Forming an impression of persons is not only a question of matching most adequately categorical and individual information; it is also a matter of being entitled to judge. In other words, there are social rules which decide whether or not the judges fulfill the conditions to make a judgment. Elsewhere (Leyens, Yzerbyt, & Schadron, 1992), we have shown that judgeability may be influenced by meta-informational cues such as the illusion of being informed or the rhetorical structure of the information. Here, we have focused upon the link between social judgeability and motivation.

There are conditions when judges are reluctant to express a judgment on the basis of the information received. This is for instance the case when judges and targets are outcome-dependent and when the information is inconsistent with expectations (Fiske & Neuberg, 1990). It is also the case when the decision may jeopardize the integrity of the group of membership; in the latter case, the ingroup is considered less judgeable than the outgroup and more information is needed before a decision is made.

We have reviewed the classical literature on prejudice and accuracy of perception by offering a new interpretation of these data. We defended the idea that, far from being an artifact, these results are better understood as an exclusion from the ingroup in case of doubt than as some special vigilance against the outgroup. This may have little to do with prejudice against other people, but is linked to the value attached to some targets which renders them less easily judgeable. Finally, we have applied this reasoning in the interpersonal domain and have shown that, in a culture which values differences more than similarities, targets dissimilar to the judges are more judgeable than similar targets, and this

202

happens despite the fact that the information is considered as equally diagnostic in both cases.

References

Allport, G. W., & Kramer, B. M. (1946). Some roots of prejudice. *Journal of Psychology, 22*, 9-39.

Berry, J. W. (1967). Independence and conformity in subsistence-level societies. *Journal of Personality and Social Psychology, 7*, 415-418.

Brewer, M. B. (1979). Ingroup bias and the minimal group paradigm: A cognitive-motivational analysis. *Psychological Bulletin, 86*, 307-324.

Bruner, J. S., Goodnow, J. J., & Austin, G. A. (1956). *A study of thinking.* New York: Wiley.

Carter, L. F. (1948). The identification of "racial membership". *Journal of Abnormal and Social Psychology, 43*, 279-286.

Clark, K. B., & Clark, M. P. (1947). Racial identification and preference in Negro children. In T. Newcomb & E. L. Hartley (Eds.), *Readings in social psychology* (pp. 169-178). New York: Holt.

Codol, J.-P. (1975). On the so-called "superior conformity of the self" behavior: Twenty experimental investigations. *European Journal of Social Psychology, 5*, 457-501.

Codol, J.-P. (1987). Comparability and incomparability between oneself and others: Means of differentiation and comparison reference points. *Cahiers de Psychologie Cognitive/European Bulletin of Cognitive Psychology, 7*, 87-105.

Cousins, S. (1989). Culture and selfhood in Japan and the U.S. *Journal of Personality and Social Psychology, 56*, 124-131.

Dorfman, D. D., Keeve, S., & Saslow, C. (1971). Ethnic identification: A signal detection analysis. *Journal of Personality and Social Psychology, 18*, 373-379.

Elliott, D. N., & Wittenberg, B. H. (1955). Accuracy of identification of Jewish and non-Jewish photographs. *Journal of Abnormal and Social Psychology, 51*, 339-341.

Fiske, S. T. (1980). Attention and weight in person perception: The impact of negative and extreme behavior. *Journal of Personality and Social Psychology, 38*, 889-906.

Fiske, S. T., & Neuberg, S. L. (1990). A continuum of impression formation, from category-based to individuating processes: Influences of information and motivation on attention and interpretation. In M. P. Zanna (Ed.), *Advances in experimental social psychology* (Vol. 23, pp. 1-74). New York: Academic Press.

Haslam, S. A., McGarty, C., Oakes, P. J., & Turner, J. C. (1992). *Social comparative context and illusory correlation: Testing between ingroup bias and social identity models of stereotype change.* Unpublished manuscript, Australian National University, Canberra.

Higgins, E. T., & Bargh, J. A. (1987). Social cognition and social perception. *Annual Review of Psychology, 38,* 369-425.

Himmelfarb, S. (1961). Studies in the perception of ethnic group members: I. Accuracy, response bias, and anti-semitism. *Journal of Personality and Social Psychology, 4,* 347-355.

Hogg, M. A., & Abrams, D. (1988). *Social identification: A social psychology of intergroup relations and group processes.* London: Routledge.

Jarymowicz, M. (1991, September). *The self/we schemata and social categorization effects.* Paper presented at the small group meeting of the European Association of Experimental Social Psychology on Changing Stereotypes, Paris.

Judd, C. M., & Park, B. (1988). Out-group homogeneity: Judgments of variability at the individual and group levels. *Journal of Personality and Social Psychology, 54,* 778-788.

Leyens, J.-P. (1983). *Sommes-nous tous des psychologues? Approche psychosociale des théories implicites de la personnalité.* Bruxelles: Mardaga.

Leyens, J.-P. (1990). Jean-Paul Codol's approach to social psychology. When *social* cognition resembles social *cognition* more than social *cognition* resembles *social* cognition. *Revue Internationale de Psychologie Sociale, 3,* 253-272.

Leyens, J.-P. & Dardenne, D. (in press). Le jugement social. In M. Richelle, J. Requin & M. Robert (Eds.), *Traité de psychologie expérimentale.* Paris : Presses Universitaires de France.

Leyens, J.-P., & Schadron, G. (1980). Porque discriminam mais os grupos que os individuos? Categoriza o ou pretexto? *Psicologia, 1,* 161-168.

Leyens, J.-P., & Yzerbyt, V. Y. (1992). The ingroup overexclusion effect: Impact of valence and confirmation on stereotypical information search. *European Journal of Social Psychology, 22,* 549-569.

Leyens, J.-P., Yzerbyt, V. Y., & Schadron, G. (1992). A social judgeability approach to stereotypes. In W. Stroebe & M. Hewstone (Eds.), *European Review of Social Psychology* (Vol. 3, pp. 91-120). New York: Wiley.

Lindzey, G., & Rogolsky, S. (1950). Prejudice and identification of minority group membership. *Journal of Abnormal and Social Psychology, 45,* 37-53.

Linville, P. W. (1982). The complexity-extremity effect and age-based stereotyping. *Journal of Personality and Social Psychology, 42,* 193-211.

Linville, P. W., & Jones, E. E. (1980). Polarized appraisals of out-group members. *Journal of Personality and Social Psychology, 38,* 689-703.

Linville, P. W., Salovey, P., & Fischer, G. W. (1986). Stereotyping and perceived distributions of social characteristics: An application to ingroup-outgroup perception. In J. F. Dovidio & S. L. Gaertner (Eds.), *Prejudice, discrimination, and racism* (pp. 165-208). Orlando, FL: Academic Press.

Markus, H., & Kitayama, S. (1991). Culture and the self: Implications for cognition, emotion, and motivation. *Psychological Review, 98,* 224-253.

Marques, J. M. (1990). The black sheep effect: Out-group homogeneity in social comparison settings. In D. Abrams & M.A. Hogg (Eds.), *Social identity theory: Constructive and critical advances.* London: Harvester-Wheatsheaf.

Marques, J. M., & Yzerbyt, V. Y. (1988). The black sheep effect: Judgmental extremity towards ingroup members in inter- and intra-group situations. *European Journal of Social Psychology, 18,* 287-292.

Marques, J. M., Yzerbyt, V. Y., & Leyens, J.-Ph. (1988). The "black sheep effect": Extremity of judgments towards ingroup members as a function of group identification. *European Journal of Social Psychology, 18,* 1-16.

Miller, J. G. (1984). Culture and the development of everyday social explanation. *Journal of Personality and Social Psychology, 46,* 961-978.

Mullen, B., Brown, R., & Smith, C. (1992). Ingroup bias as a function of salience, relevance, and status: An integration. *European Journal of Social Psychology, 22,* 103-122.

Mummendey, A., & Schreiber, H. J. (1983). Better or just different? Positive social identity by discrimination against or differentiation from outgroups. *European Journal of Social Psychology, 13,* 389-397.

Mummendey, A., & Simon, B. (1989). Better or just different? III: The impact of comparison dimension and relative ingroup size upon intergroup discrimination. *European Journal of Social Psychology, 29,* 1-16.

Peeters, G., & Czapinski, J. (1990). Positive-negative asymmetry in evaluations: The distinction between affective and informational negativity effects. In W. Stroebe & M. Hewstone (Eds.), *European Review of Social Psychology* (Vol. 1, pp. 33-60). New York: Wiley.

Pettigrew, T. F., Allport, G. W., & Barnett, E. O. (1958). Binocular resolution and perception of race in South Africa. *British Journal of Psychology, 49,* 265-278.

Quanty, M. B., Keats, J. A., & Harkins, S. G. (1975). Prejudice and criteria for identification of ethnic photographs. *Journal of Personality and Social Psychology, 32,* 449-454.

Schadron, G. (1991). *L'impact des stéréotypes sur le jugement social: l'approche de la jugeabilité sociale.* Unpublished doctoral thesis, Université Catholique de Louvain, Louvain-la-Neuve, Belgium.

Schadron, G., & Yzerbyt, V. Y. (1991). Social judgeability: Another framework for the study of social inference. *Cahiers de Psychologie Cognitive / European Bulletin of Cognitive Psychology, 11,* 229-258.

Schadron, G. & Yzerbyt, V. Y. (in press). Les stéréotypes et l'approche de la jugeabilité sociale: un impact des stéréotypes sur le jugement indépendant de leur contenu. In J.-L. Beauvois, R. V. Joule & J.-M. Monteil (Eds.), *Perspectives cognitives et conduites sociales* (Vol. 4). Cousset : DelVal.

Scodel, A., & Austrin, H. (1956). The perception of Jewish photographs by non-Jews and Jews. *Journal of Abnormal and Social Psychology, 54,* 278-280.

Secord, P. F., & Saumer, E. (1960). Identifying Jewish names: Does prejudice increase accuracy? *Journal of Abnormal and Social Psychology, 61,* 144-145.

Serino, C. (1988). Stratégies et structure de la comparaison sociale: quelques aspects de l'asymétrie Soi/Autrui dans les relations entre groupes. *Cahiers de Psychologie Cognitive / European Bulletin of Cognitive Psychology, 8,* 627-648.

Shapiro, P. N., & Penrod, S. (1986). Meta-analysis of facial identification studies. *Psychological Bulletin, 100,* 139-156.

Skowronski, J. J., & Carlston, D. E. (1989). Negativity and extremity biases in impression formation: A review of explanations. *Psychological Bulletin, 105,* 131-142.

Swann, W. B. (1990). To be known or to be adored? The interplay of self-enhancement and self-verification. In R. M. Sorrentino & E. T. Higgins (Eds.), *Handbook of motivation and cognition: Foundations of social behavior* (Vol. 2, pp. 408-448). New York: Guilford.

Tajfel, H. (1969). Social and cultural factors in perception. In G. Lindzey & E. Aronson (Eds.), *Handbook of social psychology* (Vol. 3) (2nd ed.). Reading, MA: Addison-Wesley.

Tajfel, H. (Ed.) (1978). *Differentiation between social groups: Studies in the social psychology of intergroup relations.* London: Academic Press.

Tajfel, H., Billig, M., Bundy, R. P., & Flament, C. (1971). Social categorization and intergroup behaviour. *European Journal of Social Psychology, 1,* 149-177.

Tajfel, H., & Turner, J. C. (1986). The social identity theory of intergroup behaviour. In S. Worchel & W. G. Austin (Eds.), *Psychology of intergroup relations* (pp. 7-24). Chicago: Nelson-Hall.

Tesser, A. B. (1988). Toward a self-evaluation maintenance model of social behavior. In L. Berkowitz (Ed.), *Advances in experimental social psychology* (Vol. 21, pp. 181-227). New York: Academic Press.

Turner, J. C. (1978). Social comparison, similarity and ingroup favouritism. In H. Tajfel (Ed.), *Differentiation between social groups: Studies in the social psychology of intergroup relations.* London: Academic Press.

Turner, J. C., Hogg, M. A., Oakes, P. J., Reicher, S. D., & Wetherell, M. S. (1987). *Rediscovering the social group: A self-categorization theory.* Oxford: Basil Blackwell.

Wilder D. A. (1981). Perceiving persons as a group: Categorization and intergroup relations. In D. L. Hamilton (Ed.), *Cognitive processes in stereotyping and intergroup behavior* (pp. 213-257). Hillsdale, NJ: Erlbaum.

Yzerbyt, V. Y. (1990). *De l'exploitation des informations dans la formation d'impression : vers un modèle de jugeabilité sociale.* Unpublished doctoral thesis, Université Catholique de Louvain, Louvain-la-Neuve, Belgium.

Yzerbyt, V. Y., & Leyens, J.-P. (1991). Requesting information to form an impression: The influence of valence and confirmatory status. *Journal of Experimental Social Psychology, 27,* 337-356.

Zebrowitz, L. A. (1991, September). *Differentiating same versus other race individuals.* Paper presented at the small group meeting of the European Association of Experimental Social Psychology on Changing Stereotypes, Paris.

PART THREE

QUESTIONING

THE SOCIAL COGNITION APPROACH

INTRODUCTION

TOWARDS A SOCIAL PSYCHOLOGY OF COGNITION?

Jean-Marc Monteil

Blaise Pascal University, Clermont-Ferrand, France

The redefinition or recategorization of objects and issues previously considered well established or well understood often stimulates new research or revitalizes a field of study. Subsequent changes in the meaning of objects are likely to have deep and lasting repercussions on any discipline. Such changes may reduce or extend the field of study, highlight neglected objects, introduce new perspectives, or alter prevailing theoretical conceptions. A process of this type has been at the root of some of the most extensive alterations in several areas of social psychology within the past fifty years. Such a renewal first took place at the end of the sixties and beginning of the seventies when Heider's original work (1958) gave birth to the concept of attribution. Researchers then began to look at how people in their daily lives assign causality to their own behavior, to the behavior of others, and to impersonal events which occur in their environment. Once stated, this problem generated a great deal of research.

With the emergence of social cognition at the end of the seventies, the objects studied in social psychology underwent a new transformation. The quest then became to understand how people perceive the world and the social relationships assumed to be its foundation. With this trend (see Higgins & Bargh, 1987; Sherman, Judd, & Park, 1989; Schneider, 1991), mainly derived from the theories and research paradigms of cognitive psychology, the question of attribution became just another issue in the field of social cognition. Supported by the metaphor of information processing, the popularity of this trend was to some extent a reflection of the growing influence of cognitive psychology. Social psychologists began to direct their research activity towards new objects: encoding, organization, storage, recall, and recognition of social information. These new directions raised issues that required the development of more rigorous and more complex methodologies which could help provide insight into more subtle cognitive processes and mechanisms.

The social psychology that began in the forties – at least its experimental end – has a cognitive orientation. Asch's early work on impression formation is still being quoted. Despite this past, the social cognition trend in some sense "redefined" the questions faced by social psychologists by drawing their attention to the work done in cognitive psychology. However, this increasing preoccupation with intrapsychological processes became (and probably still is) the basis of some exceedingly vivid controversies about the nature of social cognition. Although some social psychologists like Simon (1976) see no substantial difference between cognition and social cognition, others like Zajonc (1980) clearly differentiate the two. The former consider every cognitive phenomenon to be governed by the same general process. The latter think that the characteristics of human beings, both as objects of knowledge and "knowing" subjects, make social cognition and perception qualitatively distinct from the cognition and perception of inanimate objects.

The social cognition trend has been criticized in many other respects, including its immoderate use of information processing theory, its neglect of affect, motivation, and other social practices, and its failure to consider the context in which cognitive phenomena take place (social interactions, group membership, norms and values, etc.). In short, the matter is still hotly debated. But the debate is largely fruitless, that is why I shall not get involved in a confrontation of arguments of this kind. I wish instead to defend a point of view which neither integrates nor differentiates cognition and social cognition. I would now like to put forward certain reflections which will hopefully launch a debate in a less conventional area of social psychology.

In my opinion, the problem is not knowing whether the structure and content of the knowledge involved in information processing depend on the social or non-social nature of that information. The question is not one of choosing between individual cognition and collective cognition, i.e., between individual knowledge structures and content, and collective or shared knowledge structures and content. Rather, our first objective should be to describe and understand how individuals construct their cognitions through interaction with the environment, and what mechanisms and skills they use to construct this cognitive universe. At this functional level, the distinction between cognition and social cognition is not very meaningful. Our second objective should then be to describe and understand how the products of that cognitive universe are exchanged and shared, i.e., how they are "socialized" and act in return upon the individual cognitive apparatus, via some kind of social constructivism. At this level also, the preceding distinction is somewhat meaningless. However, the social psychology of cognition can find the bases for its existence in the conjunction of these two objectives.

Indeed, human cognition has a highly specific characteristic, namely, it occurs in a social and cultural context defined by the social situations individuals experience. The ambition of scientific psychology must necessarily be in keeping with the need to comprehend and explain human behavior. Consequently, it must take into consideration the status and other social positions of individuals in order to apprehend them as "socially inserted" beings. What does social insertion mean? In my mind, it means that a social position or condition has become dynamic by means of a modification in the interaction place or situation of the subject. This now-dynamic position or social state (i.e. which has been transformed into a social insertion) becomes a psychological event or episode. As such it is encoded and stored in memory and later mobilized, should the conditions for its activation arise.

The salience of a social insertion varies, depending not only on the structure and features of the situation in which it takes place, but also on the events or sequence of events it may activate in long term memory. In short, conceiving of humans as socially inserted beings means understanding them as historical individuals, i.e. as persons endowed with memory. But the content of human memory does not result only from the processing of the intrinsic properties of objects, whether those objects are social or not. They are first and foremost the products of the relationships subjects have with objects, which in turn depend on their social insertions. In other words, the human cognitive universe is a reflection of the processing and integration of an environment whose properties individuals store together with the significations which ensue from the nature of their social insertions.

If social psychology is to participate in the study of the human cognitive system, then it must deal with a socially inserted one. The study of cognition cannot be envisaged without taking stock of the significations upon which cognitive processes are based and the places in which they occur. These places are not to be taken as physical locations, but as psychological spaces through which individuals experience their social insertions in a human community. Accordingly, social comparison, socio-categorical memberships, interpersonal and intergroup confrontations ..., all are melting pots of these experiences.

1. Which Object for a Social Psychology of Cognition?

No matter how scientific psychology approaches the study of knowledge, whether through the processes allowing its construction or through those involved in its application, the prevailing theoretical paradigm is still that of cognitive psychology. As in every scientific procedure, the objective is to interrelate theoretical models and empirical facts. This dialectic is expressed through the confrontation of two approaches. The first, essentially a modelling approach, shares a common goal with artificial intelligence, namely, the simulation of behaviors of varying complexity. The second, an experimental approach, seeks to validate its hypotheses through empiricism. I shall not discuss the validity of these methodological and theoretical orientations. Both are essential and fruitful, and provide insight into human mental activity. And both state the problem of the acquisition, construction, and use of knowledge in the following terms. On the one hand, we have a subject with allegedly universal cognitive properties, and on the other hand, we have an object endowed with intrinsic properties. The subject is assumed to apply these universal properties to the intrinsic properties of the object. The research procedure consists of setting up, either by simulation or by experimentation, the necessary conditions for observing the subject's implementation of the cognitive properties used to process the object. The object may be a person, a physical object, or a problem to solve. In some cases it is presented in various contexts in order to test for differences in the way the processing is done by the subject. Admittedly in such paradigms, the social situation is at best viewed as a derived or a reactive element. Note that one entire facet of the social psychology inspired by Heider is essentially based on a general paradigm of this type. The fact that the object (and therefore the information) is social does not allow us to differentiate social and cognitive psychology. The social dimension can simply be said to complicate the models likely to account for cognitive functioning.

Opposing this approach is the socio-determinist approach in which cognitive competence and its development are said to depend solely on influences from the environment and on the place occupied by the individual in social relationships. For the social psychologists of cognition, both of these approaches, if considered as mutually exclusive, are unsatisfactory. Neither the intraindividual level, nor social positions and societal relationships should be neglected.

Cognition covers a large number and wide range of objects of study, including judgments, inferences, attributions, perceptions, attitudes, ideologies, representations, goals, intentions, and values. It can also refer to a reality shared by a given community (the scientific community, for instance). In this sense, although it subsumes intrapersonal cognitions, it is also concerned with interpersonal and social cognitions. Indeed, many individual cognitions are acquired through relationships with others, via confrontation with their beliefs and their vision of the world. The facts and events in our experience are also social. Accordingly, both their meaning and their organization are related to previously constructed concepts and categories.

The social psychology of cognition must study knowledge *per se*, as well as the social and cognitive processes by means of which that knowledge is formed and transformed. Of a broader scope than the trend of social cognition, it is concerned with the processes supporting mental activity (for instance, the encoding and retrieval of information in memory for persons and impression formation), the content of the knowledge base (for instance, causal attribution categories, inference goals in reasoning based on conditional implication rules), and the situations in which these processes and knowledge are at stake.

Research on the processes underlying mental activity is obviously fundamental because it allows us to discover trans-historical and trans-cultural regularities, and thereby establish the rules proper to the human species. Research on knowledge content is also fundamental since it enables us to construct cognitive maps of individuals and groups, and thereby improve our understanding of reciprocal influences. And research on social situations is important because it allows us to define and apprehend the relationships which support cognitive activity between subjects and objects. One of the major contributions of the social psychology of cognition is its ability to associate these three levels of investigation. Thus, even when it adopts the predominant information processing theory, the social psychology of cognition is able to account for individuals as socially inserted beings who not only contemplate the world, but act in it.

2. The Social Dimension of Neuronal Man

A new, highly active and fruitful line of research focusing on the construction of the brain is rapidly gaining new knowledge. This research trend informs us about the structure and functioning of this organ which, up to very recently, was regarded as an impenetrable black box. Moreover, some people consider that the development of neurosciences, which includes the neurobiology of behavior, marks a real intellectual revolution: the neuronal revolution (Changeux, 1981). As a body of research focusing on the structure, development, and behavioral effects of the central and peripheral nervous systems, neurosciences have understandably fascinated psychologists. Unfortunately, this fascination has sometimes led them to adopt its line of reasoning despite their lack of scientific expertise in this area. Consequently, rather than subjecting psychology to neurosciences in an attempt to give it some kind of new legitimacy, our knowledge of human functioning would no doubt be more effectively enhanced if we retained those contributions which justify the interest of psychologists, particularly of social psychologists.

2.1 A Neuronal Postulate and Cognitive Approaches

No one now questions the fact that the development of the brain is the result of genetic programming. However, everyone also agrees that in the human species more than in any other, the execution of that program is relatively flexible. This flexibility, known as epigenesis, precludes discussion of a strict determinism: "Every human being has inscribed in the very structure of his brain by means of specific neuronal networks, the unique affective, social and cultural history which is his" (Lecourt, 1989). Certain studies provide a striking illustration of this determinant role of epigenesis. For example, consider the study on the Japanese brain, which showed hemispheric specialization for the use of two different writing systems. The alphabetic system, known as Kana, relies on the left hemisphere, whereas the ideogrammatic system, known as Kanji, relies on the right hemisphere. In humans, this indeterminable part attributable to epigenesis makes it possible to act upon the program, which itself *is* transmitted. Indeed, the higher up the evolutionary ladder one moves, the more the epigenetic component gains importance in the construction of individuals. The greater this component, the tighter the link between the structure of the nervous system and the individual's history. "Man's central nervous system forms a kind of engram of his personal history, and the human individual, unique and thus "unclonable", is the product of his social history [...]. This history is marked in the individual's physical structure, i.e. it is written in the cerebral matter itself, due to the importance of epigenesis which will stabilize one circuit or another" (Prochiantz, 1989, p. 18).

If, as suggested by these studies, the social dimension has an impact on the construction of neural networks to the point of being indissociable from their development, strictly neuroscientific psychologists should find therein some matter for serious thought. Don't they postulate a one-to-one correspondence between each individual mental state (situated in time and space) and a specific neurophysiological state? Cognitive psychology, which to some extent still keeps its distance from neurosciences, views this identity relation merely as occasional (in which case we speak of functionalism). Such a functionalist conception allows cognitive psychology to reconcile two requirements: one is to be part of the natural sciences, by virtue of which it claims to share a materialistic or physicalistic ontology; the other is the necessity of maintaining a certain degree of explicative autonomy *vis-à-vis* neuropsychology. Consequently, it is difficult to ascertain the reasons why cognitive psychology would regard social dimensions as outside its domain, for their importance is emphasized in the sciences which use them as a point of comparison or even of reference.

If physical matter bears the mark of the individual's social history, then it becomes conceivable that a symbolic memory trace of the social dimension might exist in long-term memory and might affect the development and cognitive functions of the human being. It therefore seems difficult in psychology to exclude "the social" from the study of cognition. More specifically, cognitive psychology acknowledges the existence of a highly structured internal life and the need to seek explanations based on well-ordered sequences of internal states. Classical cognitivism indeed recognizes that propositional attitudes (i.e. mental attitudes related to propositional content such as *believe that, wish that,* etc.) are real states of organisms, ones which determine behavior. The value of taking the subject's social history into account thus becomes apparent, since it is at the very root of the construction of propositional content.

As a conclusion to this brief entry into the field of neurocognitivism, it would be worthwhile to temporarily set aside the rivalry between the different approaches to cognition and imagine the human individual as a *socially "inserted" neurophysiological and psychological system.* As such, the subject constructs mental representations, and processes and stores information which will later be activated (either automatically or consciously) in order to act in the real world. If this view is utilized in the understanding of human cognitive functioning, social insertion cannot be neglected.

3. What Role Does the Social Dimension Play in the Study of Human Cognitive Functioning?

If we acknowledge that one of the specific aims of social psychology is to understand the functioning of humans as participants in and partakers of the social world, we should not have too much trouble agreeing with the following statement: Studying the human individual from a social-psychological point of view means first considering the individual as a socially inserted being, and then striving to find explanatory systems which take that social insertion into account. It is legitimate to assume that a given social insertion is the basis of specific representations liable to orient as well as guide cognitive activity during the processing of current events. Let us return for a moment to neurosciences. Behavioral neurobiology informs us that the affective and social history of individuals is ingrained in the cerebral matter itself. Yet this social history is the result of a succession of individual insertions which may vary in permanence and specificity, but which at any rate exist. Consequently, it seems perfectly logical to consider that if social and affective history finds a means of expression in the stabilization or form of specific neural networks, it also finds its symbolic expression in man's permanent memory. This leads us to hypothesize that, at the time of information encoding and storage, emotional and social experience is closely linked to the subject's corporal environment. There is good reason to believe that this hypothesis is not a frivolous one. From the work by Jacoby (1983) and Tulving (1976; 1983), we know that what is stored corresponds not only to information *per se*, but also to the way in which that information was processed and placed in memory. Endowed with a representational content, social and emotional experience (probably interrelated) are part of the domain of mental representations. Accordingly as Thomson and Janigian (1988) suggest, human individuals cognitively represent their lives in terms of the events they experience, the goals they achieve, their failures, successes ..., forming as it were a life schema which, like every schema, is assumed to act as a processing unit for incoming information. The notion of episodic memory is applicable here, for it reminds us that information is coded both temporally and in reference to the person who is doing the memory storing. It thus appears legitimate to contend that one's personal history, which results from one's social history – because it depends on the corresponding social insertions – is strongly imprinted in memory. This history is subsequently activated and implemented in the form of a system of responses found in the behavioral repertory of the subject. In order for this to happen, it is sufficient for the subject to be in the presence of certain socio-psychological input or configurations which act as cue retrievers for knowledge related to previous social insertions. We should therefore direct more of our interest towards contextual information of an episodic nature, especially in the contextualist trend of cognitive psychology. But most likely for reasons of methodological convenience, contextual information of a semantic nature has been given greater importance. The difficulties encountered in taking this episodic dimension of human memory into account is an understandable explanation of why cognitive psychology has left the social history of humans out of its field of research. In the study of the processes underlying the construction and utilization of knowledge, these difficulties have also led us to view the social dimension merely as a source of external variation liable to modulate behavioral responses but never to generate them. The use of the mnemonic system to understand and explain human behavior has received substantial support. The social-psychological approach views this system simply as a socially inserted one. This perspective inevitably leads us to take the social history of subjects into consideration in order to comprehend their cognitive behavior and social conduct. Such a requirement has implications not only on the theoretical models used to support the scientific activity of social psychologists, but also on the experimental paradigms employed, especially with regard to the way in which variables are defined and manipulated (see Monteil, 1991).

4. Conclusion

Adopting the view that humans are "socially inserted" beings presupposes that all consequences of that insertion should be considered in the study of cognitive activity. If we agree with Tulving that what is stored in memory is not just information but also the way in which that information was processed and retained, we can reasonably assume that the subject encodes both the information and its context. In the concept of the "inserted" individual, that context is mostly composed of the emotional and social conditions in which the subject finds himself when faced with information to be processed, or with the necessity of forming an attitude, devising a strategy, or even managing a mechanism to render coherent the environment. The fact that this "context" has an impact is not a new idea, if we consider the work initiated by Rosenzweig in 1933! But we must go further. We can refer to the models derived from multiple trace theory (see Hintzman, 1986). This theory assumes that each experience produces separate memory traces which are specific to the encoding situation. This suggests that in every information processing situation, what is written in memory depends on the properties of the information available at the time of the retrieval and encoding episodes (see Hintzman & Block, 1971). These properties are not just objective, they are also subjective. Hence, social insertions may condition the nature of the mnemonic traces stored in and retrieved from memory.

In short, in a perception situation (whether social or not), the subject is always confronted with the reality of a social insertion which accompanies the information to be processed. The construction of a rule or of a piece of knowledge is thus specific to that insertion. What is imprinted in memory is a representation which associates the insertion (or its characteristics) with the rule or the knowledge (or its characteristics). We could consider the possibility of processing this representational content separately, but to do so we would have to acknowledge the total independence of the to-be-processed information from the whole of which it is a part.

And what becomes of social psychology in all this, one might ask? This is where social psychology finds its *raison d'être*, for the idea is to give the social dimension a preponderant place in the construction and use of structures and knowledge content. When I say construction and use, I am implying that two distinct types of processes are at stake. Indeed, the point here is that acquisition processes deal with the information to be encoded, i.e. with the knowledge to be constructed, and that the social dimension we are talking about here thus contributes to and draws from that construction. Retrieval and activation processes refer to attempts to establish a correspondence between problem situations and previously constructed knowledge. This distinction is important. It determines two research approaches which are complementary but nevertheless heuristically separate. The first is aimed at understanding how and by means of what mechanisms the social dimension affects the construction of cognition. The second focuses on two facets of the problem: a) understanding cognitive production through the study of the means used to establish a correspondence between the current situations in which the subject is inserted and what may have been constructed and stored at a given moment in the same subject's history, and b) identifying and understanding what happens when this correspondence is not established.

The classical trend of social cognition may lead one to raise the question: What is social in social cognition? We may wonder whether memorizing the characteristics of other individuals or judging a person or a group is very different from memorizing the characteristics of Picasso's paintings or judging the similarities between the objects in a set.

These questions have led some to advocate a "more social" social cognition. But the social psychology of cognition is not concerned with whether such and such a piece of information is more or less social, and thus, whether we are dealing with cognition or social cognition. Taking the viewpoint that individuals are socially inserted beings necessarily involves considering the relationships subjects have with the objects around them. These relationships are mainly determined by each subject's current insertion and by the representation of prior activated or to-be-activated insertions. In other words, the human cognitive universe is the outcome of the processing and integration of an environment whose properties subjects store in memory along with the meanings generated by the nature of their social insertions. Consequently, the problem of the social versus non-social status of cognition no longer arises, for the construction of reality is nothing other than a human production.

References

Changeux, J.-P. (1983). L'homme neuronal. Paris : Fayard.
Heider, F. (1958). The psychology of interpersonal relations. New York: Wiley.
Higgins, E. T., & Bargh, J. A. (1987). Social cognition and social perception. Annual Review of Psychology, 38, 369-425.
Hintzman, D. L. (1986). "Schema abstraction" in a multiple-trace memory model. Psychological Review, 93, 411-428.
Hintzman, D. L., & Block, R. A. (1971). Repetition and memory: Evidence for a multiple-trace hypothesis. Journal of Experimental Psychology, 88, 297-306.

Jacoby, J. L. (1983). Perceptual enhancement: Persistent effects of an experience. *Journal of Experimental Psychology: Learning, Memory and Cognition, 9,* 21-38.

Lecourt, D. (1989). Introduction. In A. Prochiantz (Ed.), *La construction du cerveau.* Paris : Hachette.

Monteil, J.-M. (1991). Social regulations and individual cognitive function: Effects of individuation on cognitive performance. *European Journal of Social Psychology, 21,* 225-237.

Prochiantz, A. (1989). *La construction du cerveau.* Paris : Hachette.

Rosenzweig, S. (1933). The experimental situation as a psychological problem. *Psychological Review, 40,* 337-354.

Schneider, D. J. (1991). Social cognition. *Annual Review of Psychology, 42,* 527-561.

Sherman, S. J., Judd, C. M., & Park, B. (1989). Social Cognition. *Annual Review of Psychology, 40,* 281-326.

Simon, H. A. (1976). Discussion: Cognition and social behavior. In J. Carroll & J. Payne (Eds.), *Cognition and social behavior.* Hillsdale, NJ: Erlbaum.

Thomson, S. C., & Janigian, A. S. (1988). Life schemes: A framework for understanding the search for meaning. *Journal of Social and Clinical Psychology, 7,* 260-280.

Tulving, E. (1976). Ecphoric processes in recall and recognition. In J. Brown (Ed.), *Recall and recognition.* London: Wiley.

Tulving, E. (1983). *Elements of episodic memory.* Oxford: Oxford University Press.

Zajonc, B. (1980). Cognition and social cognition: An historical perspective. In L. Festinger (Ed.), *Retrospective on social psychology.* New York: Oxford University Press.

ON THE RELATION
BETWEEN COGNITIVE PSYCHOLOGY
AND SOCIAL COGNITION

Jonathan St. B. T. Evans

Polytechnic South West, Plymouth, U.K.

What is social cognition and how does it relate to cognitive psychology? A recent argument that I (a cognitive psychologist) had with a cognitive social psychologist went along the following lines:

> I - *I see social cognition as a form of applied cognitive psychology. That is to say, cognitive psychologists study the cognitive representations and process associated with all kinds of knowledge, whereas the social psychologist is interested only in knowledge of the social world. In other words, social cognition is no more and no less than cognition of social things.*
>
> He - *On the contrary, all behaviour – even your laboratory experiments – takes place within a social context. Cognitive psychology is hence a part of the domain of social psychology.*

We will return later to the question of which discipline – if either – subsumes the other. First, let us try to define the domains of the cognitive and social psychologists and identify the regions in which interests overlap.

Most – or certainly many – cognitive psychologists nowadays see themselves as cognitive scientists. Hence, they perceive their role as part of a multidisciplinary approach to the study of intelligence and are more likely, it must be said, to look upon a linguist or an artificial intelligence researcher as a colleague than they would a social psychologist. Cognitive science focuses upon the nature of mental representations and processes involved in a highly abstract manner and assumes that these are largely independent of the actual domain of knowledge to which they are applied. If cognitive scientists think about social knowledge at all, they will assume its basis to be no different from any other form of knowledge.

At the same time, there have been developments in cognitive psychology in the past 20 years or so which bring at least some of its researchers towards common interests with social psychologists. The trend of interest here is the increasing concern of researchers in language, memory and reasoning with the influence of real world knowledge or *pragmatic* influences in cognition. For example, the use of highly abstract problem materials to study both memory and reasoning processes in the 50's and 60's has fallen out of favour and psychologists are much more interested in the role of domain specific knowledge. Note that cognitive psychologists still assume that the nature of cognitive processes is quite general. The difference is that they recognise that since in real life context is almost always present, then there must generally be an influence of prior knowledge on any process which is studied. Specific examples in the study of deductive reasoning are discussed below.

Links with social cognition are most apparent for researchers of the "higher" cognitive processes such as reasoning, judgement and decision making. It is harder to link work on colour vision or word recognition to the level of analysis of a social psychologist. A clear example of overlapping interest lies in the famous work of Amos Tversky and Daniel Kahneman on heuristics and biases in intuitive statistical judgement (see Kahneman, Slovic, & Tversky, 1982). This work was of considerable interest to cognitive psychologists like myself who are interested in thinking and reasoning, but as it turned out was of equal interest to the growing band of cognitive social psychologists (see Nisbett & Ross, 1980). What really happened here – and in similar cases – is that cognitive psychologists who were increasingly interested in the influence of pragmatics, and social psychologists who were wishing to find cognitive accounts of social behaviour achieved some common interest.

Consider as another example, the phenomenon of hindsight bias or the "knew-it-all-along-effect". This is the tendency for people with outcome knowledge to overestimate what they could have forecast in advance of an uncertain event. When I discovered the seminal work of Fischhoff (1975) I immediately saw this as an interesting piece of cognitive psychology which I could link with evidence of bias in reasoning tasks and of rationalisations in subject protocols (see Evans, 1989, Chapter 5). Social psychologists saw the same work as providing a possible explanation for a large range of social behaviour, and a large number of "social" studies of hindsight bias were spawned as a result (see Hawkins & Hastie, 1990).

What these examples show is that at least some cognitive and social psychologists should be taking an interest in each others' work. However, this happens a lot less than it should. Psychological research is on the whole a tribal affair: the journals that one reads and the conferences one attends depend largely on where you did your PhD and with whom. Our prejudices are inherent and our reading time finite.

I will briefly consider two topic areas: one (verbal reports) in which I think cognitive psychology owes a debt to social psychology and a second (pragmatic factors in reasoning), an area of cognitive psychology that should be of interest to social psychologists if only they knew about it.

1. Interpretation of Verbal Reports

The terms "cognitive" and "cognition" are used in two quite different ways by psychologists. Most cognitive psychologists refer simply to the notion of underlying representations and processes with no assumptions about consciousness. Many non-cognitive psychologists, however, seem to use the terms to refer to *conscious thoughts*. This, for example, is the usage when a clinical psychologist refers to a cognitive approach to the treatment of anxiety: the patient is taught consciously to suppress negative thoughts at the onset of an anxiety attack. To take a quite different example, a "cognitive", as opposed for example to a learning theory, approach to gambling behaviour is one in which the belief and theories held by the gamblers are studied (e.g. Wagenaar, 1988).

In social psychology, the equation of cognition with conscious thought has been far more common than in cognitive psychology, as in the widely influential "cognitive" attribution theory of H. Kelly. This notion was, however, strongly challenged in the famous paper of Nisbett and Wilson (1977) who claimed that (a) subjects lack access to their own cognitive processes and (b) that introspective reports reflect *a priori* causal theories about their own behaviour. Although themselves social psychologists, the authors referred also to some work in cognitive psychology and published in a highly visible journal. As a result, the paper was widely read and discussed in cognitive as well as social psychology.

In social psychology, the Nisbett and Wilson paper led to many critical if not downright hostile reactions, most of which are ably summarised in the review paper of White (1988). In cognitive psychology, the reaction was rather different, with widespread (though not universal) acceptance of their basic arguments. Although introspective reports are not widely used in cognitive psychology, some researchers have persisted with the notion that they can usefully supplement behaviour data (e.g. Kosslyn, 1980). The Nisbett and Wilson paper hence struck a chord with cognitive psychologists such as myself who were profoundly unhappy with this practice and believed that it resulted in misinterpretation of the evidence. Indeed, the twin arguments of the Nisbett and Wilson paper map closely on to those of Wason and Evans (1975) in their discussion of deductive reasoning. Wason and Evans had argued (a) that subjects were biased by factors of which they were unaware and (b) that their verbal justifications of response were *post hoc* rationalisations.

The second benefit of Nisbett and Wilson's contribution was that it forced psychologists to think hard about when verbal reports might be used and how they might be interpreted. A tradition of verbal protocol analysis based on "think aloud" protocols – extensively used, for example, in Newell and Simon's (1972) major work on problem solving – appeared to be endangered by the Nisbett and Wilson attack. However, as Ericsson and Simon (1980) pointed out, many cognitive processes produce an output in verbal form, and to deprive ourselves of the use of verbal data in cognitive psychology would be absurd.

The Ericsson and Simon (1980) paper was in fact of great importance in clarifying the nature of verbal protocols and their analysis in cognitive psychology. Whilst a response to Nisbett and Wilson, the later paper has been widely misunderstood as a criticism or refutation of it. In fact, there is no inconsistency between the two arguments. Ericsson and Simon argue that reports collected retrospectively and in which subjects are asked to interpret their will tend to be both incomplete and misleading. These are precisely the types of reports with which Nisbett and Wilson were concerned. The collection of concurrent think aloud protocols whose content is interpreted by the psychologists rather than the subject is the kind of protocol analysis for which they convincingly argue.

I like to use the term "mentalism" to refer to the belief that behaviour is mediated by conscious thought and the term "introspectionism" to refer to the associated methodology of self-reporting mental processes and self-interpreting of one's behaviour. My view is that mentalism exists in all areas of psychology but is stronger in social than in cognitive psychology. The debate in social psychology initiated by Nisbett and Wilson helped clarify the thinking of cognitive psychologists in this area, although it is doubtful whether social psychology is much less mentalistic as a result.

It is, of course, unlikely that behaviour is mediated by conscious, reportable thoughts in social but not in cognitive psychology experiments, at least when the same level of cognition (e.g. judgement, inference, decision) is involved. Hence, this is an area in which debate should continue across the two traditions. We can take no comfort from a situation in which social psychologists resolve one view of the issue and cognitive psychologists another.

2. Pragmatic Factors in Reasoning

Cognitive and social psychologists share an interest in inference. Take for example the case of inductive inference in which we form generalisations, rules and categories on the basis of our observations of the world. A cognitive psychologist might well study such phenomena using a wholly abstract or artificial problem such as the Wason (1960) "2 4 6" task. The interest would lie in how subjects formulate and test hypotheses, and whether they are prone to systematic error such as the controversial "confirmation bias" (see Evans, 1989, Chapter 3; Klayman & Ha, 1987). The social psychologist is interested in inductive inferences because they lead to social categorization and may form the basis of stereotypes, prejudice and so on.

If one takes the notion of social cognition as cognitive psychology applied to social knowledge, then one can see some obvious mappings between phenomena in cognitive and social psychology. For example, there is quite a lot of research using non-social materials which shows that subjects extrapolate too easily from the evidence of small samples (see Evans, 1989, pp. 33-39). If this is a general cognitive bias, then in a social domain it could lead to stereotyping and prejudice formation. Similarly, if there is a general confirmation bias, consisting of biased information seeking, then this could explain the belief maintenance effects discussed in the social psychological literature. This kind of thinking clearly underlies the extended discussion of social inference provided by Nisbett and Ross (1980).

Many social psychologists will, however, be suspicious of cognitive research performed in the abstract, which is why research on pragmatic influences on reasoning will be of more interest. One example is the so-called "belief bias" effect in deductive reasoning, in which there has been a recent resurgence of interest. The effect arises in experiments where subjects are given the premises of an argument and asked if a conclusion follows logically from them: a judgement of validity. Logically, the empirical truth of the conclusion is irrelevant to this task. All that matters is whether the conclusion must be true *if* the premises are true. If so, the argument is valid; if not, it is invalid.

The belief bias effect, first reported by Wilkins (1928), is that subjects' validity judgements are biased by the believability of the conclusion. Hence, believable conclusions tend to be endorsed and unbelievable ones rejected regardless of their validity. This occurs in spite of clear instructions to the subject to disregard beliefs and decide whether the conclusion follows from the premises. A number of demonstrations and replications of the bias were published – mostly in social psychological journals – following the Wilkins paper. Cognitive psychologists became interested in the effect in the late 1970's, but were highly critical of the methodology of earlier studies (see Revlin, Leirer, Yopp, & Yopp, 1980; Evans, 1982).

In a tightly controlled series of experiments, Evans, Barston and Pollard (1983) managed to demonstrate the reliable and sizeable belief bias effects in intelligent adult subjects. They used four types of syllogism whose conclusions were either valid or invalid and either believable or unbelievable. An example of their problems is the following:

> *No addictive things are inexpensive*
> *Some vitamin tablets are inexpensive*
> *Therefore, some addictive things are not cigarettes.*

This argument is invalid, but the conclusion is believable. By rearranging the terms one can produce a syllogism of the same logical form but with the unbelievable conclusion *"Some cigarettes are not addictive"*. Over the three experiments reported in the paper, Evans, Barston, and Pollard found that the percentage of conclusions accepted on the four problem types was as follows:

Valid-Believable	89%
Valid-Unbelievable	56%
Invalid-Believable	71%
Invalid-Unbelievable	10%

As is fairly apparent subjects are highly influenced in their decisions both by the validity of the argument and by the believability of the conclusion. Moreover, there is a significant interaction: the belief bias effect is larger on invalid arguments. The most striking figure is the acceptance of invalid but believable conclusions at over 70%.

Are cognitive psychologists studying the effects of belief doing research into social cognition? Maybe so, but the objectives are subtly different. The cognitive psychologist is interested in the process of reasoning. The effect of belief upon this process is then used to modify theoretical accounts of how people reason. For example, proponents of the mental models theory of reasoning (Johnson-Laird, 1983; Johnson-Laird & Byrne, 1991) have tried to account for belief bias within their general theory of deductive inference (see Oakhill & Johnson-Laird, 1985; Oakhill, Johnson-Laird, & Garnham, 1989). The theory supposes that subjects formulate mental models to represent possible world states in which the premises hold and infer putative conclusion from these models. There then follows a stage in which subjects try to find counter-examples, i.e. models in which the premises are true but the conclusion is false. If no such counter-example is found then the conclusion is declared valid.

The mental models account of belief bias supposes that when subjects find a putative conclusion which is believable they lack motivation to search for counter-examples to it: hence the large acceptance rate of invalid-believable. In most studies including Evans, Barston, and Pollard (1983), these problems have conclusions which *could* be true given the premises but are not necessitated by them. The explanation offered by Evans, Barston, and Pollard (see also Barston, 1986; Evans, 1989) has become known as the Selective Scrutiny Model and has features in common with the mental models account. The assumption of this model is that when presented with an argument whose conclusion is believable, the subject will accept it uncritically without reasoning at all. An unbelievable argument, however, is subject to rigorous examination involving an attempt to reason from the premises. Hence, subjects are less likely to reject a valid conclusion which is unbelievable than to accept an invalid one which is believable.

The social psychologist looking at this literature would probably be bored by some of the detailed theoretical arguments about the nature of reasoning processes which lies therein. However, theoretical ideas as well as empirical findings may well be relevant. The Selective Scrutiny Model is an idea capable of easy application to social inference, and its authors have pointed to one clear parallel finding in the social cognition literature. This was a study by Lord, Ross, and Lepper (1979) in which subjects were asked to evaluate reports of research studies finding evidence for or against capital punishment – an issue on which subjects were themselves polarised. Although the research methods attributed to pro and anti studies were counterbalanced, the subjects produced far more criticisms of the methodology of the study which went against their own belief than the one in favour.

The Lord, Ross, and Lepper study seems to show a selective scrutiny of the evidence for a conclusion which closely parallels the findings in the belief bias literature, if we can take the premises of a syllogism as the "evidence" for its conclusion. Taken together, the belief bias and confirmation bias research in the cognitive literature provides a potential account of a range of belief maintaining biases in the social psychological literature.

Another set of studies in the deductive reasoning area has concentrated on pragmatic influences on performance on the Wason selection task (Wason, 1966) – one of the most intensively studied problems in the area. The problem, which tests understanding of conditional logic, is simple in appearance but remarkably difficult to solve in its standard form using abstract problem materials. However, many studies have shown that logical performance can be facilitated when certain types of realistic problem content are used (see Evans, 1989, Chapter 4). One of the major theoretical accounts to have been presented is that of Cheng and Holyoak (1985) who claim that subjects are utilising *pragmatic reasoning schemas* to solve the problem.

The notion of schema is of course an old one, familiar to social as well as cognitive psychologists. The notion of a pragmatic reasoning schema has some interesting specifics, however. The idea is that we learn how to reason in a given class of situations and include a set of production (if...then) rules in our schema. When we encounter a new situation, if a schema is induced and its variable instantiated to the specifics of the situation, then inferences are triggered by the stored production rules. For example, Cheng and Holyoak discuss a permission schema which concerns action and preconditions. The schema includes production rules such as

If an action is to be taken then the precondition must be met
If the precondition is not met then the action may not be taken.

If subjects are given a particular problem to which this schema can be applied then their reasoning is affected accordingly. For example, Griggs and Cox (1982) found that selection task performance was enhanced using a rule such as "If a person is drinking alcohol then that person must be over eighteen years of age" preceded by a brief scenario in which the subject is asked to image that he is a police officer checking people drinking in a bar. Subjects correctly decide that they need to investigate any one who is drinking alcohol or who is *under* eighteen years of age for violation of the law. The latter choice is the logical equivalent of the one they fail to make in abstract formulations of the task. The Cheng and Holyoak account is that a permission schema is invoked, with "drinking alcohol" instantiated to the action and "being over 18 years of age" instantiated to the precondition. Thus the second of the production rules quoted above becomes

If a person is not over 18 years of age then they may not drink alcohol.

Thus subjects immediately recognise that people under 18 are potentially violators of the law whose drinks must be examined.

Like all cognitive theories that of pragmatic reasoning schemas has its critics (e.g. Cosmides, 1989; Johnson-Laird & Byrne, 1991). However, the idea does seem of great relevance to the study of social cognition. If subjects use pragmatic reasoning schemas then some of these will be applied to social situations and thus account for social inferences. An interesting aspect here is that the theory assumes that we learn how to reason in specific ways in different kinds of situations. Hence, we do not necessarily reason in a way which is consistent with logic or with the way we would reason in a different domain.

3. Final Thoughts

In this brief discussion, I have considered one area in which cognitive psychology has benefited from the work of social psychologists, and one in which I feel the reverse ought to be true. It follows that I do believe that researchers in the two domains share common interests and thought fruitful exchanges can and should occur. We return now to the question of what is the real connection between the two subjects.

Returning to the argument that I quoted at the outset of this paper, I was not convinced by my opponent. It is true that cognitive psychological experiments take place in a social context and can be influenced by social factors – a problem of which most experimentalists are well aware. The domain of cognitive psychology is not within that of social, however, since the cognitive psychologists must be concerned with all forms of knowledge and all forms of inference. Clearly, social knowledge and social inference mare subsets of these.

The interesting question is whether social cognition is different in nature from any other form of cognition. For example, a stereotype can be looked at as a cognitive structure (e.g. schema, mental model, prototype or concept) which is formed by inductive inference to represent a view of a particular social group and to facilitate inferences about this group. Would the structure be any different in kind to that which we induce to represent our knowledge of say motor cars? From our experience of cars, we must induce some kind of abstract generalisation of what a car consists of and what it does. Of course, we would not say that we had formed a *stereotype* of car or that this would *prejudice* our view of a new car we had not seen before, but this is just terminology. Is there any reason to suppose that the cognitive structures and processes are any different just because the objects are of a social nature?

I see no reason why social cognition should be different, and hence maintain my stance – implicit in the discussion of pragmatic influences on reasoning – that social cognition is a form of applied cognitive psychology. This is not to demean the status of the field which is both important and very demanding. This conception does, however, provide a model – by analogy to other areas of applied research – for how work should proceed. Applied researchers need to combine two sources of knowledge: underlying theory and knowledge of the domain of application. The second requirement obviously implies that social cognition research requires a good knowledge of the social behaviour to be explained, but the former that a solid base in cognitive theory is also required. Thus theoretical debates in cognitive psychology about the precise nature of cognitive representations and processes are of direct relevance to the field of social cognition.

References

Barston. J. L. (1986). *An investigation into belief biases in reasoning.* Unpublished Ph. D. thesis, Polytechnic South West, Plymouth, U.K.

Cheng, P. W., & Holyoak, K. J. (1985). Pragmatic reasoning schemas. *Cognitive Psychology, 17,* 391-416.

Cosmides, L. (1989). The logic of social exchange: Has natural selection shaped how humans reason? Studies with the Wason selection task. *Cognition, 31,* 187-276.

Ericsson, K. A., & Simon, H. A. (1980). Verbal reports as data. *Psychological Review, 87,* 215-251.

Evans, J. St. B. T. (1982). *The psychology of deductive reasoning.* London: Routledge and Kegan Paul.

Evans, J. St. B. T. (1989). *Bias in human reasoning: Causes and consequences.* Brighton: Erlbaum.

Evans, J. St. B. T., Barston, J. L., & Pollard, P. (1983). On the conflict between logic and belief in syllogistic reasoning. *Memory and Cognition, 11,* 295-306.

Fischhoff, B. (1975). Hindsight ≠ foresight: The effect of outcome knowledge on judgment under uncertainty. *Journal of Experimental Psychology: Human Perception and Performance, 1,* 288-299.

Griggs, R. A., & Cox, J. R. (1982). The elusive thematic materials effect in the Wason selection task. *British Journal of Psychology, 73,* 407-420.

Hawkins, S. A., & Hastie, R. (1990). Hindsight: Biased judgements of past events after the outcomes are known. *Psychological Bulletin, 107,* 311-327.

Johnson-Laird, P. N. (1983). *Mental models.* Cambridge: Cambridge University Press.

Johnson-Laird, P. N., & Byrne, R. (1991). *Deduction.* Hove & London: Erlbaum.

Kahneman, D., Slovic, P., & Tversky, A. (1982). *Judgment under uncertainty: Heuristics and biases.* Cambridge: Cambridge University Press.

Klayman, J., & Ha, Y. W. (1987). Confirmation, disconfirmation, and information in hypothesis testing. *Psychological Review, 94,* 211-228.

Kosslyn, S. M. (1980). *Image and mind.* Cambridge, MA: Harvard University Press.

Lord, C., Ross, L., & Lepper, M. R. (1979). Biased assimilation and attitude polarization: The effects of prior theories on subsequently considered evidence. *Journal of Personality and Social Psychology, 37,* 2098-2109.

Newell, A., & Simon, H. A. (1972). *Human problem solving.* Englewood Cliffs, NJ: Prentice-Hall.

Nisbett, R. E., & Ross, L. (1980). *Human inference: Strategies and shortcomings of social judgment.* Englewood Cliffs, NJ: Prentice-Hall.

Nisbett, R. E., & Wilson, T. D. (1977). Telling more than we can know: Verbal reports on mental processes. *Psychological Review, 84,* 231-295.

Oakhill, J., & Johnson-Laird, P. N. (1985). Rationality, memory and the search for counterexamples. *Cognition, 20,* 79-94.

Oakhill, J., Johnson-Laird, P. N., & Garnham, A. (1989). Believability and syllogistic reasoning. *Cognition, 31,* 117-140.

Revlin, R., Leirer, V., Yopp, H., & Yopp, R. (1980). The belief bias effect in formal reasoning: The influence of knowledge on logic. *Memory and Cognition, 8,* 584-592.

Wagenaar, W. A. (1988). *Paradoxes of gambling behaviour.* Hove & London: Erlbaum.

Wason, P. C. (1960). On the failure to eliminate hypotheses in a conceptual task. *Quarterly Journal of Experimental Psychology, 12,* 129-140.

Wason, P. C. (1966). Reasoning. In B. M. Foss (Ed.), *New horizons in psychology I.* Harmandsworth: Penguin.

Wason, P. C., & Evans, J. St. B. T. (1975). Dual processes in reasoning? *Cognition, 3,* 141-154.

White, P. A. (1988). Knowing more than we can tell: "Introspective access" and causal report accuracy 10 years later. *British Journal of Psychology, 79,* 13-46.

Wilkins, M. C. (1928). The effect of changed material on the ability to do formal syllogistic reasoning. *Archives of Psychology,* No.102.

THE COGNITIVE APPROACH
TO SOCIAL CATEGORIZATION

AN EVALUATION

Anne-Marie de La Haye and André Duflos

René Descartes University, Paris, France

Social cognition studies have undergone considerable expansion in the last 15 years due to the spreading influence of recent cognitive psychology in the field of social psychology. This evolution is not unamimously welcomed by social psychologists. Some serious objections have been raised, and, if we understand them correctly, what underlies these objections is the idea that the cognitive approach cannot be adapted to the complexity of social-psychological processes. We do not share this *a priori* stand on cognitive social psychology, but do agree that certain conditions must be fulfilled for a cognitive approach to be scientifically fruitful. In this paper, we are going to review these conditions, and illustrate our thesis with examples taken from the social categorization domain.

1. From Tajfel's Social Categorization to "Social Cognition" Studies

1.1 Tajfel's Cognitive Orientation
The notion of social categorization was introduced by Henri Tajfel, and, from the very beginning of his work, was explicitly intended as a cognitive account of stereotyping and inter-group discrimination. Stereotypes had already been studied when Tajfel entered the field, but his "social categorization approach" introduced a radical shift. Previous studies concentrated on two problems: the content of stereotypes and how to reduce them. In fact, stereotyping was considered pathological, and social psychologists devoted their time either to nosography or therapeutics.

Tajfel was strongly opposed to this. He wrote: "our image of a social man is that of a man who has lost his reason; [...] It is difficult to see why it should be assumed that men lose their cognitive capacity as soon as they confront human groups other than their own" (Tajfel, 1969, pp. 80-81, cited by Oakes & Turner, 1990). So, Tajfel decided to try to identify the cognitive processes which potentially contribute to prejudice and stereotyping. It was assumed that social categorization was one of those processes.

The term "cognitive", as Tajfel and his co-workers and followers employ it, essentially means two things. First, it means that phenomena related to social categorization can be explained by very basic processes, underlying any kind of categorization. What is supposed to be basic is an "accentuation" mechanism, i.e., whenever objects are cast into different categories, within-class similarities and between-class differences are over-estimated. This mechanism was partially demonstrated by Tajfel and Wilkes (1963), in an experiment bearing on line-length estimates. Results do show an exaggeration of between-class differences, but no within-class homogeneization. Moreover, between-class differentiation is entirely due to a contrast effect at the category border, which implies that this presumably "basic" process can only be generalized to the perception of distributions which do not overlap. This seems to be a very stringent condition if applied to social categories. Tajfel and Wilkes's experiment has been replicated several times, with the same pattern of results, whenever judgments bear on physical dimensions of non-social objects: no categorization effect when distributions overlap, no within-class assimilation (see Fabre, 1990). Though experimental results, all things considered, do not completely corroborate the hypothesis of a basic, perceptive accentuation mechanism, the generality of this mechanism has been reasserted a number of times by those who hold this theory, and has become a kind of ritual invocation in any textbook or review on the topic. If we scrutinize the published evidence, we must admit that the generality of this mechanism is more a basic postulate, or even an article of faith, than it is the conclusion of a large-scale demonstration.

The term "cognitive", under Tajfel's pen, has a second important implication: that intergroup discrimination, which follows social categorization as it is operationalized in the Minimal Group Paradigm (MGP), is not the effect of any material condition. It is not the result of a mutual dependence on achieving some goal, as Sherif (1966) would have said, and it is not the result of receiving or expecting similar reinforcements, as Rabbie (Rabbie, Shot, & Visser, 1989) maintains, nor is it the result of sharing the same environment. These determinants may exist in a number of natural settings, and of course Tajfel does not deny this; but the fundamental aim of his experimental work was to demonstrate that one can induce discrimination exclusively by manipulating the way the situation is defined. In this case, discrimination results from a "purely cognitive" determinant, which is the fact that subjects are considering people as belonging to different categories, even if they are completely arbitrary and meaningless, such as a "Klee group" and a "Kandinski group" might be.

This very important point could be discussed along two lines. The first one was thoroughly developed by Rabbie and his colleagues (see the article just cited for a detailed bibliography). They outrightly contest the claim that the independent variables manipulated in Tajfel's MGP are of a purely cognitive nature. And in fact they show that the subjects' reward-allocation strategy varies when they are led to believe that their own reward will be allocated either by ingroup members, or by outgroup members, or by both. The classical condition in Tajfel's experiments most likely corresponds to the last case.

Terminology also calls for a discussion, and we will come back to this problem at the end of this paper. For the time being, however, it should be noted that in the above, the qualifier "cognitive" is applied to "determining factors", which must be distinguished from other "non-cognitive factors". This way of speaking seems very problematic to us. We will come back to this discussion later on.

1.2 Two Separate Sets of Problems...

Despite Tajfel's claim that social categorization should be conceived of as being based on general mental mechanisms, this line of research never actively interacted with general cognitive research on categorization. And yet, categorization was a very active field in cognitive psychology, in the same years as the ones when Tajfel was developing his concept of social categorization. If you look at the main references on the topic, you will notice, in chronological order: Posner and Keele (1968), Reed (1972), Itoooh and Mervis (1975), Hayes-Roth and Hayes-Roth (1977), Medin and Shaffer (1978), and so on. This is not a complete bibliography, of course, but is just some important names and important dates to show that general and social studies were being conducted at the same time. Tajfel and his followers continued saying "these phenomena are based on very general mechanisms" and never made explicit reference to general categorization studies.

Why did these parallel developments occur on very similar topics, yet without any interaction? A partial explanation could be that social psychologists and cognitive psychologists were not interested in the same aspects of categorization processes. Cognitive psychologists were interested in two problems: (a) How are categories represented in memory? (b) How does the subject decide that a given object belongs to a given category?

Social categorization studies, inspired by Tajfel's work, focused on the next stage of the categorization process, that is, on the cognitive consequences of putting people into categories. In the classic "Minimal Group Paradigm", subjects are told that they themselves and the other subjects in the experiment have been divided into two groups. Sometimes this distribution is supposed to be based on some objective criterion, such as preferring Klee to Kandinski or the reverse, and other times, the experimenter provides no justification. Thus, subjects find themselves and their co-subjects in a socially categorized environment. This situation has noticeable effects both on the way subjects perceive the other persons and on the way they behave toward them. A clear in-group favoritism bias is observed, both on personality judgments and on money allocation behaviour. In-group favoritism obviously cannot be explained by referring exclusively to "a basic, perceptive, accentuation mechanism"; one needs a further assumption to account for the fact that social categorization induces the accentuation of differences which is always to the benefit of the subject's group. Tajfel's theory assumes a need to preserve a positive social identity. The problem with this further assumption is that it is by itself a sufficient explanation for in-group favoritism, and does not even need to refer to a "basic, perceptive, accentuation mechanism", which in any case does not account for much in physical perception, and cannot wholly account for social categorization.

1.3 ...which Finally Join.

Since the late 70's, social categorization studies have become more varied. They are no longer concerned exclusively with the consequences of categorization, but deal with other kinds of problems, e.g. how do we construct categories, under what conditions do categories influence person perception, and how can we describe the internal structure of categories. However diverse, all these studies are part of the so-called "social cognition" trend. When discussing the conditions under which a cognitive approach can be scientifically fruitful, examples will be taken from these recent cognitive works.

2. Conditions for a Fruitful Cognitive Approach

2.1 Do we Really Test Processes?

Our first condition seems almost tautological in its phrasing, but is not so easy to accomplish. A cognitive approach can only be scientifically fruitful if procedures are developed which give us insight into cognitive processes. Roughly speaking, there are two ways of dealing with mental events. One can consider them as hidden, hypothetical, inaccessible things that occur somewhere between stimulus and response, and, thanks to their inaccessibility, one can feel free to elaborate one's own conception of them, with no other constraint than making one's discourse coherent. This was a fairly common practice among social psychologists in the 50's and 60's. There was a very problematic gap between the content of these theories which referred to mental activities, and the choice of methods which conformed to behaviorist standards. As Shelley Taylor (1976) stated it: " We have used an S-R methodology to test S-O-R theories " (p. 70). The other way of dealing with mental activity is to make cognitive processes the domain of inquiry. Of course, a cognitive process is by definition a hidden thing. One cannot see or touch a cognitive process. However, one can construct experiments in such a way that collected evidence comes as close as possible to the ongoing process. If we speak about cognitive processes, we must try to test them; if we do not test them, then talking about them is nothing more than spreading rumors.

Let us give an example. Illusory correlation is a rather well-established phenomenon. It has been repeatedly demonstrated that when two dichotomous variables are uncorrelated, and each one presents an uneven distribution, subjects tend to overestimate the co-occurrences of infrequent alternatives on both variables. This results in an erroneous perception of a correlation between them (Hamilton & Gifford, 1976; see Fiedler, 1991, for more complete references).

Hamilton proposed that this phenomenon was a possible model for the development of stereotypes. This interpretation is conjectural, but grants importance to the phenomenon. The process which is responsible for this type of illusory correlation is not yet clearly known, though it is currently designated as "Distinctiveness-based Illusory Correlation", or DIC for short. This label not only refers to the phenomenon itself, but also to the hypothetical model formulated by Hamilton. The main points of this model are the following:

(1) Infrequent events are distinctive
(2) Jointly infrequent events are jointly distinctive
(3) Distinctiveness induces attention and deeper encoding
(4) Consequently, retrieval of jointly distinctive events is easier
(5) Frequency estimates for a category of events are based on the number of spontaneously retrieved exemplars (this hypothesis refers to Tversky and Kahneman's (1973) "availability heuristic")
(6) The frequency of jointly distinctive events is overestimated.

Until 1990, the authors who worked on the phenomenon referred exclusively to Hamilton's model. However, although nobody tried to contest this model, no real attempt was made to validate it in detail. Only the last stage was borne out repeatedly. We know of 12 articles which report 19 experiments on DIC. Not a single experiment examined the hypothesis of selective attention. Only one experiment dealt with selective retrieval (Hamilton, Dugan, & Trolier, 1985), with favorable results, we must admit. All the others jump directly from stimulus to response, from item-list structure to frequency estimates of item categories, without examining what is going on in between. Hence the question: Why refer to a cognitive process if you do not test it?

Things have recently begun to change. Hamilton's model was challenged by E. Smith (1990) and Fiedler (1991). La Haye and Lauvergeon (1991) discussed the validity of some usual dependent variables. These might appear as converging attacks on Hamilton's theory. But the polemical aspect of these papers is not the most important. The best thing that could result from this discussion would be more direct attempts to analyze the cognitive process which underlies illusory correlation. We are fairly confident that it is about to be done.

2.2 Testing Models at the Individual Level

A second requirement for a fruitful cognitive approach is assessing hypothesized processes at the individual level, at least on some occasions. The habit of aggregating data, the habit of testing theories by comparing means, was deeply rooted in the behaviorist postulate. As long as the only legitimate model for scientific psychology was to predict behavior from the situation, there were no means to deal with between-subject variability, except as a random, meaningless occurrence, strictly equivalent to within-subject variability. The black-box postulate not only allowed the researcher to neglect inter-subject variability: it made such neglect compulsory.

In cognitive analysis, on the contrary, one is much more careful about aggregating data, whether they are produced by several subjects or by a single subject (Matalon & La Haye, 1992). A mean behavior can make sense, but a "mean process" does not make sense. Unfortunately, the cognitive approach can entail the unquestioned conviction of tapping "very general" processes, that is to say, processes postulated as both unique and universal: everybody has them, and nobody has anything else. The "social cognition" trend is not free from such naïveté. In her inventory of paradigms in interpersonal cognition, La Haye (1991) was able to show that the cognitive paradigm very rarely takes individual differences into account.

Nevertheless, we consider that the ultimate goal in studying cognitive processes must be to construct models which can fit individual data. This implies that a good model is one which includes parameters to account for inter-individual variability. This objective still seems far from being reached in the social categorization domain. However, analyzing data at the individual level is not impossible, and when this is achieved, considerable progress can be expected. Two recent examples are the studies by Andersen and Cole (1990) and Pavelchak (1989). We will pay particular attention to the latter, which deals with the relative strength of category-based versus piecemeal treatment of social information.

It is not very difficult to show that when a category is activated, person perception is modified. But to what extent does category activation determine the final impression of a given person? How do category-based expectations combine with the specific information one receives on a given person? Fiske and Pavelchak (1986) developed a model of this problem, called the "two-mode model". It states that person evaluation can be obtained in two different ways. If there is a good enough match between specific information and an available category schema, the person is evaluated according to the schema. If there is no possible match between the information about a person and any available schema, the evaluation will be computed on the basis of every piece of information. In a recent article, Pavelchak (1989) presented an "idiographic technique", which he devised in order to test this model at the level of each individual set of responses. The main independent variable was the timing of the experimenter's request for a category label. The results clearly provided evidence of two different modes of processing, one based on combining every piece of information, the other based on category evaluation. However, the degree to which the stimulus fits the schema was not related to the degree to which the evaluations were category-based. The decisive factor seems to be the timing of the request for the subject to make a category decision. This is a very nice study, and it demonstrates that it is possible to test a model with individual data, on a problem which is very classically considered as a social-psychological one. We all know that such studies are very costly. It would not be realistic to require that every study conform to this standard. But we are convinced that the question of model validity at the individual level must be a constant preoccupation for us, if we claim we are doing cognitive social psychology.

2.3 Referring to General Cognitive Theories

A third condition which has sometimes been formulated involves borrowing models from general cognitive theories. This is the point which causes a number of our colleagues to disagree. The reservations about the "social cognition" trend, to which we alluded above, are rooted in the fear that social psychology will be absorbed by cognitive psychology if we borrow too much from it. We have already borrowed a number of experimental techniques, and we occasionally borrow one concept or another. What if we also borrow theories? Where could the specificity of social psychology seek refuge if we do that ?

These reactions must not be taken as purely self-defensive. There is a real epistemological problem behind them. The major argument against adopting general cognitive theories is that social psychology is not only a subdivision of psychology; it is not only a special kind of psychology, concerned with a special kind of problem, as, for example, ornithology is a subdivision of zoology, concerned with a special kind of animal. We are confronted with psychological functioning in general, as any psychologist could be, which is to say, that every aspect of psychological functioning interests social psychology. But we analyze psychological phenomena in terms of their contribution to social functioning. What makes social psychology specific is not a special subject matter; it is a more complex level of analysis. In order to achieve this goal, we have to bring specific notions and specific models into play. If we merge our social-psychological problems into general cognitive theories, we will inevitably stoop to lower levels of analysis, and cease, sooner or later, to do social psychology.

This argument is quite convincing. However, it is not certain that every aspect of social psychology can be described in such terms. There are a number of social-psychological studies that bear on topics which are also dealt with by general cognitive theories. Categorization is one of these cases. When working on such a topic, it would be completely fruitless and self-limiting to ignore this possible theoretical background. Confronting social-psychological phenomena with a general theory does not force researchers to neglect the specifically social aspects of the matter. On the contrary, it should help make these specific aspects more explicit.

In reading social psychology literature, one currently runs into two general assumptions which might be contradictory though both are part and parcel of our common faith as social psychologists. The first assumption is that cognitive processes are necessarily the same, whether they apply to social or non-social objects, matters, domains, etc. The second assumption is that social "things" have some"thing" special about them which allows us to sharply contrast them to other "things". What these two assumptions have in common is that they both lack empirical support. We call on one or the other, depending on which one seems handier in the situation, but we are not so foolish as to try and demonstrate either of them. In fact, such general assumptions are probably not capable of proof. However, if we want to gain some knowledge about these questions, the best strategy is still to base our work on general theories. If some basic process is in fact at work in the phenomena we are studying, our chances of identifying it will improve, if we confront our results with the results of other researchers, and work on the same problem within different settings. Moreover, if social-psychological phenomena do in fact need a wider set of explanatory factors in order to be understood, referring to a general theory will lead us more directly to identifying and defining those factors, and to formulating hypotheses about the way our "specifically social" parameters interact with the other ones which the theory has already dealt with.

Recent research on perceived intra-group variability is a good example of the stimulating virtue of general theories on a social-psychological problem. Implicit in the notion of stereotype is the idea that members of a stereotyped category are seen as less diverse than they really are. However, the perceived variability of social categories was not studied explicitly before 1980. The first studies on the topic focused on differences between perception of ingroups and outgroups, and showed that outgroups were perceived as less complex (Linville, 1982) and more homogenous (Park & Rothbart, 1982). Park and Rothbart (1982) proposed that information about groups is stored in two parallel configurations: as memories for individual members of the group are stored, an abstract representation of the group is built up simultaneously. They hypothesized that a variability dimension is included in the abstract representation of the group.

In more recent articles by the same authors (Park & Hastie, 1987; Judd & Park, 1988; Linville, Fisher, & Salovey, 1989; Park, Judd, & Ryan, 1991), references to general theories of category construction were made more explicit and stated in greater detail. Let us briefly review the currently available theories on the topic. They can be distinguished by the way they answer the question: What kind of information is stored in LTM and constitutes category representation? This storing process might consist of keeping a distinct trace for each exemplar presented to the subject (Hintzman, 1986; Medin & Shaffer, 1978); or it might concern only the feature values of exemplars, with no memory for their configural aspect (Hayes-Roth & Hayes-Roth, 1977); these feature values might be stored as distributions (Fried & Holyoak, 1984) or on the contrary the subject might only memorize the central tendency on each feature value: in this last case we are faced with a prototype model (Posner & Keele, 1968; Reed, 1972); finally, one might even consider that category representation relies on dual coding, so that the subject simultaneously abstracts a category prototype, and keeps traces of instances (Medin, Altom, & Murphy, 1984). Park and Hastie (1987) discuss these models from the point of view of social categorization. In their view, two kinds of models are not equipped to deal with the acquisition and actual structure of social categories. Models based exclusively on memory for instances (Hintzman, 1986) cannot be applied to social category learning, since in real-life situations, subjects are often provided with information regarding the general characteristics of groups. Prototype models (Posner & Keele, 1968; Reed, 1972), as popular as they may be, especially among social psychologists, do not provide a realistic account of category representation, since they have nothing to say about category variability. So, Park and Hastie appear to favor either a model which allows for both instance-storage and construction of an abstract category representation (Medin, Altom, & Murphy, 1984), or a model which conceives of abstract category representation as including variability, namely, Fried and Holyoak's (1984) "category density model".

The main question is whether perceived variability results from the variability of recalled instances, or whether it is an intrinsic characteristic of the abstract group representation. Judd and Park's (1988) results are more consistent with the second alternative. However, an exemplar-based model is tenable, too, as Linville, Fischer and Salovey (1989) have demonstrated. These authors developed a model for perceived category distribution. It is based on Smith and Medin's (1981) formulation of a multiple exemplar process, in which exemplars can represent both knowledge of individual instances and abstractions about different types of category members. It assumes that people form perceived distributions by activating a set of category exemplars.

In short, Park and her co-workers assume that variability is stored as an aspect of group representation, and Linville and her colleagues assume that it is retrieved. It is not our place to decide who is right: this is a current debate, and readers are waiting for the next experiments to be published. We chose this topic as an example of how a typical social-psychological problem may be enriched by referring to general theories. Perhaps some of you will think that such a discussion steers us away from social reality. We are not at all convinced of that. Just think of a social problem like "how to change stereotypes". We believe that finding the best strategy for changing stereotypes depends on discovering which process is responsible for perceived variability.

3. What Is Social in Social Categorization?

The three conditions we just reviewed were in fact conditions for a truly cognitive approach. Last but not least, a further condition must be stated: that what is studied under this label must be truly social categorization. This means that it must have something to do, first, with the cognition of human beings, and second, with the place of these human beings in a social system.

The idea that general cognitive processes underlie any categorization process may be heuristically stimulating. However, we cannot *a priori* exclude the converse alternative, that some process may be specific to perceiving or cognizing human beings. Our knowledge on categorization of non-human objects cannot be uncritically generalized to social cognition without at least empirical verification. Conversely, when and where there are reasons to inquire into whether human objects would not trigger very specific processes (as in the case of face perception) this "specificity" hypothesis must be taken into consideration.

The notion of "social categorization" also means that the subject and the persons to be categorized are actors who are taking part in social functioning. Thus, social categories cannot be conceived of as free products of individual cognitive activity. The possible categorization systems are socially determined, and the meanings of categories refer to the actors' respective positions in a defined social situation. Social categories are always, more or less, status categories: they always refer to differences in rights and duties, differences in prestige, differences in reinforcement expectations for different required behaviors. Thus, each time a subject categorizes a person, he/she by the same token activates expectations on the kind of scripts which might take place in his/her interaction with the categorized person. In a number of cases, the subject will initiate the interactional routine which will confirm or infirm these expectations. So, conceiving of categorization as nothing more than information processing is a very incomplete view of the process. The subject is also a very efficient information elicitor, i.e. a good deal of the information processed has been produced by others in reaction to the subject's behavior.

Moreover, one characteristic of social categorization is that, most of the time, people may be categorized in several different manners. Which kind of categorization will be brought into play depends on several factors. For example, Taylor has suggested that we preferentially categorize persons according to what makes them more distinctive (Taylor & Fiske, 1978). It seems highly probable that categorization also depends on the subject's goals (Oakes & Turner, 1990). However, this last hypothesis has not yet received much attention. In fact, the greater part of social categorization literature, if not all of it, seems to consider categorization as a purely receptive and non-motivated process which has little or nothing to do with what the subject does, wants, seeks, or prefers.

Here, we can come back to a point we alluded to when speaking about Tajfel. Some social-psychological authors use the term "cognitive" in a very special way, which implies excluding a number of determinants from their study's scope. The best example of this is Hamilton, but Tajfel contributed to this usage too. A typical formulation by Hamilton is the following: "Not all stereotyping necessarily originates in the learning and motivational processes emphasized in the stereotype literature; cognitive factors alone can be sufficient to produce differential perceptions of social groups" (Hamilton & Gifford, 1976, p. 405). The very construction of this sentence clearly states that there are two kinds of factors which can produce stereotypes: cognitive factors on the one hand, learning and motivational processes on the other. In our view, this kind of formulation does not make sense. Cognitive processes are always at work; they may be simultaneously determined by the informational characteristics of the environment, and/or by the reinforcing characteristics of it, and/or by the subject's affective state, etc. But in any case, whatever determinant you are considering, cognitive processes are going on. However, which kind of cognitive process is going on might very well depend on the subject's affective state or current goals, on the reinforcement schedule he is experiencing, or on his/her preferences for this or that cognitive strategy, preferences which might be rooted in previous experience, either recent, moderately old, or extremely primitive, etc.

Until fairly recently, a large part of cognitive research was devoted to the effects of informational determinants. It does not necessarily follow that manipulating variables pertaining to the informational characteristics of the environment is the only valid way of studying cognitive processes. The study of motivational and reinforcing determinants rightfully belongs to cognitive psychology. Within social psychology at least, it seems that people who follow the cognitive approach have chosen to work on situations where the subject's motivational state is low or unknown, as are the reinforcing values of alternatives. Apart from reasons of feasibility, this option is based on the implicit postulate that cognitive processes are best studied under the lowest possible motivational, "drive", or "involvement" levels. This idea, that the less the subject is concerned with the situation, the more he/she will resort to "basic" processes, is completely unquestioned, and probably groundless.

Two kinds of logical mistakes may ensue from this gratuitous postulate. Some cognitive processes, brought to light by experiments which have carefully eliminated any kind of emotional involvement on the subject's part, might be unduly considered as general, though the conditions for their appearance are in fact extremely restrictive. Some very well-known effects, obtained in such a social vacuum, appear to be extremely fragile, as soon as some social flesh is put onto the informational skeleton. For example, Shaller and Maass (1989) have shown that the Distinctiveness-based Illusory Correlation disappears when subjects are told they belong to one of the categories to be learned; in this case, responses are biased by ingroup favoritism.

The second kind of mistake is the converse of the above. Some social phenomena are overly attributed to so-called "cognitive factors", with the restrictive meaning we already underscored. And, since cognitive processes are defined from the beginning as something intrinsically different from motivational, affective, or reinforcement-governed processes, explaining a social phenomenon by the cognitive processes underlying it implies that we deny the crucial importance of these "other factors". However, this exclusion is not the result of an empirical demonstration, but only the consequence of a self-limiting decision the researcher imposes on the meaning of words.

A very worrisome example of this kind of circular reasoning is the following quotation by Oakes and Turner (1990): "It is now widely recognized that the phenomena of stereotyping and prejudice are best kept conceptually distinct, i.e. stereotyping is viewed as a normal process of social cognition which may or may not operate on a hostile, prejudiced, attitudinal content." (p.117). We would agree with this statement, if it had implied an intention to study positively loaded stereotypes as well as negatively loaded ones, and to examine whether or not the strength and orientation of the subject's attitude affects the stereotyping process. But this is not what Oakes and Turner intended to do. Two lines further, they wrote: "The present chapter discusses stereotyping process [...] and not prejudice attitudes" (p. 117). In other words, in order to "keep stereotyping and prejudice conceptually distinct", they will first restrict the study (but not the definition) of stereotyping to the cases where the attitude is not hostile, and afterwards extend their conclusions to any kind of stereotypes, whether they operate on a favorable or hostile content. This kind of reasoning is not logically valid.

People who try to reduce social-psychological phenomena to underlying cognitive processes are often motivated by the contention that cognitive explanations are simpler; but it might well only be that their conception of cognition is simple and false. An example of this simplistic cognitivism is the common idea that the fundamental function of categorization is to "reduce the amount of information we must contend with" (Hamilton & Trolier, 1986). Human cognition is supposed to be inherently constrained by a limited information-processing capacity, hence the necessity to use information-processing shortcuts, which unfortunately introduce bias into social perception and judgment. Oakes and Turner (1990) developed a very subtle discussion of what they call " the currently dominant metatheory of social cognition" (p. 118), i.e. Taylor's (1981; Fiske & Taylor, 1984) model of the person as a "cognitive miser". Though we have some serious objections to Oakes and Turner's position, as stated above, we certainly agree with them when they write "Far from reducing or impoverishing perceptual experience, categorization enriches and expands it", appealing to Bruner's patronage. The notion of "limited information-processing capacity" is often referred to in a very loose and allusive manner, without serious consideration of Shannon's original model (cf. Duflos & Lauvergeon,

1988). In our view, this model cannot be called upon for explaining one major characteristic of stereotypes: their stability. In Shannon's theory, the information processed is a function of the number of elements to be processed and of their subjective probability. But the definition of "elements" on which probabilities are evaluated varies considerably, depending on learning. The more the subject becomes familiar with a given environment, the more he learns complex patterns of conditional probabilities, and the more he will be able to treat as informational units what previously appeared to him as co-occurrences of several events. Consequently, though the human cognitive capacity is certainly limited, there is no objective definition of the quantity of information which would make the channel overflow: it depends on the way the subject treats information. Any learning process might appear to an external observer as an exponential growth of processing capacity. Of course, it only appears to be so. But when, on the contrary, we notice that subjects seem to be content with their rather modest cognitive performance, the limited information-processing capacity should not be too quickly used. A much more interesting question would be: Why did they stop learning? What kind of reward did they get for stopping? And one cannot even guess any sensible answer to this question unless social reality is considered.

As long as social psychologists equate "studying cognitive processes" with "neglecting societal functioning and motivational determinants", they will be victims of such logical mistakes. The implicit postulate, that cognitive processes are best studied under conditions of the lowest possible motivational levels, far from allowing us to unearth the most general mechanisms, might very well carry us along the blind alley of curiosities.

References

Andersen, S. M., & Cole, S. W. (1990). "Do I Know You?": The role of significant others in general social perception. *Journal of Personality and Social Psychology, 59*, 384-399.

Duflos, A. & Lauvergeon, G. (1988). Variabilité comportementale, théorie de l'information et interaction sociale : ou des us et abus d'un modèle. *Revue Internationale de Psychologie Sociale, 1*, 113-128.

Fabre, J.-M. (1990). Specificity and categorization in judgments: A cognitive approach to stereotypes. In J.-P. Caverni, J.-M. Fabre, & M. Gonzalez (Eds.), *Cognitive biases* (pp. 401-422). Amsterdam: North-Holland.

Fiedler, K. (1991). The tricky nature of skewed frequency tables: An information-loss account of "distinctiveness-based illusory correlations". *Journal of Personality and Social Psychology, 60,* 24-36.

Fiske, S. T., & Pavelchak, M. A. (1986). Category-based versus piecemeal-based affective responses: Developments in schema-triggered affect. In R. M. Sorrentino & E. T. Higgins (Eds.), *The handbook of motivation and cognition: Foundations of social behavior* (pp. 167-203). New York: Guilford Press.

Fiske, S. T., & Taylor, S. E. (1984). *Social cognition*. Reading, MA: Addison-Wesley.

Fried, L. S., & Holyoak, K. J. (1984). Induction of category distribution: A framework for classification learning. *Journal of Experimental Psychology: Learning, Memory and Cognition, 10,* 234-257.

Hamilton, D. L., Dugan, P. M., & Trolier, T. K. (1985). The formation of stereotypic beliefs: Further evidence for distinctiveness-based illusory correlations. *Journal of Personality and Social Psychology, 48,* 5-17.

Hamilton, D. L., & Gifford, R. K. (1976). Illusory correlation in interpersonal perception: A cognitive basis of stereotypic judgments. *Journal of Experimental Social Psychology, 12,* 392-407.

Hamilton, D. L., & Trolier, T. K. (1986). Stereotypes and stereotyping: An overview of the cognitive approach. In J. F. Dovidio & S. L. Gaertner (Eds.), *Prejudice, discrimination, and racism* (pp. 127-163). Orlando, FL: Academic Press.

Hayes-Roth, B., & Hayes-Roth, F. (1977). Concept learning and the recognition and classification of exemplars. *Journal of Verbal Learning and Verbal Behavior, 16,* 321-338.

Hintzman, D. L. (1986). "Schema abstraction" in a multiple-trace memory model. *Psychological Review, 93,* 411-428.

Judd, C. M., & Park, B. (1988). Out-group homogeneity: Judgments of variability at the individual and group levels. *Journal of Personality and Social Psychology, 54,* 778-788.

La Haye, A.-M. de (1991). Problems and procedures: A typology of paradigms in interpersonal cognition. *Cahiers de Psychologie Cognitive / European Bulletin of Cognitive Psychology, 11,* 279-304.

La Haye, A.-M. de & Lauvergeon, G. (1991). Processus mnésiques dans la formation des corrélations illusoires. *Psychologie Française, 36,* 67-77.

Linville, P. W. (1982). The complexity-extremity effect and age-based stereotyping. *Journal of Personality and Social Psychology, 42,* 193-211.

Linville, P. W., Fischer, G. W., & Salovey, P. (1989). Perceived distributions of in-group and out-group members: Empirical evidence and a computer simulation. *Journal of Personality and Social Psychology, 57,* 165-188.

Matalon, B., & La Haye, A.-M. de (1992). *Swans, swallows, and statistics.* Unpublished manuscript.

Medin, D. L., Altom, M. W., & Murphy, T. D. (1984). Given versus induced category representations: Use of prototype and exemplar information in classification. *Journal of Experimental Psychology: Learning, Memory and Cognition, 10,* 333-352.

Medin, D. L., & Shaffer, M. M. (1978). Context theory of classification learning. *Psychological Review, 85,* 207-238.

Oakes, P. J., & Turner, J. C. (1990). Is limited information processing capacity the cause of social stereotyping?

Park, B., & Hastie, R. (1987). Perception of variability in category development: Instance versus abstraction-based stereotypes. *Journal of Personality and Social Psychology, 53,* 621-635.

Park, B., Judd, C. M., & Ryan, C. S. (1991). Social categorization and the representation of variability information. In W. Stroebe & M. Hewstone (Eds.), *European Review of Social Psychology* (Vol. 2, pp. 211-245). New York: Willey.

Park, B., & Rothbart, M. (1982). Perception of out-group homogeneity and levels of social categorization. *Journal of Personality and Social Psychology, 42,* 1051-1068.

Pavelchak, M. (1989). Piecemeal and category-based evaluation: An idiographic analysis. *Journal of Personality and Social Psychology, 56,* 354-363.

Posner, M. I., & Keele, S. W. (1968). On the genesis of abstract ideas. *Journal of Experimental Psychology, 77,* 353-363.

Rabbie, J. M., Schot, J. C., & Visser, L. (1989). Social Identity Theory: A conceptual and empirical critique from the perspective of a behavioural interaction model. *European Journal of Social Psychology, 19,* 171-202.

Reed, S. K. (1972). Pattern recognition and categorization. *Cognitive Psychology, 3,* 382-407.

Rosch, E., & Mervis, C. B. (1975). Family resemblances: Studies in the internal structure of categories. *Cognitive Psychology, 7,* 573-605.

Schaller, M., & Maass, A. (1989). Illusory correlation and social categorization: Toward an integration of motivational and cognitive factors in stereotype formation. *Journal of Personality and Social Psychology, 56,* 709-721.

Sherif, M. (1966). *In common predicament: Social psychology of intergroup conflict and cooperation.* Boston, MA: Houghton Miffin.

Smith, E. R. (1991). Illusory correlation in a simulated exemplar-based memory. *Journal of Experimental Social Psychology, 27,* 107-123.

Smith, E. R., & Medin, D. L. (1981). *Categories and concepts.* Cambridge, MA: Harvard University Press.

Tajfel, H. (1969). Cognitive aspects of prejudice. *Journal of Social Issues, 25,* 79-97.

Tajfel, H., & Wilkes, A. (1963). Classification and social judgment. *British Journal of Psychology, 54,* 101-114.

Taylor, S. E. (1976). Developing a cognitive social psychology. In J. S. Carroll & J. W. Payne (Eds.), *Cognition and social behavior.* Hillsdale, NJ: Erlbaum.

Taylor, S. E. (1981). The interface between social and cognitive psychology. In J. H. Harvey (Ed.), *Cognition, social behavior, and the environment* (pp. 189-211). Hillsdale, NJ: Erlbaum.

Taylor, S. E., & Fiske, S. T. (1978). Salience, attention, and attribution: Top of the head phenomena. In L. Berkowitz (Ed.), *Advances in experimental social psychology* (Vol. 11, pp. 249-288). New York: Academic Press.

Tversky, A., & Kahneman, D. (1973). Availability: A heuristic for judging frequency and probability. *Cognitive Psychology, 5,* 207-232.

CONTEXT, CATEGORIZATION, AND CHANGE

CONSEQUENCES OF CULTURAL CONTRASTS
ON COMPLIANCE AND CONVERSION

William D. Crano
Texas A&M University, U.S.A.

Can the encoding of fundamental perceptual events be influenced by social factors? From its inception as a scientific discipline, social psychology has been obsessed with this issue, and our literature is replete with attempts to provide a definitive resolution to this question. In his work of more than a half-century ago, for example, Muzafer Sherif (1935, 1936) attempted to determine the manner in which enduring and shared response tendencies, or social norms, were developed. Sherif made use of the autokinetic illusion in his studies to learn whether subjects' perceptions of the illusory movement of a stationary light source could be mediated by imposition of a response norm advanced by the socially supplied judgments of others.[1]

Sherif was partly successful in his quest. Hood and Sherif (1962) disclosed that when an experimental accomplice consistently made either very high or low distance estimates of autokinetic movement, the subsequent judgments of subjects who merely had witnessed these responses were affected, even though these subjects' estimates were made after the confederate had been removed from the experimental context. Because Sherif's perceptual stimuli were completely illusory, it is impossible to know the precise extent to which social or perceptual factors influenced respondents' reports; at a minimum, however, his results suggest the possibility of social influence of basic perceptions.

---

[1] The illusion operates as follows: when a person fixates on a small pinpoint of light in an otherwise totally darkened room, the light appears to move. The perception of movement occurs even though the light source is stationary. The autokinetic effect is a compelling illusion – the illusory movement of the light is perceived even by those who *know* the light is fixed.

Later research by Solomon Asch (1951, 1956), perhaps better known than Sherif's, has also fueled the debate on the issue of the effects of social influence on primitive perceptions. Whether Asch intended his research to be used in this manner is open to discussion (cf. Campbell, 1990), for it is clear that the basic methodology of his line judgment studies rendered them incapable even of addressing the issue of persistence of social influence in a scientifically credible manner (cf. Festinger, 1953). Indeed, corollary data (Asch, 1956) suggest that subjects' reports, not their perceptions, were mediated by social influence.

Thus, the issue of the impact of social actors on perception remained unresolved. However, recent research promised to provide a definitive resolution of this issue, and in so doing, to detail the manner in which influence processes operated in mediating social behavior. This work, undertaken by Moscovici and Personnaz (1980), grew out of a theoretical orientation that held that the influence tactics of majorities and minorities were fundamentally different, and furthermore, that their influence stimulated fundamentally different change processes in the targets of their persuasive treatments (Moscovici, 1976, 1980, 1985). Theoretically, these cognitive processes had implications for the manner in which change was brought about, and for its persistence and resistance in the face of counterpressures.

1. The Spectrometer Research

In terms of design, results, and implications, Moscovici and Personnaz's (1980) study was remarkable. Let us consider its design in detail, since it forms the foundation for all that follows. The basic procedure of this study required subjects simply to judge the color of a series of slides. The slides were inevitably blue. After a brief session of independent judgments, female subjects learned that the individual with whom they were to respond subsequently (actually, an accomplice of the experimenter) had made a series of judgments that placed her in the majority, or in the minority, of prior respondents. Subject and accomplice then began an interactive (public) judgment session, during which they responded in concert to another series of slides. After each stimulus presentation, confederate and subject announced their judgments.

In this public response session, without exception, the slides were blue – and just as inevitably, the confederate, whose earlier judgments had placed her either in the minority or the majority, insisted that they were green. Results indicated that this ruse had no obvious impact on subjects' judgments, no matter what the confederate's status. Despite the fact that some subjects were paired with an individual whose judgments placed her in the apparent majority, almost no one could be persuaded to report that an obviously blue slide was green.

This is not to say, however, that the accomplices had no impact. In keeping with Festinger's (1953) admonition to differentiate public compliance from private acceptance, Moscovici and Personnaz employed a follow-on condition in their experiment, in which the subject judged the colors of yet another slide series *after* the confederate had been removed from the experimental context. In addition to the standard judgment, subjects reported the *chromatic afterimage* they experienced when the colored slide was removed from the screen. When subjects responded in private, in this final phase of the experiment, some interesting deviations from this essentially null pattern of results began to emerge. Again, on the color naming task, there was little evidence of influence by either majority or minority confederates. Almost everyone always responded "blue" when the slides were flashed onto the screen. However, the visual afterimages subjects perceived were significantly affected by the minority or majority status of the confederate with whom they had been paired in the influence section of the study. Subjects paired with the majority confederate reported afterimages that tended toward the complement of blue, which is orange. This is an informative result, because it suggests that these subjects were reporting what they saw – they said the slides they saw were blue, and the afterimages they reported after each slide were the complement of this color.

However, the subjects in the minority confederate condition reported afterimages that corresponded to having been exposed to green slides. Rather than being orange, that is, the afterimages these subjects (who had responded in concert with an accomplice of minority status) reported tended toward the red end of the spectrum, and red is the complement of green. Despite the fact that they continued to report seeing blue slides, their afterimages suggested that they had been influenced by their (minority status) response partner, because they reported the complement of green, the color the minority accomplice apparently had perceived. Since subjects were unwilling to acknowledge this influence (either to the confederate or to themselves, perhaps), they continued to respond "blue" on their verbal reports. However, on a measure that they did not consciously monitor or control, the influence of the minority was manifest.

2. Critical Reaction

This is an extraordinary finding. Yet, the study of Moscovici and Personnaz (1980) has had relatively little impact. Why is this so? Clearly one reason is because the Moscovici/Personnaz research was followed immediately, in the same issue of the journal in which it was published, by two experiments that failed to replicate its findings (cf. Doms & van Avermaet, 1980; Sorrentino, King, & Leo, 1980). It is my purpose to examine the empirical controversy surrounding this group of studies, and to propose an explanation based on results from social comparison research and the study of small groups. This integrative alternative explanation of the lack of fit between the competing studies is based on a consideration of the different laboratory "cultures" that characterize social psychological research in France and North America (cf. Peabody, 1985).

2.1 Social Comparison

We begin with some recent research on social comparison theory conducted by Gorenflo and Crano (1989), who hypothesized that people might be differentially sensitive to ingroup or outgroup influence as a consequence of the nature of the judgment required of them. If subjects believe the judgment they are to make is subjective (dependent upon personal attitudes or values, not capable of objective verification), they were hypothesized to be relatively more open to communications from people like themselves; if the task is objective (factual, capable of verification), however, information or communications from outsiders were hypothesized to prove more influential.

To test this theory, Gorenflo and Crano (1989) conducted a series of experiments. In the second of their studies, subjects were asked to play the role of a juror in a criminal trial, whose task was to judge the guilt or innocence of an individual charged with the capital crime of murder. Subjects made individual judgments, but were studied in a group context. A minimal group procedure was employed as the first exercise in the research, in advance of any other activity. After being placed into one group or another on the basis of a dot estimation task (cf. Howard & Rothbart, 1980), all subjects read an extensive collection of materials relevant to the case, including testimony of prosecution and defense witnesses. Before beginning this task, some subjects were told that these materials were insufficient to allow them to form an objective appraisal of guilt or innocence. As such, they were to rely upon their own subjective values in coming to a decision about the defendant. The other subjects were informed that the information provided was similar to that available to the typical jury member. They were told that they had sufficient data on which to base an objective judgment, and they were to rely on this information in coming to their judgment of guilt or innocence. Of course, all subjects received precisely the same information, only its characterization differed.

After reading the information, subjects individually decided the fate of the defendant. They then wrote a defense of their decision. After all had completed this task, the experimenter explained that jury members typically did not work in isolation, but in concert with other jurors. Accordingly, each subject was given the opportunity to compare his or her judgment with that of another participant. The critical issue of this experiment was the subjects' choice of comparison partner. Were subjects influenced by the apparent subjective or objective nature of the task, and if so, was this influence consistent with expectations?

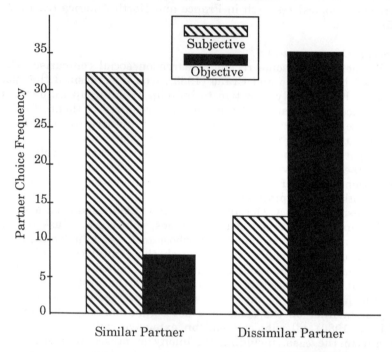

Figure 1. Preference for ingroup or outgroup comparison partner as a function of the subjective or objective nature of the required judgment.

The answer to this question, the main result of this study, is summarized in Figure 1. As illustrated, those who thought their judgments were fundamentally *subjective* chose to compare their decision with others *like themselves*, irrespective of the particular minimal group to which they were (randomly) assigned. Quite the opposite pattern was evident among the subjects who assumed that their judgments were objective. These subjects overwhelmingly preferred outgroup comparison partners.

2.2 Small Groups Research

Although this work suggests a preference for ingroup or outgroup comparison on the basis of considerations of (objective vs. subjective) task type, it is mute with respect to differential *susceptibility* to ingroup or outgroup influence sources. However, converging evidence from research on small groups reinforces the task-type distinction, and bolsters the findings derived from the study of social comparison theory (e.g., Goethals & Darley, 1987; Gorenflo & Crano, 1989; Olson, Ellis, & Zanna, 1983). The small groups data suggest that task or issue variations render targets differentially susceptible to different types of influence sources. Kaplan (1989), for example, maintains that the effectiveness of an influence source will depend on the nature or type of decision task. Accordingly, it is critical to detect features of tasks that are responsible for influence targets' differential susceptibility. Laughlin and Ellis (1986) provided one useful attempt at task categorization when they suggested that tasks or issues be ordered along a continuum ranging from *intellective* to *judgmental*. In Laughlin and Ellis' terms, intellective tasks or issues are those for which there is a demonstrably correct, objective solution. Such definitive resolution is not feasible on judgmental tasks; rather, peer consensus defines validity (McGrath, 1984). Building upon this work, Kaplan (1987, 1989; Rugs & Kaplan, in press) has shown that when the judgment task involves intellective issues, people *prefer* exposure to materials that Deutsch and Gerard (1955) have termed *informational*, i.e. to materials that involve arguments and interpretations concerned with evidence about reality. Conversely, people are less concerned with obtaining informational evidence on judgmental tasks. Instead, they clearly prefer normative materials, i.e. information about the predilections or subjective attitudes of others *within their social group*. These differential preference findings parallel those obtained in research on social comparison.

And there is more to it than this. In addition to preference differences, the small group researchers have found evidence that suggests that *susceptibility* to these different forms of information is affected by task type. For example, Mills and Kimble (1973), Laughlin and Ellis (1986), and Kaplan (1989), among others, have shown that subjects engaging in an objective (or intellective) task are more susceptible to informational influence, while those participating in subjective (or judgmental) tasks are more vulnerable to normative (i.e., subjective, peer-based) influence. These findings map precisely onto the evidence developed in the study of partner preference in social comparison.

3. Generalization and Extension: A Possible Solution to the Controversy

What have these results to do with the blue-green controversy? With the acceptance of a modest and plausible assumption, the findings suggest that the underlying cause of the dispute might have had nothing to do with the reasons offered by the researchers whose results did not replicate those of Moscovici and Personnaz (1980). It is the position of this report that the Moscovici/Personnaz study was conducted in a laboratory culture that differed from that of Doms and van Avermaet (1980) and of Sorrentino, King, and Leo (1980), and these differences fostered culture-specific variations in subjects' attributions regarding the nature of the task. If these culture-based differences were systematic and specific, then the nonconvergent results observed in this area are not only predictable, but inevitable.

What are these differences? Suppose that we hypothesize that the French subjects in the Moscovici/Personnaz experiment were accustomed to researchers insisting that they attend closely to the task at hand, take it seriously, and labor to arrive at the correct answer. On the basis of personal communication (with B. Personnaz) and an understanding of the ways in which social research is conducted in France, this is not an unreasonable assumption. The implications of such an approach is to suggest to subjects that the task involves judgments of objective reality. Why else would they be entreated to strive for accuracy? In other words, for the French subjects of Moscovici and Personnaz (1980), the blue-green task involved objective judgments. In objective-judgment situations, we know from research reviewed earlier that people prefer, and are more susceptible to, information provided by representatives of the outgroup. In the specific circumstances of Moscovici and Personnaz' study, the outgroup was of minority status. Hence, we would expect that the minority would exert greater influence than the majority on subjects' judgments – and this is precisely the result that was obtained.

It is more difficult to predict the experimenter-subject dynamics in the laboratories of Doms and van Avermaet and of Sorrentino, King, and Leo. To be sure, in North American laboratories we insist that subjects take their roles seriously. On the other hand, we often inform subjects that their task has no right-or-wrong answer, that we are interested in their personal feelings or judgments, etc. In such instructional contexts, subjects must infer that their task is fundamentally subjective. And under such circumstances, we know that the ingroup will enjoy a persuasive advantage.

Which context operated in the laboratories of Doms and van Avermaet and of Sorrentino, King, and Leo? It is impossible to tell. At a minimum, however, it is unlikely that subjects' perceptions of the subjective or objective nature of the experimental task were as explicitly controlled as in the French laboratory. As such, subjects' task attributions were free to vary, and such variations could be responsible for the unpredicted data patterns observed in these studies.

In summary, I have proposed an integrative resolution to the paradoxical findings observed in the research concerned with Moscovici and Personnaz' (1980) blue-green experiment. The resolution is based on well-established findings, which suggest differential susceptibility to ingroup or outgroup influence as a function of the nature of the critical task or issue. I postulate that the laboratory cultures of France and North America differ substantially in their subjective organizational climate, and that these differences are responsible for the paradoxical findings that characterize the unsuccessful attempts at replicating the research of Moscovici and Personnaz (1980). My approach strongly suggests that predicting the outcome of an influence attempt without understanding subjects' reflexive sense of self (and others!) is short-sighted. To understand the dynamics of self-change, we must understand reflexivity *and* self-regulation, as Codol demonstrated time and again in his own research.

References

Asch, S. E. (1951). Effects of group pressure upon the modification and distortion of judgment. In H. Guetzkow (Ed.), *Groups, leadership, and men.* Pittsburgh: Carnegie Press.

Asch, S. E. (1956). Studies of independence and conformity: I. A minority of one against a unanimous majority. *Psychological Monographs, 70,* No. 9 (whole No. 416).

Campbell, D. T. (1990). Asch's moral epistemology for socially shared knowledge. In I. Rock (Ed.), *The legacy of Solomon Asch: Essays in cognition and social psychology.* Hillsdale, NJ: Erlbaum.

Deutsch, M., & Gerard, H. B. (1955). A study of normative and informational social influence upon individual judgment. *Journal of Abnormal and Social Psychology, 51,* 629-636.

Doms, M., & van Avermaet, E. (1980). Majority influence, minority influence and conversion behavior: A replication. *Journal of Experimental Social Psychology, 16,* 283-292.

Festinger, L. (1953). An analysis of compliant behavior. In M. Sherif & M. O. Wilson (Eds.), *Group relations at the crossroads* (pp. 232-256). New York: Harper.

Goethals, G. R., & Darley, J. M. (1987). Social comparison theory: Self-evaluation and group life. In B. Mullen & G. R. Goethals (Eds.), *Theories of group behavior* (pp. 21-47). New York: Springer-Verlag.

Gorenflo, D. W., & Crano, W. D. (1989). Judgmental subjectivity/objectivity and locus of choice in social comparison. *Journal of Personality and Social Psychology, 57,* 605-614.

Hood, W. R., & Sherif, M. (1962). Verbal report and judgment of an unstructured stimulus. *Journal of Psychology, 54,* 121-130.

Howard, J. W., & Rothbart, M. (1980). Social categorization and memory for ingroup and outgroup behavior. *Journal of Personality and Social Psychology, 38,* 301-310.

Kaplan, M. F. (1987). The influence process in group decision making. In C. Hendrick (Ed.), *Review of Personality and Social Psychology: Group Processes* (Vol. 8, pp. 189-212). Beverly Hills, CA: Sage.

Kaplan, M. F. (1989). Task, situational, and personal determinants of influence processes in group decision making. *Advances in Group Processes, 6,* 87-105.

Laughlin, P. R., & Ellis, A. L. (1986). Demonstrability and social combination processes on mathematical intellective tasks. *Journal of Experimental Social Psychology, 22,* 177-189.

McGrath, J. E. (1984). *Groups: Interaction and performance.* Englewood Cliffs, NJ: Prentice-Hall.

Mills, J., & Kimble, C. E. (1973). Opinion change as a function of perceived similarity of the communicator and subjectivity of the issue. *Bulletin of the Psychonomic Society, 2,* 35-36.

Moscovici, S. (1976). *Social influence and social change.* New York: Academic Press.

Moscovici, S. (1980). Toward a theory of conversion behavior. In L. Berkowitz (Ed.), *Advances in experimental social psychology* (Vol. 13, pp. 209-239). New York: Academic Press.

Moscovici, S. (1985). Social influence and conformity. In G. Lindzey & E. Aronson (Eds.), *The handbook of social psychology* (Vol. 2, pp. 347-412) (3rd ed.). New York: Random House.

Moscovici, S., & Personnaz, B. (1980). Studies in social influence V: Minority influence and conversion behavior in a perceptual task. *Journal of Experimental Social Psychology, 16,* 270-282.

Olson, J. M., Ellis, R. J., & Zanna, M. P. (1983). Validating objective versus subjective judgments: Interest in social comparison and consistency information. *Personality and Social Psychology Bulletin, 9,* 427-436.

Peabody, D. (1985). *National characteristics.* Cambridge/Paris: Cambridge University Press/Maison des Sciences de l'Homme.

Rugs, D., & Kaplan, M. F. (in press). Effectiveness of informational and normative influences in group decision making depends on group interactive goal. *British Journal of Social Psychology*.

Sherif, M. (1935). A study of some social factors in perception. *Archives of Psychology, 27*, No. 187.

Sherif, M. (1936). *The psychology of social norms*. New York: Harper & Row.

Sorrentino, R. M., King, G., & Leo, G. (1980). The influence of the minority on perception: A note on a possible alternative explanation. *Journal of Experimental Social Psychology, 16*, 293-301.

A SOCIONORMATIVE INTERPRETATION
OF ILLUSORY CORRELATION EFFECTS

François Le Poultier

University of Haute Bretagne, Rennes, France

People who hear about bad deeds committed within a community willingly attribute them to a minority group even if no information is available to justify their conclusion. This kind of phenomenon is well known by social psychologists. It is a result of an illusory correlation which is a biased processing of information that causes people to establish a relationship between two variables or events when in fact the relationship is either much weaker than perceived, nonexistent or even the opposite of what was believed to be true. For about fifteen years, studies on illusory correlation have been inspired mostly by a cognitive approach and have been carried out using an experimental paradigm which manipulates the rare or distinctive aspects of falsely associated elements. Just like the positivity bias (Boucher & Osgood, 1969), the effects of persistence (Ross, Lepper, & Hubbard, 1975) or the fundamental attribution error (Ross, 1977), the illusory correlation is also perceived as one of the random activities of information processing carried out by people who have neither the time nor the means to be real scientists. Recent experimental data suggest that such a conception is insufficient to explain the effects of illusory correlation, especially concerning variations which affect the intensity of false associations. Furthermore, all of Heider's theory, which is the basis of social cognition analysis, would have to be re-examined if in fact the so-called biases, errors or other distortions are not the mere result of disfunctions attributable to weaknesses in encoding, storage or recall processes, but also result from a normative activity which implicates people's social positions.

1. A Cognitive Standpoint Based Upon Distinctiveness

In 1967, Chapman introduced the concept of illusory correlation to explain how people organize their knowledge of the world around them and especially how they elaborate their judgements or beliefs. Results of an initial experiment showed that during a word pair recall exercise, subjects created word associations which were not presented in the original material. According to Chapman, the errors in word pair recall were due to certain characteristics of the falsely associated words such as their semantic proximity or their resemblance. Later on, Chapman and Chapman (1969) illustrated how the illusory correlation works in the field of psychological diagnostics based on Rorschach test answers. They found no difference between professional psychodiagnosticians and inexperienced students when they asked them to indicate what Rorschach signs were indicators of male homosexuality. Professional psychodiagnosticians had a tendency to choose popular signs with no clinical validity in the associations made between test answers and symptoms. These types of errors which affect judgements made by professionals and laymen alike are assumed to originate from the distinctive nature of two falsely correlated pieces of information. Does illusory correlation occur during the process of encoding or during retrieval and recall, or does it happen while information is integrated into a global judgement? This question was to be clearly examined later (La Haye & Lauvergeon, 1991).

Following the work of Hamilton and Gifford (1976), illusory correlation was the subject of a series of experiments and the cause of a whole set of theoretical considerations which gradually concerned social psychology less and less as it took on a more cognitive focus. A more social-psychological approach could have been derived from Golding and Rorer's experiment (1972) when they tried to explain the phenomenon of illusory correlation in relation to the subject's preconceptions or to his/her implicit personality theory. But they immediately limited the theoretical impact of their work to an *a priori* bias. Thus, subjects tested on the interpretations they would make of Rorschach test answers and on the four symptoms they would associate to those answers showed very strong anticipations. When the subjects were led to make the most out of the answers, they were more susceptible to the expected relationships than to others. After the subjects had been repeatedly exposed to training materials, the illusory correlation did go down, but even so, it was extremely powerful since it resisted the effects of an intensive training period which normally should have reduced subjects' interest in false relationships in order to give way to truer associations.

For about ten years most of the research on illusory correlations was dominated by Hamilton's model (Hamilton & Gifford, 1976; Hamilton, 1981). This model is based upon two principles: (a) phenomenon which closely resembles stereotypical productions habitually studied by social psychologists is liable to purely cognitive explanations whenever only intrinsic properties of processed information and subjects' processing capacities are involved; (b) the assumed illusory correlation at the root of these stereotypical events or behaviors depends on a salience or distinctiveness effect which affects two falsely correlated pieces of information. This effect is triggered by the rarity or the statistical infrequency of one of the two pieces of information. In a pioneer experiment whose basic framework has been replicated many times, subjects examine a series of 39 behaviors consisting of 27 socially desirable behaviors and 12 socially undesirable ones. These behaviors are attributed to two groups of people, one group of 26 being the majority group and the other of 13 being the minority group. The behaviors are assigned to each group in such a way that the rates of the socially desirable and undesirable behaviors are the same for each of the two groups. During recall, when subjects have to re-attribute behaviors to each group, a significant increase in undesirable behaviors attributed to the minority group is observed. According to Hamilton and Gifford, the attribution of undesirable behaviors to the minority group is due to the statistical infrequency of the types of information and not to any obscure motivations or desires that the subjects may have which would cause the minority group to be held responsible for the socially undesirable actions. The results of an experimental variation strongly reinforce their argument because when the numerical relationship between the two types of behavior is reversed, subjects attribute more of the socially desirable behavior, which has become statistically rarer, to the minority group.

Distinctiveness theory has become a necessary reference in the study of illusory correlation. The effects observed by Hamilton and Gifford have been replicated (Hamilton, Dugan, & Trolier, 1985), reexamined in terms of encoding (Pryor, 1986), and put into a more general theoretical perspective (Acorn, Hamilton, & Sherman, 1988; Schaller & Maass, 1989; Mullen & Johnson, 1990). They have also been studied with schizophrenics (Brennan & Hemsbley, 1984), in performance tasks (Sanbotmatsu, Shavitt, Sherman, & Roskos Ewolden, 1987; Smither, Collins, & Buda, 1989) and in relation to induced moods (Mackie, Hamilton, Schroth, & Carlisle, 1989). Hamilton's theoretical model and the experimental paradigm developed with Gifford have also inspired studies containing more social variables, with variations in the instructions or in the tasks instead of just having the subjects learn the types of behavior associated with the two groups.

In a series of experiments using Hamilton and Gifford's experimental procedure, subjects had to deal with some types of information which had a certain value in regard to their opinion (Spears, van der Pligt, & Eiser, 1985; Spears, Eiser, & van der Pligt, 1987). This self-relevance variable has effects on the illusory correlation bias. Thus, subjects whose attitudes are the same as those of the minority group produce greater illusory correlation effect when they have to re-attribute favorable versus unfavorable statements to a majority or a minority group. But the analysis of the results follows the same reasoning as in the preceding explanations since the increase or decrease in the illusory correlation due to the introduced self-relevance variable is essentially interpreted in terms of information distinctiveness. When a subject has the same attitude toward a given type of information as that of a group, this information is more salient and therefore more likely to be associated with another equally distinctive piece of information because of its statistical rarity.

2. Reductions in Bias Intensity

There are nevertheless limits to a strictly cognitive analysis of illusory correlations. Some authors have experienced difficulties in reproducing effects with the classic procedure (Feldman, Calburn, & Gatti, 1986). Others having conducted an experiment on illusory correlation between educational attitudes and different types of people consider that the observed effects cannot be ascribed to inherent laws of cognitive functioning but could be attributed to arbitrarily chosen and acquired strategies (Fiedler, Hemmeter, & Hoffman, 1984). Finally, appreciable variations in the magnitude of the illusory correlation have been observed when subjects have had to deal with information connected with their future professional activity (Le Poultier, 1990). It appears that there is a smaller illusory correlation between a minority group and socially undesirable behavior for social work students than for a control group composed of biology students. During the same study it was also observed that senior social work students made re-attributions of behavior which were less affected by the illusory correlation bias than first year social work students. In the light of these factors the measured rate of the illusory correlation goes down as a function of the degree of commitment people have in their professional training. Several interpretations can be made of these kinds of effects.

An initial interpretation could be based on an extension of the notion of distinctiveness as tightly defined in Hamilton's conception. Social work students may be less sensitive than other subjects to the statistical rarity such as a minority group or an undesirable behavior for instance, because of their professional training which familiarizes them with these kinds of phenomena. They may partially ignore the statistical aspect of the experiment making the most of the general knowledge they have acquired about social groups and behavior. Moreover, at the end of the experiment more future social workers than biology students thought that the two groups were the same size (37.50 % as opposed to 18.20 %) and that the number of socially desirable behaviors was the same as the number of socially undesirable ones (35.42 % of the subjects as opposed to 22.73 %). In summary the illusory correlation effect may be weaker for certain subjects because the information dealt with is less distinctive for them. A second interpretation gives a different explanation to the decrease in the magnitude of the illusory correlation for the social work students in comparison with the biology students. The distinctiveness of the information may not be the only element involved because the use of a general strategy determined by shared professional values of social workers (such as helping minority groups and respecting differences) may come into play. Indeed, future social workers may refer to norms based upon these values, so they would avoid stigmatizing or penalizing minority groups. This interpretative hypothesis is also supported by other data. Social work students had a tendency not to attribute as many socially desirable behaviors to the majority group, as their attributions of these types of behavior to the minority group rose correlatively. Such an effect has never been observed, or if it has, it has not produced any particular interpretations (Spears, van der Pligt, & Eiser, 1985). In any event, this effect cannot be explained by the distinctiveness theory because there is an underlying global strategy used to process information. Furthermore, in a complementary exercise which is usually presented during illusory correlation experiments, subjects had to use a list of traits to describe each of the two groups to whom socially desirable versus undesirable behaviors were attributed. The biology students described the majority group in a very positive manner whereas they described the minority group very negatively. This effect was greatly attenuated, to the point of being almost nonexistent, with the future social workers. All of these findings consequently converge towards a rather socionormative interpretation of the variations in the illusory correlation bias. Even during their training, future social workers adopt professional attitudes which oblige them not to make *a priori* judgements about people or groups; they are also compelled to reduce inequality, marginality, isolation, and deviance.

3. An Experiment with Future Teachers

An experiment obeying the same principle was conducted with the following objectives: (1) to verify the persistence of the reduction of the illusory correlation with another group of subjects who were professionally involved with the presented information, and (2) to more finely analyze subjects' response methods in the re-attribution of behaviors to the groups, and identify the types of strategies used.

3.1 An Experimental Design Inspired by Hamilton's Paradigm

Two groups of subjects took part in an illusory correlation experiment following the classic procedure initiated by Hamilton and Gifford. The first group was composed of 21 second-year psychology students who did the proposed exercise as part of a course requirement which included the construction of an observation grid. The second group was made up of 24 first-year teaching students who participed in the experiment during their free time.

The material was a list of 36 behaviors selected from an assortment of behaviors observed in school children ranging in age from 7 to 9 years. The behaviors were chosen in a polarization exercise which was done by other groups of psychology students and teaching students. The list contained 24 school behaviors judged to be the most desirable and 12 school behaviors thought to be the most undesirable. Twenty-four behaviors were assigned to a group called A and 12 behaviors were allocated to another group labelled B. In each group there was the same proportion of desirable and undesirable behaviors. The distribution of 36 behaviors is summarized in Table 1 below.

Table 1
Initial Distribution of 36 Behaviors

Behaviors	Group A	Group B	Total
Desirable	16	8	24
Undesirable	8	4	12
Total	24	12	36

Each of the 36 behaviors was presented on slides for a duration of 8 seconds. While viewing a slide, subjects could see a name and the label of the group (A or B) to which the person belonged. After the slide presentation subjects had to re-attribute all of the 36 behaviors to group A or B. The illusory correlation effect is considered to have taken place when subjects significantly decreased the number of undesirable behaviors attributed to group A, where they were the most numerous, and when they increased to the same extent the number of the same behaviors assigned to group B, where they were the least numerous.

3.2 Response Patterns Affected by Normative Strategies

Examination of the results from the psychology students and the future teachers showed: (1) There were illusory correlation effects in both groups; (2) however, depending on the group of subjects, these effects were not of equal intensity; (3) the teaching students also re-allocated desirable behaviors from the majority group to the minority one.

Table 2

Re-attribution of 36 Behaviors by Psychology Students (initial distribution in italics)

Behaviors	Group A		Group B		Total
Desirable	17.05		6.95		24
		16		*8*	
Undesirable	4.34		7.66		12
		8		*4*	
Total	21.39		14.61		36

Table 3

Re-attribution of 36 Behaviors by Future Teachers (initial distribution in italics)

Behaviors	Group A		Group B		Total
Desirable	13.50		10.50		24
		16		*8*	
Undesirable	6.20		5.80		12
		8		*4*	
Total	19.70		16.30		36

Comparisons were made on the average deviation from the initial distribution, shown in the lower right-hand corner of each cell in Tables 2 and 3. The second-year psychology students increased the number of undesirable behaviors attributed to the minority group by an average of 3.66 and the teaching students produced an average of increase of 1.80 for the same type of attribution. The difference between the two averages is significant ($t(43) = 1.88$, $p < .07$). The psychology students decreased the number of socially desirable behaviors attributed to the minority group by 1.05 whereas the teaching students increased that number by 2.50. This difference is also statistically significant (t (43) = 2.02, $p < .05$). The pattern of these findings is comparable to the one obtained with the social work students. Future professionals, destined to be social workers or teachers, treat information according to the egalitarian or humanistic values which underlie their vocations in education or social assistance. Here the distinctiveness theory based upon the statistical scarcity of information also appears to be insufficient to explain such variations.

The subjects were obviously unable to retain all of the information supplied in the initial material. During the re-attribution phase they seem to have adopted a normative recall strategy. The correlation between the distribution of the scores for the increase in the number of undesirable behaviors attributed to the minority group and the distribution of the scores for the increase/decrease in the number of desirable behaviors attributed to the majority group is .90 for the psychology students and .87 for the teaching students. In other words, the more the minority group was made undesirable the more the majority group's desirability increased for certain subjects. Inversely, other subjects tended to cause the difference between the two groups to decrease. The study of the subjects' individual answers showed in fact that some subjects, mostly the psychology students, chose straightaway to attribute all the desirable behaviors to group A and all the undesirable behaviors to group B. On the other hand, more balanced answer patterns seen among the teaching students revealed other recall strategies perhaps just as normative as the preceding ones but based on different values.

3.3 Errors as Numerous but of a Different Nature

The differences observed between the two groups could be explained by the properties of the information itself. Future teachers, who were already familiar with statements of school behaviors, may make less errors than other subjects. This explanation is insufficient for two reasons. Firstly, it does not explain the phenomenon of the transfer of desirable behaviors from the majority group toward the minority group. Secondly, it appears that the two groups had approximately the same overall error rate: 45.47 % among the psychology students and 47.70 % among the future teachers. In short, subjects made a mistake almost every other time when re-attributing a behavior to a group. But the rate was not the same in the two groups of subjects if we consider the type of error.

Table 4

Error Rate in the Re-Attributions of Psychology Students (%)

Behaviors	from A to B	from B to A
Desirable	28.29	70.24
Undesirable	61.90	32.14

Table 5

Error Rate in the Re-Attributions of Future Teachers (%)

Behaviors	from A to B	from B to A
Desirable	41.58	57.23
Undesirable	49.54	50.00

The difference in the error rate of the two groups of subjects actually reflects differences in the above-mentioned normative strategies. The errors of psychology students seem to indicate greater discrimination between group A and group B, perhaps even the systematic stigmatization of the group spotted as a minority. The error rates were more homogeneous among the teaching students. They were probably the product of a less visible normative functioning which includes underlying preconceptions about associations between school performance, class attitudes, and behavior toward other pupils, all being determined, however, by a general plan of treatment which tends to balance the groups or, at least, not to attribute all the undesirable behaviors to the group containing the least number of pupils.

3.4 Different Impressions in the Two Groups of Subjects

One last piece of data reinforces this socionormative interpretation of variations in the illusory correlation. As in Hamilton and Gifford's experiments, subjects had to reveal their impression of the two groups by using a list of 30 traits, 15 of the most positive one and 15 of the most negative one. These traits were taken from Beauvois' evaluative weight scale (1984). The results are presented in the tables below.

Table 6
Average Number of Traits Attributed by Psychology Students

Traits	Group A	Group B	Total
Positive	6.90	1.57	8.47
Negative	1.67	4.86	6.53
All	8.57	6.43	

Table 7
Average Number of Traits Attributed by Future Teachers

Traits	Group A	Group B	Total
Positive	4.65	3.58	8.23
Negative	3.08	2.73	5.81
All	7.73	6.31	

On the whole, the psychology students revealed a differentiated perception of the two groups, thus conforming to the illusory correlation effects. The larger group, labelled A, was perceived in a clearly positive manner whereas the smaller one, called B, was described with a majority of negative traits. This effect was nonexistent among the teaching students. They attributed a significantly greater number of positive traits to group B, which the psychology students did not do ($t(43) = 1.95, p < .06$). They behaved exactly like the future social workers questioned during the experiment mentioned earlier.

Generally speaking, taken with different material, the response patterns obtained for the teaching students are analogous to those observed for the social work students. This resemblance leads one to think that the social position of people in organizations, the social practices pertaining to the positions, and the ideologies which underlie the exercise of the practices can intervene in the functioning of the illusory correlation bias when the data to be treated is information relating to those positions and practices. One must then admit that the distinctiveness theory concerning statistical rarity of information throughout the studies on illusory correlation can not alone explain such effects. More generally, the findings of these experiments and others also set limits on approaches of social cognition which, like Hamilton's, attempt to explain the formation of social productions such as stereotypes, beliefs, and impressions about others, in a purely cognitive manner.

4. Toward a Socionormative View of Social Cognition

The variations of the illusory correlation bias are also liable to a sociocognitive interpretation in which the subject's activity is not merely viewed as an erroneous treatment of distinctive stimuli, even if the stimuli are socially "colored" and related to people's attitudes. Positional and ideological factors susceptible to affect the intensity of a bias as powerful as the illusory correlation also affect its functioning. In other words, subjects do not only deal with information which is more or less salient *vis-à-vis* their own values but they also integrate daily social relations which they maintain regarding the data which are proposed to them in an experimental situation. They are implicitly driven to reduce the intensity of the bias if their habitual social or educational practices with groups or people refer to values which are opposed to the ideological implications of the functioning of illusory correlation, in this case believing that only members of a minority group can exhibit undesirable behavior. The results obtained in the experiment presented above along with those gathered in the earlier study show that the subjects who have or will have professional conducts of assistance or education tend to decrease the stigmatization of people who are the least numerous. Consequently, it seems difficult to reduce the functioning of the illusory correlation bias in a social situation to a simple matter of handling contextualized information by a subject having some opinions on the issue.

It is necessary to conceive of social cognition in a different way from the ones previously evoked, in order to explain effects that depend on values or norms attached to the production of social conducts of assistance and education. The post-Heiderian models of social cognition are limited by their theoretical framework: limits which stem from a conception of man as rational or scientific and which ignore social conducts, the effects of position, methods of integration in various situations, social utility – in fact, everything that is social in social psychology. Biases, distortions and errors are found throughout the activity of social judgement or of others perception but they vary in intensity from one group to another, from one situation to another, according to the material or even according to explicitly normative or counter-normative instructions given to the subjects. The tendency to favor internal causes to explain behaviors and events, usually treated like a fundamental error or a self-serving attribution bias in the wake of attribution theories, can also be interpreted as the product of a normative acquisition, namely, the norm of internality (Beauvois, 1984; Beauvois & Le Poultier, 1986; Dubois, 1987). The tendency to prefer to say good things about people where logically it would be more suitable to say bad things is probably as much the expression of a norm of non-hostility regarding others as the effect of a positivity bias ascribable to the greater availability of positive data in memory. Such a re-interpretation of the illusory correlation is difficult to make in the light of the current state of the art in this field. The bias is powerful because most subjects obliged to find a strategy to compensate for the inadequacies of their memory adopt the one that seems the most rational to them in their situation of uncertainty and the one which appears most capable of responding to the intentions that they have implicitly ascribed to the experimenter. This consists of attributing, in a preferentiel manner, undesirable behaviors to a minority group. Other subjects, such as future social workers or teachers, distribute desirable and undesirable behaviors in a different manner. They are probably more sensitive to the norms of their own professional practices, activated by the content of the test material, than to norms which they could infer from the instructions and the experimental situation. This cannot be considered as negligible, and cannot be reduced to the effect of some interfering variables which are difficult to control. Its interpretation implies a revision of the dominating paradigms of social cognition. Making it work experimentally offers new perspectives of research which must lead to the more direct manipulation of independent variables such as the subject's social conducts, position or organizational membership, and adherence to socially shared values. These perspectives should also aid us in gaining a better understanding of how subjects usually deal with information in a socionormative manner.

References

Acorn, D. A., Hamilton, D. L., & Sherman, S. J. (1988). Generalization of biased perceptions of groups based on illusory correlations. *Social Cognition*, 6, 345-072.

Beauvois, J.-L. (1984). *La psychologie quotidlenne*. Paris : Presses Universitaires de France.

Beauvois, J.-L., & Le Poultier, F. (1986). Norme d'internalité et pouvoir social en psychologie quotidienne. *Psychologie Française*, *31*, 100-108.

Boucher, J., & Osgood, C. E. (1969). The Pollyanna hypothesis. *Journal of Verbal Learning and Verbal Behavior*, *8*, 1-8.

Brennan, J. H., & Hemsbley, D. R. (1984). Illusory correlations in paranoid and non-paranoid schizophrenia. *British Journal of Clinical Psychology*, *23*, 225-226.

Chapman, L. J. (1967). Illusory correlation in observational report. *Journal of Verbal Learning and Verbal Behavior, 6,* 151-155.

Chapman, L. J., & Chapman, J. P. (1969). Illusory correlation as an obstacle to the use of valid psychodiagnostic signs. *Journal of Abnormal Psychology, 74,* 271-280.

Dubois, N. (1987). La psychologie du contrôle : les croyances internes et externes. Grenoble : Presses Universitaires de Grenoble.

Feldman, J. M., Calburn, A., & Gatti, M. (1986). Shared distinctiveness as a source of illusory correlation in performance appraisal. *Organizational Behavior and Human Decision Process, 37,* 34-59.

Fiedler, K., Hemmeter, U., & Hoffman, C. (1984). On the origin of illusory correlations. *European Journal of Social Psychology, 14,* 191-201.

Golding, S. L., & Rorer, L. G. (1972). Illusory correlation and subjective judgment. *Journal of Abnormal Psychology, 80,* 249-260.

Hamilton, D. L. (1981). Illusory correlation as a basis for stereotyping. In D. L. Hamilton (Ed.), *Cognitive processes in stereotyping and intergroup behavior* (pp. 115-144). Hillsdale, NJ: Erlbaum.

Hamilton, D. L., Dugan, P. M., & Trolier, T. K. (1985). The formation of stereotypic beliefs: Further evidence for distinctiveness-based illusory correlations. *Journal of Personality and Social Psychology, 48,* 5-17.

Hamilton, D. L., & Gifford, R. K. (1976). Illusory correlation in interpersonal perception: A cognitive basis of stereotypic judgments. *Journal of Experimental Social Psychology, 12,* 392-407.

La Haye, A.-M. de, & Lauvergeon, G. (1991). Processus de mémoire dans la formation des corrélations illusoires. *Psychologie Française, 36,* 67-77.

Le Poultier, F. (1990). *Recherches évaluatives en travail social.* Grenoble : Presses Universitaires de Grenoble.

Mackie, D. M., Hamilton, D. L., Schroth, H. A., & Carlisle, C. J. (1989). The effects of induced mood on expectancy-based illusory correlations. *Journal of Experimental Social Psychology, 25,* 11-28.

Mullen, B., & Johnson, C. (1990). Distinctiveness-based illusory correlation and stereotyping: A meta-analytic integration. *British Journal of Social Psychology, 29,* 11-28.

Pryor, J. B. (1986). The influence of different encoding sets upon the formation of illusory correlations and group impressions. *Personality and Social Psychology Bulletin, 12,* 216-226.

Ross, L. (1977). The intuitive psychologist and his shortcomings: Distortions in the attribution process. In L. Berkowitz (Ed.), *Advances in experimental social psychology* (Vol. 10, pp. 174-221). New York: Academic Press.

Ross, L., Lepper, M. R., & Hubbard, M. (1975). Perseverance in self-perception and social perception: Biased attributional processes in the debriefing paradigm. *Journal of Personality and Social Psychology, 32*, 880-892.

Sanbotmatsu, D. M., Shavitt, S., Sherman, S. J., & Roskos Ewolden, D. R. (1987). Illusory correlation in the perception of performance by self or a salient other. *Journal of Experimental Social Psychology, 23*, 518-543.

Schaller, M., & Maass, A. (1989). Illusory correlation and social categorization: Toward an integration of motivational and cognitive factors in stereotype formation. *Journal of Personality and Social Psychology, 56*, 709-721.

Smither, J. W., Collins, H., & Buda, R. (1989). When rate satisfaction influences performance evaluations: A case of illusory correlation. *Journal of Applied Psychology, 74*, 599-605.

Spears R., Eiser, J. R., & van der Pligt, J. (1987). Further evidence for expectation-based illusory correlations. *European Journal of Social Psychology, 17*, 253-258.

Spears, R., van der Pligt, J., & Eiser, J. R. (1985). Illusory correlation in the perception of group attitudes. *Journal of Personality and Social Psychology, 48*, 863-875.

STEREOTYPES AS COGNITIVE HEURISTICS

A PEEK INSIDE THE TOOLBOX

C. Neil Macrae
University of Wales, Cardiff, U.K.

Miles Hewstone
University of Bristol, U.K.

"Stereotypes are tools that jump out of the toolbox when there is a job to be done." Gilbert and Hixon (1991, p. 510)

Despite the pre-eminence of the "cognitive miser" metatheory in contemporary social cognition (Fiske & Taylor, 1991), the notion of stereotypes as functional entities, residing in some sort of mental toolbox, has its origins in much earlier times. Lippman (1922), for instance, suggested that reality is too complex for any person to represent accurately. Stereotypes, accordingly, serve to simplify perception, judgment, and action. For Lippman, then, stereotypes are energy-saving devices which spare perceivers the ordeal of responding to an almost incomprehensible social world. Seventy years on, these sentiments are characteristic features of cognitive writings on the topic. As Fiske and Neuberg (1990, p.14) note, *"we are exposed to so much information that we must in some manner simplify our social environment [...] for reasons of cognitive economy, we categorize others as members of particular groups – groups about which we often have a great deal of generalized, or stereotypic, knowledge"*. The hallmark of this miserly approach to social cognition is the belief that given our limited pool of cognitive resources, it is both simpler and more efficient to deal with people in this manner. Individuation, treating each person as a unique entity, devours cognitive resources at an alarming rate. Stereotyping, in contrast, is relatively resource-free and enables perceivers to evaluate, and respond to, others rapidly with the minimum of mental effort or cognitive fuss (Allport, 1954; Tajfel, 1969).

The roots of this approach, of course, can be found elsewhere; most notably in work in social and cognitive psychology (e.g., Bruner, 1973; Tajfel, 1969). Of particular relevance is the contention that categorization is a fundamental process in both object and social cognition (see Lingle, Altom, & Medin, 1984; Rosch, 1978; Smith & Medin, 1981). Just as we possess categories for furniture, musical instruments, and fast-foods, we also hold comparable mental structures for social groups (e.g., doctors, women, and the elderly). Moreover, these social categories serve identical functions to their counterparts in the object domain. In particular, they simplify complex stimulus arrays and provide maximum information for minimum cognitive effort. Once categorized, a range of stereotype-based information about a target becomes available to the social perceiver. A *Scotsman*, for example, will likely be deemed to be mean, aggressive, and inebriated. In addition, minimal cognitive resources are expended in acquiring this information; it is simply plucked from its permanent residence in the mind.

Category systems are represented in long-term memory by generic knowledge structures termed schemata (Brewer & Nakamura, 1984; Cantor & Mischel, 1979; Fiske & Taylor, 1984; Neisser, 1976; Rumelhart, 1984; Taylor & Crocker, 1981). Although several definitions have been proposed since Bartlett's (1932) influential usage of the term, most researchers would consider a schema a cognitive structure containing perceivers' knowledge and beliefs about a particular stimulus domain. In this sense, then, stereotypes are little more than particular instances of cognitive schemata. As Hamilton and Trolier (1986) note, a stereotype is *"a cognitive structure that contains the perceiver's knowledge, beliefs, and expectations about some human group"* (p. 133). Furthermore, as a rapidly expanding literature testifies, like other schematic structures, stereotypes affect all stages of social information processing (i.e., encoding, representation, retrieval, see Hamilton, 1979; Hamilton & Trolier, 1986; Hamilton, Sherman, & Ruvolo, 1990; Higgins & Bargh, 1987; Sherman, Judd, & Park, 1989).

One of the primary functions of a schema is to render new information meaningful by relating it to knowledge gleaned from previous experience (Bartlett, 1932). Consider, for example, students' temptation to malign a new tutor on the basis of their interactions with her lacklustre colleagues. For most of us these temptations are frequently overwhelming and irresistible. The ability to understand new individuals in terms of old, pre-established beliefs is undoubtedly a useful cognitive skill. Establishing exactly when perceivers are likely to dip into their mental toolbox and apply stereotypical modes of thinking, however, is quite another matter.

As Fiske and Neuberg (1989, p. 85) argue, *"once a category is cued, category-based cognitions (e.g., stereotypes), affect (e.g., prejudices), and behavioral tendencies (e.g., discriminatory potential) become activated, although not necessarily acted upon"*. Thus, the provision or activation of stereotypic information does not imply that this information will invariably impinge upon perceivers' judgmental processes (Brewer, 1988; Fiske & Neuberg, 1990). Stereotype-based information can be ignored, inhibited, or discarded (Devine, 1989). Indeed, under certain conditions, individuating information can assume a more prominent role in judgmental outcomes (Eagly & Wood, 1982; Locksley, Borgida, Brekke, & Hepburn, 1980; Locksley, Hepburn, & Ortiz, 1982; Nisbett, Zukier, & Lemley, 1981). In the present chapter, however, we outline studies where stereotype-based beliefs quite explicitly and unambiguously dominate perceivers' decision processes. In particular, we focus upon studies demonstrating the apparent heuristic utility of stereotypes in difficult or demanding task environments. In this way, we will consider the claim that stereotypes are tools, residing in some sort of mental toolbox, that social perceivers apply when they are short of cognitive resources (Gilbert & Hixon, 1991).

1. Stereotypes as Simplifying Structures: Effects on Judgmental Outcomes

Recently, Pratto and Bargh (1991) noted that a contributory factor in the use of stereotypes is that they, as cognitive schemata, are useful in simplifying our complex interactions with others. Here, then, we have an explicit exposition of the stereotypes-as-tools metaphor. It was in this general spirit that Bodenhausen and his colleagues (Bodenhausen & Wyer, 1985; Bodenhausen & Lichtenstein, 1987) proposed an *heuristic* model of stereotyping whereby perceivers activate and apply stereotypical modes of thinking when processing tasks are effortful or cognitively demanding.

At the outset, in the experimental context of explanation-giving, Bodenhausen and Wyer (1985) considered three main variants of stereotype-based effects on judgmental outcomes. The first *heuristic hypothesis* suggests that people use stereotypes as simplifying rules of thumb in difficult or demanding task environments. In their attempts to interpret the behavior of others, for instance, perceivers may only search for alternative or competing explanations to the extent that precomputed stereotype-based interpretations are inappropriate or unavailable (Macrae & Shepherd, 1991). Moreover, this tendency might be exacerbated as task complexity increases. Thus, according to the heuristic hypothesis, if available and applicable, perceivers will favor stereotype-based interpretations for behavior despite the presence of additional information implying the existence of potentially competing interpretations. The second *default hypothesis* claims that perceivers only utilize stereotypes in their interpretations of behavior "as a last resort" when more diagnostic information is lacking or unavailable (Locksley et al., 1980, 1982). In a sense, then, perceivers' ignorance drives their utilization of stereotypic information. If other judgmentally-relevant information were available, stereotype-based effects on explanation-giving would be eliminated (cf. Macrae, Shepherd, & Milne, 1992). The final *integration hypothesis* argues that perceivers consider both stereotypic and non-stereotypic information when interpreting the behavior of others (Pratto & Bargh, 1991). Their final judgments, accordingly, are simply based on an algebraic integration of the implications of the available information.

To evaluate these competing hypotheses, Bodenhausen and Wyer (1985) requested subjects to provide explanations for events (i.e., criminal action and job-related infraction) which were either stereotypic or counterstereotypic with respect to a target's category membership. Their results provided strongest empirical support for the heuristic hypothesis. That is, the effects of activating a stereotype appeared to override the effects of other target-related information which was available. Thus, even in the face of additional information subjects used the target's stereotype to drive their interpretations of his behavior (Macrae & Shepherd, 1989). Other decision-relevant information was only considered relevant when a stereotype-based explanation for the event was unavailable. Bodenhausen and Wyer speculate that the complex decision tasks which faced their subjects (i.e., Expt 2, parole recommendations) facilitated these heuristic effects on decision processes.

Further support for the role of task difficulty in the moderation of stereotype-based effects on judgmental processes comes from subsequent work by Bodenhausen and Lichtenstein (1987). They presented subjects with ambiguous trial evidence concerning a defendant in a case of alleged assault. Importantly, the incident was either stereotypic or nonstereotypic with regard to the defendant's group membership (i.e., Hispanic or ethnically non-descript), and prior to receiving the case details, subjects were given different task objectives. While some subjects were required to determine the defendant's aggressiveness (i.e., simple task), others judged his likelihood of guilt (i.e., complex task). Bodenhausen and Lichtenstein reasoned that the guilt objective was more complex and cognitively demanding than the trait inference task: after all, multiple factors impinge upon the computation of a person's guilt (e.g., the presence of a motive, ability to undertake the criminal action, veracity of the evidence, etc.). The assessment of perceived aggressiveness, in contrast, only relies upon people's ability to interpret behavior as falling somewhere along a single trait dimension. As such, it is a relatively simple task. The reasoning behind this experimental manipulation was quite straightforward: when faced with a complex task objective rather than a simple one, perceivers should be correspondingly more likely to use an available and applicable stereotype as a means of simplifying the judgment at hand. Bodenhausen and Lichtenstein's results provided direct support for this prediction. Subjects with the complex task objective (i.e., guilt) considered the defendant to be more aggressive, more likely to be guilty, and recalled more incriminating evidence about him when he was Hispanic (i.e., stereotype-applicable) than when he was ethnically non-descript (i.e., stereotype-inapplicable). In contrast, subjects with the simple task objective (i.e., aggressiveness), as predicted, failed to display appreciable judgmental or memorial biases with respect to the target's category membership. Again, then, stereotypes were used by perceivers to simplify complex judgmental tasks.

The complexity of the judgmental task at hand, of course, is only one factor engendering a cognitive need for simplification. Others readily spring to mind: time pressures and informational/attentional overload, for example, to name but a few (Bargh & Thein, 1985; Gilbert & Hixon, 1991; Pratto & Bargh, 1991; Rothbart, Fulero, Jensen, Howard, & Birrell, 1978). Consider, for instance, a situation where perceivers have to monitor information from a number of competing channels and sources. Here we might reasonably expect some form of stimulus simplification to occur. Moreover, stimulus simplification in this context has some obvious practical implications as many of our daily interactions unfold in this sort of processing environment. When dealing with others, we are frequently engaged in a number of potentially resource-usurping concurrent mental tasks. While attempting to impress our new partner, for example, we may simultaneously: (1) monitor her reactions to our behavior; (2) monitor our reactions to her behavior; (3) think about which movie to attend later that evening; and (4) ruminate over her physical resemblance to Meryl Streep. Given the mentally debilitating nature of these concurrent activities, as energy-saving devices or tools, stereotype-based effects on social cognition should be most likely to occur under these conditions. We might conclude (erroneously), for example, that Meryl Streep types are least likely to enjoy action movies featuring car chases, inane one-liners, and muscle-bound actors pretending to be alien assassins.

To investigate the relationship between resource-depletion and stereotype application, Gilbert and Hixon (1991) presented subjects with behavioral information in an experimental setting which attempted to capture the complexity of everyday social interaction. Specifically, subjects' cognitive resources were depleted through the introduction of a debilitating concurrent mental task: in this case a digit rehearsal task. The reasoning behind this manipulation was as follows. If stereotypes function as energy-saving devices, then perceivers should be most likely to apply them when their cognitive resources are scarce (i.e., when a need for simplification has been created). Importantly, this is exactly what Gilbert and Hixon found. The subjects in their study were required to observe, on videotape, a woman (Caucasian or Asian) describing a number of mundane life events. While viewing the tape some subjects mentally rehearsed an 8-digit number (i.e., busy-condition), the others simply observed the material (i.e., non-busy condition). Their task was then to evaluate the target on a number of stereotypic and counterstereotypic trait dimensions. As predicted, busy subjects evaluated the Asian woman more stereotypically than non-busy subjects. This, then, seems to provide unequivocal empirical support for the view that stereotypes operate as simplifying mental structures which come into operation when the characteristics of the task environment create a need for cognitive simplification.

Stereotypes can, then, usefully be characterized as tools, residing in a mental toolbox, that serve the function of simplifying information-processing and response generation. Moreover, importantly, these heuristic effects have been reported under a variety of conditions. The theme, common to all these conditions, seems to be an obstruction in perceivers' ability to engage in systematic information-processing modes. Specifically, when these modes are disrupted or bypassed, stereotype-based effects on social cognition seem especially likely to prevail. Factors shown to limit perceivers' ability to process information systematically include: (1) task difficulty (Bodenhausen & Lichtenstein, 1987); (2) information overload (Stangor & Duan, 1991); (3) concurrent mental tasks (Gilbert & Hixon, 1991); and (4) attention overload (Pratto & Bargh, 1991). The general message emerging from these studies is a consistent one: when cognitive resources are depleted, stereotype-based effects on social cognition are amplified or accentuated.

In a provocative extension to this cognitively oriented line of research, Bodenhausen (1990) suggested that biological factors may also affect perceivers' propensity to activate stereotypes as simplifying mental structures. In particular, there may be regular circadian variations in people's daily pattern of stereotype activation and application. Time of day effects, after all, have already been demonstrated in a range of other tasks and activities which depend upon resource availability for their successful execution. Through circadian-based effects on the arousal system, perceivers achieve optimal performance levels at different times of the day. That is, arousal levels moderate the overall availability and quantity of processing resources. Quite conceivably, as Bodenhausen notes, the tendency to stereotype others may follow these circadian fluctuations in arousal levels. Specifically, when processing resources are scarce, as a consequence of circadian variations in arousal levels, perceivers may be particularly susceptible to stereotypical modes of thinking. Thus, while individuals identified as *morning people* may be more prone to stereotypical thinking as the day progresses, individuals identified as *night people* may be most stereotypical first thing in the morning. To investigate this possibility, Bodenhausen (1990) tested people who reached their optimal arousal peak at different times of the day. Thus, he measured the stereotype-based responses of members of each group (i.e., morning/night) at either 9 a.m. or 8 p.m. As expected, subjects' judgments were most stereotypic when they were tested during times at which they were not at their peak level of circadian arousal.

These results, then, provide further empirical insight into the functioning of stereotypes in social cognition. As energy-saving mental devices, stereotypes are likely to be applied when processing resources are scarce and people are unable to engage in systematic information-processing strategies (Chaiken, Liberman, & Eagly, 1989; Macrae et al., 1992). In this particular instance, differences in circadian-based arousal levels limited perceivers' ability to instigate elaborate and effortful processing modes. Thus, in addition to cognitive and motivational factors determining the heuristic application of social stereotypes, biological forces may also seemingly be implicated in this regard.

While the emerging picture is a consistent one, a slightly different interpretation of the effects of resource depletion on judgmental processes can be found in some recent work by Pratto and Bargh (1991). Specifically, they posit a dissociation between trait-level and global (stereotypic) components of people's impressions of others. That is, perceivers represent, quite independently in long-term memory, trait-based and category-based information about a target. When they have sufficient time and energy to process each item of target-related behavioral information, their subsequent trait and stereotypic impressions tend to be relatively independent. When cognitive resources are depleted, in contrast, trait-level impressions are guided by perceivers' stereotypic evaluations of the target. Thus, when resources are depleted, perceivers are generally unable to integrate or reconcile individuating information with prevailing categorical expectancies. When this is the case, as Pratto and Bargh (1991, p. 44) note, *"they may fall back on group or behavior-based stereotypes which have chronic, if small, influences on their impressions of others"*. As we show in the following section, similar elements determine the effects of stereotype activation on memorial processes.

2. Stereotypes as Simplifying Structures: Effects on Memory

As simplifying mental structures, stereotype-based effects have also been noted on people's memory for social information. Moreover, these effects have considerable practical implications for issues of stereotype maintenance and change. Motivated by the equation of stereotypes with cognitive schemata, researchers have been eager to demonstrate schematic effects on social memory (see Hamilton et al., 1990; Higgins & Bargh, 1987; Sherman et al., 1989; Stangor & McMillan, 1992). Surprisingly, therefore, until quite recently the empirical picture in this domain remained rather muddled. The problem, it would appear, stemmed from the appearance of inconsistent and contradictory findings in the literature. Sometimes it seemed that perceivers preferentially recalled stereotype-consistent information; on other occasions inconsistent information was more readily retrieved from long-term memory (e.g., Belmore & Hubbard, 1987; Bodenhausen & Wyer, 1985; Cantor & Mischel, 1977; Hastie & Kumar, 1979; Macrae & Shepherd, 1989; Rothbart, Evans, & Fulero, 1979).

The characterization of perceivers as *cognitive misers* or *mental sluggards*, however, has helped, in part, to disambiguate many of these findings. Most notably, it has contributed to our general understanding of the conditions under which perceivers preferentially recall stereotype-confirming or disconfirming information. Stangor and Duan (1991), for example, make some interesting predictions in this regard. While under conditions of high processing load perceivers should display preferential recall for stereotype-consistent information, under low loads, in contrast, a memorial advantage for inconsistent information should accrue. These predictions are derived, in part, from Srull and Wyer's (1989) influential model of person memory. The model asserts that preferential recall of expectancy-congruent information is a consequence of the elaboration this information receives during processing. In their attempts to reconcile incongruent information with an existing expectancy, perceivers allegedly think about the information more *deeply*. This process of inconsistency resolution, in turn, fosters the formation of associative links between items of information in long-term memory which, ultimately, enhances the memorability of the information. When perceivers possess insufficient cognitive resources to drive this process of inconsistency-resolution, different memorial processes determine the ultimate fate of stimulus information (Bodenhausen & Lichtenstein, 1987; Bodenhausen & Wyer, 1985). In particular, the need for simplification seems to result in the preferential representation of confirming information in stereotype-based knowledge structures. Such a state of affairs is, however, unsurprising as one would expect the representation of confirming information within a knowledge structure to make relatively minimal demands upon a diminishing pool of cognitive resources.

To investigate these predictions, Stangor and Duan (1991, Expt 2) asked subjects to form impressions of two groups under either resource depleting or normal processing conditions. The resource depleting manipulation involved subjects attending to a distracting news broadcast while forming impressions of the groups. It was anticipated that the introduction of this secondary task would usurp perceivers' processing capacity (Petty, Wells, & Brock, 1976). As expected, processing load moderated subjects' recall of stereotype-based information. While disconfirming information was preferentially recalled under normal processing conditions, this tendency was reversed when a resource depleting secondary task was introduced. These effects, then, seem consistent with the assumptions of Srull and Wyer's (1989) memory model. When the attenuation of cognitive resources precludes perceivers' instigation of inconsistency-resolution, a memorial advantage for stereotype-confirming information accrues.

As well as revealing the role of inconsistency-resolution in the mediation of stereotype-based effects on memory, these findings have a number of worrisome practical implications. Most notably, in effortful and cognitively demanding social interactions, it would appear that stereotypical beliefs are likely to be maintained through people's preferential recall of confirming information. As Stangor and Duan (1991, p. 375) note, *"stereotypes are formed and maintained in part because perceivers are likely to preferentially remember information that is congruent with those expectations"*. This assertion, of course, implicitly posits some sort of relationship between people's judgments and recall. Specifically, that the utilization of stereotypes might be related to the enhanced memorability of confirming information in memory. While such a relationship is intuitively appealing, researchers have consistently experienced difficulty in demonstrating its existence. In particular, the appearance of judgment-recall correlations seems to depend upon whether the judgment is made "on-line" or is "memory-based" (Hastie & Park, 1986).

If stereotypes do indeed function as simplifying mental structures, however, then one might reasonably expect to obtain judgment-recall correlations in situations where processing demands are high. That is, through stereotype application perceivers would: (i) simplify complex task domains; and (ii) base their subsequent judgments upon the products of this simplification process (i.e., information stored in memory). In a sense, perceivers would use the theme of the stereotype-based representation in memory as a basis for all their subsequent target-related judgments and evaluations. This, then, would reveal the heuristic utility of stereotypes in demanding task environments. Not only do they simplify complex stimulus arrays, but they also help to provide the raw materials for a range of subsequent social judgments. Interestingly, Stangor and Duan (1991) failed to obtain significant judgment-recall correlations in their study. As they acknowledge, however, this was probably because subjects were computing judgments "on-line".

In related research, however, Macrae, Hewstone, and Griffiths (1993) have demonstrated a significant relationship between perceivers' judgments and recall, but only under high processing loads. In their study, subjects were presented with a videotape depicting a conversation between two women. Attention was focused on only one of the women, who was described as either a doctor or a hairdresser. With respect to the particular occupational prime subjects were given, half of the target's utterances and behaviors were stereotypic and the others were counterstereotypic. In addition, half of the subjects viewed the videotape while also engaging in a cognitively demanding digit rehearsal task (i.e., high-load); the others simply viewed the videotape (i.e., low-load). As anticipated, when processing resources were depleted subjects: (i) displayed preferential recall of consistent information; and (ii) were more stereotypic in their evaluations of the target. While inconsistent information was more memorable under low loads, this was largely unrelated to subjects' target-related judgments. This suggests, then, that perceivers make greater use of target-based information in memory when it has been encountered in difficult or demanding processing contexts. Evidence for the heuristic utility of stereotypes in demanding processing environments also comes from an earlier study by Rothbart et al. (1978). They presented subjects with the task of forming an impression of a fictitious group and varied the amount of information available (16 vs. 64 trait presentations). Whereas subjects organized their impressions around individual group members in the low memory-load condition, under high memory-load they switched instead to the group as a whole as the unit of organization. Thus, the group became the basis for evaluations of individual members under conditions of information overload.

This effect turns out to have crucial implications for stereotype change. A series of studies have demonstrated that stereotypes tend to change more in response to a pattern of stereotype-disconfirming information that is dispersed across several group members, rather then concentrated in a few (Johnston & Hewstone, 1992; Weber & Crocker, 1983). This effect disappears, however, when subjects cannot "track" information by person. Thus, Weber and Crocker (1983, Expt 4) reported no difference between concentrated and dispersed conditions under high memory load. As we have shown in recent research (Hewstone, Macrae, Griffiths, & Johnston, 1992), the relative weakness of the concentrated condition appears due, at least in part, to the fact that subjects can, and do, organize information around persons (they cluster items by person in free recall). If this kind of organization is made impossible, then subjects in both conditions organize information around the group as a whole, resulting in comparable reductions in their stereotype-based beliefs.

Taken together these findings suggest that the magnitude of stereotypic effects on judgmental processes may depend upon the characteristics of the task environment. When cognitive resources are depleted, heuristic processes are instigated, resulting in the magnification of stereotype-based judgmental biases. Moreover, the enhanced memorability of consistent information under these conditions provides a processing mechanism through which these effects may operate (cf. Gilbert & Hixon, 1991). While seemingly pessimistic for researchers interested in stereotype change or prejudice reduction, these findings are largely consistent with an emerging conception of the functional role of stereotypes in social cognition (see Brewer, 1988; Fiske & Neuberg, 1990). As simplifying mental structures, stereotypes guide information processing and response generation in difficult or demanding task environments.

3. Stereotype Activation: Effortful or Effortless ?

Like much of contemporary social psychology, the present chapter has tacitly accepted the utility of the *cognitive miser* metaphor and assumed that stereotyping is driven by the demands of cognitive economy and parsimony. As such, it is an efficient process which simplifies task demands and preserves a limited pool of cognitive resources. Moreover, the ability to categorize others into social groups is as fundamental a skill as the ability to recognize apples, pears, and plums as pieces of fruit. As such, for many researchers, stereotype activation is considered to be a relatively automatic, resource-independent process (Brewer, 1988; Devine, 1989; Fiske & Neuberg, 1990). Devine, for example, states that a stereotype *"is a well-learned set of associations that is automatically activated in the presence of a member (or symbolic equivalent) of the target group"* (p. 6). As we have shown in the present chapter, stereotypes, as energy-saving mental devices, are most likely to be utilized when perceivers are short on processing resources. Or to reiterate Gilbert and Hixon's (1991, p. 510) point, *"stereotypes are tools that jump out of the toolbox when there is a job to be done"*.

Recently, however, some doubts have been cast over the supposed automaticity of stereotype activation. While accepting the pragmatic message of the stereotypes-as-tools metaphor, Gilbert and Hixon (1991) fail to adopt the widely held view that they are automatically and effortlessly plucked from a mental toolbox (i.e., long-term memory). Instead, they argue that stereotype activation is conditional upon the presence of sufficient cognitive resources to make activation possible. Thus, swimming against the tide somewhat, Gilbert and Hixon make the seemingly counterintuitive prediction that cognitive busyness (i.e., resource depletion) can inhibit rather than facilitate stereotype activation. To test this assertion, they presented subjects with a word-fragment completion task while exposed to either a Caucasian or Asian female laboratory assistant. Importantly, some of the fragments could be completed with words that were stereotypic of Asians (e.g., S_ORT could be completed as SHORT). While completing the test, half of the subjects performed a resource depleting digit rehearsal task, the others simply performed the task. As expected, Gilbert and Hixon observed that, in contrast with busy-subjects, non-busy subjects made more stereotypic word-fragment completions when exposed to the Asian than Caucasian assistant. Thus, resource depletion appeared to inhibit the automatic activation of subjects' ethnic stereotypes.

While compelling, these findings stand as a single exception to conventional wisdom in this domain: as such, they require replication. It is worth noting, however, that researchers are slowly moving away from the "inevitability of stereotyping" view which seemed to characterize early cognitive writings on the topic. As Fiske (1990) recently remarked, *"this well-taken perspective creates an all-to-common misinterpretation. The cognitive view is too easily misinterpreted to mean that people automatically stereotype others without express intent simply because built-in or overlearned factors make them 'wired' to categorize"* (p. 253). Recent models of stereotyping (e.g., Devine, 1989) do recognize that perceivers can actively inhibit the effects of stereotype activation on their judgments and behavior.

These recent developments do not imply, however, that stereotype activation is invariably a resource dependent cognitive process. Indeed, there is much to be gained from the possession of an inferential system in which schematic beliefs are accessed and activated in a relatively effortless fashion (see Gilbert, 1989). A legacy of evolutionary processes, after all, would be the development of a cognitive system that: (i) comprises relatively rigid and inflexible mental structures; and (ii) implements stereotypical thinking when processing resources are scarce. It is, perhaps, rather fortuitous that pre-existing mental structures are highly resistant to modification or change. Perceivers continually strive to impose order and meaning on a phenomenal world characterized by flux and change (Heider, 1958). The development and maintenance of relatively rigid, inflexible mental structures undoubtedly facilitates this process. Were schematic beliefs (e.g., stereotypes) to be overridden with consummate ease, then their utility as cognitive structures guiding and shaping social cognition would disappear. In addition, the implementation of stereotypical thinking under conditions of resource depletion has some obvious processing advantages. Most notably, inferences can be made quickly and effortlessly.

4. Conclusions

In a sense, then, stereotypes can usefully be characterized as tools residing in a cognitive toolbox. Moreover, when there is a job to be done, they leave the toolbox and get to work. From available research in the social judgment and memory literatures, we have outlined the heuristic properties of stereotype activation in difficult or demanding information-processing contexts. While serving a valuable cognitive function, stereotypes nonetheless play a critical role in the causation and moderation of judgmental and memorial biases. Notwithstanding the often pernicious consequences of these biases, a complete understanding of stereotyping, we suggest, can only be obtained through a consideration of the origins and development of a cognitive system which actively sustains this mode of thought.

References

Allport, G. W. (1954). *The nature of prejudice*. Reading, MA: Addison-Wesley.
Bargh, J. A., & Thein, R. D. (1985). Individual construct accessibility, person memory, and the recall-judgment link: The case of information overload. *Journal of Personality and Social Psychology, 49*, 1129-1146.
Bartlett, F. C. (1932). *Remembering*. London: Cambridge University Press.
Belmore, S. M., & Hubbard, M. L. (1987). The role of advance expectancies in person memory. *Journal of Personality and Social Psychology, 53*, 61-70.
Bodenhausen, G. V. (1990). Stereotypes as judgmental heuristics: Evidence of circadian variations in discrimination. *Psychological Science, 1*, 319-322.
Bodenhausen, G. V., & Lichtenstein, M. (1987). Social stereotypes and information processing strategies: The impact of task complexity. *Journal of Personality and Social Psychology, 52*, 871-880.

Bodenhausen, G. V., & Wyer, R. S. (1985). Effects of stereotypes on decision making and information processing strategies. *Journal of Personality and Social Psychology, 48*, 267-282.

Brewer, M. B. (1988). A dual process model of impression formation. In R. S. Wyer & T. K. Srull (Eds.), *Advances in social cognition* (Vol. 1, pp. 1-36). Hillsdale, NJ: Erlbaum.

Brewer, W. F., & Nakamura, G. V. (1984). The nature and function of schemas. In R. S. Wyer & T. K. Srull (Eds.), *Handbook of social cognition* (Vol. 1, pp. 119-160). Hillsdale, NJ: Erlbaum.

Bruner, J. S. (1973). *Going beyond the information given.* New York: Norton.

Cantor, N., & Mischel, W. (1977). Traits as prototypes: Effects on recognition memory. *Journal of Personality and Social Psychology, 35*, 38-48.

Cantor, N., & Mischel, W. (1979). Prototypes in person perception. In L. Berkowitz (Ed.), *Advances in experimental social psychology* (Vol. 12, pp. 3-51). New York: Academic Press.

Chaiken, S., Liberman, A., & Eagly, A. H. (1989). Heuristic and systematic information processing within and beyond the persuasion context. In J. S. Uleman & J. A. Bargh (Eds.), *Unintended thought* (pp. 212-252). New York: Guilford.

Devine, P. G. (1989). Stereotypes and prejudice: Their automatic and controlled components. *Journal of Personality and Social Psychology, 56*, 5-18.

Eagly, A. E., & Wood, W. (1982). Inferred sex differences in status as a determinant of gender stereotypes about social influence. *Journal of Personality and Social Psychology, 43*, 915-928.

Fiske, S. T. (1989). Examining the role of intent: Toward understanding its role in stereotyping and prejudice. In J. S. Uleman & J. A. Bargh (Eds.), *Unintended thought* (pp. 253-286). New York: Guilford.

Fiske, S. T., & Neuberg, S. L. (1989). Category-based versus individuating processes as a function of information and motivation: Evidence from our laboratory. In D. Bar-Tal, C. F. Graumann, A. W. Kruglanski, & W. Stroebe (Eds.), *Stereotyping and prejudice. Changing conceptions* (pp. 83-103). New York: Springer-Verlag.

Fiske, S. T., & Neuberg, S. L. (1990). A continuum model of impression formation from category-based to individuating processes: Influences of information and motivation on attention and interpretation. In M. P. Zanna (Ed.), *Advances in experimental social psychology* (Vol. 23, pp. 1-74). San Diego, CA: Academic Press.

Fiske, S. T., & Taylor, S. E. (1984). *Social cognition*. Reading, MA: Addison-Wesley.

Fiske, S. T., & Taylor, S. E. (1991). *Social cognition* (2nd ed.). New York: McGraw-Hill.

Gilbert, D. T. (1989). Thinking lightly about others: Automatic components of the social inference process. In J. S. Uleman & J. A. Bargh (Eds.), *Unintended thought* (pp. 189-211). New York: Guilford Press.

Gilbert, D. T., & Hixon, J. G. (1991). The trouble of thinking: Activation and application of stereotypic beliefs. *Journal of Personality and Social Psychology, 60*, 509-517.

Hamilton, D. L. (1979). A cognitive-attributional analysis of stereotyping. In L. Berkowitz (Ed.), *Advances in experimental social psychology* (Vol. 12, pp. 53-84). New York: Academic Press.

Hamilton, D. L., Sherman, S. J., & Ruvolo, C. M. (1990). Stereotype-based expectancies: Effects on information processing and social behavior. *Journal of Social Issues, 46*, 35-60.

Hamilton, D. L., & Trolier, T. K. (1986). Stereotypes and stereotyping: An overview of the cognitive approach. In J. Dovidio & S. L. Gaertner (Eds.), *Prejudice, discrimination, and racism* (pp. 127-163). New York: Academic Press.

Hastie, R., & Kumar, P. (1979). Person memory: Personality traits as organizing principles in memory for behaviors. *Journal of Personality and Social Psychology, 37*, 25-38.

Hastie, R., & Park, B. (1986). The relationship between memory and judgment depends on whether the judgment task is memory-based or on-line. *Psychological Review, 93*, 258-268.

Heider, F. (1958). *The psychology of interpersonal relations*. New York: Wiley.

Hewstone, M., Macrae, C. N., Griffiths, R. J., & Johnston, L. (1992). *Cognitive models of stereotype change: Evidence of subtyping from person-memory paradigms*. Unpublished manuscript.

Higgins, E. T., & Bargh, J. A. (1987). Social cognition and perception. *Annual Review of Psychology, 38*, 369-425.

Johnston, L., & Hewstone, M. (1992). Cognitive models of stereotype change: Subtyping and the perceived typicality of disconfirming group members. *Journal of Experimental Social Psychology, 28*, 360-386.

Lingle, J. H., Altom, M. W., & Medin, D. L. (1984). Of cabbages and kings: Assessing the extendability of natural object concept models to social things. In R. S. Wyer & T. K. Srull (Eds.), *Handbook of social cognition* (Vol. 1, pp. 71-118). Hillsdale, NJ: Erlbaum.

Lippman, W. (1922). *Public opinion*. New York: Harcourt & Brace.

Locksley, A., Borgida, E., Brekke, N., & Hepburn, C. (1980). Sex stereotypes and social judgment. *Journal of Personality and Social Psychology, 39*, 821-831.

Locksley, A., Hepburn, C., & Ortiz, V. (1982). Social stereotypes and judgments of individuals. *Journal of Experimental Social Psychology, 18*, 23-42.

Macrae, C. N., Hewstone, M., & Griffiths, R. J. (1993). Processing load and memory for stereotype-based information. *European Journal of Social Psychology, 23*, 77-88.

Macrae, C. N., & Shepherd, J. W. (1989). Stereotypes and social judgments. *British Journal of Social Psychology, 28*, 319-325.

Macrae, C. N., & Shepherd, J. W. (1991). Categorical effects on attributional inferences: A response-time analysis. *British Journal of Social Psychology, 30*, 235-245.

Macrae, C. N., Shepherd, J. W., & Milne, A. B. (1992). The effects of source credibility on the dilution of stereotype-based judgments. *Personality and Social Psychology Bulletin, 18*, 765-775.

Neisser, U. (1976). *Cognition and reality.* San Francisco: Freeman.

Nisbett, R. E., Zukier, H., & Lemley, R. E. (1981). The dilution effect: Non-diagnostic information weakens the impact of diagnostic information. *Cognitive Psychology, 13*, 248-277.

Petty, R. E., Wells, G. L., & Brock, T. C. (1976). Distraction can enhance or reduce yielding to propaganda: Through disruption versus effort justification. *Journal of Personality and Social Psychology, 34*, 874-884.

Pratto, F., & Bargh, J. A. (1991). Stereotyping based upon apparently individuating information: Trait and global components of sex stereotypes under attention overload. *Journal of Experimental Social Psychology, 27*, 26-47.

Rosch, E. (1978). Principles of categorization. In E. Rosch & B. B. Lloyd (Eds.), *Cognition and categorization* (pp. 27-48). Hillsdale, NJ: Erlbaum.

Rothbart, M., Evans, M., & Fulero, S. (1979). Recall for confirming events: Memory processes and the maintenance of social stereotypes. *Journal of Experimental Social Psychology, 15*, 343-355.

Rothbart, M., Fulero, S., Jensen, C., Howard, J., & Birrell, P. (1978). From individual to group impressions: Availability heuristics in stereotype formation. *Journal of Experimental Social Psychology, 14*, 237-255.

Rumelhart, D. E. (1984). Schemata and the cognitive system. In R. S. Wyer & T. K. Srull (Eds.), *Handbook of social cognition* (Vol. 1, pp. 161-188). Hillsdale, NJ: Erlbaum.

Sherman, S. J., Judd, C. M., & Park, B. (1989). Social cognition. *Annual Review of Psychology, 40*, 281-326.

Smith, E. R., & Medin, D. L. (1981). *Categories and concepts.* Cambridge, MA: Harvard University Press.

Srull, T. K., & Wyer, R. S. (1989). Person memory and judgment. *Psychological Review, 96*, 58-83.

Stangor, C., & Duan, C. (1991). Effects of multiple task demands upon memory for information about social groups. *Journal of Experimental Social Psychology, 27*, 357-378.

Stangor, C., & McMillan, D. (1992). Memory for expectancy-congruent and expectancy-incongruent social information: A meta-analytic review of the social psychological and social developmental literatures. *Psychological Bulletin, 111*, 42-61.

Tajfel, H. (1969). Cognitive aspects of prejudice. *Journal of Social Issues, 25*, 79-97.

Taylor, S. E., & Crocker, J. (1981). Schematic bases of social information processing. In E. T. Higgins, C. P. Herman, & M. P. Zanna (Eds.), *The Ontario symposium on personality and social psychology* (pp. 89-134). Hillsdale, NJ: Erlbaum.

Weber, R., & Crocker, J. (1983). Cognitive processes in the revision of stereotypic beliefs. *Journal of Personality and Social Psychology, 45*, 961-977.

THE SOCIAL DETERMINATION
OF ATTRIBUTION JUDGMENTS

Elizabeth S. Sousa

Instituto Superior de Psicologia Aplicada, Lisboa, Portugal

1. Introduction

Causal attribution is an inferential process but also a form of social behavior. Causal inferences are strategies derived from evaluations of the immediate judgment context and the roles the perceiver attributes to him/herself and to others. A main component in this process is self-protection or enhancement, given socio-affective constraints. In this case, the need for cognitive control (widely considered in the attribution field, cf. e.g. Heider, 1958; Bains, 1983) is defeated by distortions whose purpose seems to be the social construction of a positive individual image.

The social determination of attributions often has been studied under the heading of social identity theory. Deschamps (1977, 1983) suggested that attributions tend to be based on social categorizations (a phenomenon already illustrated by Thibaut and Riecken in the fifties, cf. Thibaut & Riecken, 1955). Hewstone, Jaspars and Lalljee (1982) illustrated the fact that causal attributions relate to socially shared representations. On the other hand, Hewstone and Jaspars (1982) and Hewstone (1989) suggested that one of the functions of attributions is to restore or enhance a positive social identity. But the links between attribution and intergroup relations are still not fully understood. Indeed, intergroup attribution studies inherited the problems and open questions of the field of intergroup relations.[1]

1.1 Social Identifications in the Realm of Intergroup Relations

Research on intergroup relations currently has a cognitive tone (Messick & Mackie, 1987). Social Identity Theory (SIT) which combined

---

[1] Thanks are due to Guido Peeters for valuable comments on an earlier draft.

both motivational and cognitive determinants of group behavior also became the study of "cold" cognitions. However, there is now growing evidence casting doubts on the pervasive character of purely cognitive explanations of the phenomenon. The widely reported asymmetries associated with ingroup and outgroup perceptions emphasize the importance of other behavior mediators such as the affective significance of group memberships. These are the focus of the present paper. Specifically, we will consider the affective nature of group identification and its relationship to context effects.

1.1.1 Social Identification and Ingroup Bias. The Social Identity approach to group relations states that group membership refers mainly to the cognitive operation of social categorization by which the individual locates himself or herself within a value-loaded system of categories. According to Tajfel and Turner (1979), people continually seek positive self-concepts, which leads them to compare their group with relevant others. Social identification has been the backbone of the field. It may be defined as the process by which a person is bound to a social group and by which the social self is achieved. But, given that it was easily taken for granted, social identification may also be considered the Achilles' heel of the field.

Social identity was defined by Tajfel (1972, 1978, 1982) as that part of an individual's self-concept which derives from knowledge of membership of a social group, together with the value and emotional significance of that membership. In other words, social identification was conceived of as a multicomponent process. Interestingly, the valence of group memberships has been neglected by researchers. SIT research has emphasized a unidimensional view of social identifications based on the cognitive aspects of group membership (cf. Hogg & Abrams, 1988; Turner, 1982; Turner, Hogg, Oakes, Reicher, & Wetherell, 1987). Turner (1982; Turner et al., 1987) and Deschamps (1982), for instance, state that the first question determining group membership is how we perceive and define ourselves and not how we feel about others. The social identification model (Turner, 1982) emphasizes the collective perception of social uniqueness as the criterion for intergroup behavior. Accordingly, social categorization has been conceived of as a three-step process: (1) categorization of both the self and others as members of social groups, (2) settlement of the common, typical or representative attributes, behaviors and norms that define the group and distinguish it from others, which leads to stereotypical, extreme perceptions of groups, and (3) self-attribution of the stereotypic characteristics of the group (Turner et al., 1987). In other words, the individual not only acknowledges membership of a social group but also redefines his/her identity in terms of the group when interacting with others. Moreover, both the Social Identity Theory (SIT) and the Self-Categorization Theory (SCT) (its recent extension mainly directed towards group behavior) postulate strong assimilation between exemplars of the category and intergroup differentiation. Thus, identification has been conceived of as leading individuals to adopt interpersonal strategies that enhance the distinctiveness between groups in ways that favor their own group (Brewer & Kramer, 1985; Hogg & Abrams, 1988). Indeed, this proved to be the case in experimentally-induced settings and social groups (Brewer & Kramer, 1985). Daily life, however, shows a more complex pattern.

1.1.2 Social Identifications: Some Flaws and Ebbs. The existence of group identification has been traditionally and indirectly inferred from the occurrence of ingroup favoritism (cf. Hogg & Abrams, 1988) or even from the acceptance of a source of influence (cf. Mugny, Kaiser, & Papastamou, 1983).

Turner (1973) suggested that under certain circumstances group identification may be strong enough to replace more individualistic orientations. After having displayed ingroup favoritism, subjects allocated more money to an ingroup fellow than to an outgroup fellow – even against their personal interests (Turner, 1973). Further, Hogg and Turner (1985) reported that the emergence of group behavior depends on the likeability of the group. Likewise, Brown and Ross (1982) reported ingroup bias to be negatively correlated with the desire to leave the group.

The direct measure of social identifications has not been a matter of concern. Lau (1989) and many others (e.g. Hewstone, Fincham, & Jaspars, 1981; Marques & Yzerbyt, 1988; Linville, 1982; Linville & Jones, 1980) have operationalized group identification as the "objective" membership of a group such as gender, race, age, class and ideology. In a different vein, Skevington (1981) operationalized group identification as the difference between ratings of the ingroup and of the self. But, the meaning of the score is open to question. Also, Kelly (1988), Marques, Leyens, and Yzerbyt (1988), and Brown, Condor, Mathews, Wade, and Williams (1986) measured the cognitive component of social identification. Intuitively, however, it seems difficult to accept that membership of a social group does not imply affection. As suggested by Billig (1976), social identification is not just a matter of passively accepting the object of identification into one's own subjective consciousness. Groups with which a person interacts have different valences. These are associated with one's motivation to be accepted as a member of the group and represent the power of the group to influence the person (Jackson, 1981). More recently, Sachdev and Bourhis (1991) included feelings related to membership of a social group on their measure of social identification.

They found that membership in a high status group triggers more positive feelings than does membership in low status groups.

To our knowledge Hinkle and colleagues (Hinkle, Fox-Cardamone, Taylor, & Crook, 1989; Hinkle, Taylor, & Fox-Cardamone, 1989) are the only researchers to have directly addressed the multicomponent nature of identification. They empirically showed its multidimensional nature and suggested that the affective component may be more important than was previously thought.

Assuming that people attempt to gain self-positivity from membership in social groups, there is strong reason to believe they tend to identify with superior groups. Some empirical support for this idea is available in the literature. Rijsman (1983) reported that individuals assigned to an inferior group tend to disassociate themselves from their category whereas subjects assigned to a superior group increase the quality of their performance as a means of justifying their inclusion in the superior group (cf. also Ng, 1986; Snyder, Lassegard, & Ford, 1986; Turner, Sachdev, & Hogg, 1983; Waddell & Cairns, 1986). Furthermore, high status groups discriminate more than low status groups (cf. Commins & Lockwood, 1979; Doise & Sinclair, 1973; Hewstone & Jaspars, 1982; van Knippenberg & Wilke, 1979; Sachdev & Bourhis, 1985, 1991; Skevington, 1981). Often, the latter display outgroup favoritism (cf. also Deaux, 1984, 1985). Members of low status groups are less satisfied with group than members of high status groups (cf. Sachdev & Bourhis, 1991). Membership in a low status group seems to have a negative effect on people's self-esteem (Brown & Lohr, 1987; Wagner, Lampen, & Syllwasschy, 1986). Likewise, intergroup differentiation which favors one group is related to an increase in self-esteem (Lemyre & Smith, 1985). Finally, Gurin, Miller, and Gurin (1980), and Ellemers, van Knippenberg, DeVries, and Wilke (1988) reported that members of low status groups identify less with their groups when group boundaries are pervious than when they are impervious.

These studies suggest that even though individuals behave in group terms sometimes their behavior may be aimed at generating differentiation from the features recognized as defining the group in specific contexts (Tajfel & Turner, 1979). Also, they indicate that individuals' appraisals of a group are by no means a secondary determinant of group behavior. These studies point out the importance of separating the cognitive and the affective components of identification with a social group.

Stated schematically, the interplay between attraction to the group (Thibaut & Kelley, 1959) and external pressures on social categorization, keeping the relevance of group membership constant, may produce different situations.

One such situation is that individuals identify in a strong and positive way with the group. The person acknowledges membership in the group and is emotionally attached to that membership. In this context, pressure to belong in the social group may influence the emergence of ingroup favoritism. Under strong pressures such as threat, ingroup favoritism may be more accentuated (Turner & Brown, 1978; Brown, 1978).

Another alternative course of events is acknowledging membership in a group to which one would rather not belong. Interestingly here, the perviousness of group boundaries seem to be a powerful determinant of behavior. Studies on the outgroup favoritism pattern support the judgmental consequences of low attraction to the group is combined with high pervious group boundaries. A quite different situation arises when low attraction to the group is combined with impervious group boundaries. Membership in the group is perceived as externally determined but impossible to alter. Pressures lead to acceptance of the group label. Some real life examples may be found. Group boundaries are rather impervious for some structurally-valued dimensions such as gender, age or nationality. Furthermore, some groups have a rather pervasive effect in the social matrix. In these cases, in pursuit of social recognition individuals may bias their perception. Rather than seeing themselves in negative terms, individuals may reduce the importance of this membership to social identity. One functional strategy is to interact with others in terms of the personal rather than the social pole of social identity (cf. Tajfel, 1978). The affective component of the person's identification with the group may play a central role here in creating an incongruence between the cognitive and the affective components of social identity. According to the reasoning developed here two situations may exist: one characterized by congruence of the cognitive and affective components of identification, which we shall call hot identification, and one characterized by incongruence of these components, which we shall refer to as cold identification.

One may speculate about the interpretations and evaluations of unlikeable situations people make in the latter condition. One may reason that because people would prefer not to be a member of the group, they become observers therefore changing the context of evaluation (cf. Harvey & Weary, 1984). They evaluate situations on the basis of the type of outcome: what is good is good, what is bad is bad, the group is "guilty" or some external circumstances are to be blamed. On the other hand, if one considers that membership of this group is important for the person's social identity, and that the group may sanction the person, then he or she has to be more careful and subtle. The strategies used here may be more variable. They will depend on the type of audience.

This reasoning apparently contradicts Marques, Leyens, and Yzerbyt's (1988) rationale for the black-sheep effect (B.S.E.), a recent extension to social identity theory (cf. however Fraczek & Linneweber, 1989). According to Marques and Yzerbyt (1988), extreme negative evaluations of unlikeable ingroupers occur when individuals are highly identified with the group. Low identified members display more moderate evaluations of an unlikeable group member. However, only the cognitive dimension of social identification was measured. Furthermore, in both cases the assumed goal was to preserve a positive social identity, although this hypothesis was not empirically considered by the authors.

1.2 Bias and Context Effects

Another point in case is the very fact that studies in this tradition focusing on intergroup behavior have assumed that threat to social identity stems from other groups. Yet, no clear link has been established between ingroup bias and context effects. There is empirical support for the idea that a same target episode may be framed in reference to different background instances (cf. McGill, 1989; Tversky, 1977). Mackie (1974) suggested that the factor which is seen as the cause may depend on the context. In a different vein, Marques, Yzerbyt, and Rijsman (1988) have shown that experimenter's membership in a social group may influence the occurrence of ingroup biases in a situation of social comparison. Following their point of view if the experimenter is perceived as sharing a positive orientation towards the subject's ingroup, subjects belittle the ingroup when facing undesirable situations. In contrast, when they perceive the experimenter as not sharing their perspectives they display ingroup favoritism.

According to the reasoning we have developed above, hypothesis one was formulated as follows: given a negative event or performance by some ingroupers, hot identified individuals will express less negative evaluations of the ingroup than will cold identified subjects. In the same vein, the explanations given for the negative event related to the group will follow this rationale: hot identified subjects will tend to attribute a negative event to external factors whereas cold identified subjects will attribute it mainly to internal factors (hyp. 2). Another hypothesis concerns the effects of social threat: social threat will influence attribution patterns.

Subjects' identification with their group was directly addressed by studying individuals to whom membership in a specific social group is externally determined and important, but who differ in terms of their feelings about that membership. In study 1, subjects were asked to describe their national group and explain a negative event related to it. In study 2, subjects were asked to explain a socially undesirable behavior pattern held by some ingroupers. Also, a source of threat to social identity was manipulated.

2. Study 1: Ingroup Identification and Ingroup Derogation

2.1 Method

2.1.1 Subjects. Thirty-nine Portuguese individuals (20 males and 19 females) volunteered to participate. One male subject was dropped from the analysis for incomplete answers.

2.1.2 Procedure. The investigation took place in Lisbon when crisis was an extremely relevant topic of discussion among Portuguese.

Subjects were tested individually. They were led to believe they were participating in a study carried out by a foreign institution. Subjects filled in a booklet consisting of (1) meanings associated with the stimulus "Portugal"; (2) explanations for the crisis in the country. Twelve explanations had been classified *a priori* according to their "locus of causality" (internal vs. external) and were to be rated on a five-point scale ranging from 1 (=disagree) to 5 (=agree); (3) the subjects' identification with the category "Portuguese" (on a five-point scale). The third measure was obtained by asking subjects "To what extent do you feel Portuguese". Answers were given on a five-point scale ranging from not at all (=1) to entirely (=5). After completion of the booklet, the experimenter checked for subjects' membership in the national group.

2.2 Results

2.2.1 Classification of Subjects According to Type of Identification. Subjects were divided into hot vs. cold identification groups by means of a median split on the distribution of scores on the question "To what extent do you feel Portuguese" ($M = 3.84$; $SD = 1.15$).

2.2.2 Semantic Contents Evoked by "Portugal". A factorial correspondence analysis (Benzécri, 1973; Greenacre, 1984; Lebart & Morineau, 1985) was performed on a logically coded matrix containing subjects × associations with "Portugal" (subject stated the idea or did not). Correspondence analysis is a principal components method which unlike other methods, simultaneously accounts for the distributions of both the variables and the subjects by using an inertia principle derived from a chi-squared rather than euclidean metric. In our case, lexical proximities express common discourse whereas lexical distances reflect

296

content opposition. Furthermore, the discourse is assigned to subjects. Thus, the interpretation of the configuration of the space allows one to identify the subjects who said "x" by opposition to subjects who said "z".

From the 37 factors extracted, the first four reached significance. They account for 39% of the variance of the matrix.

The first factor (horizontal axis of Figure 1) opposes a positive image of Portugal mainly defined by "I am proud of our history", "the country", "the people", and "the beach" to a negative portrait: "lack of concern for education", "crisis", "youth", "difficult economic situation", "unemployment", "lack of jobs", and "bad use of tourism" (T% = 10.5; 97% of Lambda 1).

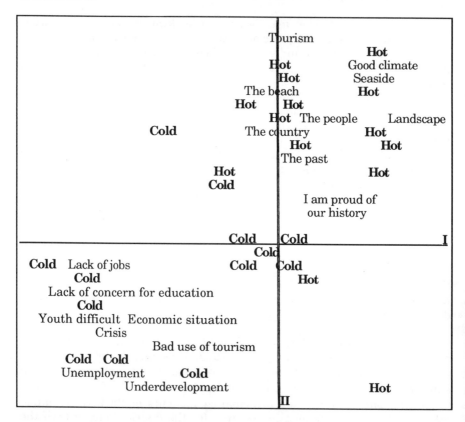

Figure 1. Factorial correspondence analysis on the free contents associated to "Portugal" (*N* = 38).

Factor 2 (vertical axis of Figure 1) again opposes the positive and negative conceptions: "tourism", "nice weather", "the seaside", "the beach", and "the landscape" oppose "the people", "under-development", "unemployment", "difficult economic situation", and "youth" (T% = 9.4; 95% of Lambda 2).

The third factor opposes "I am proud of our history", and "corruption" to "the people", "nice weather", "the beach", "the seaside", "lack of concern for education", "youth", "bad use of tourism", "crisis", "difficult economic situation" (T% = 9.4; 95% of Lambda 3).

Finally, the fourth factor opposes "bad use of tourism", "tourism", "the landscape", "the people", "the persons", and "nice weather", to "poor organization", "crisis", "the seaside", "the beach", "damaged" (T% = 8.5; 96% of Lambda 4).

In order to detect whether this structure of the subjects' views about Portugal corresponds to different types of affective identification with the national group, subject space and the lexical unit space were considered simultaneously. As may be seen in figure 1 "cold" and "hot" identified subjects clustered respectively at the negative and positive poles of the represented factors. In spite of its purely descriptive scope, these results clearly show that the negative and positive features of the representations of Portugal are correlated with the type of social identification.

2.2.3 Type of Identification and Patterns of Causal Attribution. The second step in the analysis was aimed at testing whether these two patterns of identification also correspond to different patterns of attribution.

The scores of 6 "internal" and 6 "external" items were summed and averaged as a means of getting a global score for the internality and externality of the subjects' attributions (Table 1).

A two-way multivariate analysis of variance (MANOVA), identification (cold vs. hot) × locus of causality (internal vs. external) was computed on the average scores of internal and external items. No main effects emerged for identification ($F(1,36) < 1$, ns), or for locus of causality ($F(1,36) < 1$, ns). However, as expected, the interaction between those two factors was significant ($F(1,36) = 8.73$; $p < .01$). Cold identified subjects attributed crisis less to external factors ($M = 3.02$; $SD = 0.61$) than hot identified subjects did ($M = 3.31$; $SD = 0.63$). The former ($M = 3.55$; $SD = 0.74$) attributed crisis more to internal factors than the latter ($M = 2.97$; $SD = 0.96$).

Table 1
Explanations as a Function of Affective Identification

	Identification			
	Cold (n = 19)		Hot (n = 19)	
Items	M	SD	M	SD
Internal explanations				
1.The Portuguese do not value work	4.32	0.95	3.53	1.17
2. The Portuguese are not competitive	3.16	1.57	2.79	1.65
3. The Portuguese are incapable	3.47	1.43	2.74	1.45
4. The Portuguese do not make an effort	3.05	1.78	3.16	1.50
5. The Portuguese lack prof. qualifications	3.00	1.67	2.16	1.54
6. The Portuguese way of life	4.32	0.95	3.47	1.39
External explanations				
7. Crisis is all around the world	3.11	1.45	3.84	1.26
8. Portugal lacks natural resources	2.42	1.64	2.16	1.50
9. The crisis results from bad luck	1.58	1.31	1.84	0.96
10. The population is aging	2.42	1.47	3.26	1.20
11. Portugal lacks political stability	4.16	1.26	4.53	1.02
12. Portugal lacks economic strength	4.42	0.69	4.21	0.98

The data suggest that the use of internal and external attributions is related in a significant manner to the affective component of group identification. This finding is mainly due to person factors. Indeed, the univariate analysis yielded a significant effect of identification on the internal pattern of explanations ($F(1,36) = 4.35$; $p < .05$) but not on the external attributions ($F(1,36) = 2.08$; $p = .16$). Furthermore, the pattern found for external attributions complements the pattern for internal attributions. Subjects in the cold identification condition agreed less with external explanations than subjects in the hot identification condition did. Thus, although results only provided significant support for the hypothesis in terms of internal explanations, the pattern found for external explanations still goes in the predicted direction.

One might argue that the source of the study (a foreign scientific institution) may have affected the results. Yet, following Marques, Yzerbyt and Rijsman (1988) one would expect the occurrence of an ingroup bias in an outgroup context of response but not in an ingroup context. Furthermore, one should not expect differences as a function of the affective component of social identification (cf. Marques et al., 1988; Marques & Yzerbyt, 1988). Study 1 did not support this idea.

3. Study 2: Ingroup Derogation and the Evaluation of Unlikeable Ingroupers

3.1 Overview

A source of threat to social identity was manipulated in the second study. This study further explored the relationship between expressed ingroup favoritism tendencies and social identification. The hypotheses were as follows: The emergence of ingroup favoritism will depend on type of affective identification. A source of threat influences the emergence of behavior patterns. According to our point of view, one may expect cold subjects to denigrate bad ingroupers in both the ingroup and the outgroup threat condition. This is not to be expected in the case of hot identified subjects. The latter will denigrate bad ingroupers in the ingroup threat condition but not in the outgroup threat condition.

3.2 Method

3.2.1 Subjects. The subjects were 95 Portuguese graduate students in the arts at the University of Lisbon. Gender of subjects was a controlled variable.

3.2.2 Procedure. The investigation took place in Lisbon at a time when the behavior patterns of some Portuguese had been publicly challenged (leading to a TV debate).

Subjects were asked to evaluate the national group on a series of five-point scales which stemmed from a previous pilot study. The measure of their identifications with the group was similar to the one reported in study 1. Source of threat was manipulated as follows: Half of the subjects were told that a Portuguese institution was conducting the study, the other half, that a foreign institution was heading it.

3.3 Results

The procedure for dividing subjects into hot versus cold identified was the same as in study 1 ($M = 3.9$; $SD = 1.49$).

The scores of 6 "internal" items and 6 "external" items were summed and averaged as a means of getting a global score of internality and externality of the subjects' attributions (Figure 2).

A three way multivariate analysis of variance for identification (cold vs. hot) × source of threat to the social self (ingroup vs. outgroup) × locus of causality (internal vs. external) was computed. The latter was a within-subject factor. No main effects emerged for source of threat to the social self ($F(1,92) = 1.42$; $p = .24$), which goes against our hypothesis. However, as we expected identification and locus of causality produced significant main effects ($F(1,92) = 7.86$; $p < .01$ and $F(1,92) = 8.26$; $p < .01$, respectively).

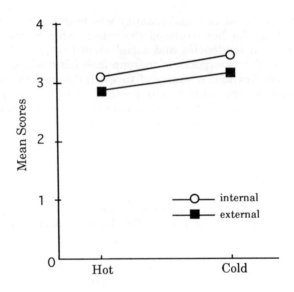

Figure 2. Mean scores of internality and externality for hot and cold subjects.

The data thus suggest that the explanations which are taken into account do vary as a function of individual's emotional involvement with a group. This finding is mainly the result of the internal items as shown by the univariate analysis of variance ($F(1,92) = 7.23$, $p < .01$, for internal items; and $F(1,92) = 2.45$, $p = .12$, for the external items). Hot identified subjects attributed the unlikeable behavior of some ingroupers less to internal factors than cold identified subjects did. Furthermore, they displayed similar patterns of response for external attributions. This pattern of results is qualified by a significant interaction: source of threat × identification type for the external attributions ($F(1,92) = 4.55$; $p = .04$). In support of our hypothesis, hot identified subjects attributed fewer external causes to the behavior of unlikeable ingroupers when they were in an ingroup context than in an outgroup context. However, cold identified subjects attributed more external causes to the behavior of unlikeable ingroupers in an ingroup context than in an outgroup context. Thus, our hypothesis was partially supported. Cold identified subjects considered more internal factors for the behavior of unlikeable ingroup members than hot identified subjects did. Furthermore, they made more external attributions in the ingroup condition than in the outgroup condition.

4. Discussion

Taken together, our results highlight the multidimensional nature of social identification and emphasize the importance of the affective component of social identity. In support of our hypothesis, individuals who were cognitively and affectively identified with a group did not belittle unlikeable ingroupers whereas individuals who were not committed to the group (cf. Striker, 1977) degraded unlikeable ingroupers in an outgroup context. Also, the findings of study 1 provide support for the idea that causal explanations and social representations follow the same rationale (cf. Hewstone, Jaspars, & Lalljee, 1982; Moscovici & Hewstone, 1983). Our subjects described and evaluated their group favorably when they were affectively identified with the group. This was not the true when they were not committed to the group. In this case we found ingroup derogation. This pattern was also expressed in the causal attribution judgments. Subjects who strongly identified with their group attributed the negative event more to external factors than did subjects with a low level of affective identification. Subjects who were committed to their group attributed the negative event less to internal factors than did cold identified subjects.

Study 2 replicated study 1. Subjects were more ingroup derogating when they were not committed to the group. They attributed the unlikeable behavior of some ingroup members mainly to internal factors. Interestingly, the emergence of this pattern was influenced by a source of threat. Hot identified subjects were less critical of the unlikeable ingroupers in an outgroup threat context than in an ingroup context. This was not the case for cold identified subjects, who displayed the opposite pattern: they were harsher in an outgroup context than in an ingroup context. The reasons for this pattern of behavior are open to question. One may speculate that because of the importance of this membership, cold identified subjects fear group sanctions such as the black-sheep effect. On the other hand, they are not very happy with the state of affairs and the outgroup may validate their point of view. In this sense, our studies qualify a recent derivative of social identity theory proposed by Marques and his colleagues (Marques, Leyens, & Yzerbyt, 1988; Marques &

Yzerbyt, 1988). Marques and colleagues did not distinguish the affective and the cognitive components of social identity. They claim that individuals who identify with a group display ingroup favoritism through denigration of unlikeable ingroupers. Our studies showed that this behavior pattern is characteristic of hot identified individuals and occurs in an ingroup context. When individuals are cognitively identified but affectively disidentified, they may also display a similar behavior pattern when interacting in an outgroup context. Further studies should address the links between type of identification with a group, derogation of unlikeable ingroupers, and ingroup favoritism.

Moreover, the present findings are consistent with Tajfel's (1972, 1978, 1982) and Tajfel and Turner's (1979) point of view concerning the multidimensional nature of social identifications. They provide empirical support for Hinkle et al.'s (Hinkle, Fox-Cardamone, Taylor, & Crook, 1989; Hinkle, Taylor, & Fox-Cardamone, 1989) emphasis on the affective component of identification with a group. Also, our results are inconsistent with cognitive conceptualizations of groups which do not predict differences as a function of the affective component of social identification (e.g. Linville, 1985; and in a different vein, Hogg & Abrams, 1988; Turner, 1987). The distinction between the affective and cognitive components of identification seems quite promising. Further studies should investigate the conditions under which the affective component opposes the cognitive one.

Some might argue that we are not dealing with social groups but with social categories (cf. Hogg & Abrams, 1988; Rabbie & Horwitz, 1988). Indeed, national groups are also social categories. Nevertheless, as far as we know, the social identity approach does not distinguish them for the purpose of social identification. Furthermore, we were able to replicate the patterns described here with other types of groups.

Finally, our results provide support for the idea that causal attribution patterns are not stable properties of groups. This idea has been implicit in studies done under the heading of social attribution (cf. e.g. Hewstone, 1989). Causal explanations vary as a function of the audience (Weary & Arkin, 1981). In this sense, they are impression management strategies.

References

Bains, G. (1983). Explanations and the need for social control. In M. Hewstone (Ed.), *Attribution theory: Social and functional extensions.* Oxford: Basil Blackwell.

Benzécri, J.-P. (1973). *L'analyse des données* (Vol. 2). Paris : Dunod.

Billig, M. (1976). *Social psychology of intergroup relations*. London: Academic Press.

Brewer, M., & Kramer, R. (1985). The psychology of intergroup attitudes and behavior. *Annual Review of Psychology, 36,* 219-243.

Brown, B. B., & Lohr, M. J. (1987). Peer group affiliation and adolescent self-esteem: An integration of ego identity and symbolic-interaction theories. *Journal of Personality and Social Psychology, 52,* 47-55.

Brown, R. (1978). Divided we fall: An analysis of relations between sections of a factory workforce. In H. Tajfel (Ed.), *Differentiation between social groups* (pp. 395-429). London: Academic Press.

Brown, R., Condor, S., Mathews, A., Wade, G., & Williams, J. (1986). Explaining intergroup differentiation in an industrial organization. *Journal of Occupational Psychology, 59,* 273-286.

Brown, R., & Ross, G. F. (1982). The battle for acceptance: An exploration into the dynamics of intergroup behaviour. In H. Tajfel (Ed.), *Social identity and intergroup relations* (pp. 155-178). Cambridge/Paris: Cambridge University Press/Maison des Sciences de l'Homme.

Commins, B., & Lockwood, J. (1979). The effects of status differences favoured treatment and equity on intergroup comparisons. *Experimental Journal of Social Psychology, 9,* 281-289.

Deaux, K. (1984). From individual differences to social categories. *American Psychologist, 39,* 105-116.

Deaux, K. (1985). Sex and gender. *Annual Review of Psychology, 36,* 49-81.

Deschamps, J.-C. (1977). *L'Attribution et la catégorisation sociale*. Bern : Peter Lang.

Deschamps, J.-C. (1982). Social identity and relations of power between groups. In H. Tajfel (Ed.), *Social identity and intergroup relations* (pp. 85-98). Cambridge/Paris: Cambridge University Press/Maison des Sciences de l'homme.

Deschamps, J.-C. (1983). Social attribution, In J. Jaspars, F. Fincham, & M. Hewstone (Eds.), *Attribution theory and research: Conceptual, developmental and social dimensions*. London: Academic Press.

Doise, W., & Sinclair, A. (1973). The categorization process in intergroup relations. *European Journal of Social Psychology, 3,* 145-153.

Ellemers, N., van Knippenberg, A., DeVries, N., & Wilke, H. (1988). Social identification and permeability of group boundaries. *European Journal of Social Psychology, 18,* 497-513.

Fraczek, A., & Linneweber, V. (1989, June). *Social identity and some aspects of ingroup hostility: Perceptual biases against black-sheep.* Paper presented at the East/West Meeting of the E.A.E.S.P., Warsaw, Poland.

Greenacre, M. J. (1984). *Theory and applications of correspondence analysis.* London: Academic Press.

Gurin, P., Miller, A. H., & Gurin, G. (1980). Stratum identification and consciousness. *Social Psychology Quarterly, 43,* 30-47.

Harvey, J., & Weary, G. (1984). Current issues in attribution theory and research. *Annual Review of Psychology, 35,* 427-459.

Heider, F. (1958). *The psychology of interpersonal relations.* New York: Wiley.

Hewstone, M. (1989). *Causal attribution: From cognitive processes to collective beliefs.* Oxford: Basil Blackwell.

Hewstone, M., Fincham, F., & Jaspars, J. (1981). Social categorization and similarity in intergroup behaviour: A replication with "penalties". *European Journal of Social Psychology, 11,* 101-107.

Hewstone, M., & Jaspars, J. (1982). Intergroup relations and attribution processes. In H. Tajfel (Ed.), *Social identity and intergroup relations* (pp. 99-133). Cambridge/Paris: Cambridge University Press/Maison des Sciences de l'Homme.

Hewstone, M., Jaspars, J., & Lalljee, M. (1982). Social representations, social attribution and social identity: The intergroup images of "public" and "comprehensive" schoolboys. *European Journal of Social Psychology, 12,* 241-269.

Hinkle, S., Fox-Cardamone, D. L., Taylor, L. A., & Crook, K. (1989, June). *Studies in social identity theory: Group identification and dimensions of intergroup comparison.* Paper presented at the East/West Meeting of the E.A.E.S.P, Warsaw, Poland.

Hinkle, S., Taylor, L. A., & Fox-Cardamone, D. L. (1989). Intragroup identification and intergroup differentiation: A multicomponent approach. *British Journal of Social Psychology, 28,* 305-317.

Hogg, M., & Abrams, D. (1988). *Social identifications.* London: Routledge.

Hogg, M., & Turner, J. C. (1985). When liking begets solidarity: An experiment on the role of interpersonal attraction in psychological group formation. *British Journal of Social Psychology, 24,* 267-281.

Jackson, S. (1981). Measurement of commitment to role identities. *Journal of Personality and Social Psychology, 40,* 138-146.

Kelly, C. (1988). Intergroup differentiation in a political context. *British Journal of Social Psychology, 27,* 319-332.

Lau, R. (1989). Individual and contextual influences on group identification. *Social Psychology Quarterly, 52,* 220-231.

Lebart, L. & Morineau, A. (1984). *Système portable pour l'analyse des données (SPAD)*. Paris : CESIA.

Lemyre, L., & Smith, P.M. (1985). Intergroup discrimination and self-esteem in the minimal group paradigm. *Journal of Personality and Social Psychology, 49,* 660-670.

Linville, P. (1982). The complexity-extremity effect and age-based stereotyping. *Journal of Personality and Social Psychology, 42,* 193-211.

Linville, P. (1985). Self-complexity and affective extremity: Don't put all of your eggs in one cognitive basket. *Social Cognition, 3,* 94-120.

Linville, P., & Jones, E. (1980). Polarized appraisals of out-group members. *Journal of Personality and Social Psychology, 38,* 689-703.

Mackie, J. (1974). *The cement of the universe: A study of causation.* Oxford: Clarendon Press.

Marques, J., Leyens, J.-Ph., & Yzerbyt, V. (1988). The black-sheep effect: Judgmental extremity towards ingroup members as a function of group identification. *European Journal of Social Psychology, 18,* 1-16.

Marques, J., & Yzerbyt, V. (1988). The black-sheep effect: Judgmental extremity towards ingroup members in inter- and intra-group situations. *European Journal of Social Psychology, 18,* 287-292.

Marques, J., Yzerbyt, V., & Rijsman, J. (1988). Context effects on intergroup discrimination: Ingroup bias as a function of experimenter's provenance. *British Journal of Social Psychology, 27,* 301-318.

McGill, A. (1989). Context effects in judgments of causation. *Journal of Personality and Social Psychology, 57,* 189-200.

Messick, D., & Mackie, D. (1987). Intergroup relations. *Annual Review of Psychology, 40,* 45-81.

Moscovici, S., & Hewstone, M. (1983). Social representations and social explanations: From the naive to the amateur scientist. In M. Hewstone (Ed.), *Attribution: Social and functional extensions.* Oxford: Basil Blackwell.

Mugny, G., Kaiser, C. & Papastamou, S. (1983). Influence minoritaire, identification et relations entre groupes. *Les Cahiers de Psychologie Sociale, 9,* 1-30.

Ng, S. H. (1986). Equity, intergroup bias and interpersonal bias in reward allocation. *European Journal of Social Psychology, 16,* 239-256.

Rabbie, J. M., & Horwitz, M. (1988). Categories versus groups as explanatory concepts in intergroup relations. *European Journal of Social Psychology, 18,* 117-123.

Rijsman, J. (1983). The dynamics of social competition in personal and categorical comparison situations. In W. Doise & S. Moscovici (Eds.), *Current issues in European social psychology* (Vol. 1). Cambridge: Cambridge University Press.

Sachdev, I., & Bourhis, R. Y. (1985). Social categorization and power differentials in group relations. *European Journal of Social Psychology, 15,* 415-434.

Sachdev, I., & Bourhis, R. Y. (1991). Power and status differentials in minority and majority group relations. *European Journal of Social Psychology, 21,* 1-24.

Skevington, S. (1981). Intergroup relations and nursing. *European Journal of Social Psychology, 11,* 43-59.

Snyder, C. R., Lassegard, M. A., & Ford, C. E. (1986). Distancing after group success and failure: Basking in reflected glory and cutting after failure. *Journal of Personality and Social Psychology, 51,* 382-388.

Stryker, S. (1977). Developments in two social psychologies: Toward an appreciation of mutual relevance. *Sociometry, 40,* 145-160.

Tajfel, H. (1972). La catégorisation sociale. In S. Moscovici (Ed.), *Introduction à la psychologie sociale* (Vol. 1, p. 272-302). Paris : Larousse.

Tajfel, H. (Ed.) (1978). *Differentiation between social groups: Studies in the social psychology of intergroup relations.* London: Academic Press.

Tajfel, H. (Ed.) (1982). *Social identity and intergroup relations.* Cambridge/Paris: Cambridge University Press/Maison des Sciences de l'Homme.

Tajfel, H., & Turner, J. C. (1979). An integrative theory of intergroup conflict. In W. G. Austin & S. Worchel (Eds.), *The social psychology of intergroup relations.* Monterey, CA: Brooks/Cole.

Thibaut, J. W., & Kelley, H. H. (1959). *The social psychology of groups.* New York: Wiley

Thibaut, J. W., Riecken, H. W. (1955). Some determinants and consequences of the perception of social causality. *Journal of Personality, 24,* 113-133.

Turner, J. C. (1973). *Competition and category conflict: Self versus group for social value versus economic gain.* Unpublished manuscript, University of Bristol.

Turner, J. C. (1981). Towards a cognitive definition of the social group. In J. C. Turner & H. Giles (Eds.), *Intergroup behaviour.* Oxford: Blackwell.

Turner, J. C. (1982). Towards a redefinition of the social group. In H. Tajfel (Ed.), *Social identity and intergroup relations* (pp. 15-40). Cambridge/Paris: Cambridge University Press/Maison des Sciences de l'Homme.

Turner, J. C., & Brown, R. (1978). Social status, cognitive alternatives and intergroup relations. In H. Tajfel (Ed.), *Differentiation between social groups* (pp.201-234). London: Academic Press.

Turner, J. C., Hogg, M. A., Oakes, P. J., Reicher, S. D., & Wetherell, M. S. (1987). *Rediscovering the social group: A self-categorization theory.* Oxford: Basil Blackwell.

Turner, J. C., Sachdev, I., & Hogg, M. A. (1983). Social categorization, interpersonal attraction, and group formation. *British Journal of Social Psychology, 22,* 227-239.

Tversky, A. (1977). Features of similarity. *Psychological Review, 84,* 327-352.

van Knippenberg, A., & Wilke, H. (1979). Perceptions of collégiens and apprentis re-analysed. *European Journal of Social Psychology, 9,* 427-434.

Waddell, N., & Cairns, E. (1986). Situational perspectives on social identity in Northern Ireland. *British Journal of Social Psychology, 25,* 25-32.

Wagner, U., Lampen, L., & Syllwasschy, J. (1986). In-group inferiority, social identity and out-group devaluation in a modified minimal group study. *British Journal of Social Psychology, 25,* 15-23.

Weary, G., & Arkin, R. (1981). Attributional self-presentation. In J. Harvey, W. Ickes, & R. Kidd (Eds.), *New directions in attribution research* (Vol. 3). Hillsdale, NJ: Erlbaum.

EVALUATIVE KNOWLEDGE
AND THE SOCIAL COGNITION PARADIGM

Jean-Léon Beauvois

Pierre Mendès France University, Grenoble, France

Nicole Dubois

University of Nancy 2, France

Social psychologists have often considered evaluative activities to be part of affect. Connotative meaning theory (Osgood, Suci, & Tannenbaum, 1957) thus includes an object's value as part of the "emotional" component of word meaning. The two- or three-component view of attitudes combines the affective component and the evaluative component (Rosenberg, 1960). It is therefore not surprising that in research on impression formation or on the social cognition paradigm, cognitive social psychologists have considered the global evaluation of persons – which has been overpowered by the omnipresent assessment of likableness – to be the result of a judgment of an affective nature. This holds for two main research trends in social cognition: cognitive algebra (Anderson, 1981, 1982) and information processing (Srull & Wyer, 1989).

The affective view of evaluative activity fits very well with the postulate of the unicity and homogeneity of knowledge. According to this postulate, knowledge about an object is seen as a mere reflection of the nature of the object, and scientific knowledge in particular is deemed to be the ideal kind of knowledge. Accordingly, a piece of knowledge (e.g. "Donald is an honest person") will be seen as either true (or tending to be true) or false (biased). Any piece of knowledge is thus conceived of as an excerpt of descriptive knowledge, i.e. the kind of knowledge used in science. For a social psychologist, when individuals receive information about another person (about his or her behavior, for example) they

This research was made possible by grants from the Programme Pluriannuel en Sciences Humaines PPSH 33, CNRS Rhône-Alpes, France.

(1) process that information in order to gain descriptive knowledge about that person (e.g. knowledge expressed in terms of traits which are instantiated by the target's behaviors: Wyer & Gordon, 1984; Srull & Wyer, 1989), and then (2) infer the evaluative-affective consequences of that knowledge (this person is likable, because I like people who behave that way or who are like that). From this point of view, (affective) evaluation is a *post-knowledge process*.

If we reject the postulate of the unicity of knowledge by introducing the notion of "evaluative knowledge", which is both different from descriptive knowledge and non-reducible to the affective value of objects, we find another representation of cognitive activity which mediates knowledge of social objects and may be another way of conceiving of social cognition. We shall not review the distinction between descriptive and evaluative knowledge here, as it has been largely discussed in other papers (Beauvois, 1984; Beauvois, 1990; Beauvois & Dubois, 1991). In the field of person perception, this distinction implies that personological information provides knowledge which, right from the beginning, is both descriptive *and* evaluative. The affective component of personological judgments, whose existence cannot be denied, can either be based on knowledge of what the target person is (descriptive knowledge) or on knowledge of his/her value or social utility (evaluative knowledge), or it can be independent of both of these types of knowledge.

We shall start by recalling some empirical data concerning the notion of evaluative knowledge in social cognition. Then we shall see what the implications of this notion are for our view of the cognitive activity which mediates knowledge about social objects.

1. Evaluative Encoding and Personological Cognition

Three types of data will be discussed in this empirical section. We shall start by reviewing several studies which have shown that efficient evaluative encoding of personological information is possible. We shall then report some of the consequences of this encoding observed in experiments using the subliminal priming paradigm. Lastly, we shall emphasize the relevance of evaluative knowledge to internalization processes.

1.1 Traits and the Encoding of Social Utility

In the "standard" view recalled above in the introduction, a trait stored in permanent memory can be considered as a sort of category whose elements, which vary in their degree of typicality, are the potential behaviors of individuals which are supposedly characterized by the trait (Mischel, 1973; Buss & Craik, 1983; Wojciszke & Pienkowski, 1991). Thus, in experiments attempting to describe episodic memory for persons (for a model of memory organization, see Srull & Wyer, 1989; for a model of memory elaboration, see Klein & Loftus, 1990), lists of behaviors are presented to subjects. Their first cognitive task is to decide which traits are instantiated by those behaviors. If we tell subjects that the famous Donald has turned in a lost wallet to the police station, they will infer that Donald is an honest person.

Researchers have therefore treated encoding on the basis of the categorical links that exist between one or more *behaviors of the target* and the traits they instantiate. We can argue, however, that this cognitive activity concerns a particular type of encoding (that related to descriptive knowledge) and that another type of encoding may exist, one which involves the knowledge of the target person's social utility, i.e., the (evaluative) knowledge of *what we can or must do with the person*, rather than knowledge of his or her behaviors. This means that a new, (evaluative) category register is activated by trait constructs, like the one involved in the standard view. But here, the elements of the category are behaviors that other persons *may or must manifest towards the person characterized by the trait* (Labourin & Lecourvoisier, 1985). For example, if I know that Donald is honest, I immediately know that I can lend him my credit card or the keys to my house, just as I know that he will turn in a lost wallet to the police station. Unfortunately, this type of behavior (which is part of evaluative knowledge) is never included in the lists given to subjects, except in cases where the researcher mistakenly paraphrases the trait to avoid naming it (e.g., we can trust him).

The first study we shall report here (Beauvois & Dubois, 1992) was aimed at showing that a trait can be instantiated both by a target person's behaviors and by behaviors that people may have towards that target person.

In a pretest, for each of 33 traits read aloud, half the subjects had to write down a behavior they considered characteristic of a person defined by the trait, and the other half had to write down a behavior that people may or must have towards that person. For each of the stimulus traits, we thus obtained two lists of behaviors. The first list will be called the target's behaviors or "TB", and the second, the other person's behaviors towards the target or "OB". It is interesting to point out that the subjects found the second task as natural as the first one, and that an equivalent number of non-responses was obtained in each case. Note simply that there was a greater variety of behaviors mentioned on the TB lists than on the OB lists, and more overlapping on the OB lists (the same behavior was proposed for two different traits: e.g., "We must know how to encourage him" for both "ambitious" and "hard working").

Then, in the experiment proper, new subjects were asked to choose, from among the behaviors on the TB and OB lists, *those they considered the most representative of the traits*. They were also asked to give a confidence rating on a five-point scale for each of their choices. The results showed that the TB and OB hierarchies (which ranked the behaviors by frequency of choice) were perfectly comparable since they had the same degree of entropy. The TB and OB conditions are therefore comparable at the statistical level. These results show that a trait can be instantiated in permanent memory by OB behaviors as well as by TB behaviors. The remarkable statistical similarity of the two categorical systems (cf. Beauvois & Dubois, 1992, Figures 1a and 1b) casts some doubt on the validity of the claim that one of these sets of behaviors (OB) can be inferred from the other (TB). The results obtained with other paradigms (person memory paradigm, categorical decision paradigm) accentuate this doubt.

These experiments were based on another theoretical hypothesis. In addition to the opposition between evaluative and descriptive knowledge, we introduced the hypothesis that the OB register is more pertinent for some traits (thereby called "evaluative") than for others (thereby called "descriptive"). This distinction (cf. Beauvois, 1984; Beauvois & Dubois, 1991) cannot be confounded with the opposition between "neutral" traits and highly polarized traits. This opposition (cf. Anderson, 1981, 1982) is an integral part of the "affective-connotative" conception of evaluative activity. "Neutral" traits are only negatively defined when there is no affective valence. Our distinction is based on the assumption that all traits involve both kinds of knowledge, but to varying extents: evaluative traits more specifically concern evaluative knowledge and OB behaviors, whereas descriptive traits pertain more specifically to descriptive knowledge and TB behaviors. Various criteria (Beauvois & Dubois, 1991) can be used to classify traits in the evaluative or descriptive categories. The most useful criterion opposes traits which contribute massively to the activity of personological characterization (i.e. an activity which is highly evaluative) to those (often different ones) that immediately evoke a specific person.

This distinction can be related to the distinctions defined in more recent research, where an attempt has been made to establish criteria to differentiate traits from a descriptive standpoint on the basis of their confirmability (Rothbart & Park, 1986) or visibility (Funder & Dobroth, 1987). Even though it is not easy to establish a correspondence between criteria derived from different theoretical frameworks, it appears legitimate from our point of view to assume that the most confirmable or visible traits (relaxed, talkative, etc.; cf. Funder & Dobroth, 1987) may also be the most descriptive ones. The distinction proposed here between evaluative and descriptive traits does not actually differ from the one proposed by Semin and Fiedler (1988) between interpretative and descriptive verbs. In fact, while these authors advocate the affective-connotative view of evaluative activity, their distinction in the end involves criteria which resemble the visibility criterion (presence vs. absence of behavioral invariance in the meaning of verbs). This distinction, although based on very different theories, is correlated with our distinction between evaluative and descriptive adjectives. In the experiments presented below, traits assumed to be very evaluative are opposed to traits assumed to be very descriptive.

Our experiments, which deal with person memory (Beauvois & Mira, 1991; Beauvois, Dubois, Mira, & Monteil, 1992), consisted of presenting subjects with a list of behaviors associated with a person. Half of the behaviors were TB and half were OB. The behaviors on the list were in fact paired on the basis of the data obtained in the previous experiment so as to instantiate "very evaluative" traits (honest, nice, dynamic, sociable, etc.) or "very descriptive" traits (shy, sensitive, passionate, etc.). Thus, each trait was exemplified by both TB and OB behaviors. The results showed that in the pure memorization situation and in the impression formation situation, there was a highly significant interaction ($p < .00001$ in all experiments) between the nature of the instantiated trait (evaluative vs. descriptive) and the type of behavior recalled (TB vs. OB). Subjects remembered more TB behaviors which instantiated the so-called descriptive traits, and more OB behaviors which instantiated the so-called evaluative traits.

Another experiment, this time using the categorical decision paradigm (Beauvois & Dubois, 1992), consisted of the tachistoscopic presentation of TB and OB behaviors followed by an evaluative or descriptive trait. Subjects had to decide as quickly as possible whether or not the behavior was representative of the trait. Each trait was paired to ten TB and ten OB behaviors chosen on the basis of previous data for their ability to trigger positive or negative decisions. The dependent variable was the decision time. As expected, the categorical decisions were equally quick for OB behaviors and TB behaviors when highly evaluative traits were being judged (nice, honest). However, decisions about TB behaviors were made more rapidly on highly descriptive traits (shy, sensitive). The quickest decisions mainly occurred on OB behaviors paired with evaluative traits, and TB behaviors paired with descriptive traits.

These experiments led us to believe that personological information ("Donald is an honest person") may either directly activate both categories, or activate a composite category which contains both "descriptive" information about the target person (Donald can do this and that) and "evaluative" information about his or her social utility (This is what we can do with Donald).

Can we conclude that the OB and TB encoding systems have the same properties? Several facts lead us to answer "No" to this question. Again, we saw in the pretest that subjects came up with fewer OB behaviors than TB behaviors for the majority of the 33 traits. We also noted that OB behaviors produced more overlapping across traits than TB behaviors did. It follows that the OB categorical system, although smaller than the TB categorical system, may be more fuzzy and involve a greater number of linked categories. We should therefore expect the two systems to be asymmetrical when a trait => behavior task (like the one reported above, which shows equal statistical consistency in TB and OB) is compared to a behavior => trait task (which, on the contrary, should produce less statistical consistency in OB than in TB). Another experiment was conducted to test this hypothesis.

Subjects had to indicate which traits corresponded to the behaviors presented. The behaviors used were the ones that had been chosen the most frequently in the first experiment as representative of the traits. The results showed, as expected, that subjects more often indicated the original trait for TB behaviors than for OB behaviors.

The OB categorical system (which denotes social utility and provides evaluative knowledge) therefore seems to be different from the TB categorical system, which contains descriptive knowledge. Because of categorical overlap, the traits that can be attributed under it are probably less univocal than the ones supported by the TB categorical system. However, once a trait has been attributed, the categorical information it activates is equally well defined in both registers.[1]

The hypothesis of the dual encoding of personological information brings up some interesting perspectives. There is no reason to consider the OB evaluative register, as it is described here, as an "affective" register. Both OB and TB are representations of behaviors which form categories, and thus can be used to process personological information. But, unlike TB, the OB behaviors provide evaluative (utilitarian) knowledge of others rather than descriptive knowledge. In fact, people may be more inclined to encode personological information from an evaluative point of view than from a descriptive one. This can be inferred from the evaluative structure of implicit personality theories, which may take on a new theoretical meaning in this context. It is possible that the locations where evaluative categories intersect are in fact definitional of what researchers call "conceptual similarity" between traits (D'Andrade, 1965; Ebbesen & Allen, 1979), from which co-occurrence matrices are extracted to establish the hierarchical or dimensional cognitive constructions called I.P.T.

---

[1] This is compatible with the logic of social evaluation practices, where evaluative knowledge probably originates (Beauvois, 1976, 1984). This logic must involve both flexibility before evaluative labelling occurs and univocal transmission of information. For example, teachers must be flexible about their knowledge of a student's label as "independent" or " lazy". Inversely, when a teacher says "This student is lazy", other people must understand the same thing.

personological information, they can be placed at the end points of a metatheoretical continuum which extends from cognitive functioning *per se* (evaluative priming effects) to its social implications (internalization and processing of evaluative information).

1.2 Evaluative Knowledge and Priming Effects

It is well known today that personological concepts can be automatically activated by subliminal priming (cf. Croizet, 1991a for a review). Many studies have shown that when word traits are presented subliminally during a "priming" task (phase A) which is followed by an allegedly independent impression formation task (phase B) in which subjects are faced with so-called "evaluatively ambiguous" behaviors,[2] we observe an increase in the use of the "primed" concepts, and *a fortiori* an evaluation bias favoring the affective polarity (positive or negative) of those concepts in person evaluation. Researchers who have explored this paradigm, all advocates of the standard view, think that the activation by priming of any personological concept (e.g. hostile) is equivalent to the activation of its descriptive component. The priming effect is only possible if the behavior presented in phase B is a relevant descriptive instantiation of the primed concept(s). If so, the target will be said to be hostile, and will thereby be degraded (because we do not usually like hostile people). In short, the evaluative bias (here, an affective one in fact) is nothing but the consequence of the pertinence of a behavior that is necessarily descriptive. Thus, these researchers think that evaluative biases are unlikely to be observed after priming of descriptively irrelevant concepts (Smith, 1984; Wyer & Srull, 1986). If this were to happen, they would assume that it was solely the outcome of a purely affective phenomenon (Bargh, 1988) whereby the primed traits, because of their affective polarity, produce a "mood" which orients (biases) the search for relevant concepts during the impression formation phase. This brings us again to a conception in which the only cognitive component is the descriptive one (the reason for the importance of descriptive relevance), which in turn can only be accompanied by an affective component, called evaluation.

The dual cognitive encoding hypothesis (descriptive *and* evaluative encoding) may lead to another way of conceiving of the priming process. Remember that the evaluative register is fuzzier than the descriptive register. So, if we agree that priming makes the primed ideas more accessible – in both the descriptive and evaluative categories (and perhaps in the evaluative one above all) –, it is very likely that the memory search

---

[2] This means that the behavior presented in the impression formation phase can instantiate a "positive" trait (e.g., nice) as well as a "negative" one (e.g., hypocritical).

during the impression formation phase evokes OB behaviors which are correct responses to the behavioral stimulus (even if those OB behaviors are recalled by activation of descriptively irrelevant concepts). This would not only orient the search in memory towards finely descriptive, relevant constructs, but also towards constructs which are evaluatively consistent with the primes. This means that evaluative priming could be observed even with personological concepts which are descriptively irrelevant to the behavior attributed to the target (of whom an impression is being formed). This effect was observed by Croizet (1991b).

In Croizet's experiment, subjects were confronted in phase B with a target person's evaluatively ambiguous behavior, after subliminal priming of personological concepts (positive or negative, descriptively relevant or irrelevant) in phase A. As Croizet expected, the evaluative polarity of the traits attributed to the target person in the impression formation phase was highly affected by the polarity of the primes, whether they were descriptively relevant or not. The effect of the irrelevant primes was actually more stable.

This evaluative priming effect cannot be interpreted in terms of a positive or negative mood, induced solely by the affective polarity of the primed constructs (in which case it would be an affective prime). This was demonstrated by the fact that no effect on trait attribution was found for non-personological but very positive ("spring", "present") or very negative ("accident", "corpse") primes. An "affectivist" interpretation of evaluative priming would assume that these words, which are highly polarized from an emotional point of view, make equally good primes as the traits "generous" or "selfish", which are not descriptively pertinent here. This is not so.

1.3 Internalization and Evaluative Information Processing

The experiments that we shall now review were conducted in a very different research tradition: the study of sociocognitive processes (Beauvois, 1991; Beauvois, Joule & Monteil, 1989). Evaluative knowledge must be assumed to contribute to all aspects of cognitive functioning, and in particular, to the most significant ones for social activity. It is well known now that children (pupils up to age 10 or 11) tend to rely on increasingly internal causal explanations. This developmental trend has been interpreted as the acquisition of a social norm: the norm of internality (cf. Dubois, 1987; Beauvois & Dubois, 1988). Recall also that, while descriptive knowledge is dependent on a validity criterion (true/false), evaluative knowledge is dependent on another, different criterion, the criterion of social acceptability (Beauvois, 1990; Beauvois & Dubois, 1991).

It is unlikely that the reason why children acquire the norm of internality is to make them more efficient at processing descriptive knowledge. Nothing allows us to contend that internal explanations are more valid (true) than external ones. We may, however, assume that when children give internal explanations, they are giving more socially acceptable explanations, ones that are more accepted in the academic environment. Moreover, several researchers have insisted on the fact that the internalization of values and moral rules is mediated by the appropriation of an internal mode for the causal explanation of psychological events (cf. Grusec, 1983). This leads us to believe that the function of the acquisition of the internality norm by children is to further the internalization of values and social utilities rather than to gain valid, descriptive knowledge of the environment.

If we jointly consider implicit personality theories and the notion of trait on the one hand, and the distinction between evaluative and descriptive knowledge on the other, the above hypothesis becomes clearer. It is assumed that during the initial stages of normative learning, children detect the value of events (and behaviors in particular) on the basis of the environment's reactions to the events. Very early, the child learns to use language to describe the utility of behaviors (a "brave" act, a "dishonest" act). Nisbett and Ross (1980) showed how the properties of the personological lexicon allow us to characterize acts and people. Also, and probably during formal evaluation practices (Beauvois, 1976), the same words can be used to characterize the people performing those acts (a brave man, a dishonest man). This transfer of value from the act to the person, via language, is only possible if an internal mode of causal explanation, facilitated by the norm of internality, has been acquired and is implemented in the practice of evaluative activities. It seems, then, that the main foundation of the explanatory constructs (the traits) of I.P.T., which are the most representative constructs in our culture of internal explanations (Shweder & Bourne, 1982), is the utility of behaviors passed from acts to individuals by means of an internal explanation process.

We would therefore expect an internalizing orientation to deal more with the evaluative knowledge involved in implicit personality theories than with descriptive personological knowledge. It should be noted that the inverse is not theoretically implied. The detection of the value of events does not imply, *sui generis*, internality. It is based on a very general kind of learning which occurs during what Hoffman (1983) calls discipline encounters, the essence of adult-child relationships until old age. Internality requires another type of learning, one which is based on the implementation by the adult of a particular mode of disciplinary contact, i.e., what Hoffman (1970, 1983) calls the inductive mode, which is characteristic of a liberal kind of execution of power. Other education[3]

---

[3] Le Poultier (1991) was able to induce internal and external orientations by modelling with effects that can be tendentially compared with those just described.

practices (such as the mere affirmation of power) enable the child to detect values and utilities without producing internalization (cf. Beauvois, Monteil & Trognon, 1991).

In a research program initiated by Le Poultier some years ago (cf. Le Poultier, 1989), we attempted to show that internality in causal explanation is associated with a predisposition for the processing of evaluative (rather than descriptive) information. The initial studies in this project dealt with the quasi-differentialist detection of "internal" and "external" children. We must admit that they did not always produce the expected results. In the most recent studies in the program (Beauvois & Dubois, 1991; Bekaddour, 1992), we decided to cease using the differentialist approach and to experimentally induce an internal or external orientation. The induction of the orientation was done by giving subjects an internality questionnaire that had supposedly been filled out by an adolescent. Obviously, this questionnaire exemplified either internal or external choices. Immediately after the induction of an (internal vs. external) orientation, the subjects were asked in a subsequent task (target characterization) to act as if they were that teenager. More specifically, they were requested to guess how that teenager would process personological information about a target person by choosing the item that best characterized that target person. The personological information presented immediately after the induction of an orientation consisted of traits considered as more or less "evaluative" based on certain a priori criteria (e.g., sociable, sensitive, sincere vs. dreamer, curious, shy). The induction of an internal orientation made subjects predisposed to choosing the most evaluative traits (Beauvois & Dubois, 1991) and OB behaviors rather than TB behaviors (Bekaddour, 1992) to characterize the target person, at least when positively polarized traits were used.[3]

2. Evaluative Knowledge and Social Cognition

Consideration of the concept of evaluative knowledge and, a fortiori, acceptance of the fact that personological constructs convey information about the value or utility of people are likely to modify (1) the way in which personological information processing is modelled, and (2) our metatheoretical conception of social cognition.

2.1 Limitations to Modelling

The standard conception seems to lead to some extravagance in the models and theories which are influential in the field of social cognition.

In his cognitive algebra, Anderson (1981) had difficulty defending the idea that evaluative activity (function V in Information Integration Theory), which is based on (descriptive) knowledge of the stimulus, depends on (1) individual differences (the value of the stimulus varies across individuals) and (2) the goals and problems involved in the judgment. Anderson seems to be fond of the following example: Someone who is "descriptively" known to be happy-go-lucky will not be evaluated in the same fashion by a player than by a statistician! In fact, if we refer to Anderson's experimental data, we can see that nothing confirms this statement; of course, individual differences and judgment rationality sometimes affect the overall evaluation of a target person, but these effects only concern the absolute values of the stimulus traits (which can hardly be interpreted as stemming from response scale unreliability), and never the relative values. Let us consider the example in the study by Oden and Anderson (1971, cited by Anderson, 1981) in which several judgments (effectiveness, liking, respect) had to be made concerning some naval officers who were known by their academic performance and personality traits. Of course, the weight of this information varied across judgments, as its empirical value did, but there was no change in its relative value. Anderson's standard conception implies that a piece of information can be positive for one judgment and negative for another, and vice versa for a second judgment. At best, Anderson can mention a few studies in which information was positive in certain cases (e.g. "persuasive" for a lawyer) and irrelevant in others ("persuasive" for a plumber, or "mechanically inclined" for a lawyer) (Anderson & Lopes, 1974, cited by Anderson, 1981). But such constructs are probably among the most descriptive constructs used in psychological description. It would be unlikely to observe this kind of effect with traits such as "honest", "intelligent" ..., which are highly evaluative (and frequent!). And Anderson must be well aware of this, because these words do not appear any more often than "happy-go-lucky" in the likableness norms that he himself established (Anderson, 1968, reproduction of norms by Anderson, 1982). Their principle is intrinsically contradictory with the idea that evaluations vary as a function of individual differences and of the rationale of the judgment. Thus, contrary to what he might claim on the basis of the standard view, Anderson's data show that a trait stimulus is inherently valued, this value being only marginally affected by the judgment's specificity and by individual differences.

In the same line of thinking, accepting that trait constructs directly provide information about the value or utility of the described person could avoid certain difficulties which the standard conception might encounter in information processing models like the one proposed by Srull & Wyer (1989) for episodic memory of person-related information. Evaluative activity, always secondary to the descriptive knowledge provided by the traits, functions as an additional encoding of the behaviors presented under a global evaluative label. After all, since evaluative activity concerns only one judgment (obviously, the likableness judgment), the dual encoding hypothesis may seem convenient. On the other hand, imagine a particular impression formation situation (a recruitment situation[4]) in which the perceiver would like to recruit a supervisor who (1) seems nice, and at the same time seems (2) suited to the company environment, (3) likely to be appreciated by his subordinates, (4) likely to satisfy his department boss, and (5) apt to progress towards a white-collar position, etc. (these being only some of the elementary requirements). One of two cases exists:

– Either we are consistent with the standard conception, in which case each of these evaluative requirements will require its own calculation. To remain consistent with Srull and Wyer's model, this means we do not have to deal with dual memory encoding, but with a six-point encoding. Each behavior is first encoded descriptively in terms of traits. Then it is added to the five evaluative labels, each with a distinctive level of rationality. We can see here how the convenient model of these two fundamentalists in fact masks an evident violation of the rules for economic encoding. Also, we are prone to accept the potential lack of contradiction between the five evaluative labels and the possibility of finding a simple integration rule to arrive at a single decision.

– Or, we accept that in such a situation, a single evaluative label remains possible. But in this case, we must also assume (Oden & Anderson's, 1971, see the brief review above) that a piece of personological information (a personality "trait") has a homogeneous evaluative meaning, i.e. that it is more or less constant.[5] Then, why should we retain the dual memory encoding hypothesis and not accept that this evaluative information is an integral part of the personological information itself? This leads us to drop the standard conception, which places evaluative activity in the area of affective idiosyncrasies, and accept the notion of evaluative knowledge.

Briefly, accepting the existence of evaluative knowledge, and *a fortiori* the simple idea that a trait provides information about the utility or value of the described person, amply simplifies the modelling of social cognition. The cost of this acceptance is only ideological.

---

[4] This situation is curiously mentioned by Srull and Wyer in a primitive fashion, we must say. They seem to consider that a representation such as "corresponds well to the job" is descriptive knowledge! Nothing is said about the evaluative knowledge that enables the perceiver to derive such a statement.

[5] This is in fact what the epistemological-cognitive analysis of trait construction shows (Beauvois, 1976, 1984).

2.2 Biases and Social Acceptability

This approach would no doubt also modify our conception of social cognition. The notion of "bias" (not to say "error" or distortion), which is so essential to the tradition that generated the concept of social cognition, should be revised in the light of the notion of evaluative knowledge. When a piece of knowledge must be judged, this judgment is based on a different normative criterion than that of descriptive validity, which has so long fascinated social psychologists (cf. Nisbett & Ross, 1980). This normative criterion is the social acceptability of the decisions that involve the piece of knowledge (for a more detailed discussion, see Beauvois, 1990; Beauvois & Dubois, 1991). Yet, knowledge which is biased from a descriptive point of view (thereby failing to meet the truth value criterion) can be perfectly acceptable from the evaluative knowledge perspective (thereby meeting the social acceptability criterion). If our subjects were confronted with Donald or Barbara (the prototypical target persons in social cognition) in an experiment, they would be more prone to function in the evaluative mode than in the descriptive mode. Instead of asking whether their inferences are biased (this is not the subject's problem, but the standard theorist's), we should look ahead and attempt to determine the conditions under which they are acceptable. Consider the case of the so-called fundamental error. From a purely descriptive point of view (truth value criterion), we know that this attribution is indeed an error. As evaluative knowledge often leads to decisions about people, personological inferences are socially acceptable most of the time (this is accentuated by the fact that such decisions are often validated, since beliefs can become reality).

The duality (perhaps the plurality) of the types of knowledge – and the associated duality or plurality of the criteria which can be used to judge a piece of knowledge – may therefore lead us to revise our approach to social cognition and its biases.

References

Anderson, N. H. (1981). *Foundations of information integration theory.* New York: Academic Press.

Anderson, N. H. (1982). *Methods of information processing integration theory.* New York: Academic Press.

Bargh, J. A. (1988). Automatic information processing: Implications for communication and affect. In L. Donohew, H. E. Sypher, & E. T. Higgins (Eds.), *Communication, social cognition, and affect* (pp. 9-32). Hillsdale, NJ: Erlbaum.

Beauvois, J.-L. (1976). Problématique des conduites sociales d'évaluation. *Connexions*, No. 19, 7-30.

Beauvois, J.-L. (1984). *La psychologie quotidienne*. Paris : Presses Universitaires de France.

Beauvois, J.-L. (1990). L'acceptabilité sociale et la connaissance évaluative. *Connexions, No. 56*, 7-16.

Beauvois, J.-L. (1991). Processus cognitifs, socio-cognitifs, représentationnels et idéologie. In V. Aebischer, E. M. Lipiansky & J.-P. Deconchy (Eds.), *Idéologies et représentations sociales*. Cousset : DelVal.

Beauvois, J.-L. & Dubois, N. (1988). The norm of internality in the explanation of psychological events. *European Journal of Social Psychology, 18*, 299-316.

Beauvois, J.-L. & Dubois, N. (1991). Internal/external orientations and psychological information processing. *Cahiers de Psychologie Cognitive/European Bulletin of Cognitive Psychology, 11*, 193-212.

Beauvois, J.-L. & Dubois, N. (1992). Traits as evaluative categories. *Cahiers de Psychologie Cognitive/European Bulletin of Cognitive Psychology, 12*, 253-270.

Beauvois, J.-L., Dubois, N., Mira, L., & Monteil, J.-M. (1992, July). *Evaluative knowledge and person memory*. Paper presented at the Small Meeting on Person Memory Interest Group, Cergy-Pontoise, France.

Beauvois, J.-L., Joule, R. V. & Monteil J.-M. (1989). *Perspectives cognitives et conduites sociales: Vol. 2. Représentations et processus sociocognitifs*. Cousset : DelVal.

Beauvois, J.-L. & Mira, L. (1991, December). *La connaissance évaluative dans la mémoire des personnes*. Paper presented at the meeting of the Société Française de Psychologie, Clermont-Ferrand, France.

Beauvois, J.-L., Monteil, J.-M., & Trognon A. (1991). A. Quelles conduites, quelles cognitions? Repères conceptuels. In J.-L. Beauvois, R.V. Joule & J.-M. Monteil (Eds.), *Perspectives cognitives et conduites sociales: Vol. 3. Quelles cognitions pour quelles conduites?* (p. 203-287). Cousset : DelVal.

Bekaddour, Z. (1992). L'effet de l'induction d'une orientation interne vs. externe sur la transmission des informations psychologiques. Unpublished manuscript, Université Pierre Mendès France, Grenoble, France.

Buss, D. M., & Craik, K. H. (1983). The act frequency approach to personality. *Psychological Review, 90*, 105-126.

Croizet, J.-C. (1991a). Les effets d'amorçage dans la formation des impressions. *Psychologie Française, 36*, 79-98.

Croizet, J.-C. (1991b). *The evaluative-descriptive interface in priming effects on impression formation*. Unpublished manuscript, Université Pierre Mendès France, Grenoble, France.

322

D'Andrade, R. G. (1965). Trait psychology and componential analysis. *American Anthropologist, 67,* 215-228.

Dubois, N. (1987). *La psychologie du contrôle: les croyances internes et externes.* Grenoble : Presses Universitaires de Grenoble.

Ebbesen, E. B., & Allen, R. B. (1979). Cognitive processes in implicit personality trait inferences. *Journal of Personality and Social Psychology, 37,* 471-488.

Funder, D. C., & Dobroth, K. M. (1987). Differences between traits: Properties associated with interjudge agreement. *Journal of Personality and Social Psychology, 52,* 409-418.

Grusec, J. E. (1983). The internalization of altruistic dispositions: A cognitive analysis. In E. T. Higgins, D. N. Ruble, & W. W. Hartup (Eds.), *Social cognition and social development.* Cambridge: Cambridge University Press.

Hoffman, M. L. (1970). Moral development. In P. H. Mussen (Ed.), *Carmichael's manual of child psychology* (Vol. 2, pp. 261-359). New York: Wiley.

Hoffman, M. L. (1983). Affective and cognitive processes in moral internalization. In E. T. Higgins, D. N. Ruble, & W. W. Hartup (Eds.), *Social cognition and social development* (pp. 236-274). Cambridge: Cambridge University Press.

Klein, S. B., & Loftus, J. (1990). Rethinking the role of organization in person memory: An independent trace storage model. *Journal of Personality and Social Psychology, 59,* 400-410.

Labourin, M. C. & Lecourvoisier, A. (1985). Le rôle des traits centraux dans la formation des impressions. *Cahiers de Psychologie Cognitive, 6,* 95-102.

Le Poultier, F. (1989). Acquisition de la norme d'internalité et activité évaluative. In J.-L. Beauvois, R. V. Joule & J.-M. Monteil (Eds.), *Perspectives cognitives et conduites sociales: Vol. 2. Représentations et processus socio-cognitifs* (p. 247-258). Cousset : DelVal.

Le Poultier, F.(1991, December). *Modelage interne et activité évaluative.* Paper presented at the meeting of the Société Française de Psychologie, Clermont-Ferrand, France.

Mischel, W. (1973). Toward a cognitive social learning reconceptualization of personality. *Psychological Review, 80,* 252-283.

Nisbett, R., & Ross, L. (1980). *Human inference: Strategies and shortcomings of social judgment.* Englewood Cliffs, NJ: Prentice Hall.

Osgood, C. E., Suci, G. J., & Tannenbaum, P. H. (1957). *The measurement of meaning.* Urbana, IL: University of Illinois Press.

Rosenberg, M. J. (1960). An analysis of affective-cognitive consistency. In M. J. Rosenberg, C. I. Hovland, W. J. McGuire, R. P. Abelson, & J.

W. Brehm (Eds.), *Attitude organization and change.* New Haven, MA: Yale University Press.

Rothbart, M., & Park, B. (1986). On the confirmability and disconfirmability of trait concepts. *Journal of Personality and Social Psychology, 50,* 131-142.

Semin, G. R., & Fiedler, K. (1988). The cognitive functions of linguistic categories in describing persons: Social cognition and language. *Journal of Personality and Social Psychology, 54,* 558-568.

Smith, E. R. (1984). Model of social inferences processes. *Psychological Review, 91,* 392-413.

Srull, T. K., & Wyer, R. S. (1989). Person memory and judgment. *Psychological Review, 96,* 58-83.

Shweder, R. A., & Bourne, E. (1982). Does the concept of the person vary cross-culturally? In A. J. Marcella & G. White (Eds.), *Cultural conception of mental health and therapy.* Boston, MA: Reidel.

Wojciszke, B., & Pienkowski, R. (1991). Prototypical structure of personality trait concepts and person perception. *Cahiers de Psychologie Cognitive/European Bulletin of Cognitive Psychology, 11,* 213-228.

Wyer, R. S., & Gordon, S. E. (1984). The cognitive representation of social information. In R. S. Wyer & T. K. Srull (Eds.), *Handbook of social cognition* (Vol. 2, pp. 73-150). Hillsdale, NJ: Erlbaum.

Wyer, R. S., & Srull, T. K. (1986). Human cognition in its social context. *Psychological Review, 93,* 322-359.

LIST OF CONTRIBUTORS

Amit, Gil. Bar-Ilan University, Ramat-Gan, 52900 Israel

Arcuri, Luciano. Universita degli Studi di Padova, Dipartimento di Psicologia dello Sviluppo e della Socializzazione, Via Beato Pellegrino 26, 35137 Padova, Italia

Beauvois, Jean-Léon. Laboratoire de psychologie sociale, Université Pierre Mendès France (Grenoble 2), Domaine de St Martin d'Hères, B.P. 47X, F-38000 St Martin d'Hères, France

Bellour, Fanny. Université Catholique de Louvain, Département de Psychologie, 20 voie du Roman Pays, 1348 Louvain-La-Neuve, Belgique

Bruner, Jerome. New York University, School of Law, 249 Sullivan Street, New York, NY 10012, U.S.A.

Clémence, Alain. Université de Genève, Faculté de Psychologie et des Sciences de l'Éducation, 24 rue du Général Dufour, CH-1211 Genève 4, Suisse

Crano, William, D. Texas A&M University, College Station, TX 77843, U.S.A.

Doise, Willem. Université de Genève, Faculté de Psychologie et des Sciences de l'Éducation, 24 rue du général Dufour, CH-1211 Genève 4, Suisse

Dubois, Nicole. Département de Psychologie, Université de Nancy 2, B.P. 33-97, F-54015 Nancy Cedex, France

Duflos, André. Laboratoire de Psychologie Sociale, Université René Descartes (Paris 5), 28 rue Serpente, F-75006 Paris, France

Durand-Delvigne, Annick. U.F.R. de Psychologie, Université Charles de Gaulle (Lille 3), B.P. 149, F-59653 Villeneuve d'Ascq Cedex, France

Evans, John, St.B.T. Department of Psychology, Polytechnic South West, Plymouth PL4 8AA, U.K.

Extra, Jan. Royal Netherlands Naval College, Nieuwe Diep 8, PO Box 10000, 1780 CA Den Helder, Nederland

Greenwald, Anthony. University of Washington, Department of Psychology, NI-25, Seattle, WA 98195, U.S.A.

Hewstone, Miles. Universität Mannheim, Lehrtuhl für Sozialpsychologie, Postfach 10 34 62, D-6800, Mannheim 1, Deutschland

Hurtig, Marie-Claude. Centre de Recherche en Psychologie Cognitive, Université de Provence (Aix-Marseille 1), 29 Avenue Robert Schuman, F-13621 Aix-en-Provence Cedex, France

Jarymowicz, Maria. University of Warsaw, Institute of Psychology, ul. Stawki 5/7, PL-00-183 Warsaw, Poland

Kaminska-Feldman, Marta. University of Warsaw, Department of Social Psychology, ul. Stawki 5/7, PL-00-183 Warsaw, Poland

Karylowski, Jerzy, J. University of North Florida, Department of Psychology, Jacksonville, FL 32212, U.S.A.

Kodilja, Renata. Istituto di Psicologia, Facoltà di Lettere e Filosofia, Università degli Studi di Trieste, via dell'Università, 7, 3400 Trieste.

La Haye, Anne-Marie (de). Laboratoire de Psychologie Sociale, Université René Descartes (Paris 5), 28 rue Serpente, F-75006 Paris, France

Lauvergeon, Guy. Laboratoire de Psychologie Sociale, Université René Descartes (Paris 5), 28 rue Serpente, F-75006 Paris, France

Le Poultier, François. Laboratoire de Psychologie Sociale, Université de Haute-Bretagne (Rennes 2), 6 Avenue Gaston Berger, F-35043 Rennes, France

Leyens, Jacques-Philippe. Université Catholique de Louvain, Département de Psychologie, 20 voie du Roman Pays, 1348 Louvain-La-Neuve, Belgique

Macrae, C. Neil. School of Psychology, University of Wales, P.O Box 901, Cardiff CF1 3YG, U.K.

Mailloux, Françoise. Chemin des Prairies, F-84130 Les Taillades, France

Massonnat, Jean. UFR de Psychologie et des Sciences de l'Éducation, Université de Provence (Aix-Marseille 1), 29 Avenue Robert Schuman, F-13621 Aix-en-Provence cedex, France

Monteil, Jean-Marc. Laboratoire de Psychologie Sociale de la Cognition, Université Blaise Pascal, 34 Avenue Carnot, F-63006 Clermont-Ferrand, France

Oriol, Michel. Institut d'Etudes et de Recherches Interethniques et Interculturelles, Université de Nice, 63 Boulevard de la Madeleine, F-06000 Nice, France

Pichevin, Marie-France. Centre de Recherche en Psychologie Cognitive, Université de Provence (Aix-Marseille 1), 29 Avenue Robert Schuman, F-13621 Aix-en-Provence Cedex, France

Piolat, Michel. UFR de Psychologie et des Sciences de l'Éducation, Université de Provence (Aix-Marseille 1), 29 Avenue Robert Schuman, F-13621 Aix-en-Provence cedex, France

Poeschl, Gabrielle. Université de Genève, Faculté de Psychologie et des Sciences de l'Education, 24 rue du général Dufour, CH-1211, Genève 4, Suisse

Serino, Carmencita. Dipartimento di Scienze dell'Educazione, Università di Bari, Pal. Ateneo, Via Crisanzio 1, 70122 Bari, Italia

Vermunt, Riel. Department of Social and Organization Psychology, University of Leiden, Wassenaarseweg 52, PO Box 9555, 2300 RB Leiden, Nederland

Vinsonneau, Geneviève. Laboratoire de Psychologie Sociale, Université René Descartes (Paris 5), 28 rue Serpente, F-75006 Paris, France

Yinon, Yoel. Bar-Ilan University, Ramat-Gan, 52900 Israel

Yzerbyt, Vincent. Université Catholique de Louvain, Département de Psychologie, 20 voie du Roman Pays, 1348 Louvain-La-Neuve, Belgique